AS THE
TABLES
TURN

Then we found a $300,000.00 overring on one of his checks. I believe he has been suspended.

Wine list is 98% complete. Will begin work on captains list tomorrow 3/24/90

11 @ 11:30 Dixon
10 @ 1:00 Johnson
7 @ 6:30 Hummel
10 @ 4:15 Lyons
15 @ 5:45 Than Johnson

4 @ 1:15 Caroline
3 @ 1:45 Urbanski
3 @ 2:15 Monza

141

142

135

140

52

13

Library

SARA

ose
Fowler
eeling
Price

4 @ 12:30
3 @ 1:00 Rayburn
3 @ 2:30 Gack

Wickner

54

MICHAEL = MEGAN

GARRETT

vani

5 @ 11:15 Light
4 @ 12:45 Educ
7 @ 2:15 Michelle

7 @ 11:30 Leighton
6 @ 1:00 Meridian
5 @ 2:30 Barre

5 @ 12:00
4 @ 1:15
8 @ 2:45

bardi
zhelle

113

5 @ 11:30 Morgan
8 @ 12:30 Vanallsburg
5 @ 2:00 Riebel

114

6 @ 11:15 W
6 @ 12:45 Re
3 @ 2:15 P
7 @ 5:15 H

AS THE
TABLES
TURN
Biography of a Bistro

Sue Doody and Michael J. Rosen

Enjoy!
Sue

ORANGE FRAZER *PRESS*
Wilmington, Ohio

AS THE

Orange Frazer Press
P.O. Box 214
37 1/2 West Main St.
Wilmington OH 45177

ISBN 1-933197-28-5

Printed in the United States
of America

First printing

Book design: Gregory Hischak
Color cover photography: Will Shively
Page 320 constitutes an extension of
this copyright page.

Library of Congress Cataloging-in-Publication-
Data Pending

TABLES TURN

The Recipes

INTRODUCTION

. . . .

WHAT CAN WE START YOU OFF WITH?

THE BOOK THAT ONLY TOOK ME 25 YEARS TO WRITE

AN INTRODUCTION BY SUE DOODY

I STARTED THIS BOOK 26 YEARS AGO when the dreamy and somewhat daft notion of owning a restaurant began to take shape in my mind. Friends remember me rambling on about "my book" for decades, which I knew I wanted to call *As the Tables Turn*, almost from the moment we began to turn a profit at Lindey's. In fact, two decades ago, my managers bought me a portable tape recorder, because I was always saying to Steve and Freddie and Biff that, one day, I would have to write a book about all the crazy things that have happened in this restaurant, if only because no one would ever believe it. I can't remember actually speaking anything into the tape recorder…and who knows how many memorable moments will go unremembered. But so much has lived on in memories: mine, my staff's, my guests'.

But it finally occurred to me, as I entered my eighth decade, that the only way I was going to run a restaurant and write this book was to approach my friend Michael, who'd written so many books that I'd enjoyed over the years. I can't remember, but the first time we met may have been when Michael won Lindey's inaugural Starving Artist Competition for a menu design. It's an illustration of our bar that has signified Lindey's for more than a decade, even after we stopped using other local artists' designs.

Or it may have been when he was literary director at the Thurber House, and I was asked, as a notable community member, to read a chapter from his first collection of James Thurber's uncollected work. He introduced the readers—I was to read first—by offering thanks to various people, and referred to the *New York Times* reviewer who snidely suggested that Michael's acknowledgments page "rivaled Robert Fulghum's for squishiness." And then I came to the podium, smiled warmly and announced to the crowd, "Oh, Michael, we all love your swishiness." This produced considerable laughter, and it was only afterward, that I learned of my mistake.

It's also true that Michael's partner Mark Svede, an art historian, worked at Lindey's for more than six years. (You'll see his witty contributions throughout our book.) So we've been warming up for this collaboration for many years.

When Michael and I started this book, we considered a few directions. Was this to be a memoir by or a biography about a divorced mother of four, an "Upper Arlington den mother" (according to a feature story in the *Columbus Dispatch*) without a jot of restaurant or business experience who, within the space of a few years, would become a very successful restaurateur who'd receive the region's Entrepreneur of the Year Award by Ernst and Young, and whose business has consistently been among the highest grossing restaurants in the area?

Or was this to be a 100-year chronicle about a saloon-turned-restaurant located in one of the nation's only privately funded historic neighborhoods, and its evolution through Prohibition, the Depression, World War II, the blight of urban "renewal," and a succession of failed businesses that preceded it?

Or was this a business book about the strategic ideas of one family who grew a single restaurant into the largest chain—60 restaurants as of this writing, with ambitious projections for the coming years—of family-owned, white-tablecloth restaurants in the country?

Finally, we realized that what attracted us both to this undertaking was the very thing that has attracted guests to Lindey's for 25 years: the people. Our regular crowd. Our longtime servers. Our hysterical, eclectic, beloved community. And so we decided to create an oral history of this place using the voices of guests, chefs, servers, neighborhood regulars— and, of course, my own voice and those of family members.

I can't guess how many people Michael contacted for this book, how many joined him over the phone lines or across a table at Lindey's, how many reluctantly begged off (it's one thing to share stories of your youthful or not-so-youthful indiscretions over a glass of wine, and it's another to share them in order to have them printed in a hardcover book). But I do know we have many generous contributors to whom we owe our continuing gratitude.

One day, having reviewed a nearly completed draft, I asked Michael, "Why do you think all these things happened here, at *my* restaurant, instead of at other restaurants?" And without skipping a beat, he replied, "Because for years, people have known they can get away with murder here, and no one ever presses charges."

I laughed over that remark, as I laughed over so many stories in this book that I had no idea had taken place right under my nose at Lindey's! Along with what must total some half million meals and hundreds of thousands of delighted guests, there's a shocking amount of shenanigans, tomfoolery, inebriation, theft, indecency—to say nothing of a giddy quotient of rudeness, arrogance, ineptitude, indignation, and smartass remarks that seemed to be, like salt and pepper, just part of Lindey's seasoning.

Or perhaps those are just the oddities that make for stories: those instances when the restaurant experienced a hiccup (or maybe it's a knowing wink) in the performance that guests perceive as beautifully orchestrated and the staff perceives as breakneck and hectic.

But later, I reconsidered Michael's observation about Lindey's "not pressing charges": Had I wittingly or unwittingly condoned or even encouraged the crazy, campy, quirky behaviors you'll read about in these pages? I knew that my innocence—or call it "my learning curve"—meant that I did trust the talented people we hired. I did expect people to return my trust, too. And that extended to the guests as well as the staff. I also know that, from the start, I always wanted to do whatever was possible to accommodate guests, prepare them any meal we could, regardless of what the menu offers.

I also realize that a restaurant in a crowded, affluent neighborhood, within walking distance for many people, means that familiarity encourages a certain privilege, that can swell into pushiness.

I remember, one recent evening, my general manager Rebecca Holder came to me. "Last night, a lady with four dinner companions came in, pointed to an empty table by the window and announced that she wanted to sit there. At Table 30." Now the guest's choice was a square table that seats four. Or three. Or two. Or one. It cannot seat five. It does not have hidden leaves that fold up to make a big circular table. And even though accommodating whims, wants, and whatever is part of what has made Lindey's Lindey's, incidents such as this make us wonder. Rebecca explained to the woman how Table 30, wedged between another table and the stairs to the second floor, is especially challenging, right in a traffic pattern, and just can't seat more than four. But not only did our guest insist, but she insisted on throwing a fit in front of a crowded room. "I can't believe you're not going to take care of me!" she nearly shouted.

So, at last, Rebecca sent two servers to get Table 60 from the third dining room, which meant removing the table settings, folding up the table, carrying it out the back door, walking it up the street, around the block to the front of the restaurant, and wedging it in through the emergency door. Meanwhile, another pair of servers broke down Table 30, and carried it out the exit, walked it around the block, wedging it through the back door and into the third dining room where Table 60 had been. And then both tables had to be reset. And this is during a busy evening, when all the servers had full stations of other guests.

Finally, after the party of five left (and, as far as I can tell, never came again, thank you very much), both tables had to go through the same breaking down and setting up again. Rebecca and I had to think hard about ever doing that again. What were they thinking? And more importantly, what were we thinking?

In the following pages, we've hoped to create a portrait of a living, breathing, ever-evolving bistro whose identity is as much the community's impression as the management's intentions. Whether or not you've ever dined with us at Lindey's, I'm certain you can imagine these pages "hosted" at whatever restaurant you frequent. If you've ever worked as a server or bartender, you're bound to identify with many of the spectacles, spills, and spirited exchanges. If you've ever fancied starting a restaurant, or any business for that matter, this loose ledger of our experience might persuade you that that time is now, or, perhaps, never.

In every case, I hope that that these pages make you feel warmly invited and welcomed to that generous communion of splendid foods, raised glasses, and convivial friends.

A NUMBER OF THINGS ABOUT LINDEY'S
LET'S START WITH THE FACTS

AVERAGING DATA from the last few years at Lindey's, we can report the following figures with the degree of accuracy we've come to expect from statistics. (That is, they're the best we can manage with the spotty information we've got.) Each number reflects a year's worth of one thing or another at our one original restaurant when not otherwise specified.

Reservations taken: **45,990**

Guests served: **136,596**

Guest checks: **63,889**

Total dining room capacity, not including party rooms: **160**

People that can fit into the entire restaurant, including terrace, patio, and party rooms, but still not including folks waiting at the bar for a seat: **350**

Dollars of meals comped: **3,396**

Hours worked by employees: **115,610**

Overtime hours worked: **1,272**

Waitstaff working a busy night, including the outside terrace and courtyard (15 servers, 5 bussers, 3 hots, 4 bartenders, 4 food runners— not counting any banquet staff for the party rooms): **45**

Cars valet-parked on a busy night: **150**

Regrettable time that a valet backed one Porsche 911 into another Porsche 911: **1**

Days after the above accident that it took for Lindey's to move to a different insurance company: **1**

Chefs on duty each night (not including line cooks): **3**

Skillets used during a typical Saturday night's dinners: **260**

Days out of 365 that Lindey's closes: **5**

Number of dishes sent back to the kitchen by guests in one year: **312**

Number of dishes sent back to the kitchen by one very special guest in one year: **56**

Most times a piece of meat was recooked until it was well-done enough for the guest: **3**

Time the chef served pizza with a topping of leftover pasta for the staff meal: **1**

Seconds of patience the chef has on a busy night when a ticket pops up for a table of seven that reads "see server first" for special instructions: **1**

Birthdays celebrated, although many go undisclosed and don't allow us to bring a dessert: **1,666** *

Soup tureens broken and replaced: **200**

White wine glasses broken and replaced: **1,600**

Martini glasses broken and replaced: **400**

Cups of coffee served: **24,044**

Glasses of soft drinks served: **13,022**

Beers served (Bud Lite being the most popular): **23,210**

Cocktails served (currently, the Cosmopolitan is #1, with Grey Goose being our most requested vodka): **122,783**

Percentage of Maraschino cherry garnishes that go uneaten: **50**

Bottles of wine served (Sketchbook Cabernet and Torre de Luna Pinot Grigio being the top sellers in the red and white lists): **11,821**

Bottles of champagne served: **889**

Number of those champagne bottles uncorked on New Year's Eve: **82**

Cups of heavy cream: **24,000**

Sticks of butter: **3,250** **

Pounds of beef tenderloin: **9,301**

Pounds of Idaho potatoes: **33,800**

---

* We do not embarrass guests with an obligatory singing of "Happy Birthday" or other song of our own invention, which we have found offsets some of the disappointment.

** On the subject of butter, we have two things to report. First, we have a separate budget for the front of the house (that is, the butter served with bread). This number just reflects the butter we use in the kitchen. As for bread service, you might be amused to know that over the years, we've tried several ways of serving butter. We've rolled it into striped balls, but the balls would stick together as they neared room temperature, or roll off the plates if they were too cold, or scoot out from under a guest's slicing knife.

Pounds of Yukon gold potatoes: **9,650**

Pounds of fingerling potatoes: **2,125**

Total tater tonnage: **22 3/4**

Longest number of years that a single banquet server (Allen Jones)
has worked at Lindey's: **16**

Average number of ties a full-time employee throws out because of spills, stains,
and snags incurred in the line of work: **10**

Miles walked by one manager: **416**

Times a married manager is presented with a flattering, tempting "opportunity"
in the line of work even though his wife would kill him if he so much as flirted with
the possibility (about half each from men and from women): **12**

Most crab cakes served in 45 minutes (at a wine tasting in 2005): **800**

Parties hosted at Lindey's: **1,007**

Number of times we converted the Promo West Pavilion into a 4-star restaurant
for a wedding reception and then tore it all down after the meal
so that the guests could rock out to Grand Funk Railroad: **1**

Number of times we'd do that again: **0**

Number of shoes left after a wedding reception: **1**

Number of years in a row the U-Haul truck broke down or ran out of gas for the
Rosemount Center Skeet Shooting Event: **2**

Service calls to repair kitchen equipment: **104**

Number of karaoke songs one should sing at a corporate holiday party at Lindey's: **0**

Rank of German Village of all Columbus tourist destinations: **1**

We've whipped it, then patted it into small ramekins, topped with a paper shield...but the paper was always greasy, a nuisance to clear from the table, and the ramekins trapped butter bits and weren't always clean when they emerged from the dishwasher.

We've sliced thick square wedges from one-pound blocks and placed them, overlapping, on butter plates...but on busy nights, the dishwasher could barely keep up, so we'd be putting butter on plates that were still warm from the drying, and servers would manage to get the butter to the table in a solid form, but by the time the butter was passed around the table, the plate would be holding a pool of clarified butter.

We have never, for all our continuing attempts to improve our bread service, served puddles of olive oil in a saucer.

What Made Lindey's Lindey's for 25 Years—and Counting

GREAT RESTAURANTS, LIKE GREAT WINES, age beautifully: they mature, growing complex and balanced, with a great structure, refined tannins, and jammy notes of prune, kid-skin gloves, Chinese five-spice powder, and Twizzlers. Good restaurants, like good wines, need to be drunk within a few years or they lose their color, character, and identifying features. And trendy restaurants are more like a Beaujolais Nouveau, meant to be drunk in the year of their creation by people who think it's cool that a 10-letter word can have six vowels. Awesome.

Lindey's is among a handful of longstanding fine-dining restaurants in Columbus—perhaps the only one in recent years—that's never changed hands, names, or concepts for a quarter of a century.

How to account for this longevity is, in some ways, the subject of this entire book. Surely there's no single answer, but rather a complicated mix of reasons that includes its unique location in a historic neighborhood, the ingenuity and ingenuousness of the proprietor, the wild personalities of its employees and frequent guests, the chefs' creativity and crankiness—there are probably more factors than we can even acknowledge.

But by way of an introduction, we've gathered some testimonials from regular guests, staff, and community members. Think of it as a chorus of silver anniversary cheers.

Andrea Cambern, news anchor at WBNS: My husband Brett and I moved to Columbus from Phoenix in 1991. Channel 10 flew me out for an interview and took me to lunch at Lindey's. Brett and I knew nothing about the city. We knew Columbus was the state capital and home to the OSU Buckeyes. Period. So my first introduction to the city was Lindey's and German Village. It was a perfect fall day, crisp air, leaves crunching under your feet—there's nothing like it in Arizona!—to say nothing of the quaintness of the old homes that comprised the neighborhood. Where I'd come from there's nothing older than your oldest pair of shoes!

And then we entered the restaurant: such a contrast! Lindey's is all hustle and bustle inside, a crowd of handsomely dressed people in suits or business attire! You could feel the business buzz. Such a change from my hometown, a resort town, where everyone wears flip-flops.

We had a lovely lunch from start to finish, and the interview went very well. As I walked past the houses and cobblestone streets, I couldn't wait to get to the phone and call Brett— we were engaged then. "Brett, if I get this job, I know exactly where we're living."

And we've been coming to Lindey's from a home in German Village for 15 years.

Diane Warren, proprietor of Katzinger's Deli, and a onetime server at Lindey's: I was preparing to work a small catered party upstairs and, for some reason, Sue was setting up with me. We were putting doilies on plates. I wasn't paying much attention and I put one upside down. (Frankly, I didn't even realize a doily had sides.) Sue, with those eagle eyes, caught it right away. She turned the doily over and said, "Ninety-nine percent of the public will never notice that. We're doing it correctly for the one percent who will."

I cannot tell you the number of times I have repeated that to my staff at Katzinger's. It was an extraordinarily simple standard, and I always credit Sue for it.

She so clearly defined Lindey's that, coming onto 25 years, the restaurant still has an unmistakable identity. During the time I worked there, Sue acted more like a wonderful hostess than an owner, and she had that knack of making people want to be noticed by her. She worked the restaurant every night, walking through the dining room, saying hello and pouring coffee. Whatever else she did behind the scenes (behind my scene as a server, anyway), I don't know, other than fretting neurotically about new restaurants. Over the next few years, I know she worried as the Fifty-Five Group opened each new restaurant; huge restaurants were opening in the new Brewery District, and her own chef Kent Rigsby launched his own restaurant in the Short North. Sue was always looking over her shoulder, worrying that her business might dip in the short run, but hoping that soon her guests would be coming on home.

A few months after we opened Katzinger's and I felt certain that I'd made the biggest financial mistake of my life and that we'd never *do* enough business to *stay in* business, I stopped at Lindey's on my way home. Sue asked me about the deli, and I told her my tale of new business woes. She laughed and told me she went through the same thing when Lindey's opened. "There were nights we didn't even do 40 covers. The first night that we managed over 60, we had a party to celebrate." Seeing the kind of business Lindey's was doing then—after just two years—made me feel like maybe the deli would be okay after all. This year, we're celebrating our own 22nd anniversary.

OVERHEARD AT LINDEY'S

....

Server Nicole (speaking to manager Freddie Cortez at the end of her shift):
Freddie, I'm done. I need my report run.
Freddie: Oh, Nicole, steaks are done. People are finished.

Ric Wanetic and **David Hagans:** Since David and I lived down the street, there were days we had breakfast, lunch, and dinner at Lindey's. If we ever invited someone to "come for dinner," they knew it meant dinner at Lindey's, at Table 30. (God forbid we'd ever have to cook.)

Some mornings, I'd have my breakfast meeting, and Al Deitzel, who also considered Lindey's his branch office, would be having his, and then we'd have a lunch meeting together. Or we'd both be doing some diet craze together. I remember times when Sharon and Al, Cookie and Victor, Ellen Gruber, and David and I would all go to a calisthenics class with Mary Majors, right downtown, and do an hour in our sweats—this really was the start of the gym routines—and then shower and dress, and meet up at Lindey's for beers and rich dinners. And, most importantly, we'd all feel very good about the total experience.

Wine purveyor **Dan Frey:** When Lindey's opened, restaurants at that time either had house wines—jug wines in red, white, and maybe rosé—or they had a leather notebook of cellar selections that were too intimidating for anyone but a genuine aficionado. (L'Armagnac, the Top, the Wine Cellar, and the Worthington Inn fit into that second category.) I think Lindey's was among the first three restaurants in the area to pour a variety of wines by the glass. Our whole concept was to have a bistro, and a bistro's wine list. We had wines exclusive to Lindey's. We had some reasonably priced wines that were made 30 yards away from the best vineyards in France—"over the tracks," as Chris Doody would say—that allowed us to provide great varietals at a fraction of the price. And from the outset, Sue wanted her staff to be able to say a wine and recommend it with a certain dish, "So then all a guest had to do was nod, or say 'that sounds good,' and not have to choose or pronounce the wine."

Ian Brown: At the time, I was working at Bravo!, and my friend Pat Granzier (who'd started as a busboy, then became a server, a manager, and then the general manager of a Brio restaurant) was working at Lindey's. We did business with a man named Joe Koran, from U.S. Food out of Cincinnati. One day, speaking with Pat on the phone, I could hear Joe's voice in the background. Joe should have been a radio announcer; he had a powerful, but sweet, voice.

"You need any toilet paper?" Pat asks me.

"What? Did you order too much or something?" I reply.

"No, but Joe just brought over my order, and the quality...well, it's good enough for someone who eats at Bravo!, but people who eat at Lindey's need cushier toilet paper."

That's the funny thing about this job: at some point, you come to actually believe what you're saying.

Chef **Jack Cory:** Sue is the catalyst that drives this restaurant and all the people around her. She exemplifies deep-rooted strength. You go back to Columbus's "top 10" lists over the last 25 years, and most of the other restaurants are gone now. But there is Lindey's. Every year. No matter which chef was in the kitchen at Lindey's, they were always second, in the minds of the guests, to their delight at being in Sue's restaurant. They came to see her. To be here.

Michael Mizenko: The flirty, fun, noisy front room with fresh flowers and real palm trees and all the handsome waiters with the green ties and white shirts and long white aprons— the whole place was just good-looking. My partner and I met there—he came out to meet my Dalmatian whom I liked to parade in front of the window on our last walk of the night. We also celebrated our anniversary, which was New Year's Eve, for years at Lindey's, and all the servers would gather around us to sing happy anniversary. I don't know if there was another restaurant in town where that could have happened. Lindey's was always welcoming that way.

Susan Sparling, manager at Bon Vie, Michigan: When I was the Columbus Bon Vie manager, I visited most of the tables each day, and once, a rather older woman said to me, "You know, I know Sue Doody."

"Oh, you do?" I replied. Many, *many* people know Sue, and many people consider that knowledge a reason for special treatment (which is, incidentally, what we like to give every guest).

"Yes, I was there on the day she announced to her gourmet group that she was going to start a restaurant. So we were some of her first customers..."

People take such pride in having known Sue or Lindey's in those early years. They love having been there when it all began. Lindey's has that magical force. Somehow, Sue got the city of Columbus to believe they were enjoying the privileges of a country club just by coming to her restaurant. The attitude has always been that you don't have to be overly dressed or at a stuffy occasion to be at Lindey's. You can be as bold and colorful as the paintings on the wall.

Sue: One evening, the dining room is filled and everyone is table-hopping, maybe a little more than usual—but not too much more. People are pulling up chairs and buying drinks for one another—and they're talking and laughing among all the tables. And one of the regulars comes in for dinner, and on her way out, she says to me, "Sue, I didn't realize you rented out the front room for private parties?"

"Oh, we never do," I replied, but I certainly understood how she'd get that impression.

Ian Brown, general manager of Lindey's in 2004: When I joined Lindey's, I experienced nothing shy of an onslaught of the funniest folks I'd ever met. For those servers, work was an outlet for their craziness. I guess the idea was, if you surround yourself with peers who are as screwy as you are, then you all can spend most nights taking care of *other* people— I don't know: there must be something therapeutic that happens during those shifts!

Susan and **Jim Lynch:** Before we moved, for two decades, Lindey's was like our second living room.

Cookbook author and columnist **Betty Rosbottom:** Lindey's has a great feeling. The moment you walk in, you see that long copper bar, so incredibly warm, and there's no bad table in the entire place. And in 1981, Sue brought fresh fish, which was hardly common in Columbus. She featured a lamb dish, which Columbus usually didn't go for. Her menu included items that reflected the Italian wave of the '70s and '80s, as well as a few Cajun dishes (popularized by Paul Prudhomme), which were all the rage. Basically, Lindey's selected exactly what American diners were getting excited about.

Restaurant reviewer and attorney **John Marshall:** My first review of Lindey's, maybe 15 years ago, began with an evening of 12 family members gathered around two tables pushed together. We carried on until quite late, ordering at least three quarters of Lindey's menu (partly at my insistence that everyone eat something different). I remember having the waiter keep the wines on a separate check from the food so that the magazine wouldn't see how much alcohol we'd consumed. I came back a second and a third time before writing my review, but my stepmother's impression of her first meal there was the most telling: she thought it was the most elegant meal she'd ever had, and still does. "The pinnacle of gastronomy! Oysters on the half shell, Caesar salad, and lamb chops!" Around 1992, in Columbus, at least, Lindey's just about summed up what people wanted in the way of a great meal.

Bartender **Eddie Meecham:** Lindey's had such an edge. We had a dual-deck cassette player up front, and the staff supplied the music. The dining room had an eclectic mix depending on the night and who was serving: the Pretenders one hour and Prokofiev the next. And the staff matched with the clientele. Everyone in that place had a favorite waiter. And a favorite table. And they felt perfectly comfortable asking for both. And just like water seeks its own level, there were some guests who only liked the handsome, elegant waiters; some who only wanted the witty young women; and some who preferred to camp it up, night after night, with the flamboyant servers. In one dining room, you had Columbus's most wealthy alongside folks who considered the neighborhood home. You had hip, professional blacks and the nelly queens, beautiful single men looking for a date and stylish women executives networking after hours. Honestly, I don't think there was another place in town where you'd have that comfortable mix.

You've Got to Be Kidding

Another of Sue's remarkable qualities is her kid-ability. "I don't know if I invited it, or simply don't mind it, but the staff has always liked to imitate my voice, and my favorite expressions," Sue admits. "I take it as a sign of being family."

Chef **Tom Johnson:** I remember featuring "Apple Pan Doody" as a special one evening (basically recreating Jacques Pepin's recipe for apple pan dowdy—sliced apples, sugar, and brioche). I put it on the specials sheet on the menu and not only was Sue not amused, but the dish didn't sell either. (Maybe if the dish had sold, she wouldn't have minded my punning!)

Manager **Steve Gifford:** One day, Sue smashed her finger in the safe door. And broke it. And although everyone was actually concerned about her, the incident quickly devolved into people kidding about how she hurt her finger counting her money.

Banquet manager **Stephanie Wright:** What I loved about working with Sue was that her quirkiness was right there alongside her professionalism and smarts and generosity. I learned everything I know about business from her. I cherished the time we spent together. But there were also so many funny things I'll never forget. How Sue called me every morning on her way to work. Her drive was never more than 15 minutes, but she always called on the way to say she was on her way.

And then she had—and maybe still has—a huge concern about 10-dollar bills. "How did we do last night? Did we have enough tens?" "Be sure to ask for extra tens at the bank." I gather 10-dollar bills had been her bugaboo for years. All three "banks" in the restaurant start with $300. That's three cash drawers, and I can still hear her saying, "We need three packs of tens, two packs of fives, two packs of ones, and a roll of each coin." And if it wasn't right, Sue would take it all out and make sure everything was right.

I tried to tell a new manager, "Look, this may seem like a really small thing, but if you can get the banks to always look just like this, Sue is going to feel confident about you. Otherwise, she'll be saying to me, "Hon, what's wrong with him? Can't he get the tens in here? We don't need twenties!"

Remember the era when *Married...with Children* was popular, City Center had just been built, and nighttime soap operas like *Dynasty* were keeping people home at night? It was during that period that our charming, talented, and unbelievably vain host, manager, and server, Freddie Cortez, ruled at the host stand. He would pull a long strand of his curly hair down to his nose to show us all how tight his curls were, or he'd discuss the latest exploits of Harry Winston, the cat he'd named after the renowned jeweler. Well, this sort of behavior does not go unrewarded at Lindey's: the staff nicknamed him Connie Colby Carrington Cortez, as if he were one of the elite rich having catfights and falling into the duck pond on the evening soaps.

We have an intercom system at Lindey's—perhaps you've heard it. (Rest assured, we have no plans to distribute little ear microphones to everyone in the front and the back of the house so that everyone can be in constant contact like at the Taco Bell drive-through.) So one day, Sue is upstairs, and over the intercom, in a voice loud enough for much of the restaurant to hear, she says, "Connie Cortez? Could you please come upstairs?" And everyone within earshot is laughing hysterically. And Sue? Sue, the owner of the restaurant, the figurehead of this civilized place—she had neither intended to be funny nor given a second thought to using Freddie's silly sobriquet.

During our intercom era, when the kitchen, office phones, bar, and dining room all had two-digit extensions, Sue made another announcement to a dining room that was full enough that many people both recognized her voice and recalled her words years and years later: "Chris? Chris? Call me...at...Chris...call me at...at...oh, hell, where am I?"

Eddie Meecham: And then there's Sue. When Lindey's opened, independent restaurants were the norm in Columbus, but very few had an owner who cared as much as Sue, who spent as much time as Sue did, who knew the entire staff as Sue did. She spent 10 or 12 hours a day in this place, and knew all her customers and, moreover, knew how to cater to their wants. And this wasn't just for a year or two at the start-up. Year after year, she spent more time in that restaurant than any of us.

OPEN HOUSE

· ·

FROM SUE'S HOUSE TO LINDEY'S OPENING

BEFORE THERE WAS LINDEY'S THERE WAS HOPE
SUE'S CULINARY BEGINNINGS

Rick Doody's fifth birthday. Sue, Alton, and the day's catch, in Corpus Christi.

Home Cooking

Sue: For 10 years, beginning with my birth in 1934, I lived on Grafton Avenue in Dayton, Ohio, with my parents Jodie and Joe Goetz, my older brother Joe, my younger sister Gail, and my younger brother Tom, and a nursemaid/housekeeper/cook named Hope who was virtually a member of the family. She pretty much did everything for the munificent sum of two dollars a week. Hope was a terrific cook; her masterpiece was cherry pie made with fruit from our own tree. When she made pies, she'd make us kids little tarts out of the scraps of dough, dotted with jelly or preserves.

Weeknights, when my parents were at home, my brother Joe and I would sit at a little table in the dining room with our parents at the big table. Hope would serve, and the menu would be fairly simple: meat loaf, city chicken (that's veal on a skewer), Swiss steak, roast chicken, once in a while roast beef, and almost never fish—we were Catholic, so that was reserved for Fridays and, since our parents usually dined out on Fridays and Saturdays, we'd have tuna à la king or creamed crab meat or salmon patties. Occasionally, we had salads, but there was always a dessert: Hope's pies, floating islands, rice pudding, or ice cream from Maharg's, a longtime Dayton catering firm.

When Mom and Dad dined out—Dad in black tie and mother in a long but not elaborate dinner dress—Joe and I might have lunch or dinner (and sometimes both) with our maternal grandparents, who lived in a large house nearby. They employed what you'd have to call a "staff": a cook, a maid (or two), a houseman/driver, and a gardener. Grandfather took breakfast, lunch, and dinner at the dining room table, with iced water at each meal and his newspaper in a silver holder. Meals there would be a little more formal, although Mother had six brothers and sisters, so we could always count on some mealtime jockeying, and confusion, as everyone's needs and schedules were accommodated.

Sunday lunch was invariably roast chicken, dressing, mashed potatoes, peas, and ice cream with chocolate or caramel sauce. Sunday evening's menu consisted of baked beans, hot or cold ham, pickles, German potato salad, and perhaps leftover cake or cookies. Then everyone would listen to Walter Winchell in the big room.

My grandfather had a theatre business. He was the first in the Midwest to bring legitimate theater to the area. He'd book *Carousel*, *Showboat*, or *Brigadoon* for a five- or six- day run in Dayton at the Victory. So once a year, at least, my brother Joe and I would go with my grandparents on the train to New York: Joe and my grandfather would share one room, and Grandmother and I would share another. We'd all eat in the dining car with white linens, nice heavy silver, and fresh flowers on every table. Then we'd stay at the Plaza Hotel. While Grandfather negotiated his bookings with Jack Warner (of Warner Brothers) at Rockefeller Center, the three of us would see plays or visit museums. I remember once I made them take me to the Automat, so I could feed money in the slot and pull out a chicken pot pie.

When the Goetz family moved in 1943 to Dixon Avenue in Oakwood, the much-loved Hope left us for marriage. From then on, we had a series of "dailies," most of whom were pretty good cooks, but, increasingly, my mother occupied the kitchen and she prepared excellent soups, salads, and sauces. However, according to her mother-in-law, she was "terrible" when it came to baking pies or cakes.

With my father's increased income, we'd have lobsters (with races on the kitchen floor), soft-shell crabs, leg of lamb, or scalloped oysters for special occasions when we'd be allowed a glass of wine. Even in our younger days there was a sip of champagne mixed with water for us at holiday dinners.

We all remember mother's Hollandaise sauce on boiled cauliflower and, at Christmastime, a fruitcake that she'd French fry and serve with a brandy sauce. (It sounds dreadful, but it was delicious—and it did get rid of the remnants of fruitcake.)

Early Restaurants

We also dined out a lot. One of our parents' favorites was Servis's, known for its excellent fish. We often ordered the seafood platter—scallops, shrimp, and filet of sole, all deep-fried—with shoestring potatoes, and a splendid Boston cream pie that involved ice cream as well.

A favorite Sunday night activity was to visit the Canton Tea Garden, owned by a family friend, Billy Gin. Our family's company owned that building, so Mr. Gin always went out of his way to make us welcome and important. The food was American Chinese: chop suey, chow mein, egg foo yung, and wonderful almond cookies.

When our parents would dine, we children were often taken to a nearby luncheonette on Park Avenue in Oakwood, which was famous for "the Hotshot": a roast beef sandwich on white bread served with mashed potatoes, all covered with beef gravy. (The beef was sometimes past its prime and so well-done that its consistency matched the plate on which it was served.)

As a special treat, perhaps after seeing a movie, we'd be taken to Goody Goody's: great hamburgers, onion soup, and various ice cream delights. One outstanding cinematic experience was *The Wizard of Oz*, which neither I nor my brother enjoyed once the Wicked Witch appeared. It took a good deal of Goody Goody ice cream with hot fudge to calm us down.

We also ate at two steakhouses: the nearby Oakwood Grill (now the Oakwood Club), owned by my parents' friends. And then my father's cousin Jim Sullivan started Sully's as well as the Pine Club, which has some of the best steaks in the United States. The proof of that: they don't take reservations or credit cards, and they never have, and it's never hurt their business. At the entrance there is a photograph of then–Vice President George H.W. Bush and his wife Barbara waiting for a table in a line outside the restaurant. Apparently the Bushes waited for close to an hour, enjoyed their steaks, and Mrs. Bush took home a doggie bag.

And there was always the Dayton Country Club. While the food was wildly variable, depending on the manager and/or the chef, there was a pleasant hominess to the dining room where the maitre d' Frank Green was another family friend.

Sue's in the Kitchen

Youngest daughter **Beth Doody:** We didn't have the same upbringing as Mom. Mom cooked for us, but she and Dad did travel and entertain a lot. So frozen dinners or pot pies from Stouffer's weren't uncommon. When she and Dad would leave for 10 days or so, they'd leave us with these wicked women—none of them ever came more than once. Chris and I had a battle with one of these women, who told us point-blank, "You aren't going to leave the table until you finish the peas," but we protested because Mom never made us eat peas. Or anything we didn't like. I remember we opened the windows in the kitchen, and dumped them behind the shutters…and then my parents found them, like, six months later.

Oldest son **Rick Doody:** One lady came by to meet us before our folks left—the nicest, sweetest, biggest, oldest lady—and we all thought, this is going to be fun. Finally. But as soon as she arrived for real, everything changed: She brought along her nephews, who stretched out on our couches; she made up all these bizarre food rules; and, worst of all, she didn't understand when we switched from daylight saving time back to standard time the weekend she was with us, and she made us go to bed at 7:30 saying that it was really 8:30. Needless to say, we didn't see her again.

Sue: I recall that Alton would go to California on business, and once we met him in Dallas on his way back. I had three of the kids. We decided to have a crab boil when we got home, so we loaded fresh crabs in one of the suitcases. Then the airlines lost the luggage, and so we left the airport without the luggage. Of course, they called that night, as they had promised, and said, "We've found your luggage. Can we deliver it tomorrow morning?" And I said, "Oh no, I must have it tonight, it has medication for my children." And they managed to get us the luggage before the crabs died!

At other times, while Alton was teaching and consulting at Ohio State, he'd call and say, "I have forty Swedes in town, and I want them to come for a real home-cooked dinner." So I'd do one of my standbys: coq au vin or beef Wellington or boeuf bourguignon. I also made a lot of pâtés and terrines for parties, and crème caramel, since I didn't bake a lot.

Sue's holiday pâtés en croute. Clockwise from left: Chris, Grammy Doody, Rick, Kent Larsson, Sue, Grandpa Doody, Trish, Uncle Joe, and Ankie Larsson.

And the kids ate whatever I was cooking, whether it was something I wanted to try from the latest issue of *Gourmet*, or something special I was roasting or poaching or wrapping in a pastry crust for a dinner party—I never made one meal for the kids and one for the adults. Or different meals just to suit one kid's taste. Of course, there were always backup options in the fridge, but everyone pretty much shared—or indulged—my passion for cooking.

Floradelle Pfahl: Back in the '60s, when protests were the "in" thing to do, we invited friends to a party at which they could protest whatever they liked. Sue arrived wearing a chef's hat and a sandwich board protesting the mediocrity of Columbus restaurants. Her sandwich board read:

Maroon the Maramor
Lower LaBota's
Destroy Denny's
Abolish Anton's
Bomb the Beef Buffet
Kindle Kuennings
Grenade Gus's
Condemn Compass Points

Even then, she had visions of running a better restaurant than was then available in Columbus. Interestingly enough, they're all out of business now. Lindey's has outlived them all.

Younger son Chris Doody: Early on, before Mom was really interested in cooking, she watched Julia Child, and cooked up whatever Julia did. Now I was barely two at the time, but the story's been told so often, I feel as if I remember it. We were at the grocery store, in the produce department, and I was throwing a temper tantrum. (I did this rather often, apparently.)

So this lady came up to Mom to see if she could help: "What's wrong with your child?"

"Well, he wants me to buy artichokes, and I'm not going to buy them."

"He wants what?" the lady asked. (She'd never heard of artichokes, let alone prepared them for herself. Let alone for a two-year-old kid.)

"Artichokes. He just loves them. But they're much too expensive today," Mom replied.

Rick Doody: I remember Mom catering and teaching cooking classes in our kitchen. She'd take classes all around town, from any place that offered them: with Betty Rosbottom at La Belle Pomme, with Lisa Gallat at her restaurant A Matter of Taste, at Nancy Jeffrey's cooking store Good Things in Bexley, at Columbus State with chef Carolyn Claycomb.

The classes Mom offered at home, to a certain extent, were just good excuses for socializing, but Mom also had a great talent and respect for good food. She dabbled with various cuisines, and when WOSU, the PBS station, began to air *The French Chef*, I remember Mom and Dad ran out to buy a new television so we could have one in the kitchen.

Sue: I had Julia's cookbooks, so at the end of each show, when they announced the next week's dishes, I'd get all the ingredients ahead of time, and read the recipes, and make the dishes along with Julia. Of course, I couldn't always keep up, and I didn't have the finished dish already made in "the other oven." But I loved watching her in black and white, with all the practicality and pragmatism of hers that really helped bring great cooking into American homes.

Years and years later, I met Julia at one of her 90th-birthday celebrations. She was signing books at the Getty Museum. I said to her, "Ms. Child, I have been in the restaurant business for 20 years, and now my sons are in restaurants, and we owe it all to you—from watching your television show." And she said, "Darling, I'm so happy to meet you. Continued success."

Trish Elkind: Mom was totally gourmet, especially at the holidays. We didn't just have turkey, it was oyster-stuffed turkey. And cauliflower and peas with hollandaise, Yorkshire pudding, roast beef, fresh cranberry relish, chocolate pecan pie, and my Grandma's rum cake that had so much rum in it that all us kids got even sillier.

And there was always a little tension about these meals because my paternal grandmother from New Orleans had a different level of sophistication: she always brought a Jell-O mold with marshmallows and grapefruit, which Mom simply didn't want on the table. Grandma also brought her sweet potatoes, which my mother also didn't feel added anything. To this day, my mom insists on making the entire meal herself; we kids are supposed to bring nothing...except the grandchildren.

Server **Mike Higbee**, Rick's childhood friend: If I was ever at Rick's house during mealtime, Sue would call us into the kitchen, "I'm trying out this new recipe, and you're the guinea pigs." This was in the '70s, when most families were just microwaving dinner or ordering Tommy's pizza or making casseroles. The Doody house was different: Sue had the kitchen and family room combined into one great room, and the food was something you talked about.

Nancy Ross: Sue and I played tennis together. She'd drive, and on our way to the court, she'd always be saying, "Someday, someday, I'm going to have a restaurant." This was about 1975. Shortly after that, I took a few cooking classes in her kitchen at home. The one menu I especially recall is her beef tenderloin, which, to my horror, she fried! She called it "sautéing," but it looked just like frying with less fat. And we made green beans, cooking them quickly, which must have been the first time most of us heard of al dente. I remember leaving, thinking, well, I could cook the green beans the night before and reheat them the next day. A revelation!

Trish: When my husband and I lived in Minneapolis, Mom came to visit. My husband grew up in a family where food wasn't the center of attention. But he was proud of his grilling, and didn't feel the least bit intimidated about cooking for my mother, the restaurateur. So he's grilling boneless chicken breasts, and my mom is watching. Ten, fifteen minutes pass. We're talking, but I can see my mother is anxiously trying not to watch over the grilling.

Finally, she can't bear it and takes me aside, "Hon, the chicken's been on the grill for 45 minutes, and it's been done for the last 30 minutes. You've got to get him to bring it in."

Well, he'd never cooked a boneless breast before. Now, whenever someone brings up that meal, we all get a good chuckle imitating Mom trying not to bully her new son-in-law, trying to politely rescue the meal, trying to eat the utterly dried-out chicken breast.

Left to right: Sue circa 1982. Sue at five. Sue and Rick, Lindey's first New Year's Eve, 1981.

If It's New, I Need it, Don't I?

Among the many things in which Columbustown natives take pride are many "firsts," often inspired by the city's reputation as a test market. For instance, Columbus was home to the first drive-in restaurants with speakers and car service, the first ATMs, the first shopping centers, the first electric chair, the first drive-through window at a bank, and the first of several chain restaurants, including Wendy's, White Castle, York Steak House, Sister's Chicken and Biscuits, and Bob Evans.

And, to the point, Columbus is the home of Lindey's, one of the longest continuously operating, owned-by-the-same-family fine-dining establishments in the area.

In Sue Doody's own life, some moments of culinary passion and possibility pop up like those little "done" buttons on a roasted Butterball turkey amid the cluttered kitchen of progress. The following selection of foods and innovations (accompanied here by commentary from Sue) fueled the momentum that would, one day, create Lindey's.

1933	1936	1945	1947	1949
The year before Sue is born, the Waldorf Salad becomes the popular luncheon dish. **Sue:** My mother made it one of our family staples. And over 70 years later, Smoked Chicken Waldorf Salad is one of Lindey's most popular lunch dishes.	Waring blenders introduce Americans to purée, frappe, and you-should-have-secured-the-lid-more-tightly. **Sue:** In my earliest memories, I remember a blender on the counter at home. Modern efficiency grabbed my imagination, even then.	Tupperware parties begin across America. **Sue:** I was all of 11 at the time, and I found the burp of the container lid pressing closed very satisfying.	Kraft Singles debut. **Sue:** When I was in junior high school, I loved having grilled cheese sandwiches while watching James Beard's *I Love to Eat*, the first food show, which debuted that year on NBC.	Minute Rice arrives on the grocer's shelves. **Sue:** We never had it at home, and then, when I eventually married, it was to someone from New Orleans. And no one with any connection to that great city would ever have such a thing in the kitchen.

1960s	1964	1973	1981

The first microwave ovens are introduced.
Sue: Yes, I acquired one of the first ones on the market. It took up a huge amount of space, and I think that all I used it for was warming my coffee and heating soup.

Kellogg's Pop-Tarts become America's new breakfast.
Sue: Even though I'd learned to make croissants and omelets au champignons from Julia Child, I was more than happy to let the kids have the toaster pastries. But that only lasted for a couple weeks, before the novelty wore off and they wanted the croissants and omelets again.

Cuisinart creates its popular food processor.
Sue: I took a cooking class from Tom Johnson at La Belle Pomme, and he used this wonderful new machine to make an Alsatian potato soup... so, yes, I had to have one.

Lindey's opens the same year a rash of national chain restaurants debut, such as Fuddrucker's, Applebee's, and the Olive Garden.
Sue: It was the year of mud pies, blackened fish, wild buffalo wings, gourmet pizzas, and frozen yogurt. But I thought Columbus needed something else. A restaurant with fresh foods, with dishes made from scratch every day. So many of the popular dining options back then had their foods prepared somewhere else and shipped in on a truck. It's funny to look back at our first menus and remember how novel it was to have a fine restaurant emphasizing the idea of "homemade" or "made from scratch."

LINDEY'S FIRST FEW YEARS:
DIARY OF A MADHOUSE

OUR BEGINNINGS WERE HUMBLE, complete with a few tumbles and stumbles. (People who used the word "bumble," without referring to a bee on our terrace, are, even today, routinely seated by the squealing cappuccino machine.) In this chapter, we offer an oral history of our early years as our "white elephant" of a location became a thriving, spirited presence in the neighborhood.

Fall, 1979: 20 Months Before Lindey's Opens Its Doors

> "I loved the look of the building. I didn't even zero in on the
> fact that it had never been a successful restaurant." —*Sue*

Sue: I've always loved to cook gourmet food, and when I first decided to open a restaurant, I originally wanted to open a lunch place like the Gourmet Market and have lots of pâtés, pasta salads, hors d'oeuvres—things that supplement a meal. I wanted to sell that over the counter and also have a lunch business.

I wanted the look of an Upper East Side New York café: hardwood floors, white table-cloths, bentwood chairs. I wanted the waiters to wear long white aprons, and I knew from the beginning that I didn't want a gourmet restaurant where people only came on special occasions. I wanted them to be able to order what they wanted, and not worry if they mispronounced some menu item or wine that was in Italian or French.

Alton Doody: In 1980, I owned Retail Planning Associates down the street from what would become Lindey's. We did store design: everything from Wal-Mart to Saks Fifth Avenue. When our son Rick graduated from Ohio Wesleyan that year, he said, "I don't know what I want to do, but I know what I don't want to do: work for your friends in these big companies." I respected that. So Sue and I decided he might travel for the next six months. We wrote him a check and off he went to England and France. But, I told him, in case you want to meet any of these people I know in retail, I'm going to give you a few names.

In England, Rick met up with Peter O'Gorman, who took him to Capetown, South Africa, to install a HyperMarket (something like a huge Wal-Mart). When he returned to England, Sue visited him in October, and we were on the telephone about a restaurant down the block from our company that was for sale. Palmer McNeil had a government job, his mother was running the restaurant, and he was anxious to get out. Bill Scheuer, who owned the building, called me, hoping to find a buyer for the restaurant. As I recall, Palmer wanted to pay off his note at the bank, $118,000, and Bill Scheuer wanted about a quarter million for the building.

Rick Doody: When I arrived in Bologna, my father made a connection for me with a local lighting manufacturer. Vito, my contact there, figured I was the way into the Doody's worldwide business. So he decided to wine and dine me for three days straight; every lunch and dinner was a 10-course meal. Vito was unbelievably generous. I had never eaten food like that in my life, and I knew that if I ever opened a restaurant in America, the cuisine would be Italian.

Oddly enough, Mom and I talked about "our" restaurant all the time when I was in high school and college. Just throwing out ideas. Imagining how we'd do things. For instance, after I gave up the idea of going to a department-store training program in college, which would have been a disaster, Mom visited me in England. We'd be at different pubs, and I'd point to the vase of flowers on the table: "If we had a restaurant, we'd never have plastic flowers, would we?" she'd shake her head no, absolutely not.

Sue: I asked Rick, "So where do you think a good location for our restaurant would be in Columbus?" We'd probably eaten at a dozen places in England by then. Without much hesitation, he said that there was a restaurant in German Village with a corner door and a lighted canopy, but he didn't know its name.

When I came home from that trip, his father told me that the Palmer Haus was up for sale and that he thought we should buy it—the very space where Rick had imagined a restaurant.

We went to look at the building at 169 East Beck Street, and we all liked it immediately, even though we saw how much work it needed. It had been home to five different restaurants in twice as many years: Kings Rose Garden, Lindenhof, Albert P. Grubb's, Barney's, and Palmer Haus. We began talking with bankers, and we were able to use the Palmer Haus's equipment as collateral against the loan. I recruited Alton to seal the deal. By the time Rick returned from Europe for Christmas, we were in negotiations to purchase the restaurant.

Alton: When we bought the place, the first thing I realized was that everything had to go. You walked into the building and were welcomed by a pay phone. Then you'd walk down an empty corridor and end up at a plate-glass window. Finally, you'd turn into a dining room that had no windows and red flocked wallpaper. The charm of the entire place—entirely overlooked!—was to use the big windows so guests could see out and people walking by could see in.

John Smallridge, now a proprietor of the Hoggy's restaurant group: Before Rick started the renovation, that place looked like a bordello: red wallpaper, dim lights, and carpeting the color of dried blood.

Alton: I remember one controversy—the main entrance. Should the bar go in the second dining room, and be accessible to the entrance on the courtyard, so you'd walk into the bar and then pass through it to enter the dining room? Or should you come in the entrance on the corner, directly into the dining room? At the time, Deirdre, a sexy 28-year-old, worked at the Doody Company. "This isn't even up for discussion," she declared. "The door has to open right into the main room. When I walk in, I want to see who's there and what's going on."

We also had a designer on staff, Lynnette, originally from France via South Africa, who was very exotic and very talented. Our goal for Lindey's was to create an adult version of TGI Friday's. I suppose my background in retail planning guided the making of a strategy: Who are we, and who are we trying to be? Twenty-five years ago, Lindey's was the tipping point away from old-fashioned elegant to...say, smart and more casual. We thought of the old steakhouses such as Peter Luger's, or places such as the Palm or the Oak Bar at the Plaza.

Rick Doody: I remember Dad doing some slide shows, educating the rest of the family on the restaurants he thought were models for Lindey's. There was Mortimer's. Elaine's. Maxwell's Plum. And we all knew many of the New Orleans restaurants we were thinking of from so many visits there over the years.

Sue: Oh, and if someone wasn't paying attention to the slides, Alton would get so mad. Well, he was a university professor...

Chef **Tom Johnson:** It was a rickety building at the start, rather like our business. When Barry Zacks owned the building, the second floor housed a pinball arcade. The room was painted black, so that the glowing, flashing, and flickering of the machines provided all the lighting. How the ceiling supported all those early, heavy video-game machines, I don't know.

What I remember is one evening, shortly after I came to Lindey's, we hosted a prom upstairs in that space. It was packed with college students. And, of course, the kids played rock music—the sound booming through amplifiers that were as tall as the room—and started frugging up there, and downstairs, Sue and I looked up and saw the tin ceiling bowing. And then we heard this huge crashing, as if the building had become organic and was suffering a heart attack. And the ceiling heaved and bulged and we raced upstairs to sedate the party. We had vision of the entire ceiling collapsing on the dining room. But it held.

Alton Doody: We have to credit Lajos Szabó, a close family friend, for much of Lindey's design. A Hungarian who left the year of the revolution, he intended to go to England but ended up in Cleveland. The first job he did on his own was our house, and then he did some work with me in the retail business. He's the chief designer and architect of Lindey's. At each meeting with Lajos we'd tell him what we were trying to accomplish, and he'd listen, and listen, and then he'd say, "Vee draw it up."

Lajos: I think Alton always wanted to open a restaurant. And one day he called me and I met him at the Palmer Haus, and he said, "Lajos, what are we going to do with it?" And I told him, it's ugly, it's dreadful, and I don't like it. So we sat down together in one of the booths and started planning.

I made a layout. Alton reviewed it. He had people from the Doody Company review it. Someone would come to my office and say we have to change this and that. I drew up plan after plan, and the trouble was, everyone wanted to be the architect. Alton had one woman who was such a dreamer, but the problem is always: you have to make something you can put on the ground and build. And she would say "Alton, we have to have this, and this, and this," and Alton would tell her that it was all too expensive. Then she would say, we cannot be cheap! For instance, she wanted a bubbling fountain in the middle of the restaurant. But I told her a fountain doesn't bring in money, a table does.

Outside? The old linden tree was the highlight of the property, and when we finally opened the place, everyone wanted to sit out on the patio under the tree. But that meant there was no room for anything else. I had to squeeze in a staircase—it had to be a spiral staircase. There was no room for trash pickup, so I had to move the garbage inside and build a gate on the building to give the trash collectors access. The only thing I couldn't do anything about was the parking: there is none in German Village.

Alton: When Barry Zacks found out that I was buying the place, he called me: "Alton, I don't know you very well. I know you're friends with my brother Gordon. And I'll help you get out of it."

"Out of what?"

"That contract you've got. Let me tell you, you'll lose your shirt, I've tried everything there: high end, low end, and nothing you can do will make it work." At the time, Barry's restaurants included the Clarmont, and the Max & Erma's restaurants.

"Barry, even if you're right, I have to do this. My son really wants to be in the business, and I can back it for the moment. We'll do it for the experience."

Left and center: the corner of Beck and Mohawk, prior to Lindenhof's renovation. Right: Kings Rose Garden interior with bentwood chairs.

January, 1981: **Opening Day Is Six Months Away**

· ·

> "If we knew how much we didn't know, we never would
> have done what we did."   —*Alton Doody*

The initial renovations took four months and about $150,000, with a work crew consisting of Sue, her sons Rick and Chris, Ken Smith, Mark Turner, and several gentlemen Rick managed to find on the unemployment line. "Once it was known that we were paying for labor," Rick remembers, "folks just showed up at the door, hoping for work."

Sue: Each day Rick would arrive with a carload of these guys. We had about 12 men that he'd drive down to German Village. I brought in a hot plate and fixed lunch for everyone right in the middle of the construction. I grilled hot dogs and ham-and-cheese sandwiches. The workers were like my family, except we paid them $3.50 an hour, and the family was working for free!

Chris: I'll never forget—Rick and Dad were acting as general contractors. There'd be a pile of equipment or junk from the previous restaurants, and Rick would say, "Chris, take all this stuff down to the basement." And I'd make a bunch of trips hauling it down, and then Dad would come into the basement, see the pile, and say, "Chris, can you take all that up to the third floor?" So I got to triple my efforts.

Sue: Some of the workers would return the next day; some would leave after half a day. (One stayed for many years, working his way up until he was a dinner server.) And this went on for six months or so before opening. They stripped wallpaper, ripped out carpeting, scraped walls, and tossed garbage out the second-floor windows onto dump trucks.

With the awful red carpeting gone, we had hardwood floors. I knew with the tin ceiling and the wood floors, we were going to have a lot of noise. And we worried about that. Restaurants 25 years ago—in Columbus, anyway—didn't make a lot of noise. But we wanted that energetic feel of a neighborhood bistro.

John Smallridge: One day I get a call from Rick asking if I have a belt sander he could borrow; he wants to sand the floors of the restaurant he's opening. So I tell him, sure, but it's only a Sears Craftsman with something like a 4-inch surface. I tell him he should rent a professional belt sander. But, no, he tells me, they're keeping things low-budget and my sander's perfect. So that week, a bunch of us would drive by at 1:00 or 2:00 in the morning, and keep Rick company. He spent days on his knees sanding this huge room with a tiny machine meant to redo the top of a nightstand.

Architect **Lajos Szabó:** The main renovations included these major items:

- Install a new bar, purchased at auction from the Red Lion, the restaurant in the old Neil House hotel. We had to turn a long straight bar with many missing parts into an L-shaped, copper-topped bar.

- Create a vestibule, but don't give up any real space inside. We wanted the tables to look out on the street, so we created a vestibule that just passed building code: two sets of doors with the minimum, minimum space between them.

- Reassemble the original tin ceiling, which was missing panels where the room divider had been installed (forcing the removal one of the enormous chandeliers, which we stumbled upon by accident in the attic and then rehung) by adding new flat panels that created a border around each room.

- Add corner molding to give the illusion of lowering the ceiling, to give the room a cozier feeling.

- Add wainscoting around the room where the booths had been mounted. (This renovation was inspired by the bar's wooden panels.)

- Make the bar area separate by installing a divider with seating on both sides, while also incorporating the load-bearing columns into the short wall.

- Sand the wide floorboards that were worn and warped in some places (and merely dirty in others) to create an even finish and stable surface.

- Create a service stand in the only space left, under the main stairs.

- Place mirrors behind the bar, between the wine racks, to enlarge the space and "double" the crowd.

- Reconfigure the kitchen: add equipment from the Neil House auction; try to create more work space in that cramped and inefficient place.

Sue: Aside from preparing meals and stripping wallpaper, I also attended liquidation sales at various places in town. We bought our bar from the Neil House, and I've always said that if that bar could talk, it would have so many stories, because all the legislators used to drink a lot there and decide the fate of the state.

I searched the Mansion Restaurant at Woodward and Park for bargains on restaurant fixtures. I went to the auction at the Top of the Center, the restaurant on top of the Borden Building. I saw a huge copper cappuccino machine there, and I said, I'll take it, here's my credit card. I wanted to be sure no one else bought it. Then the owner Bill Maxwell arrived and told the person handling the sale, "Sell everything but the cappuccino machine." But my card had already been run through.

Turns out that the machine never did work right. Probably once a week a repairman from Italy—not all the way from Italy, but from Italy originally—would come and take the whole thing apart and put the whole thing back together and then it would work for a day—and then we'd have to explain that it was only for show.

Sue: As for decorating the restaurant, everyone had ideas for me. What about blackboards on the walls for the daily specials? What about neon lettering for the logo—maybe even neon lighting inside? What about a huge fountain inside the main dining room? One of Alton's designers actually proposed peacocks for the courtyard: a fountain, an awning, and a bunch of peacocks—*live peacocks*—in German Village! In Ohio! Year-round! But I wanted artwork. I thought about renting paintings from the Columbus Museum of Art, since they had a lender's gallery. But we found another solution.

Local sculptor Stephen Canneto had helped me find local artists who wanted a space to sell their work on consignment, so we could support "starving artists" and also have beautiful art throughout the restaurant. So every morning, once we opened, I'd have to check around the restaurant to see if there was a bare nail in the middle of an empty space where someone had bought a painting the night before. The day before we opened, we were still hanging the art.

Employee of the Mouth

Server M: When someone would ask how come there's an 'S' engraved on the teaspoons, a few of the servers would reply, 'Oh, that stands for "Sue,"' and that would seem to satisfy most folks. They loved knowing that Sue was Lindey's!

But the truth is, Rick Doody had bought the spoons at an auction for the downtown Sheraton that had just closed.

But that wasn't the only "truth" at work. Another server, "hoping only to protect Lindey's from itself," took the liberty of pitching as many of those tacky Sheraton teaspoons into the trash each night as would escape notice.

Sue: At the same time, in my home kitchen, I was developing appetizers and entrées for our first menu. I experimented with recipes from my favorite cookbooks, from classes I'd taken. I tried some new things that I thought were going to be popular. Then I'd have Rick and my managers come to the house and sample everything.

A few months prior to opening, we brought on Emil Shedlock from Engine House #5, to set up company policies, handbooks, and reservation systems. We were desperate for someone with day-to-day restaurant operation experience. So Emil identified things like what we should expect from employees and what employees should expect from Lindey's. For instance, employees could have one shift drink, and 50% discount on all meals, and paid vacations.

Aside from Emil, we opened Lindey's with no practical experience in the restaurant business. It still amazes me that we succeeded.

Kitchen renovation, 1985; the equipment spends a month on the patio.

April, 1981: **Nine Weeks Until the First Guests Arrive**

. . . .

"When she fails, and Lindey's closes, I want to buy it back.
She'll never keep it open, because people only celebrate
their birthdays once a year." —*Barry Zacks*

Beth Doody: We were all on a vacation in Key West, and even though Mom and Dad were divorced, we were all together because the restaurant was just opening. I remember at every meal, around one table or another, all anyone could talk about was silverware, plates, and glasses. "How do you like this?" "Maybe we should try a glass that's taller?" "Does this feel too breakable?" I was in seventh grade, and I couldn't have cared less.

Sue: Rick went to the Pi Beta Phi sorority house to recruit staff, and we hired several of the sorority sisters. They didn't know the difference between chicken and veal, but that was okay, since we weren't serving veal. They were just so cute and agreeable.

Joan Flower: One day Diane Bucher stopped at my sorority house with the news that a restaurant was hiring and that Andy Fugazzi was involved, who was dating one of my sorority sisters. So five of us went down, interviewed—I don't think it was more than answering a few questions—and started training.

We helped prep the restaurant for opening: washing floors, stocking, painting—building a little pride in the place. We also took what we called Emil Classes. We'd come in for a couple hours, and Emil would talk about what food went with what wine, and how to suggest bottles of wine based on what people were ordering, and how to perform a proper wine service. And he gave us each a wine server, and we each had to open a bottle, in front of everyone, so Emil could adjust our technique. And whatever you did, you could not break the cork. It was a whole show for Emil: Sniff the cork. Present the cork. Never touch the bowl of the glass. Turn and twist the bottle so there will never be a drip. Hold the champagne bottle with your thumb in the bottom. Never shoot a champagne cork because you'll lose that effervescence.

We even had a final—a final exam for a restaurant!—which, as it turns out, happened to be during OSU's spring quarter finals week. "And if you don't pass, you aren't going to get the job," he told us. Period. I remember I was taking one and a half course loads at OSU, and I knew going into the "Lindey's final" that I was in trouble. But a few of my other Pi Phi sorority sisters were servers, too, so we divided up the test. We knew what was going to be covered. I studied up on French whites; someone else did reds—everyone took a part—and then we all whispered answers back and forth during the entire test. Teamwork's the key to a restaurant, right?

SUE'S PASTA PRIMAVERA, 1981

PASTA DISHES FORMED A CORNERSTONE of our early menus, although it could be said we had a lot of cornerstones—French, Italian, Cajun, American—and not a lot of façade. We were all about having a menu with broad appeal: we wanted something excellent for most every palate.

Sue: One afternoon, months before we opened, I was scraping red velvet wallpaper from the walls, and in comes Barry Zacks, who'd owned Alfred P. Grubbs in this very space years earlier and then owned the very successful Max & Erma's restaurants. And he asks me, "What will you be putting on the menu?" So I tell him that I think pasta is going to be big in the '80s. "I'm thinking of having a pasta primavera." Within the week, pasta primavera was on the menu at Max & Erma's!

Our cannelloni recipe was so complicated, we're leaving it to memory. But our pasta primavera deserves another revival. It's a "springtime" pasta originally improvised in 1975 for a group of gourmet dinners by Sirio Maccioni, the chef of Le Cirque. His Tuscan-inspired dish involved spaghetti, fresh vegetables, frozen peas, and cream; the very next week, Craig Claiborne (then food critic of the *New York Times*) proclaimed it "the best pasta discovery in 20 years," which is how the dish captured Sue's imagination and became a springtime, and then a year-round, favorite at Lindey's for almost a decade.

serves 6

- 1/2 pound asparagus (tough ends snapped off), cut on the bias into 1-inch pieces
- 2 cups broccoli florets, cut into bite-size pieces
- 1/2 pound snow peas, trimmed and halved crosswise
- 2 small zucchini, quartered lengthwise and sliced 1/4 inch thick
- 1/3 cup pine nuts (about 1 1/2 ounce)
- 4 tablespoons extra-virgin olive oil
- 1/2 pound button mushrooms, quartered into bite-size pieces
- 1 teaspoon minced garlic
- 1 medium purple onion, halved, and thinly sliced
- 1 cup frozen baby peas, thawed
- 4 ripe Italian plum tomatoes, diced into 1/2-inch cubes (about 1 1/2 cups)
- 1 pound dried fettuccini
- 4 tablespoons unsalted butter (1/2 stick)
- 2/3 cup crème fraîche (see Note)
- 1/4 pound finely grated Parmesan (1 to 1 1/2 cups), half reserved for garnish
- 1/4 to 1/2 cup low-sodium chicken stock, as needed
- 1/4 cup chopped fresh flat-leaf parsley, plus extra for optional garnish
- 1/4 cup chopped fresh chives, plus extra for optional garnish

Prepare a large bowl of ice water and set aside.

In a large pot of boiling salted water, cook the asparagus, broccoli, snow peas, and zucchini uncovered for 3 minutes, or until the vegetables are barely tender. With a slotted spoon or sieve, transfer the vegetables into the ice water to stop the cooking. Cover the pot, and keep the water simmering on low heat for cooking the fettuccine later. Once the vegetables are cool, drain them in a colander, and return them to the mixing bowl.

In a large, heavy skillet, toast the pine nuts over medium heat, gently stirring them or shaking the pan until they are golden brown, about 4 minutes. Be careful not to brown or burn the nuts. Remove the toasted nuts and set aside.

Add olive oil to coat the surface of the same skillet. Add the quartered mushrooms and sauté until they are lightly browned, about 3 minutes. Add the mushrooms to the bowl of cooked vegetables.

Bring the simmering water to a boil.

Add the remaining olive oil to the skillet, along with the garlic and onion slices, and sauté until soft and slightly colored, about 5 minutes. Add all the drained vegetables, the thawed baby peas, and the tomato chunks, and continue to cook, stirring the entire time, for 2 minutes. Taste, and add salt and pepper as needed. Turn the heat off, cover the skillet, and keep the vegetables warm.

Cook the fettuccini in the boiling water until al dente, about 6 to 10 minutes (read the package's suggestion). Drain in a colander, but do not rinse. Immediately add the butter and crème fraîche to the empty pasta pot, stirring for 1 minute to heat. Turn down the heat to medium. Stir in half of the grated cheese and then return the hot pasta to the pot, tossing to coat. Thin the sauce with up to $1/2$ cup chicken stock to ensure a uniformly creamy coating. Add the warmed vegetables, toasted pine nuts, parsley, and chives, gently tossing to combine. Taste, adding salt and pepper as needed.

Divide the pasta among six warmed dinner plates, sprinkling each with extra Parmesan and the optional parsley and chives.

Note: *To make your own crème fraîche, combine 1 cup heavy cream with 2 tablespoons cultured buttermilk in a small bowl. Cover with plastic wrap and a towel, and set in a warm place to thicken for 12 to 24 hours. Store the finished crème fraîche in the refrigerator, where it will stay fresh for 1 week.*

Suzanne Karpus: Sue's recipe, which she'd brought from home, took forever to make. Not only did we make the fresh pasta, shape it into rolls, and stuff it with spinach that had to be hand-squeezed to remove all the water, we also had to create a béchamel sauce and a meat sauce to go with it. One day, Sharon and I were walking down the street past Lindey's on a day off, and someone saw us and shouted out from the kitchen door, "We're out of the cannelloni! You have to come in right now and make more." And we did.

Chef Tom Johnson: Our pasta was made on premises, cranked out, by hand, with *one* Atlas pasta machine. This was usually done by two colleagues who were moonlighting from college and from La Belle Pomme Cooking School: Sharon Reiss and Suzanne Karpus, the two of whom went on to found Cornucopia, a catering business now owned by Suzanne. This was long before the days of electric pasta machines and long before those divinely inspired rollers imported from Italy by KitchenAid, which snap into the end of a stand mixer. The handmade results were sublime. But as the cannelloni's popularity increased, so did the drudgery below stairs. Friendships were threatened as both ladies slowly succumbed to a condition which I have since named Karpus Tunnel Syndrome!

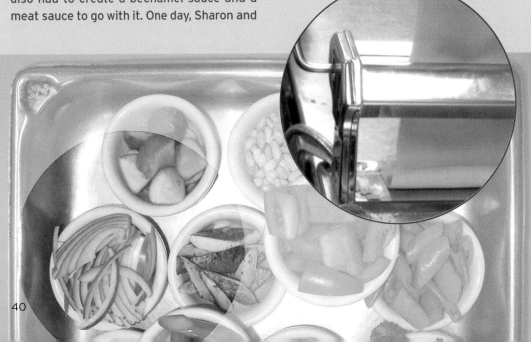

Rick Doody: The *Citizen Journal* interviewed me when Lindey's was about to open. "We want to do a story about your new restaurant," a reporter told me.

"Actually, it's my mom's restaurant," I told him.

"Well, who are your investors?"

"My dad."

"Okay, so how do you want this to be in print?"

"My mom and dad are divorced, and for a long time she didn't want to do any kind of business with Dad. Marriage didn't work, why would business? So..." We talked for a while longer, and then the next day the headline read, "Rick Doody opens a restaurant," which is exactly what I didn't want.

Actually, we all had pretty distinct roles: Mom leaned toward the food. Dad leaned toward everything—that's just how he is. Emil did the service. I did the restaurant operations. And there wasn't a day when we didn't try to fix and improve Lindey's.

June 7, 1981: Opening Day

· ·

> "I told my suppliers that I meant business and that I was going to stay in business. We just needed to survive long enough for us to get things right." —*Sue*

Sue: I don't think I had enough knowledge about how many restaurants actually fail. We had done a pretty good job the week before opening, familiarizing our servers with the different dishes—and we had a few practice dinners, serving a very limited menu to a few friends and family for free, just to rehearse. And then we opened for real.

The opening staff consisted of several ill-defined positions, all sort of jumbled together. Along with Sue (proprietor/chef/owner/mother) and Rick Doody (co-owner/manager/son) and Emil Shedlock (host/"the one person with any restaurant experience"/wine buyer— all of 21 years old), and Walter (a cook who'd answered an ad in the paper).

At the time, the restaurant seated 106 guests. The first night, Lindey's served 20 dinners.

Joan Flower: In the beginning, our uniforms were khaki pants, a white button-down shirt, and a little maroon grosgrain ribbon in a bow (the men wore maroon ties), tan docksiders, and a white apron. I lived with three other Lindey's servers at the time, and heading out to work, you just grabbed the first clean white shirt you saw, whether it was yours or not. If you were the last person to leave, you often lost out.

Six weeks after opening, the red-and-white checkered "tablecloths" (easy-to-wipe-down oilcloths) are thrown out, and white linens cover the dining room tables. Sue breaths a sigh of relief. Many, many more sighs are to come.

Joan Flower: We all had side work to do. The worst? Laundry duty. You'd see your name on the chart, and next to it: "washer and dryer," which meant you'd have to take the soiled laundry in the bags from the night before, and head down to the basement: wash, dry, and fold. You'd try to get the washing done when you came in, and time the drying so that it would be done just about the time your last tables were leaving. But if the napkins had been in the dryer too long, they'd be wrinkled, and Sue would notice that, and you'd have to give them another cycle…and you'd be folding laundry when you wanted to be home in bed.

But then, when our machines broke, which was frequently, you'd have to run up to the bookkeeper, Cathy Sisterhen, for a roll of quarters, and drive all the linens over to the Laundromat and tie up every machine there (which always made the locals coming in with their clothes unhappy), wait for the laundry, and then drive it all back to Lindey's.

Bartender **Kurt Baughman:** When Sue first opened the restaurant, I gather the only bar-ware she had was "the all-purpose wine glass." One glass for red wine and the same glass for white wine. And if you wanted a martini (although the martini wasn't so popular in 1981), that came in the wine glass, too. Twenty-five years later, some guests still order their cocktails in wine glasses—just remembering the good old days.

Sue: There were a lot of doubters. People were saying, "Who does she think she is? She has no experience! And that place is a white elephant." But I think my experience came from my volunteer work, and from running a household and a household budget.

But the real challenge was that some people didn't take me seriously. Produce vendors or suppliers would give me inferior products or less competitive deals because I was a woman. They figured the restaurant was the pet project of a bored housewife. They thought I wouldn't notice or wouldn't have the gumption to protest. But I learned very quickly to negotiate and hold out for what was right. I'd send the inferior foods right back. I told them I meant business and I was going to stay in business. I opened with my favorite recipes, and I thought I really could just go with my own recipes, and some specials and seasonal things…but I soon realized that I needed someone with more expertise. We had people in the kitchen with books open—*Mastering the Art of French Cooking* and recipes from the *Times*—while I was trying to teach people how to stir things. At that point, a good night was 150 dinners. (Today, upwards of 500 dinners is more typical.)

Joan Flower: On a busy night, you could count on Emil to step in and do the whole wine service for you. He'd present the wine list to your table with a long sweeping gesture, sort of floating it down from above the diner. He chatted up a few bottles he liked—and it wasn't as if we had an extensive cellar, at least compared to today's restaurant lists—but people were just learning about wines then.

Yes, Emil would place each wine glass on the table with such showmanship, twisting his hand so he could hold the glass by the stem and then give it a full turn on the way to the table, like a diver doing a front flip in lay-out position with a perfect landing, no splash. Then the cork-sniffing, the tasting, the pouring—it was all a drawn-out entertainment.

Sue: I knew I wanted fresh—but there were a lot of things that slipped by in the beginning. Such as quality control. Such as systems. I remember Ivan and Marci Gilbert came to lunch one day full of advice for me. (Ivan owned another Columbus restaurant.) First he told me that I should always make sure that each delivery truck drops off everything that's on the bill. He'd been keeping another place in business for months, paying for produce that the driver had been dropping off at the other restaurant.

And then he told me I should be watchful of employees as they leave the restaurant each day. "They could be walking off with profits, right out that door." He'd noticed one of his cooks walking awkwardly toward the front door after her shift, when all of a sudden a prime rib dropped onto the floor from beneath her skirt. She'd been squeezing it between her knees and trying to leave unnoticed.

Lindey's very first event in the courtyard was the wedding of a Calvin Klein model. The groom's family, from Bexley, had discovered Lindey's.

Sue: They wanted to know if we could host the wedding here, and we hadn't even begun to establish a special events business. But we set up tables in the courtyard, had someone from the awning company come out and make certain the awning wouldn't blow loose, which it always did, and their florists created a beautiful space complete with the second "awning," the chuppah, since it was a Jewish wedding.

As for the bride, Calvin Klein created a dress especially for her, and let me tell you, she was drop-dead gorgeous.

Chris Doody: I remember one time, Saturday night, busing tables, and Rick was very tense. It was an OSU football game. This was when the walk-in cooler was on the main floor, and our "chef" had four strip steaks in the locker. *Four. Four total.* We were going to need something like 40. Rick was freaking out, and he ended up sending me to every store within driving distance to get strip steaks. We just didn't know what par* was.

Mark Turner: Lindey's dining room floor was pretty worn, and Rick and I thought it could use a new finish. We started Sunday night after closing, putting down a coat of polyurethane with sponge mops. We didn't know that you were supposed to do it by hand, in a very light coating, in two or three layers, with plenty of drying time in between layers. So we finished, closed the doors, and felt terrific about our job. The floors were going to look great. The next day, a Monday, Rick called me at my day job: "It's not dry! Mom just walked in and she stuck to the floor!" So I ran over and we set up fans everywhere, opened all the doors and, amazingly, we were able to set up and open for dinner.

---

* **Speak restaurantese:** "Par," as on a golf course, refers to an average: the number you might be expected to reach on a given course. In a restaurant's case, that's the number of any given item that's likely to sell on any given night. At the start of Lindey's, we often had no idea how many of each entrée to prepare. How many people would be coming in for dinner? How many would be inclined to order each entrée? Eventually—it's a matter of practice, as in golf—we learned. We learned.

OUR OVERGLAZED ONION SOUP

ONE RECIPE FROM JULIA CHILD'S *Mastering the Art of French Cooking* that Sue adored, adapted, and added to the very first menu at Lindey's is a rich, hearty, soulful French onion soup. Sue's version, fine-tuned yet again by chef Tom Johnson, is an Overglazed Onion Soup with both port and cognac infusing a sturdy chicken stock and a substantial cache of onions. In the intervening years, various Lindey's chefs have added their own subtle touches: if you're fond of our current version, you'll want both red and yellow onions, both a veal and a chicken stock as the base, and dried oregano rather than the cloves and allspice. But if you'd like to try the original version, this is it.

makes 8 servings

- 1 1/2 pounds yellow onions peeled and thinly sliced (about 5 cups)
- 1 tablespoon dried thyme
- 3 tablespoons unsalted butter or canola oil
- 2 quarts rich chicken broth (or, if you'd rather be more French than more Lindey's, water)
- 1 bay leaf
- 1 cup tawny port or dry Madeira
- 1 tablespoon Worcestershire sauce
- 1/8 teaspoon ground cloves
- 1/4 teaspoon ground allspice
- salt and freshly ground black pepper, to taste

for serving

- 8 thick slices French bread, toasted
- 8 thin slices Swiss cheese (large enough to cover each bowl)
- 1/2 cup grated Parmesan cheese
- 8 teaspoons VS Cognac, optional

Slowly cook the onions and thyme in the butter or oil, covered, in a large heavy-bottomed soup kettle over medium heat, until they are soft, translucent, and have reduced by about one-third (about 35 minutes). The onions will give up some liquid, which contains their residual sugar.

Uncover the soup kettle, increase the heat to medium-high, and continue to cook, stirring and scraping the bottom continuously for 4 to 8 minutes as the water evaporates and the sugar caramelizes, darkening the onions. You want the onions to be golden brown, not scorched or burned.

Add the chicken stock and the bay leaf and bring the pot to a boil, then reduce the heat so that the liquid remains at a simmer. In 30 minutes, discard the bay leaf and skim off any grease which may have risen to the surface. Add the port or Madeira and the Worcestershire sauce, and simmer an additional 5 minutes. Finally, stir in the ground cloves and allspice.

Season to taste with salt, freshly ground pepper, and any of the other seasonings in order to balance the soup's flavors. (The salt, in particular, depends on the saltiness of the stock used.)

To serve, ladle portions of the soup into individual ovenproof crocks and add the optional cognac, if desired. Top each crock with a toasted French bread slice, a slice of Swiss cheese, and a sprinkling of Parmesan. Place under a broiler or in a hot oven until the cheese is crusty and brown. Serve immediately.

Now imagine, if you will, chopping enough onions to serve a restaurant the size of Lindey's. Typically, the kitchen made the soup in 80-serving batches, subduing a single 50-pound bag of onions in one fell—and tearful—swoop.

That is, until Larry Moore arrived in the kitchen.

Sue: We hired Larry as a general handyman for building maintenance—he literally held down the fort in our early days. But Chef Tom Johnson discovered that Larry had another talent: He simply wasn't allergic to onions!

Indeed, without shedding a single tear, Larry could process 50 pounds of onions in a machine called the Buffalo chopper (no, not for making ground beef—the machine was made in Buffalo, New York), which resembled a giant salad bowl with whirling knives inside.

Chef Tom Johnson: One afternoon, Larry prepped the onions for the soup, and didn't realize that he'd left open the door in the prep kitchen that leads to the restaurant's air conditioning unit. But then, in the middle of lunch, one of the servers rushes into the kitchen, saying, "Chef, something's wrong in the dining room—you have to come out here." So I follow him out into the dining room where I see that all the guests are blotting their eyes with their napkins—all the guests, and all at the same time, as if someone had just announced a terribly sad bit of news over the intercom.

Now I had no idea what had happened until I went downstairs and realized that the onion vapors had been sucked through the ventilation system into the dining room, atomizing like some invisible boo-hoo gas throughout the restaurant.

But our luck with Larry ended one day. All he really wanted to do was work as a guard at the Franklin Country Jail. And the day he finally got that job, I said to Sue, "Well, there goes our onion chopper."

For those of us at home, there are ways to decrease the amount of those volatile, irritating onion ions: use a very sharp knife, chill the onions ahead of time, and see if you can find someone like Larry to lend a hand.

Fall, 1981: **Five Months Later, a New Chef Arrives**

> "I had never worked in an inner-city kitchen before where half the staff was stealing and the owner's son was constantly sticking his finger into the sauce while I was cooking."
> —*Chef Tom Johnson*

Sue hears a review of Lindey's broadcast on WOSU by restaurant critic Tom Johnson who, at the time, was chef at Shaw's Restaurant, in Lancaster, Ohio.

Sue: Tom had more than a few kind things to say about the restaurant—and he reviewed us just five days after opening! I sent our bartender down to the station to get the tape but they had already erased it. So I called and finally reached Tom, hoping to hire him as a consultant.

Chef **Tom Johnson:** On the program, I offered on-air cooking segments, and then reviewed restaurants and also films. In both cases, I had the same philosophy: for the first long while, I wanted to be positive and establish a clear record of what I am for by giving compliments, and appreciating what each chef or filmmaker is trying to do. That way, when it came time to tell listeners that something wasn't quite right, they'd know what I stood for—and they'd know what I wouldn't stand for.

The one controversial review I did offer was of the Fontanelle, an old Columbus restaurant that decided to outfit all their servers—all females, as I remember—as if they were chorus girls in a local production of *Dames at Sea*. In the lobby, they had all these photos of the owners with nuns and parishioners doing various charity events, and then inside the restaurant were all these scantily clad, buxom women. It was an insult to my business. These were professionals, and they deserved more than this. So, on air, I said, "One of my dinner companions remarked to our server, 'Why aren't the bartenders in jock straps?' But our server begged us not to say anything because she needed the job.'"

About Lindey's, as I recall, I listed some of the dishes I'd sampled, and then I said that the restaurant was many notches above what the previous tenants had offered in that space. But it was still a little unfocused: it needed some refining touches.

So when Sue called me, I agreed to meet for lunch, and I said, sure let's try something. After a few consultations—for instance, I suggested they put petite tenderloins with béarnaise on the menu (and these tournedos are on the menu to this day!)—and since I'd tired of the commute from Columbus to Lancaster, I just hopped on board when Sue offered me the chef's position.

But did I understand the mechanics of scheduling? Not really. My style of cooking had always been more labor-intensive. Did I realize that Lindey's needed a chef as well as a line cook? Not at all. I'm really best as a teacher, I now realize. And that worked out beautifully when I opened L'Armagnac with John Bessey. But at Lindey's, no. I am an idea man, and I had never worked in an inner-city kitchen before where half the staff was stealing and the owner's son was constantly sticking his finger in the sauce as I was cooking.

Sue: Tom was good marketing. He was expertise! He was well-known, and people came to Lindey's just to taste his cooking. Immediately, business picked up on weekend nights, and Tom spent time visiting with the customers. But he didn't have a handle on the cost of things. Or how much you should order for a busy weekend. What he did during the day was sit outside behind the restaurant under the awning and chat with the neighbors, regaling them with stories of his favorite movie stars.

Tom: Sue began to have loyal customers and vocal friends. They wanted her to succeed. And Sue was determined. She read the trade magazines cover to cover. She wanted free-range chickens. She wanted an herb garden in the courtyard. She wanted anything that would work.

But her favorite trick was showing up at 11:15 in the morning, passing through the kitchen and saying, "I just took a call for a party of 50, and they're coming in at 12:30. They're going to have your chicken salad and pitas, and something for dessert." The kitchen would be furious. And I would say, I'm not going to do it, absolutely not, not this time. And just like the woman for whom I worked at Shaw's, Sue would look at me, her eyes welled up with tears—swimming pools just shimmering—and I'd say stop, stop, you're doing that to get your way. But I knew, deep down, that we were winning over guests, building a following for the restaurant. And in a few minutes, I'd have cooled off and started chopping celery for the chicken salad.

But I saw how hard Sue worked, doing what everyone said she couldn't do. It would be so easy to pity her: her husband left her to live with another woman. It was a terrible shock and it hurt. He eventually moved in with his new wife, right down the street. Plus, she continued to work with him, as a business partner, in this new venture.

But Sue did have a concept, and even if she couldn't communicate it exactly to us in the kitchen (all we knew is that she wanted to stay open all the time, and serve more guests!), she worked 17-hour days, doing everything. Nothing anyone did was something she didn't do. As we say here in Ohio, Sue didn't just fall into a tub of butter—she churned it by hand! I think her brother Joe, who is a priest, and her dear friends, like Sheila, kept her on track, even as her ex-husband would come in and complain about the artwork, argue about how this was being done, or quibble about how this or that tasted.

Winter, 1982: **Eight Months and Counting (Our Losses)**

"I tried to keep Paula Wolfert's saying in mind: 'No matter how bad things are, remember food is a love offering.'"—*Chef Tom Johnson*

Sue: We'd turn a profit one month, and then slip back the next month. I'd get my hopes up as the numbers rose, and then the numbers would slip, and my hopes would—well, I knew something else would have to be done.

Whatever profit we made I put back into the business. All the things I've done have been financed from within. I kept my debt-to-equity balance in check. If I had carried any more debt, I wouldn't have been able to sleep nights.

I knew that people wanted me to succeed, and came to Lindey's in spite of the food and subpar service. They gave me and my sons time to sharpen our skills and correct our errors. In the first year, we lost about $150,000, but within another six months after that, I was turning a small profit. The key was higher volume and lower margin.

Hell's Kitchen

Could our losses have been influenced by our lack of inventory controls? We had one young lady who worked in the kitchen before we started counting the portions of meat each night. She would take one or two filets or strip steaks each week. This went unnoticed for some time because Lindey's just didn't have any sort of system. As it turns out, she didn't want the meat to cook for her family. She wanted it to sell from her porch to folks in her neighborhood.

Actually, she wanted it for an even higher purpose: When we finally confronted her with the thievery, she flatly stated that she had to do it. "You had to be punished because Lindey's is a godless place."

Mike Higbee: To use our original inventory system, you'd feed each check into the machine each time you'd ring in an item, logging in with your employee number, and then with the running number on that check from the last time you rang it in so it would update the internal invoice. Then you'd punch whatever keys corresponded with the new food items. But half the time you couldn't even read the running number: the blue ink was too faint, the ink had smeared, or the check didn't feed correctly and printed the last line on top of a previous line. And you'd stand there and try and try to get the machine to take your check, while three other waiters are standing behind you, waiting to ring in their orders. And the whole place would be so loud—people laughing in the bar, music, crowds of people—that you couldn't even explain the problem to whoever had to come by to void the check and get the system working again.

Joan Flower: Then the Doodys found out that our head bartender was skimming money from the cash drawer. Every night. And she was skimming off more than a little bit of the booze herself, mixing herself a little something just to take the edge off. When they fired her, I believe the staff broke into a chorus of "Ding dong, the witch is dead."

Jim Finnerty: Before joining Lindey's, I bartended at Max & Erma's, where the woman I worked for stressed that a bartender should anticipate the needs of the customer, assume that they're ready for this or that. When I left there to work at the Old Mohawk, two guys from the Doody Company, Ken Smith and Mark Turner, came in once in a while. They liked the service and the repartee, and at one point, they mentioned to me they were helping to open a new restaurant down the street—but they were looking to hire all female bartenders to get businessmen in the seats. Unfortunately, after several weeks, they discovered that the bar drawer was short about 20% each night. And so one day, Mark and Ken offered me a job.

　　As head bartender, my duties were not only to train the staff, but also to order the booze. (Emil Shedlock ordered the wine.) Now Rick and Ken and Mark loved to throw parties after we'd close up. So Rick would say, we need a fifth of Dewar's, a fifth of Jim Beam, a fifth of whatever, and they'd load up. So one day Sue says to me, "Finn, your bar costs are ridiculous!" and I reply, "Well, Susie, don't talk to me, talk to the boys from home! Get Rick and his buddies to mark down what they take!" The bar costs went right down.

Crowds, Please!

Meanwhile, Rick tried a number of other ways to attract customers. He and his longtime friend Mark Turner attempted to develop a private party business.

Mark Turner: We'd get a copy of the *Columbus Dispatch*, scan the engagement listings, look up the names in the phone book, and just start talking to whoever answered. Lindey's had a room that was perfect for receptions or weddings—but we didn't have a lot of success to tout. Then I figured, if we were going to have a private party business, we ought to have connections with bakers, photographers, bands, cake makers. And that got the ball rolling.

But in the meantime, Lindey's installed a small bar on the second floor, hired the band Two Suited to play jazz on weekends, and charged a five-dollar cover.

Rick Doody: Ken Smith, Mr. Finance Guy, would do these sales projections for us. Even though we didn't have a party facility that was very lovely or even competitive with other places, Ken would show up with these insane projections, suggesting we ought to have 30% of our sales from parties within three months. Not likely.

Black and White...and Green!

And then a godsend: Rosalee and Murray Greenberg host a party upstairs. It's the very first big party at Lindey's, and it's a doozy. According to Sue, it not only filled the coffers, but "brought half the Jewish population of Columbus, plus half of everyone else" into Lindey's.

Interior designer **Rosalee Greenberg**, of Centners: Today, Columbus has become fabulous with plenty of wonderful restaurants (and Lindey's has kept up with the best!), but when it first opened, there was nothing like Lindey's in town. My husband Murray and I had dinner there one night—we loved Tom Johnson's food—and we were so excited. We had this idea that we had to have a party here. No occasion; we were just inspired. And we were Lindey's first really large party, so I know it took all kinds of work for Sue and her crew.

The theme was black and white, and people came dressed in tuxes and formal gowns, as well as in black-and-white prisoner stripes and referee outfits. It was fabulous. I think someone came in a black T-shirt that read, "I made the cut to the Greenbergs' party."

Sue: We were so strapped at that point, I went to Centners to ask Murray for a check ahead of time since we had big upfront food and liquor costs for a few hundred people.

And then, at 5:00 the day before, we installed some very bold carpeting that I'd just bought at the Top of the Center liquidation sale. Huge rolls of carpeting to cart up the long staircase to the second floor. But even with all the mess of installing things—and running the restaurant downstairs—we got it done. Then the day of the party, Rosalee comes by to see that everything's ready, and she finds me in the office: "Any chance you can change the carpeting in here before my party? It's just *godawful*."

"Sure," I reply, "if you want to donate the carpeting."

Needless to say, that party took place on the godawful carpet and no one paid it much attention. Even though we'd hired valets to run cars to various parking spaces all over the village, what with the restaurant doing a steady business downstairs and the additional party guests, we created the worst traffic jam German Village has ever known. Beck and Mohawk became Times Square.

Mark Turner: I was helping out for that party, and at one point Rick says to me, "We're completely out of ice. The whole restaurant is out of ice." So I jump in my car, race over to the convenience store, buy every bag of ice that they have on hand, load it in my car, lug it all back to the restaurant, and unload it—wearing my tuxedo, mind you.

Breakfast at Lindey's

Thinking an early breakfast might be an added attraction for the business crowd, Sue decides to serve weekday breakfasts. She opens for brunch on Sunday mornings as well, with John Bessey joining the kitchen crew. (John and chef Tom eventually bought L'Armagnac, a small French restaurant.) But the early morning business is very sporadic: some mornings it's two tables; other mornings, it's a crowd.

Sue: It was confusing to be scrambling eggs when the lunch crowd was beginning to walk in. But we served breakfast for another year until Kent Rigsby—who made getting rid of breakfast a condition of his being chef—took over the kitchen.

Congressman **Robert Shamansky:** Lindey's was the perfect place to meet for breakfast. You had the advantages of a private club—just a few familiar, discerning people sharing the room with you—and none of the disadvantages. It was very democratic—that's with a small "d."

Bartender **T.A. Anderson:** At the time of Lindey's opening, hardly anyone in Columbus had heard of cappuccino. Or heard our machine!

Joan Flower: That machine was so loud! And no one expected this wailing, screeching, shrieking in a nice restaurant. Everyone would look over, half-thinking something was about to explode. Now, we're all used to the sound of baristas' machines.

T.A.: The machine filled the entire center of the bar: gold, ugly, with all these arms, spouting steam and leaking everywhere. But there were times we could use it to heat glasses, or warm a little shot of Grand Marnier to go with the coffee. But mostly it was a centerpiece, spending much of its time waiting to be repaired (again).

Yes, the machine offered the bar patrons a variation on musical chairs: when the "music" of the screeching steamer started, the people at the bar would all raise their voices, and then, when the bartender suddenly switched off the steamer, there was always someone's voice still shouting after everyone else had readjusted their level. The loser was often the person who'd had the most cocktails.

January, 1983: **Eighteen Months of Business Behind Us...**

. . . .

"Naiveté was the cornerstone of Lindey's early successes
and difficulties."
—*Ken Smith*

Ken Smith: When I came to Columbus to work for Alton Doody, I intended to start a restaurant—Steak Escape—featuring the Philly cheese steak, which I had grown up on in Philadelphia. Since Sue had just opened Lindey's, Alton suggested I try out my interest in the restaurant business by helping out there for a few months. During downtime at Lindey's, their kitchen became my test kitchen. Mark Turner and I lived a few blocks away, and we had managed to set our own kitchen on fire. We had an electric stove top, and when we tried to make fresh-cut fries, the oil dripped over just as folks from the Doody Company were coming over to sample the food. There was fire, smoke, and dinner at Lindey's instead.

We had to wait for Lindey's chef Kent Rigsby to teach us how to blanch the fries and then do two-part frying to give the fries that great crispy crust.

Sue: We were making enough money that the company could send Rick for his masters at Cornell's hotel and restaurant school, so he could find out what his mom was supposed to know about the restaurant business. I even went to Ithaca a few times and sat in on classes with Rick, just to share the experience.

He brought back all kinds of information about the point-of-sale system, food trends in the early '80s, suggestions about commercial equipment that a full-service kitchen required, and all the most current sanitation practices.

My daughter Beth, her boyfriend, and I drove to his graduation, but Rick and his friends had failed to make a dinner reservation, and the little town of Ithaca was jammed with parents. Literally the only place we could find to eat was a former Arthur Treacher's that housed an Indian restaurant. We sat down, and the first thing we saw was a woman wiping off the wet dishes with her sari. We were hysterical with laughter: there wasn't even a dishwasher around to sterilize the dishes. So there we were: a table with recent graduates of Cornell's restaurant program sitting down to what we knew was going to be terrible food that would give us all ptomaine poisoning.

Lindey's for One

February 28, 1983: the last original episode of *M*A*S*H* aired on television, and 125 million people did not come to Lindey's for dinner. This was the largest audience to ever watch a single television program and the smallest number of guests to ever dine at Lindey's. One gentlemen arrived at 5:00 p.m., had the dining room to himself for 45 minutes, and then returned home to watch TV.

Maybe a Marquee Would Help

Michael Burns: My friend and oft-time dinner companion Janet lived and worked in Delaware, and one Monday morning, after having our Sunday dinner at Lindey's—which, by the way, has never had a street sign (it's just the foot-tall word "Lindey's" painted on the window)—she was touting its glories to one of her coworkers.

"That's so funny," the coworker said, "Our Wendy's doesn't have food or service anything like that."

"No, it's not Wendy's, it's *Lindey's*," Janet corrected.

"*Wendy's?*" the coworker repeated.

"LINDEY'S!"

It must be noted that both Janet and her coworker are speech pathologists.

Server Lincoln Workman: People never get the name right, even today, after 25 years. Or the name of the neighborhood. There was a time that certain servers would answer the phone at the host stand, "Linsey's in Germantown, how may I help you?"

Spring, Summer, Autumn, 1983: A New Chef and a New Menu

· ·

"Lindey's gave Columbus permission to be a little hotter, a lot more
fun, and a bit more like a more cosmopolitan city." —*Ric Wanetik*

This was when the fine tuning began in earnest: new menu items, new trends, new chef. "It was the time of California cuisine, nouvelle cuisine, and lighter sauces," Sue remembers. "And we made it through our second year, finally out of the red!"

But one complaint—the restaurant's noise level, both inside and outside—hadn't gone away. (And never would.) One dear friend of the restaurant, Sheila Martin, upon hearing a guest complain to the manager about the din in the dining room, turned to her companions and remarked, "If they want a quiet dinner, they should go to Egan Ryan. Some of those people do look as if the funeral home did their makeup."

Rick Doody: We had a couple guys living in one of the apartments behind Lindey's. Chef Tom would set up his prep kitchen under the awning, and while all hell was breaking loose in the kitchen, he'd be out there peeling carrots and telling stories. But that was better than *before* the neighbors were his friends and one of them contacted HVAC, who sent someone with a decibel reader: it read 74 at the property line, and then 82 at the restaurant. It was our exhaust fans making the noise. So, I suppose, Tom may have bought us a little time, softened a few of the more vocal complaints. But it was inevitable: we would have to buy those two apartments, and be our own neighbors who wouldn't mind the restaurant's noise.

Alton: When we first visualized the business on Beck and Mohawk, I thought of it as a miniature Commander's Palace. Originally, you entered that restaurant on the corner, just exactly as you do at Lindey's. It was a grocery store, probably, at the start. And they had back buildings. With a patio in between. When Sue and I each decided to purchase one of the buildings behind Lindey's, I'd imagined we'd be a small version of that New Orleans institution. But it took us a few years before we could acquire those back buildings. And just doing that helped. We got to clean up the ugliness of the tricycles and plastic toys in those back yards. Lindey's had such a great balcony. Finally, we had the chance to control what it overlooked.

Sue: So began our attempt to create the courtyard for outdoor dining between the restaurant and the buildings to the south. It would only take us another two decades of hassles with the German Village Commission in order to do so.

Employee of the Mouth

Upon seeing Lindey's kitchens 22 years later, Tom said: "I'm especially delighted that Sue has enlarged the cellar far beyond the original confines, which resembled the lower half of the last scene of *Aida*." *

Sue: When Tom Johnson left to open L'Armagnac, we hired Kent Rigsby as the new head chef. A recent graduate of the culinary school in San Francisco, Kent understood volume in a way that Tom really didn't. And he brought California food ideas, less-rich cooking, and a terrific palate. To this day, Kent has left his insignia on our cuisine.

Chef Kent Rigsby: I came back to Columbus knowing I wanted to open my own place one day. I'd moved into an apartment on Mohawk, literally cattycorner to Lindey's, and I heard they needed a chef and I interviewed for the position. So serendipitous. They hired me pretty cheap, since we were both trying things out. It was the perfect chance to prove myself.

I had trained at top professional kitchens, and the first thing that seemed obvious was that the operation at Lindey's was more "learn by doing," more homemaker-style. So it was a teeth-pulling experience to institute kitchen organization, industry-standard cleanliness, and a clear chain of command. For instance, the lunch prep cook would hide his hamburger meat in the walk-in so that the night cook didn't use it for a staff meal at night. It was very seat-of-the-pants.

---

* For the benefit of those of us with modest opera knowledge, Tom is referring to the burial place in the temple of Vulcan. Aida hides in the crypt where her lover Radames is to be buried alive. They sing a beautiful, baleful duet, bidding farewell to earth and its sorrows, while, upstairs, the holy people are jubilantly dancing.

The plot of Verdi's great opera has no special bearing on Lindey's, even if dining here has often been compared to going to the theater. In the course of our interview with Chef Johnson he also volunteered that it is not worth going to see Elton John's version of the opera should it ever come to Columbus. "Instead, just go to Lindey's, mention the word 'Aida' to the hostess on duty, and she'll give you a backstage tour of the downstairs prep kitchens."

But Sue gave me free rein, pretty much. I'll always remember bringing her something new I wanted to put on the menu, and nine times out of ten, she'd say, "Oh Kent, that's the best thing I've ever put in my mouth." (Which, of course, would send the staff riffing on every sort of joke the moment Sue left the room.)

But Sue was devoted—or her guests were!—to some dishes I couldn't abide. Specifically? The baked brie appetizer: take an unripe wheel of brie, shove it in a hot pizza oven, and then take sliced apples and poke them like spokes into the runny cheese. I just don't think people should eat cheese as an appetizer: it's too rich and filling. And brie is at its best when it's ripe and at room temperature. But I was stuck with that dish.

At the time, Lindey's wasn't doing the volume they do now. It was just one dining room, with a small second room. A few parties upstairs. And a smaller patio. We had old kitchen equipment, small kitchen space, and a basement prep kitchen that was so gloomy and challenging that the previous chef used to prep outside. Outside, that is, until the health department shut that down.

The guests also made me a little crazy. I was appalled that someone would want a tournedos—a thin, beautiful cut of filet mignon—cooked well or medium-well. I remember seeing Pierre, the grill cook, turning a piece of meat over and over until it was charred, carbonized, and juiceless. When I asked him what on earth he thought he was doing, he replied, "Someone wants it well-done, cooked through all the way—what else can I do?" So I gave him an answer: you quickly sear both sides on the grill, and then you put the meat in the oven to cook through. That's the level of teaching and the kind of changes I had to do, alongside developing a menu and getting good food into the dining room.

And if there's one other thing I remember Sue saying, time and again, it was, "I wish we could be open 24 hours a day so I could throw away the key." And the fact is, the place was only closed for about four hours a day, with breakfast at dawn and last call at 2:00 in the morning.

Server **Kaira Rouda:** Every summer during college, from the beginning of Lindey's, I worked as a cocktailer on the upstairs terrace. It was the best place in Columbus. But working there, you had to run everything up and down the spiral staircase: not just trays of food, but the entire bar setup. Every night. I'd arrive from my day job, and the terrace would be covered with fallen leaves, pollen, whatever, so it all had to be swept, and then the ice had to come up, and the glassware. It was like a movable picnic. And when it rained, it was like a removable picnic. Everything went back down...and then the next evening...

Kitchen Con

Server **Alice Mattimo:** In 1984, when the state penitentiary finally closed, Sue hired a just-released inmate to work as a dishwasher. This was someone who was supposed to have been in prison for life. He was in his mid-50s. He just showed up in the kitchen one day, and it was clear this guy was nuts. He was always hitting on the female servers (like any of us 21-year-olds were going to date a 50-something ex-con). Once, when things were slow, he came over and asked me if I could take a break and "you know, go outside and..." and then he made the motion of shooting heroin in his arm.

So after a few days of this, I said to Sue, "Um, Sue, do you know what was he in for?"

"I didn't want to ask," she replied.

"Well, what if it was for killing his boss?"

Thankfully, he didn't last long enough to find out.

1984 to 1986: Double or Nothing

> "All the wives would come out for dinner, but the husbands were afraid to come out to the Cleveland Lindey's because they'd be lured into buying furs and jewelry."   —*Sue*

Business is going well, and Rick decides to try a branch of Lindey's at Beachwood Mall, an upscale shopping venue in Cleveland. Chef Tom Callahan, who'd worked under Kent at Lindey's German Village, joins Rick in Cleveland, and Sue and her friend Sheila run up every week or so to help with the financials. The restaurant has the same wainscoting, banquettes, palms, and even some of the same artists' work on the walls.

Sue: My ex-husband owned a clothing store in the same mall, and he helped us outfit the new restaurant, including some rather extravagant, enormous decorative globes for the ceiling that required a flatbed truck for transport. We were "highly leveraged," as we say in the business. Not a good thing.

After two years of not-exactly-booming business, we closed up shop in 1986. We had opened on the second floor of a fashion mall. All the wives would come out for dinner, but the husbands were afraid to come out to the Cleveland Lindey's because they'd be lured into buying furs and jewelry.

After a few months at the Columbus Lindey's, Rick returns to Cleveland to open several Steak Escape franchises whose menu his friends Mark and Ken had tested in Lindey's own kitchen.

John Smallridge: Unfortunately, Rick was never meant to be standing behind the line, and to make ends meet as an owner of a Steak Escape, you've got to employ yourself.

Sue: Rick could never balance the books at his Steak Escapes—folks were robbing him blind. I'll never forget: one day there was a bus wreck right outside one of his buildings, and one of his cooks saw the crash, ran outside, and climbed inside the wrecked bus, holding his neck, pretending he had been hurt in the accident. That was how dishonest his employees were.

In 1986, chef Kent Rigsby leaves to start his own restaurant in the upcoming Short North neighborhood. He calls it Rigsby's Cuisine Volatile, leaving everyone at Lindey's to wonder how cuisine's volatility can ever compare with a chef's.

Jack Cory and Tim Zahler take over as co-chefs, while Sue auditions various chefs from around the country.

Meanwhile, brother Chris, who has just come from Mr. B's in New Orleans, joins the restaurant, bringing some Cajun-influenced dishes to the Lindey's menu. (See page 235, for more on Chris's time at Mr. B's.)

Soon-to-be-chef Jack Cory: In 1986, a couple months after I started working as sous chef, we knew this one Saturday night was going to be big. At the time, we were buying cheesecakes and other desserts from a local baker. So in the middle of the evening rush, with his wife working the floor, the chef at the time, Gene, says he's going to get more desserts, we're nearly out...and he leaves the restaurant. The executive chef making a run for supplies on a Saturday night? Well, he sort of overshoots the cheesecakes—and drives to Canada and we never see him again. He left his wife, his kids, and the 150 other diners we had yet to serve that night. (Obviously desserts were the least of his worries.)

Sue: Things were beginning to go very well, so I reinvested whatever profit we had into converting our courtyard into a third dining room, which added 15 tables to the restaurant; renovating the kitchen, which included excavating half of the basement so that a person could stand upright; and replacing about 75% of the kitchen equipment.

But I knew Lindey's was still losing out on the suburban customer, a guest who wants to have a quiet dinner and talk, so we carpeted the new room. (I now have people who request the back room. But other regulars would be horrified to be seated back there).

Server Mark Svede: During the renovation, we had a conveyor belt that ran from the basement through the small window in the foundation, dumping little fistfuls of dirt onto the Beck Street sidewalk, which would then have to be shoveled up into the dumpster and hauled away. It reminded me of *The Great Escape*, the Steve McQueen movie from 1963 where the prisoners burrow their way out of the German prison camp by filling their pants with dirt, and then releasing it into the prison's gardens, a tiny bit at a time, hoping no one will notice.

Chris Doody: Mom handed out hard hats to people as they came to the restaurant. They were plastic, with the Lindey's logo on them. It was a funny idea, but the construction mess got to the point that there was so much dust four layers of plastic barrier didn't seem to help. It was a classic blunder. Instead of closing, the way normal humans would have, we tried to stay open. I mean, construction was so extensive that Mohawk Street was closed in front of the restaurant because we needed a three-story lift with a crane that had these giant alien feet planted across the street in order to put new ventilation hoods on the roof.

And here's Mom, calling, "Honey, are we ready to open...? Everything ready?" But when the restaurant opened in 1981, the family didn't do any remodeling in the kitchen. So after five years, we were dying to rip the floor, redo the drains, and replace the ceiling, lights, and most of the equipment. The restaurant was expanding to add an entire new room, so the kitchen had to be up to speed. The price tag for this: $80,000. For us, that felt like a million.

Chef **Jack Cory:** Sue didn't want to close, so sous chef Big Bob and I had a tent on the patio with a huge grill, and we served burgers. But construction dust was falling everywhere, and finally we shut down for a couple weeks. Tom Harlor, the manager at the time, and I became the general contractors and workers, and we pounded away around the clock to get the kitchen renovated and the restaurant reopened.

Lindey's Pledge

At some time during Rick and Chris's management at Lindey's, they decided to print up small cards which they passed out to all the servers at a pre-shift meeting. The text read as follows:

Sue's Pledge

From this day forward, every customer that comes within 10 feet of me, regardless of what I'm doing, in this house, I'm going to look him in the eye, I'm going to greet him with a '*Good afternoon*,' or a '*Good evening*,' or a '*What can I do for you?*' — so help me Sue!

The staff recited the pledge together, not once, not twice, but three or maybe four times, until the servers managed to recite it with the right spirit. However tongue-in-cheek the sons may have intended the card, and however much they intended it to rally the staff to an even higher level of attentiveness, the rather experienced staff at the time wasted no time ridiculing the effort. The cards were never mentioned again.

Until now.

A NUMBER OF THINGS ABOUT LINDEY'S
THE EARLY YEARS

Restaurants that opened and closed at 169 East Beck Street
in the 10 years prior to Lindey's opening: **4**

Approximate percentage, nationwide, of restaurants
that close within three years: **50**

Times that Pierre, a member of the work crew, sanded and re-stained the front doors
of Lindey's until Alton was satisfied with the look: **4**

Number of times anyone other than Alton had used the word "patina"
up to that point, or used it after that point: **0**

Dollars originally paid for the building and real estate that is now Lindey's: **320,000**

Additional dollars spent in initial renovation of the place: **150,000**

Dollars spent on the bar, purchased from the Neil House,
which had gone out of business: **1,400** *

Minutes that "Rumors" lasted as a possible name for the Doody's new restaurant: **1** **

Hours that Lindey's was open for business each day in the beginning
(breakfast began at 6:00, and last call wrapped up at 2:00): **20**

Typical number of hours Sue spent in the restaurant each day: **12**

Staff members who had restaurant experience prior to working at Lindey's
(Emil Shedlock, the front of the house manager): **1**

Number of times that the recipe for Coquille St. Jacques
was changed after opening day: **6**

---

* Lindey's copper top, perhaps the restaurant's most distinguishing feature, was installed by the man repairing the gutters.

** "Rick! that sounds like a strip club!" Sue replied.

Number of dinners served the first night Lindey's opened: **20**

Times each week "the restaurant concept" was brought up
for discussion and revision: **4**

Reservations on Lindey's biggest night to date
(an Ohio State football weekend): **350**

Strip steaks and tournedos on hand that night: **17**

Additional strip steaks and tournedos purchased by a panicking Rick Doody
at area supermarkets to supplement that evening's dinners: **100**

Amount in dollars that Lindey's went into the red for the first year: **787,000**

Percentage profit margin in a typical restaurant: **3 to 5**

Times the back patio flooded, sending water down the stairs into the kitchen
and basement, usually causing the grease trap to back up: **27***

Typical percentage of liquor bottles on the terrace with dead bees
in the pouring spouts during the summer months: **100**

Thickness, in inches, of the docket one particular neighbor
brought to the German Village Commission, filled with the various
disturbances, transgressions, and irritating things perpetrated by
Lindey's and restaurant guests: **2 1/2**

Additional years it would take for the Village to grant Lindey's a zoning variance
to set up a bar in the courtyard Lindey's built in 1984: **15**

* Sue: "German Village's sewers aren't deep, and every hard rain, we'd have to move all the dry goods, lift all the wine boxes off the floor, mop, and wet-vac. The labels on the wine bottles would get wet and drop off, and there was one time when we didn't know which wet label went with what bar bottle."

FRONT OF THE HOUSE

· ·

STORIES OF HOSTING, SERVING & DINING

THE HOSTESS WITH THE MOSTEST
STORIES FROM THE CENTER OF THE STORM

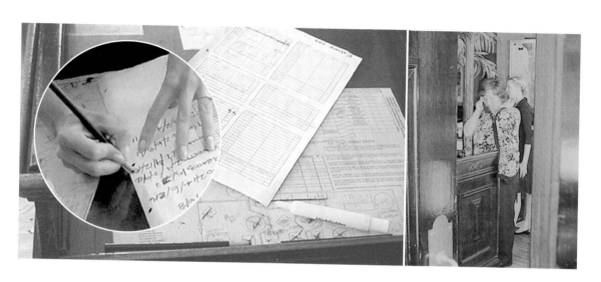

IT'S JUST A FEW STEPS ACROSS the brick sidewalk from the street curb to Lindey's front doors. From the front doors to the inside doors is an equally short distance, plus the optional weaving past the departing guests, the valets holding open the doors, and the umbrella stand. Once inside, the first seats of the bar, Table 10, and the restaurant's epicenter, the host stand, are all six feet away.

Yes, it could be argued that the host stand is the eye of the centripetal storm that is Lindey's. Or you could suggest that the hosts are the restaurant's ringmasters. Come up with whatever metaphor you'd like, but the fact is, planning where the 600 diners on a typically busy night will sit (and that's not counting the upstairs private parties, guests on the patio or the terrace, or the bar patrons), is a feat as remarkable as—oh, that's right: *you* were going to supply the metaphor.

Assistant Manager **Cathy Sheedy** (now Walsh): Standing at the host stand, the managers were really acting as the maître d'. And you'd get to the point I remember Tony Sarno was very good at this—where you'd get to know the cars that the regulars drove. We didn't have valet parking at this time. So you could see through the front door windows all the cars halting at the stop sign, or turning down Mohawk. And whenever Tony wasn't schmoozing some guest at the stand, he was watching those windows to see who might be coming in unexpectedly so he could make room for them. He had just as long as it took them to park their cars and walk back.

Lindey's was crazy busy Friday and Saturday nights. You were being bombarded with requests from every side. One evening, I even had a man call to say that his party of four

Lindey's Fables for the Famished

We thought you'd find it less bullying if we offered some observations about restaurant etiquette in the friendly form of a fable. Each one is prompted or inspired by a guest or staff member at Lindey's. History (or our fear of litigation) may have erased the customers' names, but their deeds live on in these inspirational examples of what not to do.

The Gourmet and the Grapes:

A fable inspired by waiter John Squire

Once upon a time, two gentlemen came in for dinner. John, a tall and veteran server, recognized one as a culinary teacher in town. He also remembered that the gentleman typically ordered the least expensive wine on the menu.

I know it's on Lindey's list because it's perfectly drinkable, but for a bit more money, you get a much better wine, John would think to himself. ☞

would be a little late. I noted that in the book, even as I thought the phone connection was very weird—like long-distance. As his reservation time approached, the phone rang again.

"We're going to be later still, we're caught in a holding pattern at the airport." He was calling from the cockpit of his private plane to have us hold his reservation.

Manager **Freddie Cortez**: Some nights, I tried to convince Sue that she could take an evening off. (Partly because things were a bit more relaxed when Momma wasn't around.) She'd go home midafternoon, and then call me just as the dinner crowd started arriving. "Sugar," she'd always say, "Do you need me?"

"Of course, I need you, but you can stay home tonight. Most of my reservations are in, and I'm already cutting some staff, so I think we're in good shape." And then she'd always waffle a bit, and then she'd agree, offering me some closing bit of advice like:

"All right, Sugar, but if god forbid anything awful should happen, like a robbery, you just give them whatever they want and call them a cab."

"Okay, I will."

General Manager **Tom Harlor**: When I started at Lindey's in the mid-'80s, a great night was 250 to 275 covers. When I left, we were doing 500 and knocking at the $3 million door for a year's gross. Nearly every night was a runaway—you just hung on for the ride. You certainly couldn't steer it.

We developed this reservation system that really had some personal play in it. I mean, you'd always have to be looking at the book and moving names around the tables to ensure that you had the right tables at the right times. And while you never willfully overbooked, you could book the restaurant right to capacity, figuring that the walk-ins could offset the no-shows. Your goal was to be able to quote a party a pretty short wait time—say, 15 minutes—and if the table you were waiting to give them just sat and sat, you'd have those deuces in the bar up your sleeve. I remember an assistant manager, Cathy Sheedy, who'd be saying all week, "Hey, Tom, that's enough reservations for

Saturday, don't take any more," but we had to push. At a management meeting, the chef said the same thing: "Tom, could you take a few less reservations on the weekend so we don't get slammed so hard?" And I said, "Look, it's my job: I'm supposed to get as many people in here as possible, and your job is to get the food out for them to eat." Sue agreed, and that was the end of that.

As the week progressed, Saturday started to fill in: each table had three lines on the reservation sheet, one for each turn. And you could seat some earlier and some later, but there were still only so many tables. But at one time, we had phones all over the restaurant, and anyone on staff could pick a phone and jot down a reservation on the remote reservation sheets, initial it, and then these would be entered in the one reservation book. You can see the problem already: a table getting booked even as someone is walking downstairs with a new reservation, people at lunch making reservations for a dinner in person at the host stand while someone on the phone is snatching that same table, two staff members taking calls for the same time slot. It was a mess.

So working reservations was brutal, especially when I first started and the regulars simply told me how things worked: this is when I'm coming, and this is where I sit. But after I had been at Lindey's a while, people began to respect me. I think they figured, well, he's made it this far, he must be good.

Manager **Freddie Cortez**: Tom was a genius at seating. The reservation sheet had all the deuces down the first row. All the four-tops were down the second row. And the third row had the larger tables. Next to each table, you'd have a 5:00, a 7:00, and a 9:00 slot. You could adjust the time of any slot, but then you'd have to change all the other times for that table so that there was always the two-hour slot. For instance, you could make an 8:00 reservation, but then that table couldn't have a first seating after 6:00 or have a third seating until 10:00.

Everything would go smoothly until all of a sudden the mob would arrive at the front door. But Tom was so calm and cool with his reservation sheet and yellow highlighter. "My friend will seat you," he'd say, coloring

☞ That night, the gentlemen brought a friend for dinner, and, sure enough, he ordered the same inexpensive merlot. When John uncorked it and poured him a sample taste, the man announced to his guest: "It's going to be really good when it opens up a bit."

Dude! No, it's not. The wine's not ever going to open up! John once again thought about actually saying something aloud because—come on! The man's a culinarian! A friggin' gourmet! Surely that distinction requires some responsibility?

But no, he restrained himself.

Moral: *Expense is by no means an assurance of quality...but a measly five extra bucks goes a lot farther than nonsense when it comes to drinkability.*

the slot yellow, and then turning to me, he'd say: "Okay, dude. Take them to Table X." And I'd grab the menus, take them to Table X, and most of the time everything worked. But sometimes: "Um, Tom, they don't want to sit there." And that would be it! He'd get out his bottle of Wite-Out, remove the yellow line, and I'd be standing there, waiting for it to dry—that was how he showed his displeasure—and then he'd put the party at another table, put another yellow line through that slot, and then tell me, "Okay, take them to Table Y."

The other trick I learned from Tom: On Mondays, he'd take the book and write in a few parties on all the busy nights. He'd make up names, enter them in various time slots, and then put a tiny ink mark by the names. And that was how he made certain he had a few tables in reserve that he could always give to someone without a reservation.

Before we share some stories from the host stand, consider some of the factors we weigh as we seat parties from 5:00 until 11:00 every night. ("It's probably easier to juggle flaming batons or chainsaws," one hostess liked to remark.) You plot in advance, taking reservations and charting out where each party will sit, but you also must gerrymander your various plots throughout the evening as you...

- Distribute tables evenly among the waitstaff, allowing for the fact that some parties request certain servers (and whether the feeling's "mutual"), and reconfiguring if said server is not working the table the party requested.

- Keep in mind which staff members can handle which kind of situations— veteran servers, trainees, those who will be in the weeds if you don't space out their tables with at least 15-minute intervals.

- Seat and close the early stations first and seat the later sections later and last.

- Address the evening's def tables.

Assistant manager Rachel Hollander: In restaurant lingo, "def" means "definitely," but it's mostly a verb, as in we have regulars who def certain tables, and we plot those tables first on the floor plan for the shift and then assign the other parties after that. More and more, we're finding that even nonregulars are deffing tables based on where they enjoyed sitting the one time they were here. What's hard about this is that one person takes a reservation and ignores the fact that another person booked a certain table for another guest: the table gets double deffed. So all we can do is look at who the two parties are and seat the person with the most seniority or regularity. But often, both reservations are for parties we don't already know. Then we look at who is coming in first and give them the table, because it's less awkward than if they walked in, saw the table empty, and the host told them they couldn't sit there.

- Accommodate frequent guests on the patio or the terrace if it's suddenly nice out and they'd rather "take their reservation outside"; accommodate guests who suddenly get chilly and want to move indoors.

- ❦ Ensure that parties that want the boisterous front room are seated there, that romantic couples get the secluded tables, and that guests who prefer more quiet are seated in the back room—unless we have larger parties there, in which case you...you...just seat them anywhere and hope for the best.

- ❦ Figure out how to reset a four-top for five, an eight-top for two four-tops (it's fun with fractions, kids!) and so on and so on as parties arrive with or acquire a different number of people than in the reservation they made.

- ❦ Try to seat smokers near the door—the outdoors being our only smoking section now. (When we did have smoking and nonsmoking rooms, that was always a factor for every reservation.)

- ❦ Determine where we can best serve large parties, parties with small children (which means high chairs, helium balloon, and spills), or elderly guests.

- ❦ Remember that for whatever cockamamie reason, certain regulars can not be seated near certain other regulars.

- ❦ When parties stay longer than anticipated, consider one of two options: 1) Go over to the table and say "How WAS everything?" strongly emphasizing the verb's tense, as if to reinforce the idea that their dinner took place in the past and that, surely, the time had come to move into the future. 2) Find another open table for the party that had been assigned to the lingerers' table. And then, on some occasions, we exercise a third option; one such evening involved regular guests Brett and Andrea Cambern.

Andrea: We'd made a reservation for a later dinner, a group of six, and everyone gathered at our house first for drinks and appetizers. Just before leaving, Lindey's called over—we lived catty-corner to the restaurant—to say that the party at our table was just staying on and on, and, just then, there was a knock at the door, and the valet had run over a bottle of Veuve Clicquot for us. Just to apologize and hold us over. About half an hour later, another bottle arrived, just to apologize again and keep us appeased—and I don't recall if there was a third bottle. But by the time we arrived for our extra-later dinner, we were feeling no pain.

- ❦ Oh, and figure out how to reinvent all these plans when you have one of those all too frequent bursts of "the perfect storm," where parties arrive late, the kitchen backs up, a server goes home sick, guests run into old friends and you can't get them to sit down and order—oh, the problems of popularity.

Six Feet Over

Steve Gifford: When I was 24 I became an assistant manager. I was also Lindey's wine buyer, the maître d', and the person charged with keeping the beverage costs in line. Luckily, Freddie Cortez and Allison Burgess helped me. They especially helped me let my hair down at the front door. I was as naïve about Columbus's gay community as I was of its society titans, and Fred taught me something about kissing the old ladies, and shaking hands with the influential people, and goofing around with the friskier bunch. Mostly what I remember is wiping a lot of make-up off my eyeglasses.

It's funny, but in that post, you're mostly working that six-foot distance between the podium and the front door. And a world of things happens in that small space.

There are people who come in and say they have a reservation and they don't. And that just meant we took them right to a table. We had people who'd look at the reservation list and point to a name, "Miller for four," and we'd take them to a table, knowing that they were not, in fact, the Miller party. (One of the things I learned, probably from my mother, who never worked in a restaurant, is that you have to confront things with the positive idea that you're going to find a resolution. Anything's possible.)

During slow moments, you could sidle over to Table 10, and visit with Skip and Cherie, who were always good for a little conversation. Or you'd visit with the regulars gathered at the bar: Neil Schultz, Marv Glassman, Frank Cipriano, Herb Lape—so many outgoing (and sometimes outlandish) characters. An amazing group of people, night after night.

Anywhere But Here

One Saturday evening, Jan and Jim, regulars at Lindey's, were convinced to join two of their friends at a "popular" suburban restaurant where they were cheerfully told that their 8:00 table would be ready at about 9:30. Justifiably irate, Jim called Lindey's. Jason, the maître d' that evening, answered. "Hello, Jason, we'd like to make reservations for dinner."

"Great. What day would that be for?" Jason asked.

"Today. This evening, in fact."

After a thoughtful pause, Jason asked, "And about what time?"

"Oh, in about 10 minutes?"

"We'll certainly work on it," he replied.

When the group arrived, Table 10 had apparently just turned over, and it was now set for four, and moreover, it was set with the appropriate cocktails and appetizers.

Once seated, Jan said to her companion, "Why in the world would we go anyplace else?"

It's for You

Nicole Neamand: My very first week at Lindey's, I worked as a hostess. I was as green as could be. I'm standing at the hostess stand. The bar is packed. I realize everyone seems to know everyone else, and I don't know a single soul. So I'm feeling very insecure.

The phone rings. "Good evening, Lindey's."

"I'm looking for a customer, and I believe she's at the bar there."

"What's her name? I'll try to find her." (Remember this is a decade before cell phones.)

"It's Carmen Miranda."

"Okay, can you hold?"

So here I am, all of 20, and I'm going down the bar, asking each person if he or she has seen Carmen Miranda.

Finally, this woman with a raspy, husky voice says to me, "Honey, you can't be serious?"

"Why? Do you know who Carmen Miranda is?"

"Yes...don't you? You know, the woman with all the fruit on her head? And the costumes? From the movies?" So I go back to the phone to, to...and no one is on the line.

Something to Smile About

Jimmy Cooper: Early in my time at Lindey's, I had a two-top, a man and a woman, who had a leisurely lunch, outstaying everyone else. After they left, I was standing at the host stand for Sue to wrap something up so I could check out. The phone at the host stand rings, so I pick up:

"I was just here at lunch—" I recognize the voice: it's the man I'd just waited on. "And I seem to have lost my teeth. Would you mind checking the table?"

The man left without his teeth? I hadn't noticed this? So I go back to Table 26, and there is a napkin on the chair where he'd been sitting. And, sure enough, there are his teeth. "Yes, they're here," I say, and he says he'll be right over to get them

Now tell me: How does a person eat lunch, and leave the restaurant without his teeth? It's not as if we have an all-soup buffet.

Gift Certificates

One of Lindey's favorite managers, Todd Cumbow, went through a period where he received several phone calls from a gentleman who claimed to have recently dined at Lindey's and found the service, the food, or the experience less than what he'd expected—and worst of all, his dinner companion was none other than this or that notable, well-to-do local dignitary. In fact, in various calls, he'd say that he was alternately embarrassed, disappointed, or unpleasantly surprised, but always ending with the phrase, "So is there anything Lindey's can do to make amends?" In other words, skip the contrition and the apologetic letter, just send me gift certificates, which Todd promptly sent, since it's Lindey's policy to make guests happy. This went on with some regularity: the poor man consistently had bad experiences at Lindey's, a notable person in tow to increase his embarrassment, and, oddly, no reservations—at least no one would find his name in the book on the night of his disappointing meal. Moreover, neither Todd nor any other manager remembered seeing the notable person mentioned.

At last, Lindey's interest in assuring every guest's satisfaction notwithstanding, Todd grew suspicious and phoned a few other restaurant colleagues. In fact, the gentleman had experienced a citywide blight of disappointments while hosting his distinguished dinner companions at most of the city's finer restaurants. There had been no disappointing meals, no problems with service, no famous dinner companions. Only the gift certificates were real. His scam was abruptly halted.

Identity Crisis

A woman walks into the restaurant on a particularly busy night. The bar is lined three deep with guests, and anyone entering could have discerned that every table in the dining room is occupied. "I'd like a table for four," she says, avoiding both the hostess's eyes and the reservation sheet with a full column of names waiting to be crossed out with a highlighter.

"I'm sorry, we're full right now," the hostess replies graciously. "The soonest I'll have a table will be...10:00, about 90 minutes from now. Would that be—"

"Young lady, do you know who I am?" the guest replies.

"I'm sorry?" the hostess asks, hoping that the din in the restaurant might offer the guest a chance to reconsider her remark.

Instead, the woman leans toward the hostess, and repeats herself, slowly and loudly:

"I said, do you...have any idea who I am?"

At that, the hostess raps her knuckles on the stand's wooden ledge, and calls out to the crowd huddled near: "Excuse me? Does anybody here know who this lady is? Apparently she's forgotten her name."

Regrettably, we can neither attribute this remark to any one hostess in particular, nor can anyone remember whether the guest waited the 90 minutes anonymously or left the restaurant, her secret identity intact.

TURNING THE TABLES
BY THE NUMBERS

MOST OF THE TABLES AT LINDEY'S are turned between three and five times every day—twice at lunch, and three times at dinner. Some of the most popular tables on a very busy day and night might turn seven times. But let's be conservative and say our dining rooms' core 48 tables—this doesn't include tables on the terrace, patio, or party rooms—turn three times a day. Let's factor in some slow days, a few snowy days, and a few holidays. In a given year, the restaurant's tables are set and reset 51,000 times.

We aren't privy to all the memorable moments at all these tables, but certain faces and certain events seem to be carved like initials into certain tables. Here's a brief survey of the dining rooms, compressing 25 years into one memorable evening.

Table 32

Katharine Moore: Just after I was hired as executive director of the German Village Society and moved here from Washington, D.C., I was informed that one of my first official orders of business was to meet "the popes of German Village," Fred and Howard. "What you need to do, Katharine, is call Lindey's and make a reservation for Table 32." ❦ I'd already thought this meeting rather odd, and now it seemed simply pretentious. Requesting a certain table? It's not as if I were selecting seats for season tickets at the opera. I arrived for the meeting, and the hostess pointed out my dinner companions, who were working the room. The only time I had ever seen anything close to this was Ted Kennedy working the Four Seasons in Georgetown! ❦ When we connected at Table 32, Howard extended his hand, and I was completely unsure of what to say, so I said, "Gosh, I feel like I am here to kiss the ring." ❦ He pulled his hand back suddenly and I thought, Oh great, the first words out of my mouth and I offended him. ❦ "It's customary to kneel when you do that," he replied, presenting me his jeweled hand again. "Now we've got that out of the way before dinner."

(Story continues at Table 54.)

Table 54

Katharine Moore: Fast-forward maybe two months. I came to realize that nearly everyone in the Village had a favorite table at most restaurants in the Village—particularly Lindey's, since it's been here as long as or longer than many of the residents. ❦ In fact, in no time at all, I found myself calling Lindey's regularly, making a reservation for myself and requesting Table 54 ...and thinking, how quickly the high have fallen!

Table 20

At the middle table along the windows at the front of the restaurant, Emeril once joined us for a book party. His acquaintance, our manager Ross Hall, brought the chef a bottle of good wine, the best of our hors d'oeuvres, and a large steak. ❦ This is also the table where you'll likely see Judge Janet Jackson, Jan and Jim Barnes, and Sally Blue.

Table 10

The is the first table, right inside the door, right in the front window. This is where Cherie Hungate and Skip Van Dyne spent the first two decades of their evenings at Lindey's. And this is where we'll always remember Harold Cull holding forth. "Aunt Kate," as many of the servers called him, was the self-appointed head of gay society in Columbus; he'd preside at Lindey's for hours. People from the bar or from other tables would take turns at his table, have a drink, share in a few stories. He loved listening. He loved giving advice. All the people in the front part of the restaurant became his dinner companions—dear friends, friends of friends, perfect strangers, staff. ❦ "On the other hand," one dear guest points out, "When the legislature was in session, the scene at Lindey's changed to suits and bad haircuts. One somewhat paunchy pol from up north favored white suits: white-on-white shirts, white brocade ties, and, of course, white pointy-toed wingtip shoes. He'd bring along his constant dinner guest, his mistress, a size 14 in a size 10 dress. And they always sat at Table 10 (not the least visible place to sit in the room). The other politicians were easy to spot, too. The bottoms of their vests always seemed separated from their belts by a not-so-small protuberance of shirt front. And they really did smoke cigars (or more often just chewed the ends)."

Table 30

Having given up Table 10, Skip and Cherie would arrive at Table 30 at 4:00 or so in the afternoon, and the table would be theirs for the duration. ❦ **Manager Ian Brown:** Tables 30 and 31 have selling power. Probably 90 percent of the guests are escorted past those tables on the way to other tables. "Oh, what is that she's having?" they'll ask the host. "Oh, I want whatever that was" All you have to do is drop a piece of food on Table 30 or 31—just set it on the edge of the table—and the next thing you know, everyone and their mother will order one. If I ever decide someday to make widgets, that's where I'm going to display them.

Table 17

The almost-nightly favorite of Robin and Bonnie Freeman for many years, this table is near the service bar, close to the spirit providers, their buddies the bartenders. ❦ **Eddie Meecham:** For a couple years, they had a trinket that looked like one of those photo viewers from some amusement park, where you could see a tiny picture magnified at the end of the plastic cone. Only theirs had a mirror set at an angle inside it, so it was actually a little spyglass that looked sideways down the bar. ❦ Manager **Steve Gifford:** In and around 1990, when I worked at Lindey's, at the end of the night, each server could have a cocktail at Table 17. Sue would be there going over papers. The manager would be checking over each server's receipts. We'd all debrief. Then Sue would always announce, "It's bedtime," and head home to watch Peter Jennings. Table 17 was our gathering place for war stories, sidework, an extra-large Post Mortem to share, and sometimes a little pow-wow with the chef. At that time, a "shift drink" was at the manager's discretion: "Great night, every-one, the drinks are on me." Most nights, that would just be the first of the cocktails, which the staff would continue at one of the nearby bars or clubs. You certainly can't go right to sleep after being so wired.

Table 28

"The Grumpy Gourmet," Columbus's veteran restaurant reviewer Doral Chenoweth, had a favorite table at Lindey's. In a *Columbus Dispatch* article, "My Table, Please," he named favorite tables in some Columbus restaurants. "My table is the one with a wall art light for reading. This two-top is next to a clanking ice machine and a rattling coffee pot, and adjacent to the kitchen door. It is the loudest station in notably loud Lindey's. And the table rocks back and forth from winds created by heavy server traffic. But I like it." ❦ While at Cornell in a restaurant management program, Rick Doody received a call from Doral: "You put an ice bin where I sit, you...!" It's true, the two-top that had stood against the far wall—Table 28—had been removed to accommodate a newside stand and ice bin.

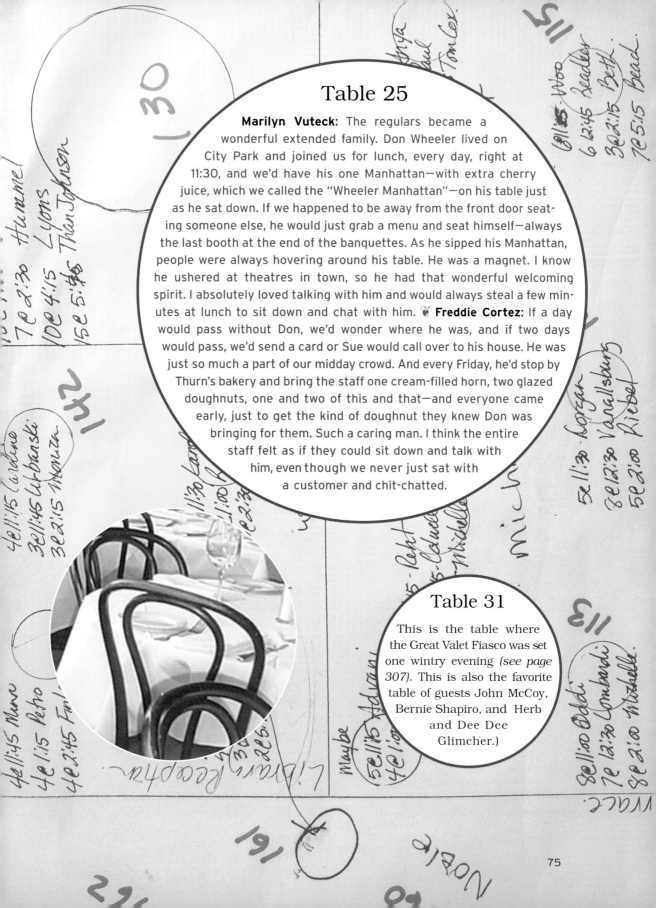

Table 25

Marilyn Vuteck: The regulars became a wonderful extended family. Don Wheeler lived on City Park and joined us for lunch, every day, right at 11:30, and we'd have his one Manhattan—with extra cherry juice, which we called the "Wheeler Manhattan"—on his table just as he sat down. If we happened to be away from the front door seating someone else, he would just grab a menu and seat himself—always the last booth at the end of the banquettes. As he sipped his Manhattan, people were always hovering around his table. He was a magnet. I know he ushered at theatres in town, so he had that wonderful welcoming spirit. I absolutely loved talking with him and would always steal a few minutes at lunch to sit down and chat with him. ❧ **Freddie Cortez:** If a day would pass without Don, we'd wonder where he was, and if two days would pass, we'd send a card or Sue would call over to his house. He was just so much a part of our midday crowd. And every Friday, he'd stop by Thurn's bakery and bring the staff one cream-filled horn, two glazed doughnuts, one and two of this and that—and everyone came early, just to get the kind of doughnut they knew Don was bringing for them. Such a caring man. I think the entire staff felt as if they could sit down and talk with him, even though we never just sat with a customer and chit-chatted.

Table 31

This is the table where the Great Valet Fiasco was set one wintry evening *(see page 307)*. This is also the favorite table of guests John McCoy, Bernie Shapiro, and Herb and Dee Dee Glimcher.)

Table 32

Server and (at the time) shuttle driver **Collin Smith:** I remember one evening, I'm standing at the front door, opening it as each guest arrives. A nice-looking man comes in with a lady on his arm and they're shown to Table 32. Then I park a few more cars. About 25 minutes later, in comes this guy again, and he has another woman on his arm. Of course, I just hold open the door and try to keep from winking. I don't know a thing. But then, about two hours later, I open the door, and out comes the man with the first woman, and then another man—ah, oh, wait! aha, his twin!—with the second woman. Apparently everyone but me knew Stan and Gary Robbins, who own a beverage company in town. ❦ On any given night, you'd have seen Fred Holdrich and Howard Burns, or Cookie and Victor Krupman (every Friday night), or Michael Block and his family at this table.

Table 44

Sue: No one ever wanted to sit here, since it meant being tucked into the corner where people were heading to and from the restrooms, so we removed it and made a side stand there.

Tables 64 and 86

On October 31, 1994, two tables in Lindey's Green Room were set aside for the foreign minister of Armenia and his security team. At Mayor Lushutka's invitation, the World Summit on Trade Efficiency was meeting in Columbus. Two Secret Service agents were stationed in the outside courtyard with an overview of the room; another watched over the curbside valet. No one parked on Mohawk while they dined. Otherwise, it was just another day at the bistro.

Table 35

Server Bob Bergandine: One New Year's Eve, I had a deuce, Table 35, which is against the wall, right at the corner that leads into the middle dining room. I had a young couple: a guy with a girl who was completely done up, her hair teased into a high profile—this was clearly the big night for her and her man. They ordered a bottle of Korbel. Now, I never had any trouble with expensive bottles of champagne, but some of the cheap ones, I don't know, they had a tendency to explode on me. Is that ironic? Maybe. So I brought their bottle of Korbel, and, I don't know how, but it just blew as I opened it. The cork flew off and missed the woman's nose by less than an inch, and the champagne blasted the wall, making a perfect silhouette of her head and her pile of hair. ❦ Her boyfriend started laughing, and that made me start laughing, even though I knew I should have been nothing but contrite. But his date? She was furious. She marched into the restroom. Unfortunately, after she returned, it was clear the left side of her hair was not going to return to its lofty self. ❦ I'm not sure there's a lesson to learn from this. Order nicer champagne if you're going to do up your hair in an important way?

Tables 36, 37 & 38

For Jazz Night, these tables, the closest to the kitchen, in the corner of the main room, are folded up to make room for the band. Where do they go? They get stacked in the kitchen, as if there's extra room to spare there. ❦ **Chef Jared Bissel:** The music and the crowd are so loud on Jazz Night that you can't even hear yourself talk in the kitchen. We have to yell out the tickets. The place is jamming, and everyone from the servers to the line cooks are hollering at the top of their lungs. And out in the dining, there's Jeannette Williams belting out Aretha Franklin. ❦ **Bartender Tony Murray:** Oh, Jeannette could draw in the crowd. Week after week. When she had her game on, the whole room would be swaying. She'd sing "R-E-S-P-E-C-T" and all the ladies would be singing along. Or she'd join her friends Kay and John Mills at Table 20, singing into her microphone right there, and in the middle of the song, just as if it were the third verse, she'd work in "Oh, Tony, uh-huh, Tony-eeee, can I get a huh, huh, Absolut and cranber-reeee...." Just part of the song. "And, Tony, Tony-eeee, can you put it on Kay's tab, ah yes-sir-eeee."

Table 64

The table farthest from the front door, looking out into the rear courtyard, this is the table for pre-shift meetings. ❦ Wine purveyor **Dan Frey:** For many years, managers would invite me to pre-shift meetings, where the chef brings out samples of the evening's specials. And I'd get there early, stick my finger in the sauces, talk with the chef about the various preparations, and then grab a wine or two that we'd try with each dish. Then I'd rush out to the car or into the cellar and grab a couple bottles of whatever wine seemed best with each dish, and join the staff at the meeting. It was all very immediate. But I could also get in trouble for that: ❦ "Um, Dan? Could we try the first pinot again? I'm not sure—" Someone on the staff could never decide which wine seemed better. ❦ "Hey, Dan, I forgot what the first wine we tasted was." ❦ So after four or five other bottles, we'd go back and retaste one. On several occasions, I poured way too much wine. "Dan!" Sue would say, "You're getting my whole staff drunk and they haven't even started working!" ❦ This mostly happened when I'd bring in a winemaker. And it would be insulting not to try each and every wine they'd intended to show off. I remember Kathleen Heitz of Heitz Wine Cellars joined us at one meeting. I believe I asked her to marry me twice during the tasting: She had everything I wanted in a woman—including her own winery.

Table 80

Shelia Wiley: Lifelong patrons the Zeiglers join us every year for New Year's Eve, and always at Table 80 with eight guests. One year, we had it reserved for them, but coincidentally, right before they arrived, a younger group of eight guests with a reservation at Table 52 was ready to be seated and they were accidentally shown to Table 80 by the host. ❦ How do I learn of this? One of my managers comes to me in tears because Mr. Z said we're casting the old folks away and giving tables to the younger folks and on and on. So I go over to the table of younger folks, explain the mistake, and find that they are more than happy to move. In fact, one member of their party knows Mr. Z.'s son. But, no, the Zeiglers don't want them to move. So now it's a power struggle, and meanwhile we're all standing in the hall, blocking everything. *(Story continues at Table 52.)*

Table 52

(continued from Table 80)

Finally, the Zeigler party settles around table 52 and orders. But, as bad luck would have it, we're now out of the two specials that they wanted, and nothing else on the menu seems right. So they decide that they want sliders for New Year's Eve dinner. Sacks of White Castle hamburgers! One of the gentlemen goes outside to the valet, gives him $50, and tells him to get as many White Castle burgers as this will buy. When I hear about this, I think, "No one is going to bring sliders into my restaurant, and not on New Year's Eve on top of that."

(Story continues at Sue's Dining Room.)

Valet Stand

(continued from Sue's Dining Room)

So I go outside and wait for the valet to return. The gentleman who'd given him the money also comes outside. And I can see he is dead set on bringing hamburgers to his table, and I know I am just as dead set against it. We have ourselves a little conversation. I turn on my Southern charm, and it's freezing cold outside, by the way, and I'm from New Orleans and I don't do cold, so finally, I say, "You give me your sacks of burgers, and I'll take them into the kitchen and bring them out to you in a proper way." When the valet pulls up, I take the sacks down the block and go in the side door to the kitchen.

(Story concludes back at Table 52 on the next page.)

Sue's Dining Room

(continued from Table 52)

So I call Sue Doody at home. She's having her own dinner party. "Sue, darling, I know it's New Year's Eve, I know you're with your family, but I have to tell you I'm putting your friends out, and I don't want you mad at me." I hadn't been her G.M. for a year, and this was my first New Year's Eve—but they had to go. 🐛 Sue replied, "Oh my. What were they thinking! Okay, hon, if you've got to put them out, you put them out. Oh...." *(Story continues at the valet stand.)*

Table 52

(continued from the Valet Stand)

The chef and I get out a big platter, put out all the sliders, dress the plates with parsley and whatnot, and then have the server take it out to the Zeigler party. And wouldn't you know, as soon as it's out there, everyone recognizes the smell, and the Zeiglers are passing sliders over to all the neighboring tables. So meanwhile, everyone in the dining room is dancing and swigging champagne from the bottles on other guests' tables and snapping pictures of one another. The evening turned out great, and the next morning, as a final happy note, Mr. Z. called when I was in doing inventory. "My wife said I had to call and apologize. She said if I didn't, I couldn't ever come to Lindey's again, and I can't let that happen."

Table 85

Robert Lazarus: For years and years, our regular Tuesday lunch group has been meeting at Table 85. We've had a few lunch spots for various days of the week, but Lindey's has always been our favorite. At the round table in the Green Room, next to the small bar there, it was always Chuck Lazarus, Bob Greene, Bill Westwater, and myself. Bob kept elaborate records for us and would bring out his index cards and make a great show of reporting who was there and who paid last time and whose turn it was next to pay. We often had the eggs Benedict, I remember, and it was Chuck's particular habit to test the poached egg with his fork to see that it was done just right. ❧ **Corde Robinson**, daughter of Bill Westwater: We always felt that Dad's lunch group had their pulse on the activities of the city. And if there wasn't anything going on, they often made things up around the table at Lindey's. Of course, there was always great secrecy about the luncheon topics. And then, whenever anyone in the family would announce the latest scoop, Dad would often say, "Oh, I knew that from Tuesday lunch at Lindey's."

Table 32

Manager Freddie Cortez: Another evening—a Monday night in the fall—Kip has a table of four businessmen. "Freddie, those guys at 32 are getting on my nerves," he tells me. "All they want to know is some stupid football score. I don't care about football!" (Now this is prior to Rick Doody putting a TV over the doorway in the bar, thereby obviating the need for servers who couldn't care less about sports to be score-runners.) Each time Kip delivers something to the table, one of the men asks him for the score. Finally, I tell him, "Just go in the kitchen and ask one of the cooks. They've got a radio. They're probably listening." And a few minutes later, I see Kip at the table. "So did you get us the score?" one man asks. "Ah, no, but..." replies Kip, "but I think someone just hit a home run." And then he scurried off back to the kitchen to get their entrées.

Table 54

Once the most requested table at Lindey's, Table 54 used to look out onto the courtyard before we added the Green Room. It's sunk down, enclosed by railings, and offers an intimate space—albeit right below the restroom traffic. Yet it's still our "engagement table." By our calculations, 43 proposals have been made at that table in our 25 years. 🍎 **Sue:** When we first opened, Table 54 sat on top of a trap door in the rear dining room. The trap door led to the basement, where the electric meter was housed. Each month, we had to ask the meter reader to come back later, after lunch, because we had to move the table, clear away the carpeting, and pull up the door in order for him to climb down the stairs into the cellar to read the meter.

LINDEY'S GARLIC MASHED POTATOES

IN A 1991 ARTICLE that the *Washington Post* entitled "Mash Notes to the Potato: Oh, How We Love the Ultimate Comfort Food," a recipe from Lindey's appeared along with other spud favorites from around the nation; Celebration Potatoes, Colcannon Cheddar Mashed Potatoes, Green Bean and Potato Purée, and Swedish Potatoes. The feature gave the recipe for our Garlic Mashed Potatoes, which the paper described as "redolent with the mellowed, sweet flavor of roasted garlic." (In our 25 years, potatoes have never appeared on a menu accompanied by the word "redolent." It's just part of our overall guest commitment.) We've never taken this "ultimate" potato off the menu ever since Chef David Tidd set it alongside our lamb chops.

makes 8 servings

- 1 large head garlic
- 1 teaspoon olive oil
- 4 pounds Idaho baking potatoes
- about 6 cups chicken stock or salted water
- 1 cup heavy cream, or more if needed
- 1 cup (2 sticks) unsalted butter, room temperature, cut into small bits
- salt and freshly ground white pepper, to taste

Preheat the oven to 325°F.

Coat the head of garlic with the olive oil, wrap in aluminum foil, and roast for 1 hour or until quite soft.

Allow the garlic to cool. Slice off the flat bottom end of the garlic and gently squeeze out the golden-brown paste into a small bowl. Set aside.

Peel and cut potatoes into large chunks. Place in a large saucepan and add chicken stock to cover. Over high heat, bring the liquid to a boil, and then reduce the heat to medium, so that the potatoes simmer until they are tender, about 30 minutes.

Drain the potatoes, discarding any remaining chicken stock, and place them back in the saucepan. Steam the potatoes for 10 minutes over medium heat, with the lid off. Stir the potatoes occasionally, so all the potatoes take a turn at the bottom of the pot. As the water steams away, it makes room for, yes, the butter and the cream.)

Adding the cream a little at a time, mash, beat, or even whip the potatoes into an even fluffier attitude with an electric mixer fitted with the whisk attachment. Beat in the butter and roasted garlic, and add salt and white pepper to taste. Add more cream (or fresh stock), if the potatoes seem dry. Turn into a heated serving dish.

We discourage you from serving this dish with a comment such as "there are over 4,500 calories in this dish, but that only means 525 per person, so it's not so bad." That's like going for a Sunday drive in the country and talking about gas emissions. However, you are encouraged to show some restraint as you fill your guests' plates. Leftover potatoes reheat beautifully. Think of tomorrow's lunch: in a hot skillet with a little olive oil, fry up a flattened disk of these potatoes. Crispy brown outside, creamy potato inside...maybe blend in a little grated Parmesan first, or some fresh herbs. Oh the joys of mashed potatoes.

OH, WE'RE GOOD FRIENDS OF THE OWNER
THAT AND A QUARTER WON'T EVEN GET YOU A CUP OF COFFEE

ON OCCASION, there is a gentleman who arrives at Lindey's, informs the hostess that his name is "Mr. Doody," and that he has a reservation for however many people he has in tow for whatever time it happens to be. Curiously, and invariably, we never have such a reservation. (Plus, the only Mr. Doodys we know are Sue's ex-husband, who lives in New Orleans, and her sons Rick and Chris—and we're pretty familiar with their faces.)

That notwithstanding, we show the man to the table he prefers, Table 54 (the round table in the middle dining room that's on a slightly lower level), as if it had been waiting for someone with an important-sounding name all night.

Our idea of hospitality is to treat everyone as if they were "dear friends" of the owners. And yet guests are often tempted to play the Doody name as if it were a trump card or get-out-of-jail-free card to see what prize, exemption, or privilege that might bestow.

Here are some priceless examples.

Patience Is a Virtue;
Impatience, a Dead Giveaway

Tim Picard: When I was a manager, some guy came in saying that he'd made a reservation in his name [not Doody], but when we looked through the list, we had no such reservation. There's always a chance that we can lose a reservation for one reason or another, but this is often a lousy ploy to get a table on a busy night at the last minute. So I tell him we'll seat him as soon as possible, but it's likely to be at least an hour. He agrees to wait at the bar with his friends. Not 10 minutes later, he's back at the host stand, indignant as can be: When the hell is my table going to be ready? When I explain that, not 10 minutes earlier, I'd said that it would be at least an hour, he says, "All right, I've had it! Where's my good friend *Sue Dooley*?" And, with that, I knew for certain that his wait was going to be at least an hour—and maybe longer.

Foreign Relations

Collin Smith, a longtime server: The one thing that always worked our nerves was when a customer would say, "Where's the owner, we know the owner." It was suddenly like having an Amway salesman at your table. And most of the people who would say that didn't have a clue who Sue Doody might be or what she looked like.

I remember Jimmy Borden hosting one Saturday night. It's 7:00, we're busy, and someone calls saying they'd like a table in a few minutes, they're nearby.

"We're full just now," Jimmy replied, "but I can seat you at—"

The caller interrupts. "I don't think you recognized my name. My wife and I are very good friends with Sue; if I could speak with her—"

And then it's Jimmy's turn to interrupt, "You could...but then, since you're such good friends with Sue, you surely know she's in Russia right now."

As I recall, Jimmy wasn't mischievous only with pretentious callers. Once Sue herself called from Europe during a busy weekend evening. "Hi, it's Sue Doody, how is everything go—"

Jimmy, who had immediately recognized her voice (no talent required), interrupted in a Chinese accent: "Who? Sue? Doody? She no here no more. We Chinese restaurant now."

Call of Duty

Sue: My first cousin's son came into Lindey's to apply for a job. He played basketball at Ohio Dominican College. I didn't see him arrive—I was upstairs in the office—but Todd, the manager on duty, took his application, glanced over it to make sure all the information was there, and thanked the young man. The next day, he called me over to ask if I'd seen the young man's application, which listed under references: "Mrs. Duty is a cousin." Needless to say, anyone with that kind of chutzpah, we had to hire!

Last Call

Manager X: We had a group of ladies who'd decided that Lindey's might be the perfect ending to a bachelorette party. They climb out of a limo, settle into a table on the terrace, and are promptly informed by the server that we've already had last call outside: "But you're welcome to go inside, where they're still serving." Not exactly pleased to have this kink in their impromptu plans, they do come inside and order drinks. In no time at all, the bride-to-be's friends are cheering her on as she performs oral sex on a beer bottle. Soon enough, one member of the party is going table to table to see if anyone has a condom to spare. When the manager catches sight of this, he politely asks the lady to please return to her table and allow the other guests to enjoy their evenings.

"Do you have any idea who I am?" she replies indignantly! "I am one of the biggest personal friends of Ms. Doody."

Amazingly, the manager did not reply, "Oh, then I'm sure Ms. Doody will be happy to hear that her dear friend came in to perform fellatio on one of her beer bottles."

The manager did, however, remember that story...oh, this many years later.

Call My Bluff

But Sue's is not the only name that gets invoked. Guests come in who announce that they went to high school with the Lindey brothers. Or that they used to babysit for Mrs. Lindey's kids when they were in high school.

Once a gentleman came in with a Lindey's gift certificate he wanted to redeem for cash. It's company policy that a guest needs to order something—even a cup of coffee—in order to receive the balance of the gift in cash. When manager Todd Cumbow graciously explained this, the guest was indignant, as if Todd had questioned his credit or reputation.

"Okay, then I'll just call Chris [Doody] right now," he said, and reached for his cell phone.

"Well, if you have to," Todd replied, remembering that Chris had once told him, "If someone's going to threaten you with my name, they're no friend of mine."

The gentleman closed his cell phone. "You're the first person that's ever challenged me."

Midnight Snack

On another occasion, a Saturday night about midnight, a guest calls in, wanting the recipe for our tuna tartare. The manager that evening says we can get him the recipe from the chef the next day, but the chef has gone for the evening. Nonetheless, he recites the basic ingredients and process for the appetizer. Yet that isn't satisfactory. The caller wants the actual recipe. Right now. The manager tries to be cheerful, even as other guests are coming and going, as servers are needing his attention. Finally the caller says, "Well, I'm just going to phone Chris at home right now, and I'll do that. You want me to do that?"

The manager replied, "Good luck. We've been trying to reach Chris all week. But if you *do* get him, tell him to drop off some more teaspoons at the restaurant because we're almost out."

THE GUEST IS ALWAYS RIGHT
...WITH A FEW EXCEPTIONS

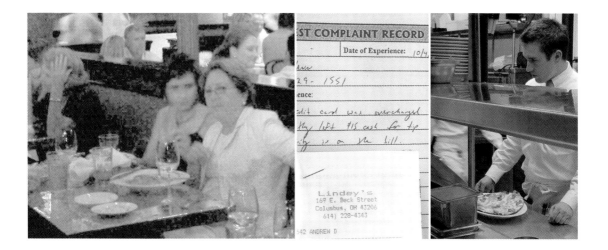

PERHAPS IT WAS A PHASE—a sign of sudden growth but lagging maturity?—when, 10 or 15 years ago, restaurants seemed to be offering a Dinner Lecture Series with their meals. Guests would comment, suggest, or complain as usual, but servers—instead of smiling, immediately resolving the issue, and contenting themselves by regaling coworkers at the side stand with what they might have said in reply to whatever was so obviously misinformed—began to correct guests, defend the kitchen, or flex their own culinary savvy.

For example, when a diner who shall remain nameless mentioned to a certain server that a salmon chowder was unbearably salty, he was quickly told, "Salmon is a saltwater fish, what did you expect?" Remaining calm, while preparing to announce that his major in college happened to have been zoology, the guest couldn't help but reply that even saltwater fish must excrete salt from their systems, and that the server was, fact, a fish out of water.

Another friend once sent back a glass of wine that held half an inch of sediment. The server brought over the manager, who took pains to explain that sediment is an integral part of winemaking. "It's what you expect with good wine."

"What I *expect*," the guest replied, "is that I will not receive a scolding from a misinformed staff member when I come to enjoy an evening in this restaurant. A glass of wine should not come with complimentary sludge."

Neither of these examples occurred at Lindey's, but lest you think we're trying to exempt ourselves from the trend, here are some stunning examples of the creative insubordination that was a part of our somewhat vainglorious past.

A Fresh Start to the New Year

Alice Mattimo: Sue has always believed that the customer's always right, as long as they *are* right. But when the customer's *wrong*, she didn't just go along because that was what was expected of a restaurateur.

One New Year's Eve, I had a lady who was incredibly difficult. She was in a group of 15—my two eight-tops. They were staying most of the night. The most galling thing was that she'd send her husband to the bar to get drinks for the table so that he could pay cash and not have to tip for the drinks at the end of the meal. This went on for a few rounds. I didn't say a thing. At the end of the evening, just to make things easier, I even took the party's check and broke it out into eight separate checks. Every other couple was fine with this, but this same woman was sure that I might have accidentally slipped someone else's drink or side dish onto her check. And she stood up and put her finger in my face, just as Sue Doody was walking past the table. "Young lady," she announced, "you are the...worst...waitress I have ever had."

"That really hurts," I replied, "because you are the best customer I've ever waited on." Sue just smiled and continued walking. As my friend and coworker Bob Bergandine would say, "We serve more attitude than food at Lindey's."

Let's Have Some Order

Server Erich K: One busy Saturday night in the back room, I had a table of older queens. There was nothing particularly noteworthy about them, other than that one gentleman, much to the dismay of his fellow diners and to my complete chagrin, ordered a soup, an appetizer, and an entrée, and then, with a great deal of flourish and volume, proceeded to instruct me as follows:

"Now, I'd like you to bring the soup out first, when everyone else is having their soup. After that, I'll have the salad as a second course. When I've finished with that, and not until I have finished with that, you can serve me my entrée."

The other three men at the table looked down in embarrassment. I eyed the offender quietly from my elevated position before leaning in just a little too close to his somewhat bloated face to reply in my very best Dunaway-does-Crawford-does-the-Pepsi-Cola-board-of-directors imitation: "Well...you think you're very clever, don't you? Trying to sweep the poor little server under the carpet? Well, think again. This ain't my first time at the rodeo."

The control queen stared up dumbfounded while his companions tittered. As I walked away from the table, I heard one of them murmur through the stifled giggles, "I think she's got it covered, Herb."

Snapper Decision

The Barneses and the Schneidermans are having dinner one night. Lenore orders the snapper, and it's dry. She raises her hand and signals the closest person, Tony at the host stand. She's motioning "could you come here?" with her fingers.

Tony crosses his arms and calls across the room. "What?"

Lenore calls back as softy as she can, "This snapper is dry."

"It's supposed to be. It's a dry fish," Tony replies.

But then he walks over, picks up her plate, and takes it to the kitchen. A few minutes later, he reappears with another plate with a newly prepared piece of fish. "Here's your snapper," he says, setting the plate in front of Lenore...and, turning to walk away, adds, "And it's going to be dry."

A Parting Shot of Coffee

Randy Manypenny, a beloved longtime waiter at Lindey's—lost to us in the early years of the AIDS epidemic—may have helped to establish the witty culture of Lindey's. (That's a refined way of saying we have a policy of tolerating what would be called insubordination, rudeness, and smart-ass behavior by most restaurants and parents of 14-year-olds.) "Randy could shred a person to pieces with his wit, but physically he was so skinny you couldn't hit him with a handful of corn," Collin Smith remembers. "And with his haircut and what he liked to wear, he could qualify as the biggest sissy on earth. In the winter, he'd walk to Lindey's from his apartment, usually wearing earmuffs from his collection: baseball earmuffs, Cabbage Patch doll earmuffs, kitten earmuffs, piglet earmuffs—you name it. Someone on staff would say, 'Randy, you're going to get yourself beaten up walking around in those,' and he would reply, 'I don't care. I like them. I think they're cute.'"

But Randy was master of the Parthian shot, the snide remark delivered as the last word (also known as a "parting shot"), derived from the Parthians,* the expert archers of ancient Asia who could fire an arrow while seemingly in retreat.

One evening, Randy had a particularly exasperating diner. And while he managed to deliver his characteristically charming, attentive service throughout the meal, when he returned the guest's credit card and the charge slip, he added, "Oh, and by the way, I took the liberty of putting some fresh coffee in a Styrofoam cup for you because I know it's a long way back to Hell."

Lindey's does not have a policy of offering coffee to go (to Hell).

On another occasion, Randy walked past a table on the way to the kitchen (it wasn't his section), and a woman reached out, grabbed him by the arm, and hissed in a low voice, "The children are hungry!"

Without skipping a beat, Randy hissed back, "And the crow flies at night."

---

* Who were these Parthians, you ask, as if this book encompassed more than just the Lindey's era? Parthia occupied the vast expanse known as Persia (what would become everything from Iran to Georgia, from Israel to Pakistan), prospering for some 500 years, half on either side of the great B.C./A.D. divide. But since our focus is on food, if Lindey's were 2,000 years older and you were having dinner here, you'd likely be served lamb or chicken, beans, and a hard, almost unrisen bread that none other than Pliny claimed "would keep for centuries." Curiously, Columbus's own Grumpy Gourmet described our bread in the mid-1980s as "akin to an Iranian terrorist—hard enough to break your face and flaky." History repeats itself—or maybe just excuses itself from the table.

Just My Luck

Collin Smith: One of our regular families comes in on a weekend night. Party of six. I walk up to the table, and the man says to me, "We're going to a play, and we're sort of in a hurry." Now I'd probably waited on them a hundred times before. So I smile and say, "The truth is, you're not in a hurry. I am. I'm going to be rushing all over this place while you relax here at the table, which is fine. But I am the one 'sort of in a hurry.'" But I'm smiling, so it doesn't really come off as hostile. They eat, get their check, walk out happy.

Funny enough, right? But then two hours later, they come back to the restaurant for dessert. And guess who gets to serve them? "So...how was the play?"

Brassy Abby

One of our favorite cocktail waitresses, Abby Pemberton, had a particularly tough job. We have a long, narrow row of tables parallel to the bar, a row of seats along the bar, and just enough space for about two people to line up in the intervening space. Negotiating the long path between the service bar at one end and the guests near the door is very difficult on a crowded night, especially with a tray of glasses. Glasses filled to the brim and garnished with something that teeters. With a stack of napkins that blow off immediately if you don't weigh them down with something like an empty rocks glass, which is also a perfect thing to hold your pens so they don't roll off the tray.

As a joke of sorts, one of our servers bought Abby some brass knuckles to keep on the tray; people were always hassling her—mostly in a nice way—so it just rested there in the rocks glass to deflect any little difficulties.

But Abby was by no means defenseless.

Abby Pemberton: A guest ordered our Caesar salad and then grabbed my arm saying, "And I want no anchovies."

So I look down at his hand on my arm, and I reply, "I'm sorry, what did you want?"

"I want—I meant, I do *not* want anchovies," he repeats, his hand still on my arm.

"I don't understand," I reply, pretending to make more notes on my pad.

"I *don't* want *anchovies* on my *Caesar salad*, okay?"

"Oh, okay. So...when I bring out the Caesar salad with the anchovies, you want me not to bring the anchovies, but you want the salad, is that right? Or do you not want the Caesar salad?"

Meanwhile, my friend Nicole over at the side stand is dying as I fake all this confusion. But, come on, you don't need to grab a server's arm just to make a point.

Another night, I'm carrying a tray of drinks to the front of the bar and some guy barks out at me, "Hey, decaf!"

So I nod and say, "I'll be right there with it—just let me deliver these."

On my way back to the coffee maker, the man barks again, "Decaf!" So I raise my finger to say, just a minute, I'll be right back with it.

A moment later, I'm back and I set two cups of coffee on his table.

"Hey, how come you brought me two coffees?"

"Because you asked me twice," I replied.

Half-Time Entertainment

At one point, Lindey's had the idea of doing half portions. Half portions to make diners happy. So anything a chef designed had to be able to be halved.

"In no time at all," recalls chef **Bob Keane**, "we created a monster. People wanted half of one thing with half of another. Or—this killed me—they wanted half apps. Appetizers are already half portions! So, in effect, they wanted half of a half. (That's called sharing, and all you do is take a forkful from your friend's plate.) Thankfully, the management eventually saw the problem."

The waitstaff certainly endured the tyranny of this monster. They may even have been the ones who slew this half-baked idea.

Mark Svede: We had been offering half portions for about two months, and the menu clearly noted which items were available as a half portion or a full portion. After some initial confusion, we were required to ask every guest who

ordered an entrée offered in both sizes which they wanted. Every guest. We asked tiny birdlike ladies if they wanted the full or half order. We asked hulking athletes if they desired the full or the half order.

One night I had a three-top. One woman ordered the pork chops, which came with the two options—essentially, one or two pork chops with the same sides. So I asked, "Would you care for the full or the half portion?"

"The full portion will be fine," she replied.

I brought their salads. I cleared their salads. I brought out the entrées and set down the double pork chop in front of the one guest. She looked down at the plate. She looked up at me.

"Oh—*this* is a half portion? This is so big." The tone of her voice clearly gave her away.

"No, *this* is the regular portion," I said.

"Oh, no. I only wanted the half portion," she replied.

The table behind theirs was unseated. I grabbed a fork from it and speared the closest of her two pork chops. "Now *that's* the half portion," I said, and marched the chop through the dining room back to the kitchen.

Separate But Unequal

Server M: It's a football Saturday, we're absolutely booked, and a ten-top of five young couples settles in my station to celebrate the Buckeye victory. We've combined tables 71, 72, and 73 for this party, right in the middle of the green room. They can see, at the outset, how busy we are and how we're stretching to make them comfortable. The staff is whirling around them, tables are being served, turned, seated—it's amazing that we can keep up.

I welcome the table to Lindey's, tell them my name, and the first thing the man directly across the table from me says is, "We're going to need separate checks."

I explain that it's the restaurant's policy—which the host surely explained when they made a reservation for 10—that we can only offer a single check for a party of this size. I then offer to take separate forms of payment for different amounts. I also offer to divide the check evenly. Finally, I apologize that I'm not permitted to do anything else because of what an order this size requires of our register system.

Clearly unsatisfied with my reply, the man mutters

from across the table, "You just won't do it because you're a fag."

The rest of the table is apoplectic at his remark.

"No," I reply in anything but a mutter, "you're going to get really super-special service tonight because I'm a fag. The one-check policy is because of the management."

For the rest of the meal, everyone else at the table gives me the most sympathetic glances, prefacing requests with "if it's no trouble," or "if you'd be so kind." The man's date scowls at him the entire night.

I believe he enjoyed the worst Buckeye victory dinner of his young life.

A Not-So-Private Joke

Michael Tsonton worked as bartender, server, and line cook at Lindey's at a couple points in his restaurant career. He is now the executive chef and owner of copperblue in Chicago.

Michael: I had this table of six in the back dining room. It was parents, their son and his girl-friend, and his son's friend and his girlfriend. I'd brought them drinks, and now it was time to take their dinner order. "If you don't mind, I'll just go around the table clockwise," I said. But I was exhausted—I was going on my 13th or 14th hour of straight work—and I inadvertently went around counterclockwise.

"Did you go to public or private school?" Out of the clear blue, the son asks me this as I'm standing there to take his order.

"I went to public school," I replied, and the entire table laughed at me.

"Yeah, that kind of figures, the way you moved around the table—counterclockwise." *You pretentious little bastard*, I thought to myself as he gave me his dinner order.

He also wanted another drink, a Jack and Coke, so I went to the bar and told John Lee as he poured the whiskey what had just transpired and what I thought about it. He agreed, of course: totally uncalled-for! So I filled a rocks glass with bunch of Maraschino cherries and an orange wheel, and took the drinks back out to the table.

"And you? Did you go to public or private school?" I asked the kid.

"I went to private school," he replied to me with great smugness and self-importance.

"Figures! Because where I went to school, we didn't mix our Jack with Coke. So here's your drink," I said, setting down the cocktail, "and here's your chaser," I added, plopping down the glass of cherries.

Then the father just hit the ceiling, but I walked away. I gave the busboy 10 bucks and told him I had no intention of going back to that table and that he should just keep them watered and get them coffee—whatever.

On their way out, the father repeated the whole incident to Sue.

And then, as soon as I was free, I went up to Sue, completely nervous and sweating, and also explained what had happened.

"Michael, you were a little excessive, but I understand. What was that boy thinking?"

Sue just expected people to act well at her restaurant. And she gave her staff more than just the benefit of the doubt. It's something I try to apply at my own restaurant, every day.

POST MORTEM

THIS DESSERT FIRST APPEARED on a devilish menu by Chef Tom Johnson the first Halloween we were open. And it's never departed, as it were.

That evening's specials included that skeletal classic, osso buco; a true dungeon-delight, RATatouille; and this decadent dessert intended to trim years off your life, the Post Mortem. Tom's story about the discovery of this concoction follows his original recipes for the two key components: the brownie, and the Kahlúa "Hot Fudge" Sauce.

serves 4*

- 4 squares Palm-Beach-Comes-to-German-Village Brownies
- 4 scoops premium coffee ice cream
- 1 cup Kahlúa "Hot Fudge" Sauce

To serve, place one brownie square on each dessert plate. Place a scoop of coffee ice cream on top, and ladle the heated Kahlúa "Hot Fudge" Sauce over the top.

Palm-Beach-Comes-to-German-Village Brownies

makes 32 generously sized brownies

- 4 ounces unsweetened chocolate, coarsely chopped
- 1/2 pound (2 sticks) unsalted butter, cut into 16 pieces
- 1 1/2 cups sifted all-purpose flour
- 1/2 cups shelled walnuts or pecans, broken into large bits
- 2 cups sugar
- 4 large eggs, lightly beaten
- 1/4 teaspoon finely ground sea salt
- 1/2 teaspoon pure vanilla extract

Preheat the oven to 350°F, and place an oven rack one-third up from the bottom of the oven. Butter a 13 x 9 x 2-inch pan.

Melt the chocolate and butter in the top of a double boiler, set over barely simmering water, stirring occasionally. (Alternatively, use a microwave oven set on half power, stirring after 1 minute, and adding addition-al time only until the chocolate is all but melted; the rest will melt as you stir.) Set the melted mixture aside.

When melted, allow the mixture to cool slightly, but not set up. Add the remaining ingredients and blend until just combined. Pour the batter into the prepared pan and smooth the top with a spatula.

Bake for 25 minutes, reversing the pan from front to back once after 12 minutes to ensure even baking. At the end of the 25 minutes, the cake will have a firm crust, but the center will be underbaked when pierced with a toothpick. That's the idea! You want a fudgelike center. Let the cake cool in the pan. Tightly cover the cake with foil or plastic wrap, and refrigerate for several hours, or overnight to create the right density.

Cut into squares—wetting the knife before each cut to create a clean edge—before serving.

Kahlúa "Hot Fudge" Sauce
makes 3 cups**

- 1 cup unsweetened Dutch-process cocoa such as Dröste (Lindey's uses Callebaut brute cocoa–available at specialty stores)
- 2/3 cup granulated sugar
- 1/2 cup light brown sugar, packed
- 1 cup whipping cream
- 1/2 cup (8 tablespoons) unsalted butter, cut into 8 pieces
- 1/4 cup Kahlúa or other coffee liqueur
- 1 1/2 teaspoons pure vanilla extract
- salt, to taste (optional)

* Or even twice that number if people are content to be "Pre-Mortem," saving room for coffee, cheese, or breakfast the next day.

** Enough for 6 servings, so there's plenty to spoon from the jar in the refrigerator when there's "nothing else to eat" in the house.

In a medium-size heavy-bottom saucepan over medium heat, combine the cocoa and both sugars. Slowly stir in the cream to make a paste, and then add the bits of butter. Bring to a simmer. Reduce the heat, simmer for another minute, stirring, and then remove from heat. Add the Kahlúa and vanilla. Season with a pinch or two of salt. Serve warm or at room temperature.

The sauce can be cooled, sealed in an airtight jar, and kept refrigerated for up to 2 weeks. Before serving, heat the sauce in a loosely covered microwave-safe bowl. Microwave at half-power, stirring halfway through the cook time—approximately 1 to 3 minutes, depending on your machine's power.

Above: Dreamy-eyed Chef Tom Johnson, circa 1982

Tom Johnson: The late Robbins Hunter, Esq., of Granville, Ohio, last of the infamous Ohio Yankees and a curmudgeon to warm the cockles of the coldest heart, hoarded his mother's receipt for a half-baked fudge cake: a thin brownie-like sheet cake that lends an oral sensation of chocolate fudge because of its limited cooking time. ("Something wonderfully half-baked this way comes!")

Casting about for any recipe for a half-baked fudge cake, I happened on a tome, awash in the giddiness of legend, called *The Palm Beach Cook Book*. Nestled among the tidbits of Mrs. So-and-So the VII, and even Countess Reventlow, then the name of Barbara Hutton, the Woolworth heiress who, save for devouring a brace of husbands, looked as if she never ate, was this Palm Beach Fudge Cake.

My days at Lindey's coincided with the heyday of bestowing homicidal names on our super-caloric chocolate confections: Death-by-Tollhouse, Serial Killer Brownies, Chocolate Narcosis, and the Fudge Vapours. Since Marjorie Merriweather Post had recently passed away, I named this humble "post mortem" tribute as a dedication to her splendid culinary accomplishments.

Pre-Post Mortem

Server Alice Mattimo: I hated making the Post Mortems. I'd often eloquently describe all our beautifully prepared desserts and then finish with "and then, there's the Post Mortem...you should order that some night when you have a big strong male server because we have to scoop coffee ice cream onto a brownie and if you get it tonight, you will get puny little shards of ice cream that will take me forever to chip out...these guys could make you a really nice one the next time you come." I quickly realized that saying this just guaranteed every table had to have one.

Server Abby Pemberton: I remember Alice had another technique. A lady would ask her, "Oh, how's this 'Post Mortem' on your menu?"

And for whatever reason, Alice thought

she could dissuade the guest since she was very busy by saying that it was awful.

"Really? *Awful?* Now, why is that?" she asked, so then Alice would explain:

"First of all, the brownies are kept on a big tray on top of the microwave, and if you aren't six feet tall, and I'm not, you have to climb up on the ice cream freezer, in the middle of everyone else rushing around with these giant trays, and grab one. And it's hard as a rock and wrapped in nine layers of plastic so it takes five minutes just to unwrap it and put it in a bowl so I can microwave it—that is, if there is a bowl. But half the time I have to run over to the dishwasher racks and find a bowl, and it's usually still warm. So then I microwave the brownie, and grab the ice cream scoop out of the nasty water and wash it under hot water and then reach down into the ice cream freezer—all the way down, and if you're not six feet tall, like I'm not, you're getting your shirt sleeve messed up in the freezer, and you have to scrape and scrape just to get two scoops of ice cream out of the bucket, which at this time of night, is almost empty, so that means I have to reach in even farther. So then I nearly bloody my knuckles trying to form two round balls of the hard ice cream and lift them out of the freezer without dropping them. And then I can see that there are ice crystals on the one scoop, which doesn't look so good, so I toss it back and make another scoop. And then the hot fudge ladle is always sticky, and drizzling the stuff always gets on the bowl rim, which means I have to wipe that up and get stickier.

"Oh, and then I have to find you a dessert spoon, and nine times out of ten, I'll have to fish around in a bus tub and wash one myself because by 8:30 or so we run out. So 15 minutes have passed by the time I get you your Post Mortem and at that point the hot fudge and the hot bowl have pretty much melted the ice cream except for the freezer-burned crystals.

"So it's awful, like I said."

Post Mortem on a Stick

Every restaurant gets lured into doing many regrettable things—hopefully, they only do each regrettable thing once.

Our banquet manager, Marilyn Vuteck, came to general manager Tom Harlor one day and said we should have a booth at Octoberfest. "We should offer something that's sort of a signature dish there. It will be great for PR." So she came up with this idea of selling our Post Mortem—on a stick! So we actually created this novelty: baked the brownies to be more like cookies, shaped the coffee ice cream in a patty, poked in a Popsicle stick, and dipped the whole sandwiched affair in chocolate. Marilyn, Tom, and a few of the line cooks made them in the basement, hundreds of them. Maybe 500? And then they took freezers packed with the treats out into the street fair and sold them at our booth—sold a few dozen. Maybe. People were there for the beer and the Bahama Mamas.

So our walk-in freezer was filled with racks of Post Mortem on a Stick for weeks. We tried to sell them as a dessert, but I think they eventually became the unofficial employee snack.

STAFF LOUNGE
THE LIFE OF A SERVER

FOR MANY YEARS, if you wanted a position serving dinners at Lindey's, you'd have to wait for someone to move or die. Sadly, because of AIDS, that did happen on more occasions than anyone would ever have imagined. But the front of house staff at Lindey's, especially in the first 15 years, was a seasoned group of men and women who spent as much of their time off together as they spent at work. And that sense of fraternity produced some truly marvelous stories. Here are a few glimpses into the on- and off-hours of Lindey's staff.

Model Behavior

Server **Jim Borden:** Andrew B. must have been the quietest person to work at Lindey's, but he inspired the most craziness because he was the handsomest man in the place. He had a great physique from serving in the armed forces, and he'd change in the staff room and no one—the girls, the guys—could resist commenting, teasing, lusting after him. He went on to model for Giorgio Armani for several years.

One evening as Andrew was walking through the dining room, some guy grabbed Andrew's arm—he must have felt Andrew's muscles beneath the white shirt—and he said, "Oh, excuse me—are you our waitress tonight?"

Andrew reached down, grabbed his crotch very conspicuously, and replied in a loud, testosterone-inspired voice: *"Waiter!* Last time I checked." The entire room came to a standstill.

Pre-Shifty Business

Server **Mark S:** Some nights, it's easy to get your shift covered. Some nights, it's impossible. And it was always each server's responsibility once the schedule was made. For a while, we had a bulletin board where people could offer their shifts or look to pick up additional ones.

I remember once a server had hepatitis and was laid up for about 10 days. For the second week, when there were still shifts that no one was picking up, his friend pinned up a place mat and wrote across it: "Little yellow different! Please cover my shifts." This was right when Nuprin, the pain reliever, ran ads everywhere with those three words: little, yellow, different. And, in fact, the laid-up server happened to be little (short), yellow (jaundiced from hepatitis), and unmistakably different.

John Squire: When I first started at Lindey's, if you needed the morning off, you called in, and the manager's answer was usually "Sure." The staff could be switched around, the person on call could be brought in. Now, it's not so easy. One server named Andy played in a band, and he had more than a few late-night gigs. He'd come in for his lunch shift just beat from the night before (which had probably only ended a few hours before the pre-shift meeting). He had no other option if he wanted to keep his job at Lindey's. I remember one morning during our meeting suddenly realizing Andy wasn't with us. We all looked around, and finally found him behind Table 64, which has the side stand partitioning it from the rest of the dining room: he'd grabbed a stack of napkins to use as a pillow, and he was fast asleep. I mean, out cold. The staff all went back and stood in a circle around him—and he woke up, completely startled...and then was promptly sent home.

Pooling Together

Server A: In the early '90s, the staff at Lindey's would have a pool for various collegiate ball games. As I recall, it was "hosted" by one waiter in particular who made no small amount of money asking servers who were students at OSU and who happened to be gay if he could buy their unused football tickets (and then resell them). There was a higher-than-usual concentration of straight waiters at the time (in addition to the kitchen staff, which was almost all straight), so the pool, which only cost a dollar a pop, netted the winner something close to $50—and that was without the gay contingent's participation. The straight waiters would come around with the mimeographed sheet that listed all the teams matched up for the weekend's games, and they'd kid and chide and pester: "Aw, come on, it's just a dollar, just do it! You can afford it!" And we'd all just shrug and keep eating or doing whatever we were doing.

Finally, one week, a Friday night, Kip and Jimmy agree to kick in. We're all sitting around Table 64, one of our two pre-meal tables in the backroom: most of the gay servers are sitting in one arc, and most of the straight waiters are sitting or standing across from us in another arc.

"Okay," Kip says, grabbing a pen to circle the word "Boston." "Let's pick Boston since it's closest to Provincetown."

Then Jimmy says, "Great, now then, how about Miami in the next game—people there are so fierce! Who are they playing—oh, it doesn't matter."

Kip: "What about San Diego in this game? I had a few hot dates with someone from there...oh, wait, I think he dumped me. You know what, let's bet on whoever they're playing."

This assessment continues throughout the entire game roster, with the knowledgeable fans/straight waiters just groaning:

"That's not how you pick teams!"

"Aw, you guys are such fruits."

"You two are so out in left field you're not even in the ballpark!"

Of course, you already know the outcome. Not that Kip and Jimmy achieved any new level of respect from the sports contingent at Lindey's, but their win that week was far sweeter than the mere $50 pool.

Oh, Horrors!

Stephanie Wright: Up on the second floor, you get a little extra time waiting for the private parties to arrive. No one will admit how it began—I gather it's a long tradition at Lindey's—but we fell into a habit of scaring one another, of concocting elaborate schemes that would allow one or another server to startle, grab, and unhinge another staff member. For instance, someone would get under the library table with the tablecloth that reached to the floor, and just sit there and wait for 20 minutes for someone to come in so they could grab that person's leg. Allen got out in the linen bin, outside in the alleys, where the linen company used to pick up the laundry. Allen waited down there, I don't know how long, and we sent Jimmy down, it's late, it's dark, and we're all hiding on the steps, and Jimmy throws the laundry bag in and Allen threw the bag back out, and Jimmy screamed and wet his pants, I think.

There was also a Mexican busboy named Jack, an OSU wrestler, who was very handsome. And a good sport about all the gay waiters fawning all over him. But he also liked to get them back, so one evening he had himself sent up in the dumbwaiter. He climbed into the tiny space, closed the doors, and had someone send him up to the second floor. Kip, who was working the upstairs parties, went to open the dumbwaiter, and Jack popped out and scared the living daylights out of poor Kip.

Day Off

Chef M: Once a month, Neil took a day off; that was his day to get drunk. That was pretty much always the Saturday after payday, and you could circle it on the calendar: that's going to be his drunk day. And there would be a phone call, "Hey, chef, I hurt my ankle, and I can't come in." And then the day after, he'd come in limping, sure enough, but by the end of the long night, somehow he'd be cured and walking just fine.

Going to the Dogs

Mark S: All the bussers knew that the tin to-go containers positioned at each bus stand were for my dogs. Each night, when I'd pull in from work, I'd give them what I called "special treat": a few bits of fancy fare snatched from the guests' unfinished meals. (The rest would go in the fridge for the next few days of treats.)

When a new server would start working, he or she would usually ask someone what the tin was doing at the side stand, and a busser would quickly answer that it was for Mark, so there was this recurring theme at Lindey's that everyone was chipping in to send food from the guests' plates to poor Mark who was putting himself through graduate school on a budget.

The biggest hauls were always those evenings when the Honda executives would come in from Tokyo for a party upstairs. Eager for large cuts of beef at prices that must have seemed as cheap as McDonald's burgers, the smallish gentlemen would rarely finish the twin tournedos or the enormous chops that the chefs would prepare for them.

Of course, the irony would be my leaving Lindey's at 1:00 in the morning, famished, and turning into the Taco Bell drive-thru to order two bean burritos, while two pounds of pheasant, crab cakes, and Hunan-glazed pork chops, still warm, are resting in the passenger's seat for the two dogs at home.

Post-Op (After Work)

> "If, after a long night of partying, you arrive at your front door and the birds are singing or the *New York Times* has been delivered, you have to figure there's no recovering that day."
> —*Dr. Jim Barnes*

Chef Matt Harding: With all the cash flowing in the restaurant business—servers walking home with a hundred or a couple hundred dollars in cash each night—temptation is pretty hard to resist. It's like fire: if you get close, it's hard not to be burned.

Another chef: Drugs are always an issue. Down the basement, in the crawl space, I'd find my cooks, smoking pot. Or out back. And if you have really great cooks, you're not going to find a quick replacement for them, so what are your choices? Fire them? Write them up knowing that the owner would fire them? From where I'm sitting, as the chef, I want cooks.

I want the kitchen positions filled. It's long hours. It's modest pay. And then it can be short hours if you have to cut staff on a slow night. And if you have the people you need, the people who can put out good food, you try to bend over backwards to keep them. You learn how to stay on top of the happiness factor, keep things working, hope nothing spins out of control.

Chef **David Tidd:** The kitchen has to break down and clean up every night. Everything. Every piece of equipment. Every refrigerator shelf. Every ingredient along the line. Sometimes I think we spend more time setting up and breaking down than we do actually cooking food. So during the closing process, our reward was a bucket of beer. We'd be stuck from 10:00 until 1:00 or 2:00 in the morning wrapping up food, cleaning equipment, and washing down the floors, with only a few late dinners to fire. Then we'd head off to Victory's or over to the Hi-Beck, and the bartenders there would be more than happy to have us, knowing they'd make more money between 1:00 and 2:30 than they'd have made all night.

All this led to a decadent lifestyle. We worked incredibly hard, and then we'd be so wired, so beat, so hungry, and was there anything to do then, like go to the hardware store or visit the library? No, we'd go to someone's house or a bar and wind down or crash.

Bartender **Tony Murray:** You have to understand that the life in restaurants is a little crazy. It used to be we'd have last call at 2:00 in the morning. So we're all getting out of Lindey's at 2:30 with a pocket full of bills, totally wound up from 8 or 10 hours of work, and just famished. Sometimes we'd all go to my house or to Tony and Ray's and drink for a while. Or to the Hi-Beck, and then over to someone's house. You have all that energy, and you'd want to tell some stories about the hectic night you just put in. We called ourselves vampires. By the time we were done, winding up and unwinding, whatever, we'd be heading for home at 7:00 in the morning, just blending with the morning rush hour.

Later in the day, you'd realize you blew two-thirds of what you made the night before, and that you needed to start treating all that nightly cash like a salary and go to the bank at the end of the week. I'm telling you, it was crazy.

Next-to-Last Call

Collin Smith: Nicole and Jimmy B. and I would head over to the Short North Tavern when we'd get out of Lindey's, so we'd basically have 45 minutes to get loaded before 2:15 rolled around and everyone had to clear out. One night, Jimmy B., a fast worker, is pretty tanked, and stands up to head out the back door. I call to him: "Hey, Jim, where you going? They still have more scotch behind the bar," and he looked at me, as if he were actually weighing the suggestion. Then he turned around, sat back down, and had another drink.

Opposites Attract

In the mid-'80s, other options after quitting time were the gay bars or one particular gentlemen's club where an exhausted server could go for a late-night steam bath. One early morning that has lived on in legend involves a server we'll call James, who often patronized this bathhouse. He checked in, stripped down, and swaddled himself in a towel in hopes of finding someone extra-special for the early morning hours. He entered the steam room in something of a post-cocktail stupor, looked around and almost immediately made contact with that certain someone. He coyly cast a glance at the fellow, who returned his furtive look. He licked his lips. So did the potential mate. He inched closer. Each man's suggestive gesture was matched by the other. Finally, after 20-odd minutes of this silliness, James realized that he was flirting with his own reflection in the steam room's mirror.

James merrily retold his "encounter" at the next staff meal, and from there, the story made the rounds among Lindey's most devoted.

Take Me Out to the Ball Game—
Oh, I'm Already out

Michael Mastracci: During the summer, every Sunday, we had the Lindey's softball team. More often than not, we'd still be wasted from the night before—up all night, probably partying at one of the bars whose staff we'd end up playing on the ball diamond a few hours later. The game would be at 10:00. On a couple hours sleep, with a fine hangover, we'd be out there in Schiller Park, all co-ed teams, playing the teams from Engine House, the Hi-Beck, Gibby's, Thurman's, Victory's, Graystone Winery, the Monk. It was softball, but it was also hardcore: we kept scores, and we even ended the season with an all-day elimination tournament. (I think we may have rested up for that one.)

Tony Murray: Twice, we won the championship, not that the league had any official name other than something like "The German Village Run Around the Bases and Get Drunk Softball League." It was all restaurants and bars in the Village, playing seven innings, and co-ed with a mandatory three girls minimum, which meant we were always calling around early Sunday morning digging for girlfriends and wives of employees.

Even staff that didn't play would come and cheer; Sue was there every Sunday after church, and great old regulars like Don Wheeler came and took Polaroids and cheered us on. It was a big party. Everyone brought coolers of beers, and as the day wore on and other restaurants played, we'd hang out, sharing beers, mooching beers...and sometimes running home to shower before dinner shift at 4:00.

PROFILES IN SERVICE
THE REMARKABLE BOB

FOR SOME EIGHT YEARS, we had a talented, generous, hilarious waiter who could craft outrageous, ridiculous, often compromising, and always vivid stories during the idle moments before and after a shift. Oh, and sometimes during. He was a seasoned professional when it came to waiting tables, but that hardly interfered with his ability to entertain both guests and coworkers alike. In hindsight, the waiter thought it best to leave behind his youthful silliness, so we've promised not to give his full name here in exchange for "stories that shouldn't be left out of the book, for crying out loud." So here are some highlights from Bob's time at Lindey's.

What's in a Name?

Bob: Once, in a perfectly nice group of people from Bexley, I recognized Bella Wexner, the mother of The Limited's Les Wexner. At the end of their meal, she handed me a Gold American Express card. (Now this was 20 or so years ago when the gold card was the top card, and very few people had the privilege of carrying such a card.) Taking it to the credit card machine, I noticed that she hadn't signed the back. So, just to be funny, I took a pencil and signed "Needa Peter," the name of a renowned drag queen at the moment. I figured I could just show my fellow waiters. "Oh, my god, look who I'm waiting on tonight!" So, yes, that was funny, everyone laughed, et cetera, but then when I tried to erase the name, I then realized that the card's little white strip makes whatever you write permanent. And I fell into such a panic. *She's going to know it's me! It's the first time she's used the card!* I was so nervous, I was just dripping with sweat as I returned the card to her. I said, "Thanks so much for joining us for dinner," and spun around and walked away.

Honestly, I don't know what ever came of "the incident." Or Needa Peter.

Meanwhile, a debate continued at the side stand: "Just what's the best drag name of all time?" Some contenders we'll always remember: Ivana B. Queen, Lisa Carmen Denominator, Sheelita Buffet, Devoida Taste, Ginger Beef, Mini Van Driver....

Now back to work.

A Crash Course in Footwear

Bob: I'd purchased a new pair of penny loafers that I was quite pleased with. Working the upstairs library one evening, I had eight businessmen who'd all ordered steak au poivre, each cooked to his liking. Kent Rigsby, the chef at the time, fired the orders, placed them in the window, and I lined them around a large tray and heaved them through the dining room and up the long flight of carpeted stairs to the second floor. About two thirds of the way up the stairs, which aren't exactly the deepest steps you've ever climbed, I felt my new, stiff, shiny-leather-soled penny loafers slip. It all happened in very slow motion: the tray dipped, the steaks slid to the edge, the plates fell, one—*clang!*—by one—*clang!*—with the loudest racket—*clang! clang! clang!*—on the wooden floor—*clang!*—at the bottom of the stairs—*clang!*—the steaks flopped off—*clang!*—the sauce spattered, and the tray landed with a final, resounding *CLANG!* The entire dining room had gone silent. Everyone's staring at the door at the bottom of the stairs, probably expecting whoever was carrying the tray to land on top of everything. But once the tray started tipping, I couldn't do anything to stop it.

I climbed the remaining stairs, turned the corner at the landing, and poked my head into the library: "Gentlemen, your dinners will be just another few minutes," which made them all break out laughing hysterically. Of course, they'd heard the crashing as well.

Then I went to the kitchen for a potentially bigger problem: "Chef, you'll need to fire the eight dinners for the library again." And without saying a word, Kent pulled eight steaks from the prep drawers and cooked the entire order a second time. Even when I retrieved the steaks and lined them up on a second large tray, Kent didn't say a word. I think he saw the look of panic on my face and figured he had nothing further to add.

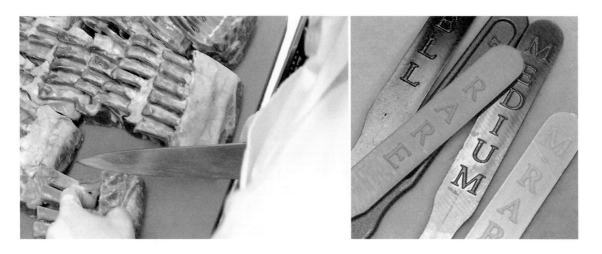

Lindey's Fables for the Famished

The Tortoise and the Harried Waiter:

A fable inspired by waiter Collin Smith

Once upon another time, we had a woman, nice as could be, lovely and generous, who'd eat at Lindey's quite often. And, just as often, she'd stop by for a take-out order for herself and her daughter. She'd arrive, grab one of the waiters, and instead of ordering, she would use the menu as the inspiration for a lovely conversation. "Now, this pesto pizza: would I like that?" she would ask.

"I think so," a server named Collin would say. "I believe you had that last night for dinner."

"Okay, good. Good. And what about a salad? Let's see what kinds you have tonight."

"We have the three printed right at the top of the menu, right there," Collin would point, leaving out the obvious fact that those three salads had not moved from their position on the menu for months—or had it been years?

☞

Excerpts from Bob's Ongoing Monologues

ON HIS TALK SHOW:

One day, when I leave Lindey's, I'm going to have my own television talk show. It's going to be called *Bob's Kitchen*, and the set will have an avocado green stove and an avocado refrigerator. And at the beginning of every show, I'll say, "And now, ladies and gentlemen, will you please help me welcome my first guest, back once again, the lovely Needa Peter." And then we'll settle down and have a wonderful interview, all about her life.

ON BEAUTY:

Bob: Who do you think is prettier, Collin: me or Nicole?
Collin, a server: Well—Nicole, I'd say.
Bob: Well… (very long pause) …Nicole is very, very, very, very pretty. But I'd have to pick me.

ON HIS WARDROBE:

Every time we had a staff get-together at Lindey's, someone would ask what Bob what he was thinking of wearing to the party. Invariably, he'd reply:

Well…(very long pause)…an acid-washed jean mini-skirt, pink jellies, and a crop top.

But then he'd never show up.

Nor can anyone forget the evening that the slender and tall Bob came through the double doors from the kitchen into the dining room with an especially wide smile, an especially prancing gait, and a huge plume of fennel stalks placed upright on top of his head. Look, I'm a showgirl! A Las Vegas showgirl! From that moment on, the chefs were more careful about leaving the unused sprays from the fennel bulbs out in the open.

Bob: Yes, and then my friend Ray and I discussed attending Tim and Kim Picard's wedding, which was to be held upstairs at Lindey's. Over a period of weeks, I believe, I told Kim that we intended to crash the affair, dressing as her two mystery aunts, wearing long flowing chiffon gowns in some shade of seafoam green. Ray was to be her short stout aunt, and I was to be her tall skinny aunt. And we'd show up, take our seats on the groom's side, and not speak to anyone but ourselves.

I actually instilled a bit of dread in dear Kimberly. Someone even told me that she half thought her aunties would show up any moment during their honeymoon.

ON HIS FAVORITE RECIPE:

Whenever someone would ask Bob what he was making for the staff potluck/holiday party/July softball game, he'd reply with the name of some exotic-sounding dish and then offer the recipe, which was always the same:

Take a pound of ground round, brown it, drain off the grease, save the grease, throw away the ground round, add a cup and a half of marshmallow cream, 3/4 cup of packed brown sugar, 2/3 cup Miracle Whip, season to taste, put in a greased baking dish, bake at 500 until done, and serve.

If someone ever challenged him—"But, Bob, you said you were bringing fish..."—he'd immediately launch back into the recipe:

That's right, You take a pound of ground round, brown it, drain off...

At a cocktail party hosted at Lindey's one evening, Bob was passing an hors d'oeuvres tray that included something like a Swedish meatball. One of the guests commented that they were the most delicious tidbit, and Bob graciously offered her the recipe:

You take a pound of ground round, brown it, drain off the grease, save... Apparently, he got as far as the Miracle Whip before the woman furrowed her brow and walked away.

ON HIS OTHER FAVORITE RECIPE:

Thanks to Bob's almost constant attention, one server, young Nicole, had been exposed to all sorts of unlikely things. She may, in fact, have been Bob's favorite person to kid, pester, provoke, set off into tears of laughter, and rub the wrong way. Among their repertoire of sillinesses, scatological jokes occupied no small part.

☛ "Oh. Now, do I like the raspberry vinaigrette one? I think my daughter does...or should we get the–"

"How about one of each? You've done that before."

"That sounds perfect. So let's see, we have the salads and the pizza–or have I had the pizza with the tomato? Would that be spicy?"

"No, not at all."

"But I think I like spicy things, sometimes. I've had something spicy here...what was it?"
[Editor's note: The rest of the dialogue has been omitted for space considerations.]

Moral: *An order is meant to be a brief exchange between someone who is mildly peckish and someone who is awfully busy.*

One evening Nicole came to dinner with her mother. Toward the end of their meal, Bob went into the walk-in fridge and found some guacamole. Then he took some brownies and formed them into small bits. Next he had a chef blind-bake a pizza crust. And Bob decorated this pizza just so, and carried it to the table under a plate cover.

Nicole's mother elbowed her daughter, clearly suggesting, *Look, honey, they're bringing something special just for you, since you work here.*

And, indeed, Bob set down the covered dish right in front of Nicole, revealed the entrée, and quickly rushed off with the cover. It was his legendary "diarrhea pizza," a fictional food he'd kidded Nicole about for months and, on a whim, decided to create "just for her."

ON THE HOLIDAYS:

If someone would ask, "Bob, what are you going to do for the holiday?" whether that implied Christmas or New Year's Eve or July Fourth or President's Day, he would reply, Me? Oh I'm going to take a covered dish and an unresolved issue, get really drunk, tell everybody off, and pass out in pool of my own filth.

ON HIS VIETNAM EXPERIENCE:

While people who work in restaurants often trade "war stories" about various difficult chefs or impossible customers, on many an idle moment at Lindey's, Bob would tell us *his* war stories: When I was in Vietnam, you see, I was the driver for gospel singer Christy Lane. You remember her song, "One Day at a Time Sweet Jesus"?

We spent days and days together on the road, traveling from one demilitarized zone to another, although she had a fit one day when she found out that I was trying on her dresses and stretching out her shoes when I'd put my feet in them.

We were crossing the jungle one day, just driving along, and the muffler hit a bump and dropped right off. So I managed to do a little repair tying it back on with a tampon string from our first aid kit, and that held it until we got back to the base.

Bob could go on and on, inventing incident after incident until someone at one of his tables needed him.

"WHAT WERE THEY THINKING!"
HAD WE ONLY KNOWN...

OF THE MANY, MANY generous things said about Sue, the quality most frequently recited by staff members is Sue's willingness to forgive and forget. According to more than one longtime employee, Sue has an ability to respond to nearly any outrageous incident with the phrase, "What were they thinking!" and then get on with more pressing matters.

So, in our callow youth, we may have overlooked a few things at Lindey's.

Or perhaps we just didn't know where to look.

Okay, maybe we even looked away a few times, trying not to make a bigger deal out of some little misadventure. All right, then, we've confessed: We might have excused, and unintentionally encouraged, a little louche or just plain lousy behavior.

For the purposes of this book, we probably should have asked our lawyers about some statute of limitations...but what the heck! Now that we're older, wiser, and a proven success, we thought we could share a few "confidential" bits from our own kitchen.

Now, we haven't endeavored to prove or disprove the truth of any of these incidents. It's simply amusing to know that Lindey's gathers such stories around it. (As you might guess, many names in this section have been omitted to protect either the innocent or the guilty.) And it's simply comforting to know that such incidents will never happen again under our watch.

Trip and a Half

Server X: For Lindey's 10th anniversary, four other guys and I went over to a buddy's house and got a buzz on. And since we all knew we weren't going to be waiting tables at the party—just bussing, basically—we decided to do a hit of acid, too. Then we got to work and waited around for the party to begin. But Rick Doody comes into the room—and we're well into our trip by now—and he says, "Okay, guys, I'm going to need four or five extra valets tonight." So we all look at each other. And I catch the eye of one of my buddies, and he's nodding and I'm nodding, *Yeah, we can do this. We can do this!* So we volunteer and head outside, where all the other valets are leaning against the building waiting for the first rush

Lindey's Fables for the Famished

The Not-So-Rare Bimbo and the All-Too-Weary Waiter

A fable inspired by server Erich Kraus

One lunch, in the front room, a waiter named Erich had a four-top: three suits and a woman who busied herself emulating Suzanne Somers: giggling a lot, batting a lot o' lash, and generally behaving in an obnoxious manner.

When it came time to order, the woman debated between the tournedos and the filet, blathering on in that ever-so-charming manner that some women resort to when they're trying to make an impression on the gentlemen. "Oh, I don't know. It's just so difficult to decide. Gee, they both sound so good. Have any of you ordered the tournedos before? Oh, yeah, me too, I just love beef!"

Erich finally got an order out of her, then added, "How would you like that cooked?"

At this point, the dining room is crowded and noisy. Servers are zigzagging around the room, guests are shuttling in and shuffling out, food runners are carrying trays above the crowd on the tips ☞

of arriving cars. By the way, it's 96 degrees in the shade. Literally.

And all I thought was, *I can do this. I've never driven a car while on LSD, but I'm going do it, and I'm going to take the first car that pulls up, just to prove it.* And I jockey to the head of the line, just as the first car pulls up: it's a 1980 Mercedes SL convertible. "I got it," I said, "I got it," and opened the guy's door, gave him a ticket, jumped in the car, and drove off.

I headed down Third Street. I drove back on Fourth. I turned back down Fifth. I drove all around downtown, just loving the breeze in the heat. Half an hour later, I made my way back to Lindey's and parked.

Next car that arrived, I took for another drive. I think I parked maybe four cars total all night.

Don't ask me how I managed to drive five other people's cars while on acid without damage to anyone or anything. Don't ask me how I managed to park the cars in the right place so the other valets could find them later. I can't remember.

Crop Dusting

Among one particular server's talents was—and maybe still is—the ability to pass gas at will. On the busiest nights, when people would be "camping" at his tables, he would pass by and pass gas. And he'd stop and say, "Oh, I'm so sorry." The guests would be so disgusted, appalled, whatever, they'd just up and leave. Night after night, the manager would take him aside in the coat room: "If you fart on one more table, I'm going to have to let you go." But at the end of the confrontation, the server and the manager giggled: two people having a fight about a restaurant policy on farting? But his ploy, which he called "crop dusting," continued on those nights when he wanted to get home a little early.

Fun with Fudge

Manager X: A few servers were known for...their creativity, let's say. If ever there was a birthday for someone they knew well—someone who wouldn't take offense—they'd take a Post Mortem and place it on a large platter. They'd reshape the brownie in a special way (rather longer and more cylindrical), add two scoops of ice cream on one end of it (rather than placing the scoops on top), and then arrange some whipped cream just so at the brownie's other end. Well, that surely had Marjorie Merriweather Post rolling in her grave.

Halfwits

For a very short time, Lindey's ran coupons in the local newspaper for a free appetizer, or maybe it was a half portion of pasta. Who can remember? What we do remember is that certain servers were coupon-clippers. They'd bring their own discount coupons to the restaurant, clip them on the checks of folks who didn't have a coupon, and ring out the meal at full-price, keeping the difference and turning in their coupon with the check.

That racket was short-lived, as was the loophole in our old computer system allowing a server to ring up a bottle of wine generically, and then enter the bottle's price. On a number of occasions, those same "certain servers" would ring in, say, $45, but serve a $35 bottle the guest had ordered, taking out the difference as a tip. Inventory control is just one of those nightmares people who dream of owning a restaurant never imagine.

Coat Checkmate

Server X: We checked coats in a small corridor that's a hard right before you enter the kitchen. This is about the time when the news often featured people throwing red paint on coats to protest that "fur is dead" and that animals should wear their own fur. Now, if a guest was particularly conspicuous and awful, saying, "Oh, please take extra good care of my coat, it's ermine" or whatever, that would make it a candidate for retribution. You'd go back there to hang up the person's coat, and down near the hem, where no one would think to look immediately, you'd hold a lit lighter, just a few seconds, and the hairs would sizzle and frizzle up. And then you'd just brush it off, and there would be a little hole in the coat, right

of their fingers....and this one guest continued to blather:

"Gosh, I don't really like it well-done...that can be so tough, you know. Although I'm sure they do a very good well-done steak here, don't they? You guys probably like it rare, don't you? Ooh, I couldn't! No, that's too bloody for me!" As her disinterested audience looked anywhere but in her direction, she turned to Erich, apparently mistaking him for someone who cared.

"Oh, I just can't decide! What do you think?" she inquired with the perfect pouting expression.

With the flattest expressionless possible, he replied, "I'm not eating it. You are."

Her silly smile disappeared.

"Medium rare," she replied very quickly and quietly.

For the rest of the meal, she managed to restrain herself, and everyone at the table looked as if they were enjoying themselves a great deal more than during the ordering. The gentleman who paid the check left Erich a very generous tip.

Moral: *One woman's meat is another man's slow-acting poison.*

down to the skin. Not that this wasn't satisfying enough, but every once in a while, the person working the salad station, which had an opening into the coat corridor, would call out, "Did someone's head get too close to the oven? Do you smell burning hair?"

Free Enterprise

Manager X: One of the managers hired his little brother to be a busser. Nice enough kid. Anyway, one day he "discovered" the walk-in, and the wonders stored therein. He would take an empty half-gallon milk carton, and go into the walk-in and snag five crème brûlées, which he would then shuttle upstairs, hidden in the carton. And then he'd offer them for sale to the waitstaff for a buck apiece. Now the price on the menu was $3.95, so even with a 50 percent staff discount, he was offering half price of half price. I'm not sure how long he kept up his little trade, but how much could it have netted him?

Know Your Audience

Assistant manager Jason Seigler: Maggie, a server who mostly worked parties, was celebrating her birthday and certain members of the staff arranged a little surprise: a male stripper for the party. Now, Maggie was very easygoing and relaxed, but she was also a little conservative and shy. And in no time at all, this completely hunky guy stripped down to his birthday suit and did a show for Maggie in the small party room. The rest of us looked on while the stripper was gyrating and so forth, nearly on top of her. Two things were clear: Maggie was going to have a heart attack and die right there, and clearly some waiters wanted to see the stripper a whole lot more than the birthday girl did.

Cutting Up

After a thousand parties at Lindey's, servers come up with little tricks to amuse themselves. For instance, at every wedding reception, the bridal couple cuts the cake. But no one in the party knows how. It's an art. You need to cut 1-inch squares. But the bride and groom are all nervous, so...instead of giving simple instructions, certain veteran servers came up with some wild goose chases: "You know, it's a tradition to give the grandmother of the groom the first piece, after you have your piece." And then they'd come back from delivering the piece, and server X would say, "And the second piece has to go to the daughter of the oldest son of the bride's family—or else the youngest male on the groom's side." And server X would invent one crazy thing after another and have the bridal couple deliver slices all around the room—it amused us—until one of them would give us this look like, *um, I don't think so.* Tradition...tradition!

Rm w/a Vu

Server X: At Lindey's, I perfected what I called my "breast view." When I was lucky enough to serve or deliver food to a woman with ample breasts, I would present the plate at her place and say, "Here's the chicken paillard...with mango chutney" or whatever it was she had ordered, and I'd have just about one and a half seconds, while everyone was looking at the plate where I was gesturing, to check out her breasts.

Tumblering

Sue: And then there was a gentleman who worked maintenance with us, and we had a little trouble with him falling down the stairs. All the time. As you might guess, he had a drinking problem and a habit of pouring himself a large tumbler of vodka. "What are you doing?" I asked him on more than one night. "I'm having a post-shift drink," he'd reply.

He'd stand at the end of the bar, and just ease himself into the after-work mood. Well, we had to fire him. But then he decided to file for workman's compensation for injuries.

Of course, we were sorry that he'd hurt himself, but, really, we tried to keep him on as long as we could, despite his constant inebriation. When the legal part began, his wife agreed to testify that, sadly, he was drunk and that, with their son, he was robbing the apartment complex where they lived. But then, when he did something nice for her and she wasn't angry at him anymore, she dropped the whole thing and never appeared at the court hearing. So we paid the settlement and vowed to be more stringent with our shift-drink policy—as in, no more shift drinks.

Love Is the Drug

Manager Courtney Chapman: Lindey's became an icon to me—no other place I'd ever worked or would work resembled it. I'd been in the restaurant business since I'd turned 18— that was 10 years before starting at Lindey's—and nothing compared to that place. I think I was in shock for the first three months, trying to figure out if the staff or the guests were doing more drugs. We'd have folks in here eating, drinking, and running to the restroom. Back and forth, back and forth, until I finally realized that those little bathroom runs had nothing to do with nature calling. We had regulars who had bad cases of Hollywood hay fever—just weren't able to shake it, no matter what season. Plus, there were the restrooms upstairs, which offered a bit more privacy. Enough privacy that seven servers got busted there, all at once, along with a manager.

Meanwhile, there's Sue, who came in from about 10:00 to 3:00 in the afternoon, knew everyone's name, asked about everyone's friends and home life, but had no idea what happened after her "shift." But once someone mentioned to Sue that Smoot Construction was doing random drug testing of their employees, and Sue didn't miss a beat: "Oh, we'd have to close our doors," she laughed.

SPECTACULAR SPILLS
AND OTHER RESTAURANT SPECTACLES

ONCE AGAIN, we are willing to stare in the 25-year-old mirror of success, shrug off all of the finesse, polish, and applause, and take a moment to laugh at our fumbles, faux pas, and fiascos.

House of Cards

Server **Abby Pemberton:** I remember working lunches with a server named John Z. He was classically good-looking—though maybe not the most personable fellow. He wanted to be an actor. One afternoon, I'm at the side stand as John carries a tray filled with drinks and waters to the first table in the back room. They're all ladies, all separate checks, of course. So he starts circling the table, taking the drinks off, one at a time, setting each in front of a guest. But he's taking them all from the front of the tray. So I think to myself, *No…you know better than that, you're going to rearrange the tray, right? You're going to take the next glass from the opposite side.* But then the next glass he takes off is from the same wrong side of the tray. *It's going to fall, all those Bloody Marys and iced teas are going over,* I think to myself. And as he reaches for the next and then the next glass, I think, *No, no, come on! You're not going to take that glass!* So I keep watching as if John were playing some house-of-cards game, always taking the most risky option. Finally, the tray spills over, dumping red juice and brown tea all over the ladies. So that's when I think to myself, *Well, I suppose I should have prevented that. I could have gone over and said something.* But John had been waiting tables for a while. And a person doesn't have to wait tables to know that when things aren't balanced they fall down and go boom!

Soup and Sympathy

Server Allen Jones: I remember my friend Mark carrying four bowls of soups upstairs, and the line cook forgot to tuck the little paper napkins between the crocks and the underliners. So, when Mark turned the corner to scale the 20 steps up to the second floor, the four full bowls of tomato-basil bisque slid straight down, directly onto Table 30, spattering four ladies, the tablecloth, the wall, the café curtains (which had just been installed!), and the window—and Mark continued walking right up the stairs as if he hadn't even felt the weight shift, hadn't even heard the soups drop, hadn't even heard the four ladies gasp in unison. Later he told me, "Well, I knew everyone *else* would have noticed and instantly jumped over to help and apologize and promise to pick up their dry cleaning tab—*what more could I have done?*" For the duration of lunch, Mark never came back down the stairs.

Those stairs are the source of more than one embarrassment. Server M. recalls the evening a bride slid down the entire flight of steps: "Remember slipping down the sliding board in the backyard on a sheet of waxed paper? Or flying down the basement steps on a sheet of cardboard from the box the new dishwasher came in? The poor bride rode the train of her satin dress, hurtling feet-first down to the base of the stairs and kicking open the emergency exit door, which broke her fall and deposited her onto the brick sidewalk of Beck Street. Amazingly, her bustle padded her descent and her landing, and she was unharmed."

The Ring of Truth

Server Collin Smith: One evening, Sue is having a birthday dinner at two tables pushed together, facing Table 80, where I have six very large men. I'm bringing over a tray of filled water glasses and, for whatever reason, the sole of my shoe sticks on the carpeting, and I dump an entire glass of water right into the waist band and down the pants of one of these guys. He bolts up, and shoves his face within an inch of my face like he's going to put me out of my misery forever. But his table breaks out laughing, so he starts laughing, too. I rush to grab him a towel, then a new glass of water, and then, *then* I see that all the men are wearing Super Bowl rings. If this man would have lost his temper and hit me...!

The entire incident started and finished within 15 seconds: a near-death experience right in front of the owner, whose entire party didn't notice a thing.

Call a Doctor—Oh, Never Mind—Just Pass the Catsup

One day at lunch, a server named Allen is seen racing from the front of the house toward the kitchen. "There's a woman choking at Table 34," he says to no one in particular. "I don't know how to do anything about that!" and he pushes open the kitchen doors and hides inside.

The next server to pass into the dining room is Jimmy, who quickly sets down his tray, grabs the woman from behind, reaches around her, clasps his hands at her diaphragm, efficiently administers the Heimlich maneuver—and out shoots a morsel of food.

Without looking behind her, without even pausing to thank Jimmy or consider the fact that she'd been without oxygen for the greater part of a minute, turning colors, the woman sits back down, resumes her conversation, and lifts her fork to her mouth.

The rest of the dining room is as stunned as Jimmy.

It's Raining, It's Pouring

There's one other memorable spill that no one seems to remember exactly. Or maybe it's just that no one wants to own up to the unfortunate moment. Our pool of oral historians can't remember who caused and who "received" the accident, and someone even made the point that Lindey's has never served the spilled item: spaghetti and meatballs. (Not even as a nightly special? Not even calling it something like *Rigatoni con Porpette di Carne*?)

But why should factual accuracy stand in the way of our amusement?

During dinner service, in the front room where two large palm trees hold sway above two rows of deuces, a tallish waiter, carrying a tray balanced above his head on the fingertips of one hand, took a marvelous spill and managed to fall in such a way that a plate of spaghetti flew up rather than down from the tray. While the pasta caught in the branches of one of the palm trees, decorating the fronds like tinsel, the meatballs, with their greater specific gravity, rained down on the couple seated at Table 21 "like record-size hail," one server remembers. "The people hardly knew what hit them, especially since they had ordered something else entirely and were not anticipating small round objects either to be set in front of them with a bed of pasta, or to be dropping from Lindey's tin ceiling."

We have no other information about this climatic disturbance.

Sauced Again

Chef **Jared Bissel:** The stairs down to the prep kitchen are the worst. You skate down them, and you skate up them. You're walking down with, say, a bucket of cream—this happened to me more than once—and you slide halfway down, spilling half a bucket right on your uniform.

Chef **Ricky Barnes:** One time I was carrying a five-gallon plastic bucket filled pretty much to the top with hot demiglaze. I had to take it from the kitchen down to the basement, down the worst set of stairs of any restaurant I've known. I fell a few steps from the bottom, and spilled the hot sauce down my pants and all across the floor. This was hours of roasting bones, simmering stock, reducing and reducing the stock into this rich meat sauce—all down the drain…literally! I quickly yanked off my chef pants, and, looking at the sauce, I was so tempted just to squeegee whatever I could back into the buckets…but Chef Bob had come running to make sure I was all right, and there was no way that was going to happen.

The Show Must Go On

Sous chef **John Martin:** It was a Saturday night in early April. We got a late, really big snowstorm. The restaurant was full and we had a large party upstairs. Which would be the perfect time for the power to go out. We lit candles and tried to decipher the waitstaff's handwriting. Most of the stoves and ovens were gas-powered, so we were able to produce all of the meals ordered. (OSHA: if you are reading this book, the ventilation system was magically spared.)

But when all the dinners had been served, breaking down the kitchen took even longer than usual: we shoveled snow off the patio and carried outside all of the expensive and perishable items from the walk-ins and freezers and the kitchen line, placing everything flat on the cold concrete. Then we buried it all under the mounds of snow. Suddenly it looked as if Lindey's patio had one more foot of snow than anywhere else in the neighborhood.

The next day, the electricity restored, we came in early and reversed the whole ordeal, unburying all the food and lugging it back into the restaurant. But we had no choice: it was either this little camping-in-the-wilderness technique, or losing hundreds and hundreds of dollars of food.

Things We've Thrown

As Helen Thurber once said of her husband James, "When he throws a party it always ends up hitting someone." Maybe we can consider accidents an unavoidable part of entertaining. For instance, server Freddie Cortez was waiting for bartender Eddie to pop the cocktail onions in a Gibson a customer had ordered, and Eddie was busy, so he tossed Freddie the **jar of cocktail onions**, not realizing the lid wasn't secured. "My 100% cotton, professionally starched shirt was soaked with pickled onion juice. Now that's a smell you can't just blot with a little soda water and ignore." So along with the spills and falls mentioned here, and in addition to the rare guest throwing a cocktail in someone's face, we have to admit to a few intentional spills: items that we've lobbed, tossed, or wrecked for some higher purpose.

When food is waiting to be picked up on the line, certain chefs, at certain times, under certain stressful conditions, have thrown things. Now maybe "tantrum" is too dramatic-sounding, but we don't believe any such behavior is a stress-management technique taught at any culinary institution.

In this spirit of candor, we'll admit that we had one particular manager and one particular chef who did not have much rapport. When the manager would poke his head into the

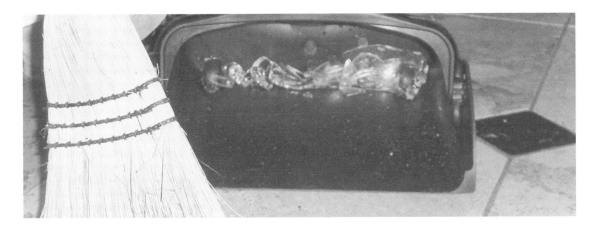

Lindey's Fables for the Famished

The Firefly and the Fire Marshal:

A fable inspired by server Mark Svede

Once upon yet another time, days after Lindey's had installed new wooden floors in the front dining room—so many years of broken glass, spills, scooting chairs, and resanding had taken their toll—one particular gentlemen disdainfully flicked his cigarette ashes directly on the new surface. During those years, a person could smoke in the front room at Lindey's—but not drop ashes on a wooden floor, in a historic building, in a neighborhood where fire safety issues are stringent because of the close proximity to other buildings. All evening, the gentleman persisted in dropping his ashes on the floor, despite the fact that the waitstaff had supplied ashtrays on his table, and ☞

kitchen with a special request for Table 54 or to inquire about the status of Table 71's appetizers, the chef thought nothing of throwing a **plate of pasta** or a **carton of eggs** across the room. The airborne articles never "connected," but they did guarantee a mess that a third party would have to clean up.

Chef **Kent Rigsby:** I remember one server—he'd been there from the beginning—who had a rather cavalier attitude toward the kitchen. And he really only wanted to sell the most expensive item on the menu: the steak with peppercorns. Night after night, his tickets would be at least 75% that one item. Not only that, but he was the slowest when it came to picking up food, so that all too often, the meat wasn't hot when it arrived at the table. One night, his order was up—three steak au poivres—and he saw it, but decided to get a pitcher of water instead. He came back to the kitchen two other times, making eye contact with me each time, while his food was sitting under the lamps. The last time, when he finally came over for his dinners, just as he reached for the shelf, I pushed the three plates out of the window and onto the floor. The **three dinner plates** shattered, the **three steaks** and all the juice and whatever starch we were serving—all that splattered across the floor. "You made me wait, so now you can wait." Of course, the customers were the ones waiting—I knew that—but it was the heat of the moment.

Likewise, there have been people who've reportedly seen the following items move with unusual velocity.

A **plate of baked brie** with almonds and apple slices had to be peeled from the wall of the kitchen on one occasion—or was it more than one occasion?

A staff member batted a **potted poinsettia** from Table 30 across tables 21, 22, 23, 24, 25, and 26, scattering soil everywhere, and requiring all the linens to be stripped and the tables to be reset with new dishes. (Apparently, his dog had crapped on the front seat of his Ford Escort—or maybe it was his Alfa Romeo—and when he walked into work, the little flowerpot was the first to greet him.)

One of the restaurant's district partners found a **plunger** in an upstairs bathroom after repeatedly telling the managers that plungers were not to be stored within sight. Unfortunately, we were having an ongoing, nightly problem with an upstairs bathroom. The plunger was tossed into the office, with the warning, "The next time I see a plunger in the bathroom, I'm firing you."

The Day I Nearly Killed Chris Doody

Sous chef **John Martin:** As in most restaurants that I have worked, some of the equipment at Lindey's was a bit antiquated. I had recently worked in one of the newest and best hotels in the city and worked part-time with a caterer who had brand new equipment.

One afternoon I went to turn on an oven. Some of the ovens had pilot lights and others needed to be lit every time they were turned on. I must have mistaken the ovens; I turned one on and left it to preheat. In the meantime Chris walked by and tried to light it. Apparently the oven had built up a lot of gas by then, and when Chris tried to light it, the ensuing explosion knocked him over, throwing him across the kitchen. Oops. Understandably, Chris got very angry but he was also scared. And I fessed up, pleading ignorance. "Oh, really? You have to light the oven? I didn't know that. I'm sooooooo sorry!"

Safe Keeping

But perhaps the biggest, heaviest thing that's ever been thrown at Lindey's was not the work of a guest or a member of the staff.

Chris Doody: One Thursday night, I was cooking here, and Marilyn Vuteck, the manager on duty, comes running down the stairs through the dining room and into the kitchen. She bursts through the doors, shouting, *"Somebody stole the safe!"* Now our safe is on the second floor, up about twenty-some steps up a narrow hallway, and then through a couple doors into an office—it's not what you'd call accessible. So I ran upstairs, and sure enough, the safe's gone. Now this is not a little tacklebox-size safe you buy at Staples. This is an 800-pound safe

☞ covered and replaced them regularly. At one point, the owner of the restaurant, a tall and lovely woman named Sue, found a hotel lobby canister, and set it on the floor, beside the gentleman's table, just beside his elbow. Nonetheless, the man rotated in his chair another fifteen degrees, and ashed his cigarette on the floor once again.

Moral: *Even if you're in a fancy place, you can still make an ash of yourself.*

The Reluctant Chef
and the
Funny Diner:

A fable inspired by guest
Ric Wanetik

Some two decades ago, there was a chef at Lindey's named Kent who hated anyone coming into the kitchen. There was also a guest at the time named Ric (how he lost his final "k" is the subject of another fable) who made it a point to go into the kitchen and irritate the chef.

"Why aren't there baked potatoes?" Ric would call. "Every restaurant has plain baked potatoes!"

The chef would look at Ric in a startled manner, and return to his work. So Ric would turn and leave.

Other times, Ric came to the kitchen door and called to the chef:

"How could you be out of the calves' liver!" It was just a friendly tormenting.   ☞

the size of an oven. Since it didn't come down the stairs and through the dining room, someone had to have lifted it out of the office, through the upstairs banquet room, out onto the back terrace, and then down a long flight of concrete stairs. And why that much weight didn't break through the floor and end up in the main dining room, I don't know.

Tom Harlor, general manager at the time: Some ex-employee must have tipped them off to the safe's location and the right time for the heist. We had a houseful of people that night, although no party in the upstairs rooms. The two guys used the back stairs, carried in a dolly, went directly over to the safe, and carried it right out, with no one noticing a thing—until the last second, when someone accidentally forgot something in the upstairs office.

Chris: At the time, on the line, we had a very large, very strong chef from New Orleans named Craig. So he and I ran outside looking for the thief. Sure enough, in the alley behind the restaurant, we saw two kids—they couldn't even have been 16—with a dolly and our safe. They must have tumbled the safe down the back stairs. Anyway, Craig and I chased after them, and caught one of the kids. Turns out they'd been set up to steal the safe and were waiting for a truck to pick them up.

Born to Be Spilled

Finally, there can be no more spectacular spill, no more told, retold, and reinvented story than the day of Skip's 50th birthday. Here are some of the many versions.

From Fred and Howard's "Scuttlebutt," *Columbus Alive*, April 3–17, 1991:

"...some days, you just shouldn't get out of bed. Skip Van Dyne's recent birthday started off in the worst possible way. Rising at 6:30 that morning, he looked out the window to admire his brand-new 45022 pickup truck—only to discover it missing. The police called later that day to report that they had recovered some of it. The week ended up very well, however. Three days later, Van Dyne was not the only one surprised when a Harley-Davidson was wheeled out of the kitchen into Lindey's dining room to the tune of 'Born to Be Wild.' He didn't know it was a birthday present until he saw Cherie Hungate riding it."

Some folks remember the details differently.

One guest: "They turned up the music, and over the loudspeakers, they played 'Born Free' and they rolled out this huge motorcycle."

Another guest: "I'll never forget that song, 'Born to be Alive'—it was perfect! Sue Doody in a motorcycle jacket."

A server: "Then, all of sudden, this music blasts over the loud speakers: it's 'Born in the U.S.A.' by Springsteen! Amazing."

Here's how Skip and Cherie remember the story, which is theirs anyway:

Cherie: One day, Skip is standing, surveying the cars in the garage: a black Rolls, a black Bricklin SV-1 (the gull-winged acrylic sports car manufactured for three years in the mid-'70s) nicknamed "Puppy," a Ferrari, a Lamborghini...and in the middle of Macon Alley, he says "I need a Harley. I have the world's finest vehicles, but I need a Harley."

So at the time, Skip has a client, the Fu Man, who was something like Minister of Defense of the Avengers Club. He looked like Mr. Clean, with a huge neck and upper arms like my thighs. He liked to solve problems. So I call Fu Man. I say, "The boss wants a Harley."

"Little darling, we'll get the boss one hell of a Harley." So he finds a black sportster, and cranks it up and customizes it, and does all this special stuff for Skip. He puts on a sissy bar, welds the Avengers Club logo on it, and—"

Skip Van Dyne: Let me take over from here. So Fu Man loads the bike with nitromethane and aviation gas—that's 114 octane. *That's racing fuel.* The exact formula is one of the great secrets in racing.

And I gather the bike stays hidden in Buddy Wolfe's garage until Saturday. And then, since none of these people rides, Cherie and Buddy and his wife Gay push the bike the

☞ However wonderfully Chef Kent performed at the stove, Sue, the restaurant's owner, wanted her chefs to circulate in the dining room. Reluctantly, at some point each night, Kent would walk table to table, and say hello.

"How is everything?" he'd ask, when he arrived at Ric's table.

Which was Ric's cue to say, every time, "It's really awful, I hate it."

And that became a joke between Chef Kent and Ric.

After Kent opened his own restaurant, Ric would dine there and the chef would come by the table and ask: "Is everything as awful as you like?"

And Ric could only reply, "Yes, I hate it very much."

Moral: *Humor is like rich food: too much will come to haunt you when you lie down at night to sleep.*

five or six blocks to Lindey's, bring it in through the back door, and set it in the kitchen.

Not two feet away are a dozen gas burners. *This bike is a fucking bomb!* But they didn't know.

Chef **Chris Domanik:** We moved the motorcycle next to the dishwashing area, which was the only place it would fit. As the servers came back with the dirty dishes, they'd toss the silverware into the wash bins, and water would splash on the bike. So I was always running over with a dish towel to wipe it off.

Cherie: This is a Saturday, about four or so, and Steppenwolf's "Born to Be Wild" is cranking so loud that the windows are vibrating.

I dressed up like a biker babe that day, in a Spandex miniskirt. I climb on the Harley, and chef Chris and Mark and Freddie push me out of the kitchen toward the front of the restaurant. And then the party really starts. Everyone gathers around the bike. Skip is so surprised he wants to hop on the bike immediately. So we try to get it out the front doors, but it won't fit, so it's back out through the kitchen. But first you have to picture Skip: he's wearing a brilliant yellow silk shirt with his usual black jeans, and a leather motorcycle jacket.

Skip: We're on Mohawk now, and we turn so we're right in front of the restaurant's windows, right outside the table where we all were sitting. I turn on the engine, start revving up the motor, put it into gear, and the bike flies off in a wheelie. Now you know you're in trouble if you're 6'2" and you're seeing rooflines beside you instead of above you—and then I feel the sissy bar kick in so I don't flip completely on my back. The bike is porpoising—skipping forward on its rear wheel like a Flipper walking backwards above water on his tail—and I'm braking, and all anyone can see is yellow and black and yellow and black, like I'm a big bumblebee tumbling until I collide into the tree right outside the restaurant, not 20 feet away.

The cycle popped the primary case on Beck Street's high curb. And that's it: the bike is broken. We're going to have to push the Harley back to the house. Meanwhile, Bob Falconi, an emergency room doctor, is part of our moving party, so he looks me over and says, "No blood, no foul, you're fine."

The fact is I had a few cracked ribs and, by the next day, I was entirely black and blue.

And, then I get a call from the Fu Man. "I heard you didn't do too well."

So I say, "Fu Man...I've got Tylenol, I've got Motrin, I've got..."

"Well, you're a full-fledged biker now."

"But what the hell did you put in that bike?" I ask him.

"Well, I loaded it up special for you. I mean, I didn't want the boss to think I didn't do you right."

Two days later, Fu Man sold at the Harley at the Easy Rider Rodeo in Chillicothe.

And I'm back at Lindey's, a little worse for wear.

TIPPING POINTS
GRATITUDE V. GRATUITY

IN 1987, THE GRUMPY GOURMET interviewed a range of servers in area restaurants, asking for their worst nights. Lindey's own Jim Borden, after a long night, replied, "This is my worst night ever. All my tables were food critics."

Now that we've all become food critics, perhaps servers live in constant fear of our snide remarks, comparisons, and caviling. Borden's other worst nights (apparently they occurred with some regularity) were "when the docs are in town." Not the medical professionals (doctors are typically pretty fair tippers), but customers who "dock you for this, dock you for that," figuring the tip on their mental calculators, and subtracting for every minute of wait time and every degree the food temperature varied from their ideal, factoring a coefficient of dissatisfaction for their table's proximity to a noisy side stand, boisterous table, or chilly door, and reducing the "standard 15%" with most any other factor beyond the server's control.

On the other hand, there are the flustering, flattering moments, when a server returns to a table to find a lacy pair of ladies underwear slid into the check presenter, demure as a napkin tucked into a napkin ring. (It's accompanied, of course, by a slightly inebriated guest at the table, winking.)

In this section, we have asked previous employees for a few moments of exceptional generosity or the lack thereof.

Bottled Gratuity

Mark Svede: A table of four from Cincinnati had spent a long night in my section, and at the end of their meal and their many glasses of wine, they called me over to the table to confess that they were "a bit shy. We don't have enough cash to leave you the right tip and to keep 'just in case' for the ride back to Cincinnati. So we can do one of two things."

I already knew neither option was one I would choose.

"We can just leave you the cash we have, which isn't enough, or we can hold onto the cash and send you back a really nice bottle of wine when we get home for your trouble."

"I really would rather have the money," I replied. "I just started working here and I'm putting myself through graduate school."

"*Humph!* You just don't trust us, that's all," the woman replied. "You're just presuming we'd never send the wine. But you know what they say: *PRESUMING* makes an *ASS* out of *YOU* and *ME*."

"No, I didn't realize they said that," I replied. The way I figured it, they'd be lucky to remember what street they lived on, let alone the address of Lindey's.

An Ample Tip

One server remembers that in addition to a respectable 20 percent tip, he was offered an additional $100 if he'd spend a little time after he got off work hanging out in the diners' hot tub for an hour. He declined.

But the most remarkable tip we've heard about occurred during a holiday party for a certain corporation. Their CEO came to town from Manhattan to take care of his Columbus office. After the bill was tabulated, the added tip came to $1,500, but he rounded it up to $3,500. (That's our kind of arithmetic.) Leaving the party, he gave the hostess $400. And when Sara, a server who'd been helping out with the party, walked through the room he handed her $100 by way of thanks. But then, staring at her breasts, he unfolded another $100. "Now there's one for each of your girls."

Hearing of this "generosity," our veteran server Allen remarked, "Next year, if I see these folks have booked a party, you can be sure I'll be in drag with even bigger tits."

Fashion Tips

The more requests a guest makes or the longer a guest stays at a given table are factors that servers think about, since each member of the waitstaff has a limited piece of real estate for a limited amount of real time in which to make his or her very real income.

One regular guest was notoriously difficult to wait on at lunch. She had servers running back and forth for this and that as long as she was there, and almost none of her "requests" added anything to the bill. *Can you check on this? Can I get more hot water? I need another spoon. Can you see if the chef is going to be here Saturday?* Endless little requests. Her favorite server was Danny Burns, and she'd run him ragged during lunch.

One day, he found out that she had taken a job at the new Henri Bendel's at City Center. Being a fashion-conscious drag queen in his off-off-hours, Danny spent an afternoon with his favorite guest at Lindey's, trying on dozens and dozens of dresses. *Do you have this in a slightly fuller cut? Can I try on the kelly green one as well? What scarves do you have that could accent this simple look? Can I get a cup of tea? Is there a phone? I want to call my boyfriend and see if this he thinks I'd look good in something this shimmery.* At the end of his session, Danny said, "Well, thank you for your time," and left his salesperson only a little more empty-handed than she had left him at lunch.

More Calculations

We had one lovely (and perhaps lonely) lady who made it a practice to join us for dinner 15 minutes before closing. Usually this would be on a Friday night, the kitchen would be shutting down, and whoever had to wait on her would put in an order at 11:30 and pretty much spend the next two hours trying not to hurry her. Suddenly, what seemed like a solid, steady night ended up dragging out for two more hours. The server at her station would be doing that disheartening calculation (total tips ÷ hours worked = a plummeting hourly wage). One night, one of the managers on duty kidded the waiter: "Let's everyone chip in and buy her gift certificates to Cameron Mitchell restaurants."

Chip on Your Shoulder? Never

Allen, a server who often works private parties upstairs, remembers one particular birthday attended by 14 very well-to-do ladies. The staff did all sorts of extra things for the guests, such as brewing an iced tea they'd requested (and then didn't touch). Their entire lunch was rather pricy—but nothing when compared to the gift the guest of honor received: her friends had bought her a diamond necklace, with matching bracelet and earrings.

When it came time to present the checks, Allen remembers quite distinctly that each lady's total came to $29.45. It was a set menu. Suddenly, the conversation changed:

"I'm going to have him put $40 on my credit card, and then you just leave whatever's left, since I owe you that from last week."

"Can you put half on this card, and then she's going to pay the rest on her card?"

"I have your $7 from last Sunday, so I'll leave the tip for both of us—can I get change?"

Finally, Allen said, "I'm sorry, but it's the house policy: you're going to have to figure out the bills yourself."

Now this was not well received.

Finally, one of the ladies comes over to Allen to reassure him and to apologize for her friends' scowls. "You did a lovely job, don't worry. Thank you."

Then, five minutes later she's back at the side stand, where Allen is straightening up. "I've looked over my bill, and mine is 25 cents too high, Allen—"

"Well, since it's already rung through, I can't very well—"

"No, I wasn't asking for it back! Not at all. I just want you to add that to your tip, since you did such a nice job."

You want to know the amazing thing? That extra quarter didn't go to Allen's head. He still works parties at Lindey's.

Flights of Not-So-Fancy

Erich Kraus: I applied to Lindey's in the spring of 1996. Ross hired me as a terrace server, as was typical, and assured me that if I proved myself there, I could likely stay on in the autumn and pick up dining room shifts.

Ten years ago—and maybe still—the terrace was a lot of work. There's the daily set-up and the daily tear-down. There's the slippery flight of stairs. There's the uneven sidewalk and a few doors standing between your tables and the kitchen. The whole deck gets napalmed nightly with insect repellent and your shift gets cancelled if it's pouring rain or sweltering hot. Not a barrel of laughs, from what I can remember.

Needless to say, the more tenured dining-room servers managed to look down at the rookies on the terrace, despite our physically elevated location. They swished about in their starched whites on the air-conditioned ground floor as we ran up and down the stairs in sweat-soaked polo shirts and khaki shorts. (But neither the ladies nor "the girls"—the gay servers—downstairs were entirely uninterested in our feeble existence: Ross had hired a few members of the OSU wrestling team to work as terrace busboys.)

One hot and humid summer evening—which they all were—I waited on a party of three gay men, the host of which was known for his spending power and generosity. It was a busy night, and their "thirst" kept me running. When their champagne tab crept over the $500 mark, my coworkers downstairs took notice.

The party's friendliness and generosity increased with each glass of champagne. Before I realized what was happening, they were ordering bottles of Veuve Clicquot for other tables...gradually, the entire terrace had joined their party.

At the end of a very lively evening, they'd racked up a tab in excess of $1,500 (of which $30 comprised food). With true style, the host didn't bat an eyelash when I presented the bill. He tipped me a flat 20 percent. That, combined with the gratuities from my other guests, was a career record that I never bettered.

At closing time, in hopes of gaining favor with the "big kids" downstairs, I bought the front and the back of the house a round of drinks. And, true to his word, soon thereafter Ross asked me to pick up a few dining room shifts.

When the weather cooled, I left the amateur class and moved inside.

How to Tell If You're a Lindey's Regular

REMEMBER THAT *NATIONAL LAMPOON* CARTOON where the hot dog is standing by the mailbox at the end of his driveway reading a postcard, and the caption says, "You may already be a wiener"?

Just wondered if you remembered. It's one of our favorites too.

But thinking of that did remind us that there have been two generations of people who've considered Lindey's their restaurant. For instance, Brooke O'Neill came as a young girl when it was her father's favorite lunch place, and now she comes with her husband Brendan for most every celebration (plus a few extra times each week just to meet friends or to have dinner).

Remembering the "first generation" of regulars at Lindey's, Stephanie Ford says, "Lindey's was our *Cheers*, and we had our weekly episodes Friday and Saturday nights just like the television program."

Fred Holdrich put it this way: "We went home to Lindey's late at night before going to our own homes. Many nights, we'd just lock the door, and whoever was inside would stay at the bar until..."

Veteran bartender **Eddie Meecham:** The managers who didn't make it here lost sight, even if it was only for a moment, that Lindey's was the one place where knowing your customers is all-important. For some people, coming and waiting an average of 45 minutes, or even twice that, was part of their evening's plan: cocktails at the bar, and then dinner a little later. But if a regular came in, wanted a table, and the manager said, "We don't have a table right now, so if you'd like to have a seat at the bar..." that would be it. They had to know who could *always* get a table and how to make that happen.

As for this younger generation, here are Brooke's own words, excerpted from an impromptu speech she gave upon accepting the title Ms. Lindey's 2004 (she also reigned in 2005, and apparently in 2006, when the intended recipient of the crown decided to wait another year before shouldering the zero responsibilities that go along with the title), a spontaneous crowning that occurred the night of the Memorial Golf Tournament.

Brooke: I'd like to thank my mom and dad for bringing me here as a child and giving me the resources to always pay my bar bill and come here dressed well, and my husband who picks up the bill now that we come four times a week. I want to thank Sue for smoking cigarettes with me in her office, and Ross for introducing me to Veuve Clicquot, which has really made a difference in my life, and everyone else who helped to raise me in this restaurant. I came to Lindey's for my prom, every one of my birthdays, my graduation from high school and from college, then while I was in college, then as a single woman in town I would save up my money so I could spend the weekend on the terrace in some fabulous outfit. I met my husband here. We had our engagement party here and took up the entire bar, and ever since then, we've celebrated all our anniversaries here, every New Year's Eve, all of our birthdays...I just feel so much a part of the love that's Lindey's.

Yes, we have had many people who've come every day for years on end. We've had people who've had two, and even three meals a day with us on a regular basis, and not simply because they lived close by and were renovating the kitchen. We've had people who come to town once or twice a year, and every time, make a reservation at Lindey's.

Ric Wanetik: In 1984, when I told my staff at Lazarus I had just been named president of subsidiary divisions for Marshall Fields, there was a general silence, and then the first words spoken were Becky Case's, "Has anyone told Sue Doody?" as if David's and my departure would mean her profits would plummet and it would be the end of her restaurant.

David Hagans: Before we left for Chicago, we had a surprise party for Ric at Lindey's. Friends had invited Ric to cocktails in the main dining room while we'd set up the party in the middle dining room. The place was packed—both the dining room and the bar—and Ric's back faced the middle room so he didn't see two large 6'5" white rabbits enter the room, although everyone else did...and fell silent. The rabbits (costumes from our Easter event at Lazarus) worked their way through the crowd and tapped Ric on the shoulder; each one took an arm and escorted Ric into the party, where everyone was wearing T-shirts in Pappagolo pink and green that read "Chicago 2, Lindey's 0."

But it's not really frequency, regularity, the number of friends you bring, or the dollars you drop that makes you a Lindey's regular. It's something less tangible, more individual. Perhaps it's how comfortable you feel. For instance:

Michael Morris: About 10 years ago, there was a fountain on the patio. A buddy of mine used to meet with me pretty regularly; we set up shop in the afternoon, and then it would

be evening, and pretty soon, we'd be a party of 10 or 12...and in no time, it would be 11:30 at night. One night, my friend kept talking about the fountain, and the next thing I know, he's found some soap, and climbed into the fountain, half-naked—and he's enticed a couple passersby to join in the "bath." It was like an episode of *I Love Lucy*, with these soaped-up people giggling in the bubbling fountain. And then, wouldn't you know, Chris Doody (the owner's son and one of the managers at the time) comes around the corner: "What the heck are you doing?" he asks. But then, as if he half expected to see a bubble bath of guests in the fountain, he just walked back into the restaurant.

Server **Alice Mattimo:** Frank and Kay Cipriano always dined at Lindey's and often shared their goings-on with the staff. For instance, we all knew all that they'd recently moved from a house that was a few doors down from Lindey's to another place a few blocks away. So one night, their son came home from college and walked into Lindey's, looking for his parents. Surprisingly, they weren't at their usual table.

"Hey, do any of you know where my parents live now?" he asked sheepishly. "I went to our house and they don't live there anymore."

Of course, we knew, and one of the waiters walked him to his new home.

So, like our friend the hot dog, you may *already* be a Lindey's regular—and not even know it! Here are some of the signs.

You're a Lindey's regular when...

☞ Looking at the evening's reservation sheet, a member of the waitstaff willingly trades stations in order to serve you.

☞ Looking at the evening's reservation sheet, a member of the waitstaff willingly trades stations in order *not* to serve you. (In fact, some regulars come with a "bounty." One server to another: "I'll give you $20 if you'll pick up the [your last name here] party on Table [x].")

☞ Lindey's is your branch office, as it was for Amy Goldstein and Marc Sigal in the early '80s, who used to come for lunch every Saturday with the week's mail and a small Sony Watchman, and sit for the better part of the afternoon working in the dining room.

☞ Your server doesn't even bother to rattle off any specials you'd never order anyway.

☞ When you say that you want the veal scaloppini, but want to substitute rice for the scaloppini, the server doesn't even consider smirking. (However, everyone at the side stand will know about the gaffe.)

☞ The bartender has called you a cab even before last call.

☞ When making reservations, the person who picks up the phone recognizes your voice and doesn't ask for your phone number.

Stephanie and **Mike Ford:** You know that you're a regular when you're at Lindey's and your son calls and asks, "Can I speak with my mom, please?" and when the host says, "I'm sorry, but I don't know who your mother is," the son replies, "Then you must be new."

☞ Your waiter says of course you can have that little biscotti that comes with the espresso even if you're only having a regular cup of coffee with skim milk instead of cream. No problem.

☞ Your server (and you do have at least one you can call "yours") knows that you are going to take the check, no matter who at the table tries to slip them a credit card. In fact, you've made arrangements ahead of time; no check is even presented.

☞ You talk to your waiter about his art history career, his dogs, and his upcoming trip to Jamaica rather than how much you're enjoying the food.

☞ You always get extra "bev naps" on the patio, just in case the glasses sweat and you're wearing silk. (That's regulars' talk for "beverage napkins.")

Brooke O'Neill: You're a regular when you realize you have accumulated a dozen Lindey's champagne glasses at home, each acquired mysteriously, accidentally, and certainly unintentionally. (Lindey's, if you're listening, you really ought to schedule a barware amnesty day every other year, when guests can bring back items that somehow ended up at their homes—no questions asked.)

- Servers who have never waited on you before know your name and that you want the sauce on the side.

- Servers ring in something that's not on the menu with a code based on your name: 1 SKIP'S CHX PARM or 1 HGLIM MARINARA.

- On your birthday, the restaurant staff buys you a bottle of champagne instead of putting a candle in a crème brûlée.

- The valets don't give you a claim ticket when you get out of your car. In fact, the valets know where you live and have offered to drive you home on certain festive occasions.

Sheila Martin: I was such a frequent diner at Lindey's that I was always poking my head into the kitchen to talk with Sue, one of my dearest friends, or to kid around with the chef. But when a new employee would come on board, there was sometimes a bit of confusion. One evening, I walked into the kitchen, and this new waiter rushed over to me, "Oh, miss, miss! I'm sorry, this isn't where the ladies room is. It's over..."

"No, it's okay," I replied. "I always pee in the kitchen."

- Your server edits the specials on your behalf, omitting anything he or she thinks is too pricy, prissy, or just plain weird.

- You stay long enough and late enough that your server sits down at the table with you.

- You always sit at the same table. And you know your table number. And you know the other regulars who also like that same table and always have to take that into consideration when making reservation times.

- In the winter, the manager takes your fur coat up to the office.

Terri Dickie: You're a regular when you can look across the street, see the place is packed, and then can call over, ask for Tony at the bar, and he says, "Yep, I've got a couple just leaving," and you can walk over, and he's put down a couple napkins and ice waters and you sit right down.

- Finally, you know you're a regular at Lindey's when your wake is held at the bar.

Lynn Elliott: When Neil [Schultz] died, we had the wake at Lindey's. He always used to say he wanted to be laid out at Lindey's so people could come by, pay their last respects, and have a drink on him! And at the funeral, we announced just that, inviting everyone to join us at Lindey's for lunch. And, Sue, bless her heart, after it was all over, she wouldn't allow me to pay a cent for it. I never in a million years would have held it there had I imagined that. Anyway, I tried to think of what I could give Sue, something of Neil's or ours to show my appreciation. Finally, in our collection of leather-bound books, I found a copy of *Alice in Wonderland*. A little treasure. Lindey's was always Neil's "wonderland."

LINDEY'S DRESS CODE DECODED,
OR, LET THE FUR FLY

PEOPLE HAVE LIKENED THE CROWD AT LINDEY'S to an Easter parade, a fashion runway, a Mardi Gras float, and any number of other colorful spectacles. We've always thought of ourselves as business casual, as a place you can come after work, assuming that you don't work as a coal miner or a cat burglar. But over the years, we have had such colorful patrons that some of us might have been grateful for a little more black and white.

In fact, there's a certain decorum at Lindey's, even in the painted subjects framed throughout the restaurant.

Sue: The first very large canvas I bought from Tony Cochran portrayed a woman with a plunging neckline. That décolleté look was very Victorian, with much of the bosom exposed. But I asked Tony if he'd consider putting a higher collar on the dress, since this building is turn of the century, when the style was more prudent. So he was happy to, and now there's a yoke in the dress and a collar. It's a beautiful work, and, in fact, people over the years have tried to buy the painting from our walls, and Tony has repainted that exact subject for several guests.

The funny thing—*and this is so Lindey's*—is that we have another painting by Tony, which has an equally beautiful woman, sitting with her knees pulled up so that her dress falls away, revealing her calves and a little thigh. Her purse sits beside her, keeping the view from being the least bit scandalous. But somehow people have taken to telling a story that, originally, Tony had painted a thin clutch purse in the painting, and that I'd insisted he paint in a much taller handbag to make the painting more respectable. Oh, please.

Lost

German Village resident Pat Groseck had a mink coat that was shedding. "I wish I could just lose it," she said one evening at Lindey's bar, only half joking.

Her friend replied, also only half joking, "Well then, go hang it by the door...?"

So Pat did, adding her mink to the layers of jackets on the coat tree in the crowded bar that's about six feet from the front door. Sure enough, by the end of the evening, she was in need of a new coat, and had to brave the few blocks to her house in the cold.

Lost and Found

Pat's wasn't the only stolen coat we remember. David Hagan and Ric Wanetik hosted a party one night, and Mrs. Garek wore a Persian lamb coat with a mink collar, which we'd hung near the host stand. But by the end of the party, it was gone, as were the trench coat and hat hung beside it. A bit of hasty sleuthing revealed the following: a couple of guys from out of town had been seated in the bar not far from the coat stand. They'd asked Jan, the cocktailer, what the hot spot for dancing was at the moment. Assessing the situation rather delicately, she figured they'd be happy at the Garage, a gay club open until 2:30, where the Lindey's staff, both gay and straight, often went after work.

The valet remembered that the perps were driving a van.

Sue: I told Mrs. Garek that insurance would cover the cost of the coat, but I wanted to find it! So chef Kent Rigsby, Tony my manager, and I climbed into my BMW, and the three of us drove to the Garage and combed the parking lot of the club.

We looked inside the windows of every van parked there, and, sure enough, we found one with the coats tossed on the rear seats.

We called the police. Someone made an announcement in the bar that was something like "Would the owner of a whatever-kind-of-van-it-was please come to the front door," and, in a few minutes, the two guys appeared.

Wouldn't you know, they claimed that they had no idea what the jackets were doing in their van. And even though we'd identified the two coats and the hat as ours—I said the lamb coat was mine, and Kent said the trench coat was his, and Tony said the hat was his—the police said that since no one saw these two guy take the articles, they were free to go. So we drove back to Lindey's, returned the items to their rightful owners the next day, and wondered about the workings of our justice system.

Found

Manager Freddie Cortez: We had an informal coat check for certain patrons or for especially fancy coats. Not that Lindey's crowd often dressed formally, but when someone arrived in a long fur coat, the managers often ran the coat up to the office and tore off a piece of adding machine tape to write down the guest's name. That system worked up to a point. But then one night Allen and Kip were working a party upstairs, and Sue and I needed something from the office, and came in only to find them trying on the various furs.

Server Allen: Checking *out* the coats is just another part of the coat check process, isn't it?

Room Temperature

Server J: First of all, if you're just reading this and haven't met Cherie, you have to picture a lean, tall, gorgeous blond with just the warmest personality and most playful spirit. She would come to Lindey's in what was essentially pantyhose and a slip (and this would be in the middle of winter), sit with her partner Skip at their favorite table, right next to the door (which was always opening and closing and letting in blasts of cold air), and complain about how cold it was. Meanwhile, the entire dining room would be roasting. And if you tried to change the temperature? More complaints. And, without a doubt, they spent more money at Lindey's than a dozen other regulars.

I think Cherie just liked to tell us how she was simply freezing. For a long time, she would go over and adjust the thermostat on the wall until we finally put a lockable cover on it. Which only meant that Cherie needed to take her knife over to the thermostat and jam it inside in order to turn up the heat.

Even in the summer, the vents, which are right next to their favorite table, would be blowing cold air on her while the rest of the place would be roasting. So the staff would take the grate out of the wooden floor, spread a napkin across the vent, and re-cover the vent. Eventually, the management replaced the vents with wooden covers that directed the air up the side of the wall.

Fun Fur

Server **Collin S:** In the early days, Skip and Cherie had best friends who often joined them at Table 30. The two couples were joined at the hip. Skip had a black Corvette then with serial number whatever-it-was-1, and his buddy had a black Corvette with serial number whatever-it-was-2. But keeping up with Skip and Cherie was a challenge, I guess—the other couple came less and less frequently. But before that happened, they all celebrated Skip's birthday at Lindey's. And what do you get someone who has everything?

They showed up with a live chinchilla. Do you know what one looks like—live? We've got this miniature kangaroo in the dining room, and it's making this eeeee!, this high-pitched squeal that could burst a glass. *Eeee! Eeee! Happy birthday, Skippeeee!* We couldn't think of what to get you, so we thought, hey, how about a live chinchilla! And I see Skip and Cherie looking at each other, like he's thinking *maybe the chef can cook it up with a little cognac demi-glaze* and she's thinking, *ooh, I could have a tiny chinchilla skirt.*

Better Red

Server **Alice Mattimo:** Skip and Cherie were always the best tippers! He would bring his law firm in and his Ferrari or Lamborghini would be parked out front. Skip had long silver and black hair, and Cherie, always provocative, wore some kind of short skirt. One time, another group of lawyers sat at my other four-top looking like law firms usually look. And they called me over and nodded toward Skip's group and asked, "Is that a famous rock band we should recognize?" I didn't want to disappoint them by saying, "Sorry, but they're just a bunch of lawyers, too," so I said, "I don't know." Meanwhile, a car enthusiast with a camera was out front taking a picture of the black Lamborghini, and Cherie excitedly headed out to get in the picture since (*coincidentally!*) she'd dressed in red leather that matched the car's interior. She lay across the hood, and suddenly more people with cameras gathered around. In an instant, a crowd appeared around Cherie and the car, and no fewer than four cameras snapped pictures of what *obviously* must have been the ride of a rock group.

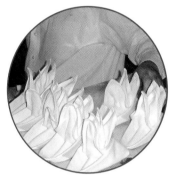

Fashion Hawk

A server we'll call Al: At one of my first parties upstairs—a Christmas party—I realized it was not our typical crowd when I overheard a woman say, "I *told* you this was a nice place; that's why I wore the pantyhose."

Figuring *I'd* probably worn more pantyhose in my life than the speaker, I pivoted and looked at the woman in amazement.

"What are *you* hawking at?" she said.

"Excuse me?" I replied.

"*Hawking*. What are you hawking at?"

"I'm afraid I don't know what hawking is."

"Oh, you know, hawking, gawking, staring—whatever you call what you're doing, looking at me like that?"

"I'm *hawking*...at absolutely nothing."

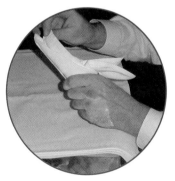

Float Me a Dress

Server Jimmy S: When Beth Doody went to New Orleans to ride in the Mardi Gras parade—her father Alton was to be King Hermes, a parade master—she needed a formal gown. And she mentioned this to her mom, and Sue said, "Honey, why don't you ask one of the boys downstairs if you can borrow one of theirs?"

And, in fact, Danny Burns did have a beaded gown he'd made by sewing Mardi Gras beads onto a full-length strapless dress. Hell, the gown must have weighed 50 pounds! Danny was exhausted when we wore it himself the first time. But he brought it in for Beth to try on. She ended up borrowing a gown from one of Sue's friends instead, though. Something a little less heavy, I think.

It's a Wrap

One afternoon a woman hailed Shelia over to her table to complain about the temperature. "It's too cold in here—can you turn up the heat or something?" A moment later, Shelia was standing behind the chilled guest and draping a folded tablecloth over her shoulders. "We call this a Lindey's mink." No one is sure if Shelia was joking or actually offering the guest a "wrap." Either way, within a few minutes, the woman's "stole" was draped over her chair. Perhaps she was suddenly warmer.

Party Dress

Server **Jimmy S:** Oh, and then there was the time I called in gay. This was a Sunday night, Labor Day weekend, and I ended up going to the Tremont, a rather scary wrinkle room in German Village. It was crock-pot night, and there were thirty crock pots on the pool table—all the regulars bringing in their famous chili and whatnot, and there were hot dogs in the back. (Withhold your comments, please.) And that morning, when I woke up, I was just in one of those moods. I put on a one-piece Catalina bathing suit—red-white-and-blue stripes, my American Gladiator outfit—with my hairy chest and my hairy ass hanging out, and I grabbed a flag, and a blond wig, and marched down Mohawk from my house over to the Tremont. (And, of course, there are still people pulling up alongside me to ask, "Excuse, me, how do you get to Schmidt's?" So of course I tell them: "You just hop on I-270 and go around until you see a sign for Lake Erie, and turn...")

So I'm over at the bar, and I'm supposed to be at work at 5:00. But I lose track of time, and at 4:15, still in skag drag and skunk drunk, I go to the payphone and call over to Lindey's. "Ross, I hate to do this, but I can't come in tonight. I've been celebrating here at the Tremont, I've had too many cocktails, I'm in a lady's swimsuit, and I think I have to call in gay." That made Ross laugh so hard, that he actually let me off.

PROFILE: SKIP AND CHERIE
LINDEY'S MOST ORIGINAL COUPLE

A GOOD NUMBER OF STORIES at Lindey's might be apocryphal. We have only the trustworthy testimonies of respectable patrons amused by the idea of having their stories put in a book. But evenings do wear on, nights are often dark, and 25 years is a long time to remember everything exactly.

But just about everyone at Lindey's has a story featuring Skip and Cherie, who were nearly always in attendance at one of the front three tables in the front of the dining room for almost our entire history. "When you eat at Lindey's four or five days a week—" Cherie says before Skip interrupts, "—and some weeks, all seven days—" and then Cherie finishes her thought, "—every day of the year, for twenty-some years, the place doesn't just feel like home, it is your home. So we've always thought of everyone here as family."

Here are a few irresistible anecdotes, which they've graciously agreed to let us print here even though no one is sure they happened exactly this way.

First Impressions

Emil Shedlock, Lindey's first manager: Before Sue really knew Skip Van Dyne and what he did for a living, she came up to me one day very worried about a conversation I was having with him.

Skip: I came to Lindey's a few times a week for dinner, but I'd also have meetings there with people from the office, other lawyers, and clients. Lindey's was part of what we called our Golden Triangle: our house on City Park, the office on Livingston Avenue, and Lindey's, the third corner.

And I always had my cell phone. Now this was 1981, so its case was one half of a Harley-Davidson set of saddle bags, which could hold the phone and one file. The battery was supposed to last for two hours of calling and six hours of standby. But I was buying batteries constantly.

Emil: So Sue is very nervous, and she says to me, "I walked by Skip's table and you two were talking about kilos and narcotics. And he's got that whole collection of expensive black cars, and that huge cell phone! *Emil, I think Skip is a drug dealer, and he's dealing in our restaurant!"*

"Sue, get a grip," I told her. "He's a lawyer. He's defending them."

Banquet manager Marilyn Vutech: I saw my first cell phone at Lindey's. Skip would haul that thing in, all 10 pounds of it, and take the occasional call at his regular table. I was just getting into real estate at the time, and I thought it would be a great sales tool. I called Skip's salesperson and purchased a phone at Skip's "good-friend rate" of $1,350. I think I was one of the first realtors to be able to make calls from the road. And it served me well until the day it was stolen from my car, when I was thrilled to replace it with a one-pounder.

Stephanie Ford: One year, the theme for Jim and Jan's Halloween party was "Come as Your Sexual Fantasy," so I decided to go as Skip Van Dyne. I went to Dick Frank, a costume designer, and sat for four hours while he resculpted my face: he put on a bald cap, and glued on Skip's hairline, moustache, chin—everything. I wore black jeans, a black shirt, black boots, and I carried a briefcase with a princess phone and Monopoly money spilling out.

Cherie: And Stephanie was accompanied by David Wirthman, who was dressed as me. Of course, it was perfect drag.

The Cat's Meow

Skip: One of Lindey's next-door neighbors owned the biggest cat, named Nessie, who liked our cars. When Cherie and I drove over in my 454 SS pickup, a hot rod with a covered tonneau, Nessie liked to jump up on the cover, and everyone in the restaurant would look out the window and freak out, but Nessie was Nessie, and he could do whatever he wanted, which included setting off the oversensitive alarm system on the car since he was so large.

Nessie also liked our Dodge viper, which he liked to sit on. And the guests and servers would freak out, and we'd say, it's okay, it's okay, the sun's warm, and it's just Nessie.

Cherie: But then one day Nessie disappeared. Skip and I put up a reward for the cat. (Not that this made the neighbor like us even a little.)

Skip: I remember another night we were gathered on the terrace at Lindey's, sitting on the fence between the terrace and the neighbor's roof. And Sue comes outside, walks right over to me, and says, "Skip, now you can't be peeking into our neighbor's window. She just called and said she saw you—" Now you have to picture my gorgeous Cherie standing right beside me when I look right back at Sue who has only known us for literally thousands of dinners in her restaurant. "Sue, I have one question: Why? Why would I do that?"

Guest **Michael Mizenko:** I can't picture Lindey's without Skip and Cherie at their table in the front window, with one of their cars parked right across the street where they, and most everyone in the restaurant, could see it lit up by the street lights...although I don't think it was a legal parking space.

One night, a cat jumped on the hood of their car. And Cherie, who had a great sense of timing, stood up at the exact moment the restaurant had a break in the noise, grabbed her napkin and threw it on her plate, and announced to the entire front room, "There's a pussy on my Rolls! There's a pussy on my Rolls!" Then she marched out the door in her teetery heels and tiny skirt, and ran across the cobblestone street, arms waving, shooing the cat and chasing it a few doors down the street—all of this very much to the delight of that evening's guests.

A Taste of Money

Bartender **John Lee:** One evening, Skip made something of a show of a particular Chateauneuf de Pape he'd brought in. Some stupendous bottle that must have been very—as in *very*—expensive. And he wanted to give everyone a taste. He offered me a taste, and I told him, "You know, it's going to be wasted on me; you can buy me a shot of bourbon."

So they finished the bottle, which apparently was even better than they'd imagined, and Cherie got it into her head that the bottle ought to be displayed over the mirror, on the wooden keystone that framed the mirror behind the bar. Now I can't explain why she wanted to do this, but she came around the bar, asked me to help her up, and for whatever reason, I made a step of my hands and hoisted her up. She tucked the bottle up there, I lowered her to the ground, and as soon as the two of us turned around to face the dining room, there's Sue, glaring at us, but smiling that smile that means, *"What are you thinking?"* But she didn't say a word. (Oh, the manager certainly did, later.)

But Skip and Cherie were part of my education at Lindey's. Their monthly house charge was more than I made annually. I mean, I didn't realize people *made* that kind of money, let alone *spent* that kind of money!

Happy Birthday Suit

Server **Jimmy Strausbaugh:** During one weekday dinner, Cherie happened to mention to me that the very next day she would have had her new breasts for exactly 10 years. So when Skip and Cherie arrived the next afternoon, the staff surprised Cherie with a 10th anniversary party for Boober and Titter, as she affectionately called them. We had ice-cream cake and champagne, and all the staff gathered around Table 30 to sing, "Happy Birthday, Boober and Titter." It was early enough that the rest of the dining room didn't actually understand what we were doing. Not that we didn't tell all of Cherie's many, many admirers later.

Largesse and Then Some

If there were a secular, restaurant version of patron saints, Skip and Cherie would be Lindey's. Especially for the staff. Late nights, weekends, holidays, and other special occasions, many servers often gathered at their home or at their table. There was always a bottle to share, a gift to give, a little pro bono legal advice, a warmth and generosity and sense of humor that only family, with all its attending tensions, can bring.

Cherie: The valets at Lindey's are princes! And there's at least one woman I remember, so they're also princesses! The cigarette machine at the restaurant never worked, or it was

A Little
Ad-ditional Fun

Advertising executive **Jim Vutech:** No restaurant as consistently popular as Lindey's even needs to advertise. For years, you could hardly get a seat in the place. So the ads we created supported the notion that "We do our own thing here at Lindey's, because we're not like the new restaurants on the block." The Doodys were eager to have the feel of a timeless restaurant such as Galatoire's or Commander's Palace. They wanted their brand to represent that kind of credibility. And if you become such an institution, you can afford not to take yourself too seriously.

In this box, and on pages 144 and 163, we've reprinted many of the headlines with a brief excerpt from the ad copy. Cheeky us.

Soon, Many Lindey's Customers Will Be Dining for Free. / The holiday season is the perfect time to give a Gift Certificate from Lindey's...

Lately, Some of Lindey's Best Customers Have Been Walking Out the Door. / And they're leaving with their favorite Lindey's carryout menu items.

At Lindey's, You Never Know What Might Show Up on the Menu. / Now at Lindey's you can expect to find a new menu daily—at lunch and dinner...

Lately, Some of Lindey's Best Customers Have Been Having Private Affairs. / We can't keep it a secret any longer. Lindey's now is available for your private party or affair...

always out of our cigarettes, so the valets would run and get us a carton and we'd tip them handsomely. But probably the valets will never forget the time we had them deliver 200 White Castle burgers to Fire Station #2, at Fourth and Fulton, which happens to be the busiest station in the country. We'd met a few of the firefighters, and learned that they often got hungry late at night, even though they do prepare dinners there. So we gave the valets some money, had them deliver this huge order of sliders to the firemen, and they came back to tell us, "The guys said it was the best food they'd ever had from Lindey's."

Two other funny "gifts" I remember. Since everyone's always talking about Skip's cars, when manager Tom Harlor had a son while at Lindey's, we bought him a Mercedes. A pedal-pushing kid's car Mercedes. And then, when Lindey's next manager Ross had a baby girl, we weren't going to buy her just a receiving blanket. I mean, Judge Taylor had married Ross and Leah in our living room! And Ross was he was like our son. So as a surprise, the servers pulled Tables 31 and 32 together, and helped us set a Lamborghini—just like ours, except child-size and pink instead of red—as the centerpiece. The car was battery powered, huge, and heavy, and Skip will never forget that "some assembly required" meant two days of tiny pieces and wrenches and pages of directions. The car even had a cell phone like ours, except it was pink and could only dial Barbie.

I guess people say, since we never had kids, that cars are our children! Plus the many, many servers we've loved over the years at Lindey's.

LIVE AT LINDEY'S

OUR COLORFUL COMMUNITY

THIRTY YEARS AGO, Warner LeRoy, the New York restaurateur who founded Maxwell's Plum, told the *New York Times* that "A restaurant is a fantasy—a kind of living fantasy in which diners are the most important members of the cast." At Lindey's, we have to admit to being a haven for some rather theatrical guests over the years.

There's the gentleman we know as Lovey Howe, a rather flamboyant gay man who often wore something like a WWII sailor suit, but custom-made in red and blue.

There's the oncologist and his wife who would come in regularly, five minutes before closing, to read the newspaper, review charts, organize bills, and say two or three words to one another over dinner.

We were home to the owners of a local ballroom-dancing studio who often brought in instructors and competitors: high-cheekboned, super-rouged women and their attending high-cheekboned, minimally rouged partners. Once a year, they filled the front room with pairs from the national ballroom dancing competition and Lindey's looked as if the dandies and demoiselles in the belle epoque paintings that cover the dining room walls had walked out of the frames.

Here are a few small tributes to some of our most colorful guests. Think of these as our Tony Awards. You can even imagine our bartender Tony Murray presenting them: the Lindey's Awards for various memorable performances.

More Ad-ditional Fun

Lately, Lindey's Customers Are Finding New Places to Eat. / Lindey's has added a new bar and dining area, and a newly remodeled terrace area that overlooks a New Orleans–style outdoor patio.

At Lindey's, We Support the Arts. We Sauté Them, Filet Them, and Marinate Them, Too. / At Lindey's we're taking great pride in our culinary art.

Nine Times out of Ten, When You Order a Meal at Lindey's, You End Up Paying for It. / But in honor of our anniversary, the tenth one's on us!

At Lindey's You Never Know Where Your Next Meal Is Coming From. / At Lindey's, we travel to the ends of the earth to find the finest, freshest ingredients.

At Lindey's, Some of Our Best Customers Never Order a Meal. / Instead, they "graze" through our menu and order à la carte...

After 10 Years of Planning, We Finally Came Up with a Great Idea for a Party. / Our 10th anniversary. As a special patron of Lindey's you're invited...

It's a Fact, Something New Is Cooking at Lindey's. / And his name is Bruce Molzan. Former head chef at...

The Pepper-Steak Lady

There are as many variations on this story as there are servers, but here are two fairly reliable renditions.

Manager S: One woman, who spoke barely a word beyond her order—usually steak au poivre, an item that was no longer on the menu—ate by herself at a deuce. I believe she had some kind of...let's say malady. But I'm no doctor. She was pleasant enough, and regular enough...but she just wasn't the usual Lindey's guest. One night when I was the manager on duty, a server rushes over to me and says that the pepper-steak lady's purse was sitting open on the seat next to her, and inside it lay a foot-long knife. "Right there, no sheath—it's just pointing from one side of the purse to the other." I didn't know what to do—I didn't think this guest seemed like the violent sort, but...so I called the police and had them wait outside the restaurant. I guess there was no problem.

She kept coming back for some time, although I changed her name to "the pepper-steak-knife lady."

Server Jimmy B: We had this one crazy lady who was certainly on some kind of major medication. She came in every day, sat at the bar, and ordered a vodka tonic, a rum and Coke, a glass of milk, a glass of cabernet, a glass of water, and scotch on the rocks—I think I have that right—and then she'd ask for either Freddie or me, and have herself a fancy dinner at a deuce along the wall, which she'd pay for with her gold AmEx. I was always nice to her, but she often had a fit that "the girls" were giving her dirty looks from the kitchen. One evening, her purse tipped over, revealing a 10-inch chef's knife inside. So I go to Freddie, who's managing that night, and tell him that our guest has a butcher knife, and I'm going to take it. But then she leaves, and the next day in the paper, they report that on the way home from Lindey's, she apparently confronted a cab driver with the weapon, and then got to her house, where she held the police at bay for something like six hours before they subdued her.

Double Time

For many years, these words appeared across the bottom of Lindey's menus: "Did you know some of our best guests are having private affairs?" This was our cheeky way of recommending the upstairs dining rooms for special events, meetings, and parties. But some people may have taken that message as a general blessing of their romantic surreptitiousness. That was not our intention. And yet, a few regular guests, who must remain nameless here, provided an ongoing challenge for our hosts and managers.

A typical predicament: The manager answering the phone recognizes the voice as that of the wife of a gentleman seated with a beautiful woman at a nearby cocktail table, and says "Oh, good evening, Mrs. So-and-So," speaking in a tone that's just loud enough for Mr. So-and-So to overhear. "No, I don't think I've seen him..." the manager says, checking to see if the husband is signaling with his eyes or shaking his head one way or the other. "But I just came on a few minutes ago—want me to check the other rooms?" Then Mr. So-and-So excuses himself from the table and swings by the manager to offer a ruse, a thank you, a twenty, a sigh of relief. "Okay, then," the manager concludes, "if I see him, I'll tell him..." and now the manager's voice increases in volume, "...that you're coming by with your mother for dinner in half an hour. See you then."

Perhaps the menu ought to read, "...having not-so-private affairs."

Singer **Jeanette Williams:** One Jazz Night, a guy came in with his girlfriend and another couple. Somebody dropped a dime and called the man's wife. And she arrived a while later, looking sharp! Sharp as could be: she had a full-length mink, her hair was coiffed, she wore diamond earrings—I mean, she looked beautiful. And she walked over to her husband's table and said, "Excuse me, may I speak to you for a moment?" I was sitting right there and she walked back to the door for a little privacy and called him every name but a child of god.

Starving Artists menu cover by Carol Schar, 1991

● ● ● ● ● ● ● ● ● ● ● ● ● ● ● ● ● ●

Lindey's
Fables
for the
Famished

● ● ● ● ● ● ● ● ● ● ● ● ● ● ● ● ● ●

**The Hot-Water Lady
and the
Two-Timing Waiter:**
A fable inspired by waiter
Collin Smith

A very slight lady of some 80 years became a frequent diner at one point, typically accompanying her husband. With few exceptions, she ordered nothing but lemon and hot water. Lots and lots of hot water. Lots and lots of lemons. No, not tea. Just pot after pot after pot of hot water and, once in a while, a few vegetables. Meanwhile, her husband had beers and a hearing problem.

To make matters more exasperating, waiter Bob would come up behind whichever fellow server was waiting on their table and just whisper, "She grows her own herbs." Each time he'd passed by he'd mutter this, as if this were an important secret. ☞

Then his friend gets up to run a little interference, talking to the wife, trying to explain or whatever, and suddenly the husband's gone—just snuck out the door.

And then the husband's girlfriend comes over, comes right up and looks his wife dead in the face, and says, "Fuck you."

All *I* know is that girl ought to have been glad that *I* wasn't his wife, because *I* would have beat the life out of her.

So the husband spent a week or so staying at the Athletic Club and apparently decided to change his ways, because if his wife had taken him to court, she would have had everything he owned. I believe they were back at Jazz Night before too long.

Tony and Ray

Bartender **Tony Murray:** Tony and Ray—even though they've moved to Florida—have to rank among the all-time great people of Lindey's golden days. They had an antique Rolls-Royce, a beautiful car from the late 1940s, and they'd drive it five miles per hour for the grand total of the block and a half between their place and Lindey's. But then everyone could see them get in and get out of their car.

I still think of Tony today: so much fun, so good-hearted. He just brought the crowd in. You could say Lindey's was his party. He'd come in with an entourage of four people, then it would be 14 people, and sometimes the whole bar, and when the tab would come, he'd say, "Tony? I want it *all*, child."

Now it is true that Tony had a voice that went through your head like a nail, and Ray was usually so tipsy I don't know how he managed to walk. He'd lean over to everyone that came along, bending close, saying, "I want to tell you a secret."

Occasionally, when the hostess was seating another party and people would walk into the restaurant, Tony or Ray would get up from Table 10, stand at the podium, greet the new arrivals in whatever stage of cocktail-consumption they were in, grab menus, and escort them to a table. Just any empty table. Raymond loved running the show.

Now Raymond's toupee, frequently separated from him, often became the center of attention at the bar. As a routine of sorts, his friend Neil liked to remove it while Ray was chatting at the bar, wear it around the restaurant on his own balding head (yes, his remaining hair was a dramatically darker color), and eventually replace it on Ray's head—all without interrupting his conversation.

One bartender used to comment that Raymond's toupee was the Lindey's sundial: On those rare evenings when his hairpiece stayed on his head, you could tell what time it was by how much it had rotated throughout the evening.

Stephanie, one of Ray's dear friends, remembers one particular night: I was walking Raymond home, down Beck Street, holding his hand. And we were both a little wobbly. And at one point, he lets go, and I keep walking, not exactly aware that he wasn't beside me. Then I hear this voice: "Help me, help me." And I turn around, and realize that he's gone. So I rush back down the street, and I see that he's flipped over a wrought-iron fence, into the bushes of one of the little houses we'd just passed. I help him up, and we walk the rest of the block to his house, where I leave him, figuring that he's safe and sound.

At 9:00 the next morning, he calls me on the phone. "Honey, *I lost my hair!*" And I think, *oh, I think I know where you lost it*, so I tell him to give me a few minutes, and I'd see what I could do. And I go retrace our walk home the night before and I see this German Village lady watering her garden. I lean over her fence, and instantly she says to me, "Are you looking for something?"

And I say, "Yes!"

"Is it this?" she says, reaching down and then holding up Raymond's toupee. "I thought it was a bird's nest—it was right in my boxwood hedge."

So I thank her, take the hairpiece, and return it to its rightful owner.

☛ Then one night a server named Collin waited on this guest, and she ended their evening together by saying,

"You did such a superb job, Collin, I want to ask for you whenever I come here."

"Thank you," replied Collin, as he thought to himself: *Lovely. Seven pots of hot water. Some lemons. And, sometimes, a few steamed vegetables.*

In the coming weeks, Collin always strove to make her meals of hot lemon water and vegetables pleasant.

Then, as time wore on, Collin began working lunches at another fine restaurant in town and, as it turned out, it was his continued pleasure to serve this very woman at lunchtime. Sometimes, as luck would have it, he would wait on this nice lady at lunch and then, a few hours later, at dinner. And she was very sweet and always appreciated that she was making special requests of Collin.

Nonetheless, shortly thereafter Collin ended his careers at both restaurants.

Moral: *Life is rarely easy and seldom fair, but should you have to wake up twice with the same recurring nightmare?*

The Popes of German Village

Fred and Howard are unanimously considered the first figureheads of the restored German Village. In 1962, they bought a frowsy building on the main street of the Village and, three years later, opened its doors as Hausfrau Haven—not merely a general store, but a community gathering place and information center in a neighborhood that was in desperate need of revitalization. They also helped to cultivate the vital, whimsical, passionate culture of this historic neighborhood.

They lived across from Lindey's for 20 years, and half a block away for many more years after that. Fred and Howard also wrote "Scuttlebutt," the gossip column for Columbus's alternative paper.

Lest anyone would think their reputation was confined to the Village, the *Columbus Dispatch*'s Dennis Feely wrote an article one Sunday morning about "The Popes of German Village," and mentioned among the men's community activities, commercial interests, and personal attributes, the fact that Fred and Howard were more than business partners.

Fred Holdrich: As I remember that morning, we went down to the store early as usual, since Sunday's a busy time for a newsstand. Seeing the story, we thought, well, perhaps we won't stay open today. It was January. We weren't that busy. So after a short morning of customers, we put up a sign, CLOSED FOR REMODELING. (Our customers were used to our fickle schedule and understood that remodeling Hausfrau Haven was in and of itself a joke.) Actually, we decided to close for an hour and attend a Weight Watchers meeting at the Christopher Inn. Now lest you think us completely inattentive, remember Hausfrau Haven was not only a newsstand but several rooms jam-packed with everything from, well, jam to greeting cards, from German Village souvenirs to silly costumes. We had snacks, coolers of wine and beverages—it was a browser's paradise, with hardly enough aisle space for two people to pass. So midmorning we switched off the lights, flipped the deadbolt in the door, and accidentally locked three ladies inside on our way out to the meeting. How did we learn of this? A friend called the store and one of the women answered the phone and described their predicament. "I'm sure either Fred or Howard will be right back," our friend suggest-ed, "but in the meantime, my goodness, you should eat something." "No, we *can't*," the woman replied. "We're going to lunch at Lindey's!" And we did get back within the hour, by which time they'd had plenty of time to select some souvenirs of their visit to quaint old German Village...and build up an appetite for Lindey's.

Sue: The next Sunday brunch at Lindey's, before Fred and Howard walked in, I cut up two menus and taped them into a pair of paper miters—which they happily wore throughout their meal.

Friends Who Drink and Drive Us Nuts

Finally, there are several German Village residents who regularly join us for a few rounds of overindulgence. It's a liquid sort of chain-smoking in which a fresh beverage arrives with the last sip of the previous beverage—but in this case, it's the consumer that gets lit.

General manager **Rebecca Holder:** On any given evening, the valets and I look at the dining room and the bar, and we can pretty much judge how late it's going to be and how many valets it's going to take to end the night: which guests look like they can still drive; who can we put in a cab; who is someone going to have to drive home; who we can encourage to walk home.

Yes, we have folks who live two blocks away, insist on driving to Lindey's, and refuse to let us drive them home when they're intoxicated. My only option is to call the police and say, "This person just left my establishment and I believe them to be intoxicated, and here's their license plate number."

Not that this absolves us of responsibility. But I'll tell you: people who want to get drunk, find a way. It doesn't matter how soon we try to cut them off. They bring other "refreshments" to accompany their drinks. They bring a spare set of keys, figuring someone's going to ask them for their keys to keep them from driving.

We had one guy here who'd had a couple glasses of wine and suddenly, the next thing we know, he's slouched over on the bar and Tony's trying to get to him to talk. But the guy just stares back. Can't speak. He doesn't show any symptoms other than he won't answer any question beyond a "yep." "Where do you live?" "Yep." "Is there someone we can call?" "Yep." "What's your name?" "Yep." So finally, we help him stumble out the door and he falls asleep on the bench. So we see his cell phone, and just start calling names in his directory, hoping someone will recognize the number and can tell us who he is and where he lives. His daughter's number is among the listings, and she calls back and gives us his address. Tony and my manager Todd jump in the cab with him, take him up to his apartment, prop him up inside, and bid him goodnight.

OUR TWENTY-FIVE-YEARS-AND-COUNTING HOUSE SALAD

WE CAN'T BE SURE, but Lindey's might have been the first kitchen in town where little lettuces with peculiar names like frisée and arugula were tossed together onto the same plate like in-laws meeting for the first time. (We know for sure that many in-laws have met across the table at Lindey's for the first time. We've always been a place where young couples trust us to replace formality with festivity.) Who knew, with a little champagne vinaigrette, those greens might create such a following. Add some hearts of palm, which had been relegated to the Odd Foods section of the grocery store, the tangy cream of gorgonzola, and you've got something winning. It's been on our menu since the dawn of our time, 1981.

As for how hearts of palm won Sue's heart, perhaps she knew that Grace Kelly, the Academy Award winner for Best Actress of 1954, included it on her favorite menu: caviar blinis, duck à l'orange, French-style green beans, and hearts of palm salad vinaigrette.

serves 4

- 8 ounces mesclun greens
  (baby spinach, oakleaf, mache,
  arugula, frisée, radicchio, mizuna,
  chard, mustard greens, or whatever
  else might prompt a guest to wonder
  if he or she should have ordered
  the less intimidating wedge of iceberg),
  washed and dried
- salt and freshly ground pepper, to taste
- 1/4 cup Lindey's House Vinaigrette
- 16 slices Roma tomato (3 to 4 whole
  Roma tomatoes)
- 3/4 teaspoon each, chopped fresh
  thyme, oregano, rosemary, and sage
  leaves, any stems removed
- 1 1/2 teaspoons chopped fresh parsley,
  stems removed
- 4 ounces, hearts of palm, sliced
  lengthwise into thin spears
- 4 tablespoons crumbled gorgonzola,
  about 3 ounces

Place the greens in a large mixing bowl and season with salt and pepper, to taste. Add the vinaigrette, tomatoes, and fresh herbs, and toss gently. Place a serving of greens and 4 tomato slices on each of four plates. Toss the hearts of palm in the bowl to lightly dress. Place a quarter of the sliced hearts on top of each salad. Sprinkle each salad with a quarter of the cheese.

Serve with the traditional Lindey's hallmark, the chilled fork, so that the diner will wonder why the big salad fork is ice-cold, but the knife, which is needed both to cut and to provide a backstop for the fork, is room temperature. Consider for a moment, that the one cold and the one warm utensil are creating some kind of weird circuit through your body. The chilled (negative?) ions from one hand are charging toward the warm (positive?) ions of the other hand, creating...creating...the need for another sip of wine. Enjoy!

Lindey's House Vinaigrette
enough for 4 salads

- 1 teaspoon Dijon mustard
- 1 teaspoon dry mustard,
  such as Colman's
- 1 teaspoon chopped fresh garlic
  (1 or 2 cloves)
- 2 tablespoons freshly squeezed
  lemon juice (about 1/2 lemon)
- 2 tablespoons champagne vinegar
- 3 tablespoons extra-virgin olive oil
- 1/4 cup canola or other
  light-flavored vegetable oil
- 1 teaspoon kosher salt

Place the first five ingredients in the jar of an electric blender or the bowl of a food processor, and pulse a few times to mix. With the machine running, add both oils gradually to create a thick emulsion. Check seasoning; add salt or dilute with tablespoons of water, as necessary.

BIG STARS, LITTLE STARS,

AND EVEN ONE TINY STAR AT LINDEY'S

WHILE WE LIKE TO THINK that we treat all guests as if they were local celebrities, like **Jack Nicklaus**, **Jack Hanna**, or **Bobby Rahal**, to name just three of Columbus's resident superstars, we have been graced by the presence of an uncanny number and variety of visiting notables from stage, screen, courtroom, stadium, gallery, and concert hall over the years. Not all of them have made us quite as nervous as when Lindey's chef Korir Russell was serving Louis Farrakhan at a nearby kitchen, with his two body guards watching her make his little sandwich. Perhaps our most anxious moment might have occurred when Sue's daughter Trish came to lunch after her graduation from Ohio Wesleyan with her roommates, one of whom happened to be the daughter of the head of the FBI.

Sometimes such distinguished patrons go unnoticed, as when **John Kasich**, who often joined us for dinner in our early years, was approached by Joan Flower, then a cocktail waitress and a junior at Ohio State. "I remember going up to take his drink order, and thinking, gosh, he looks so familiar. So I said to him, 'Do you go to OSU?'"

"No," he replied, "I'm your congressman."

And in addition to such luminaries as playwright and novelist **Eric Bogosian**, or **Barry "Copacabana" Manilow**, or tennis legend **Pete Sampras**, or the renowned director **Julie Taymor** there have been other personages who parade through Lindey's on Halloween, as well as various waiters who sportingly don the couture of the opposite sex for extra-special occasions—for instance, coming to Lindey's on a night off to use their employee discount for dinner.

Sheepishly admitting at the outset that we are forgetting and slighting many illustrious figures (if you're illustrious and a Lindey's diner, please let us know so we can add you to our next edition!), we have created a list of some of the celebs whose company we've relished, and, in some cases, garnished with stories. We've added a few historical references for both younger and older readers who might not be familiar with the other's icons.

Finally, as if to give the illusion of a most inspired dinner party, we've grouped the celebrities at lively, unlikely tables of eight. Just imagine yourself serving—or sitting nearby at your own table of two—such a boisterous gathering.

The towering, tap-dancing **Tommy Tune**; daughter of Priscilla and Gene D'Angelo, Columbus's own **Beverly D'Angelo**, who played Patsy Cline in *Coal Miner's Daughter;* **Sean Astin** (depending on your age, you'd know him as son of Patty Duke, or as Sam Gamgee from *Lord of the Rings*); OSU football coach **John Cooper** (He's joined us on several occasions, but one dinner, it was the night before the OSU-Michigan game! Many people at the bar were very worried: "What's he doing here now? Doesn't he know what day tomorrow is?" "He should be at home resting!" "PLUS! *He's* supposed to be making sure the players are in their rooms, like, sleeping and not gallivanting around town!"); and, to complete the party, the four **Pointer Sisters**. (Walking to Lindey's one day, one of our regular guests spotted Ivy, a server, in the middle of Mohawk, waving good-bye to a taxi-cab. "What are you doing, Ivy?" he asked. "Bidding them good riddance," she said, seething. "That's the Pointer Sisters, who've taken a liking to Lindey's, *and* to me. But they're high-maintenance/ low tippers. Not really a winning combination.")

Actors **Nick Nolte** and **Judd Hirsch** (two of the stars in *Teachers*, which was being filmed at the old Central High School); musicians **k.d. lang** and **Chris Isaac**; the multiple per-sonae of Dayton-born comedian **Jonathan Winters**; socialite, movie star, favorite of paparazzi, ex-love interest of Carson Daly, and party partner of Paris Hilton, **Tara Reid**, whose movies include *American Pie* and a few disaster films—at least, at the box-office—such as *Dr. T & the Women* and *Body Shots*; Ohio-born star of stage, sitcoms, and cabaret **Kaye Ballard**; and, finally, looking very much like his father and awfully tall (that could be because he was having lunch with 15 elementary-age black girls from Columbus area schools), **Robert Kennedy, Jr**.

Jon

Bon Jovi ("This was in his dark days," recalls Chef Gretchen, "*after* the time he was really, really popular, but *before* the time he became really, really popular again. He was most gracious and kind, sitting in the front room, rather than being tucked into some private space."); cult-film director **John Waters**; **Jenny Craig** (she sensibly ordered our house salad, a single crab cake, and steamed vegetables); **General McCaffrey**; Margaritaville's own **Jimmy Buffett**; mega-superstar **Dame Edna Everage** (a.k.a. Barry Humphries); Ohio senator and our favorite astronaut of all time, **John Glenn**; and the lovely golden girl, Maude herself, **Bea Arthur**.

Richard

Karn, from the cast of Tim Allen's *Home Improvement*, now host of *Family Feud*; the inimitable **Phyllis Diller**; native son and consummate singer/pianist **Michael Feinstein**; conceptual artist Joseph Kosuth; Watergate's second-to-plead-guilty, **Jeb Stuart Magruder**; **Stephen Birmingham**, the chronicler of the upper classes and author of books such as *Our Crowd* and *The Grandees*; **Spike Lee** (if he ever comes to your place, remember to hold the bacon on his club sandwich; we forgot); and **Tina Louise** (yes, Ginger Grant from *Gilligan's Island*). (Over the years, we've also enjoyed the subtly evolving presence of one other guest from that television series: a gentleman the staff affectionately called "Lovey Howell," Mr. Howell's glamorous wife. He would request a four-top for himself and three friends who would never show up, order one tournedos and a house salad, and sit for the entire Jazz Night. While we've had many makeovers and transformations at Lindey's, Lovey is still the only regular who, over a period of a couple years, actually changed sexes while continuing to enjoy almost-weekly meals in Lindey's main dining room.

Paris *Review* editor **George Plimpton**; **Rob Schneider**, from the *Saturday Night Live* cast; **John Scali**, the ABC news man, ambassador to the UN, foreign affairs advisor to Nixon, and the man often credited for a crucial intervention in the Cuban Missile Crisis; **Maureen McCormick**, best-known as Marcia Brady; music icon **Neil Diamond**; **Bob Vila**, in Columbus to shoot a Sears commercial and eat "at one of his favorite restaurants," according to a letter we received from the Chamber of Commerce; **Hanford Dickson**, the original "dog" of the Cleveland Browns; and **David Faustino** known as Bud(rick) Franklin Bundy in the TV series *Married...with Children*, or, in his other career as rapper, "D" Lil' (David is 5'3"), whose best known song may be "I Told Ya," released in 1992, just about the time of his visit to Lindey's.

Rock legend **Eric Clapton**; **Lee Grant**, the actress whose career was halted for over a decade because of McCarthy blacklisting; song-and-dance man **Ben Vereen**; **Tim Conway** and **Harvey Korman** of *Carol Burnett Show* fame; **Emeril Lagasse**, who knew our manager Ross Hall (originally from Commander's Palace), and who joined us for a book party where he signed more books than at any other city on his tour; and two World Championship Wrestling superstars, **Billy Kidman** and **Ray Mysterio Jr.**, in town to defend their tag-team title and to enjoy a meal at Lindey's on Ted Turner's TBS credit card.

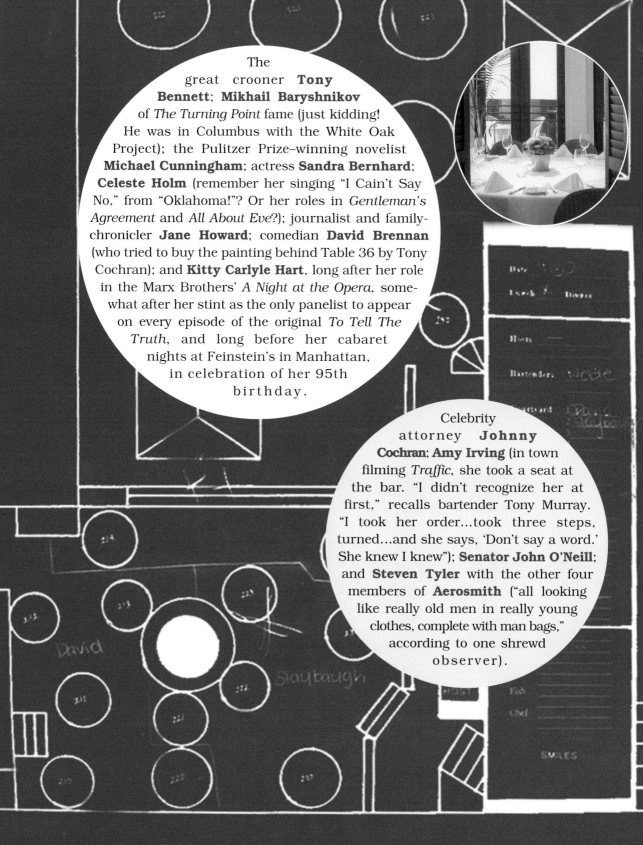

The great crooner **Tony Bennett**; Mikhail Baryshnikov of *The Turning Point* fame (just kidding! He was in Columbus with the White Oak Project); the Pulitzer Prize–winning novelist **Michael Cunningham**; actress **Sandra Bernhard**; **Celeste Holm** (remember her singing "I Cain't Say No," from "Oklahoma!"? Or her roles in *Gentleman's Agreement* and *All About Eve*?); journalist and family-chronicler **Jane Howard**; comedian **David Brennan** (who tried to buy the painting behind Table 36 by Tony Cochran); and **Kitty Carlyle Hart**, long after her role in the Marx Brothers' *A Night at the Opera*, somewhat after her stint as the only panelist to appear on every episode of the original *To Tell The Truth*, and long before her cabaret nights at Feinstein's in Manhattan, in celebration of her 95th birthday.

Celebrity attorney **Johnny Cochran**; **Amy Irving** (in town filming *Traffic*, she took a seat at the bar. "I didn't recognize her at first," recalls bartender Tony Murray. "I took her order...took three steps, turned...and she says, 'Don't say a word.' She knew I knew"); **Senator John O'Neill**; and **Steven Tyler** with the other four members of **Aerosmith** ("all looking like really old men in really young clothes, complete with man bags," according to one shrewd observer).

Mariette Hartley is an actress with innumerable film and television roles (well, they're numerable, but we're too lazy to count them), yet many of us recognized her when she came for dinner because of her Polaroid commercials with James Garner. Others knew her work as an advocate for suicide prevention, and still others remembered her from the 1978 made-for-television movie *The Incredible Hulk: Married*, for which she received an Emmy for her role as Caroline Fields, the doctor to whom David Banner comes in hopes of a cure and ends up falling in love with. (This was *not* her first time on the set with nonhumans. In a 1966 episode of *Star Trek*, censors prohibited Gene Roddenberry from showing her bellybutton. But four years later, the director got even: in his movie *Genesis II*, he had Mariette reveal her *two* bellybuttons.) (Our attorney has asked that we note that neither the subject nor her blouse came up during her visit to Lindey's. Why we are even mentioning this here confounds him entirely.)

One evening, bartender Tony Murray remembers a few gentlemen coming into the bar together, one of whom looked familiar in some way. After a good pause, Tony asked, "Are you gentlemen musicians?" They shook their heads no, Tony served them a round of drinks, and when they stood to go to their table, Tony took the extended credit card. "And I looked at the name, as I always do, so I could say *Thank you, Mr. So-and-So*, when I return the credit slip. And then I saw the card read **Branford Marsalis**! So I turned around laughing, and he said, 'I got you, didn't I?' 'Got me good,' I told him. We had a good laugh."

Each year that the Schwarzenegger Classic descends upon Columbus, **Arnold** sends his advance team. They scout out the restaurant, make reservations for close to two dozen huge men (no crowding body builders around a small table), and then, the day of the meal, it's the most amusing scene: our thin-legged Bentwood chairs suddenly look as if we'd borrowed them from Kiddie Corral Preschool, what with the two dozen bodybuilders having a tea party around our tables. Alas, Arnold never ends up at the table. As you might guess, Lindey's beef is the entrée of choice for the beefcakes.

In February of 1999, the celebrity skaters from *Celebrities on Ice* joined us at Lindey's: chef Matt Harding remembers **Michelle Kwan** in particular, but the large table was filled her fellow skaters: **Oksana Baiul**, **Nancy Kerrigan**, **Dorothy Hamill**—a who's who of contemporary female skating. "Yeah, it looked like a fourth-grade field trip," the chef remembers. "They were all so petite!"

Chef Gretchen Eiselt recalls another celebrity, who apparently arrived long after she and the party guests had left. "We often catered events at a couple's home on Schiller Park.

They had what we'd call a big mansion in Columbus terms. They were lovely, very world-ly, and eager to have us come over to prepare food. The first order of business was to get the wife tipsy (prompt service is our specialty), and then we'd have a perfect evening. She never treated us like servants. She appreciated food and the people preparing it. One evening, **Luciano Pavarotti** was to be her guest for a big benefit, and Lindey's had prepared a huge traditional Italian meal in his honor. All the guests, who had donated something shy of a small fortune, were having cocktails. "He should be here any minute," the wife would chirp. And then, during appetizers, she'd say, "Oh, that was him on the phone, he's just running late." And then, at dinner: "I can't imagine what's keeping him." Finally, at dessert: "Hasn't the food just been marvelous?" After we left, the great tenor arrived, apparently, but we never saw him, and who knows how many guests stayed that long. Shortly after that, the couple moved to Long Island.

A server named **Bobby:** I had an eight-top one night, and I'm taking drink orders. I'm eight inches from this man's face, and I look up to see that it's Lance Cumson! *Lance Cumson*, the playboy from *Falcon Crest*, which I *only watched every single week*. And I had such a crush on him at the time. And, at the time, I believe he was only on wife number three. Anyway, I took two seconds to pull myself together, take his order, and get through the evening. But I was so nervous—the very idea that I was waiting on the man who would go on to star in *Snake Eater*, *Snake Eater II*, and *Snake Eater III*, plus 50 other movies I'd never ever see.

But not everyone at Lindey's recognized **Lorenzo Lamas**, the actor who played Lance Cumson. Later that same evening, some servers and their friends were heading out to another bar for a drink toward the end of the night.

Server **Collin Smith:** I'd had the night off, so when I arrived at Lindey's I see this handsome, tall, well-dressed man standing at the host stand. He reaches out his hand as I walk in.
"Well, hello, how are you?" he says as we shake. And I'm thinking, *How can I not know we have a new manager?*
Later, when I join my friends at their table, I find out that the man is Lorenzo Lamas, son of Fernando "you rook mahvelous" Lamas and movie star Arlene Dahl. A renowned martial artist, actor, and womanizer in his own right, Lorenzo was just goofing around on his way out of Lindey's.
How do I find this out? A certain colleague had been watching Mr. Lamas rather closely, and as soon as the actor had finished his drink and left his table, my colleague darted over to grab the garnish from Lorenzo's drink: a toothpick with an olive. Now it was resting inside the cellophane cigarette packet on my friend's table. "I just wanted it."

Sue: Linda Dano, star of the soap operas *One Life to Live, General Hospital, Port Charles, As the World Turns*, and host of her own talk show, not only came to Lindey's for lunch, but brought her entire crew. I had never heard of her, having never been home during the day to watch television, but they came and filmed me all around the restaurant, shot lots of footage, and asked all kinds of questions. We treated everyone to lunch and I waited to hear from them—supposedly, I was to go to New York and appear on her show—but we never heard back. That's show biz. And, meanwhile, we were busy doing restaurant biz.

Agent and German Village resident **Tica Mitchell:** One of my clients, **Michael Roll**, a pianist, is married to another very well-known pianist in Europe, **Juliana Markova**, from Bulgaria. She was in Columbus as a soloist with the symphony. My late husband Bill and I took them to dinner at Lindey's on the very day that the Bulgarian government fell. Juliana had lived her entire life absolutely petrified. She thought there would be spies under the bed or in the shower. She was always searching for hidden microphones. And early on at dinner, I'd asked what her reaction was to the news of the Bulgarian dictator being deposed. Well, Juliana had no idea what I was talking about. She hadn't heard. She had spent her day shopping at City Center after completing her rehearsals, and had no clue that the Berlin Wall had fallen. You can't begin to imagine—I still can't!—what it must have been like to be sitting one night at dinner, in Lindey's, in Columbus, Ohio, and realize that your entire world, all the fear and nightmares and political tension, has been changed, cleared away like the dirty dishes. Amazing.

Ric Wanetik: While at Lazarus, I planned a series of events as part of "Inspiration Italy," a special series we hosted at the store. **Gina Lollobrigida** came as the honorary hostess of the events, and we also brought over a team of **Genovese Flag Throwers**: young 20-year-old guys who'd probably never been out of the country before. For each of five or six days, they performed on the statehouse lawn across from Lazarus, twirling and hurling these heavy flagged staffs in the air—they even performed at halftime during an OSU football game. *Onstage*, they were these great, athletic, symbols of Italy. *Offstage?* One evening—obviously I was not thinking clearly—I took the dozen men to dinner at Lindey's. They didn't know a word of English. I didn't really know a word of Italian. During the course of dinner, they got smashing drunk, completely rowdy and out of control...and all I remember is passing Sue on the way out the door. "Whatever it is," I said, "just bill me."

Doc Severinsen joined us one evening. "Do you have root beer?" the great bandleader asked Tony, who recognized him immediately. (Could it have been the flashy shirt and leisure suit? Tony couldn't recall.) We didn't carry root beer at the time, but Tony said,

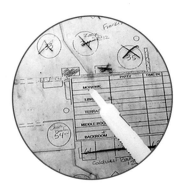

"Absolutely." He ducked under the bar, ran across the street to the pizza parlor, grabbed a few bottles of root beer, skedaddled in the back door, and appeared behind the bar with a tall foamy glass of root beer and a calm smile.

Apparently, **Jim Nabors** joined us for dinner at Table 31 one evening, where several neighboring tables remarked on his surprisingly low and very un–Gomer Pyle–like voice. Another night he joined many of the regulars at the bar—Tony and Raymond, Stephanie and Michael Ford, Mark Rinker, David Wirthman, and Harold Kull for a night of singing show tunes a cappella well past closing time.

Dick Neustadt: As you go into the new section, there's a four-top table right there. I was having lunch with Bob Shamansky, who was serving in Congress at the time. Sue stopped by to say hello, and motioned to the far corner, near the entrance to the kitchen, where three young girls were having lunch with one older gentleman. "My daughter Trish just graduated from Ohio Wesleyan, and that's her, sitting with her roommate Katie and Katie's father." So we look over, and it's **William H. Webster**, a distinguished judge who served a full 10-year term as Director of the FBI from 1978 to 1987. So suddenly we look around, and we see three or four large, suited guys from the agency, standing out like sore thumbs. The dining room seemed like a particularly safe place that day.

In June of 1987, Lindey's was graced by none other than London fashion icon **Zandra Rhodes**, in town for a retrospective exhibition of her textiles and garments. The designer, along with a bevy of fashion models from a show of wearable art at the Cultural Arts Center, joined us at Lindey's, although no one seems to remember anyone eating anything.

Tica Mitchell: I brought jazz singer **Cleo Laine** and her husband, the bandleader **John Dankworth** to Lindey's, and two fellas (two of Lindey's embedded drunks) came by the table, and one gentlemen, who thought he knew Cleo, leaned over and planted a big smacker right on her lips. Now Cleo is British by way of Jamaica, and has all the proper sensibilities of a woman of a certain class. Well, she simply froze on the spot, mortified. Actually, the whole table froze. And her greeter didn't even know what he'd done. Thankfully, the moment passed, the fellas moved onto another table, and everyone enjoyed their dinner. "Of all people to do that to, *it had to be Cleo!*" my husband railed, when we got home.

Sue: When **Robert Goulet** came into the restaurant, fresh from performing in *Anne of a Thousand Days*, I recognized him and immediately asked him how he was, since his recent prostate surgery had made him something of a spokesman for early detection. I told him my brother was recently diagnosed with the disease, and that we were very close. He could tell how concerned I was, invited me to sit with him, and told me what we might expect. He even made me laugh describing how, shortly after his surgery, he was to appear in *Camelot*, which required that he wear tights, while wearing that little catheter bag strapped on his thigh. I felt much relieved talking to him, and years and years later, I still get holiday cards from Robert and his wife Vera.

Appearing in the touring company of *The Best Little Whorehouse in Texas*, Swedish-born actress **Ann-Margret** called one evening to see if we'd be open late the next evening for dinner. Tony Murray answered, saying he'd stick around so she could come in and eat something. "She arrived late the next night, sat at the bar, and we had the nicest conversation," Tony remembers. "She even returned the following night for dinner as well, and sadly, we toasted the passing of her dear friend Walter Matthau. It was July 1, 2000."

From the **Machine Crusade Tour** Weblog: Week 3: Sunday, September 23, 2003:

> *"Working from files left by his father, Brian Herbert and bestselling novelist Kevin J. Anderson collaborated on a new set of* Dune *novels, prequels to the classic* Dune *novels—where we step onto planet Arrakis decades before* Dune's *hero, Paul Atreides, walks its sands. While Kevin is immersed in a smorgasbord of remembered and current science fiction projects, Brian and Jan go to nearby German Village and enjoy the finest meal of the entire tour at Lindey's, a European-style restaurant. The waiting staff, including Becca and Jesse, are enthusiastic and very attentive, even before they learn that Brian and Jan are on a book tour. When they both say that they are* Dune *fans, Brian gives them signed memorabilia...."*

Brian: "When I get into a town, I always ask at the hotel what's the best restaurant around: a real place, with real food. Lindey's was the recommendation. The place has the feeling of other cities: cosmopolitan, full of life."

One More Tiny Story (by Mike Harden)

It was close to 10 years ago that beloved local columnist Mike Harden paid some small tribute to one of Lindey's most *irregular* patrons, **Tiny Tim**. While we've been lucky to welcome a dizzying variety of the odd and outlandish over 25 years, Mr. Tim, as Mr. Harden recounts here, remains among our most renowned. Here's an excerpt from Mike's *Columbus Dispatch* column of December 4, 1996.

Several years ago, when Tiny Tim turned 55, I met him for lunch at Lindey's.

It takes a lot to turn the heads of the jaded sophisticates who frequent that German Village restaurant, but Tiny Tim did.

He strolled in wearing a swallow-tailed tuxedo jacket whose pattern can be described only as bad Depression-era linoleum.

He looked like an overfed toucan who had been dressed by Ray Charles.

Tiny Tim has come to town at the behest of state Senate candidate Ron Shoemaker, a Fairfield County Republican who apparently thought he could win a lot of down-home votes by dragging Tiny Tim along on the campaign trail. Strumming on his ukulele, the trilling falsetto songbird crooned:

> Ron Shoemaker, the working man's friend
> On Ron Shoemaker you can depend
> New day's comin' when Shoemaker wins
> There's a new day comin' soon.

Shoemaker got about as close to the Ohio Senate as the song did to the *Billboard* Hot 100. As long as Tiny Tim got his check, I don't suppose he cared. At Lindey's, he sipped his beer through a pair of cocktail straws.

"You never know what people's mouths are going through," he was known to say.

He had a strange habit of breaking into song in the middle of interview questions, an inclination that drew amused glances from the Lindey's crowd.

Out of nowhere, thunderstruck by the epiphanic recollection of a snatch of lyric from a failed 1920s Broadway musical, he would suddenly begin warbling. It sounded like a water buffalo floating an air biscuit through a birdcall...

Everybody Is a Star

Guests have also sighted a broad range of celebrities that, shall we say, remain "unconfirmed," since many occurred during Halloween, and many more took place not during Halloween. Oddly enough, Lindey's has employed a fair share of gentlemen who, for sheer entertainment purposes, enjoy appearing as celebrated women, legendary chanteuses, and even historic mountain ranges. Over the years, guests have seen **Carmelita Tropicana** (Carmen Miranda's younger sister); **Wilson Phillips**; **Mount Rushmore** (Allen with two additional servers joined at his hip); **Baby M**; **a pair of genies** (servers Danny and Kip, charmingly dressed in flowing veils and sheer pajama pants, and apparently quite distracting to a table of macho dudes at Table 35 who tried to get them to come over and grant them a few wishes over cocktails); and a **trio of cowgirls** (Kip, Allen, and Chickie in full cowgirl regalia, firing cap guns and riding stick horses through the dining room, around the kitchen, and back outside, shooting all the patrons).

Mark Rinker: At Halloween, we'd all stop off at Lindey's to reveal our costumes before the Barnes's annual party, and give the tourists further reason to think German Village a coven of crazies and queers, and then we'd parade down to the Barnes's house for the actual party. And often, after the party, we'd parade back to Lindey's for a nightcap.

Every year was a different theme, and the costumes were unbelievable. One year, Stephanie Ford and I came as Bonnie and Clyde (she was a very menacing Clyde and I was a very convincing Bonnie). Another year I came as Prince Charles and Jan Barnes came as my Folies Bergère escort. And yet another time, two gentleman and myself arrived as wayward nuns, in habits and red stiletto heels, and each smoking a cigar. Our first stop that

Twentieth Anniversary Ad-ditional Fun

20-Year-Olds Do It Better. / Lindey's is 20. Come join the party.

Young Enough to Get It. Old Enough to Get It Right. / Lindey's is 20. Come join the party.

Some Things Get Better With Age. Other Just Kick Ass From the Start. / Lindey's is 20. Come join the party.

Lindey's at Polaris. / The most convincing pro-cloning argument to date.

It's Martini Night at Lindey's. / Pace yourself.

Nice Brass. / Thursday is Jazz Night.

The Party Room at Lindey's. / For you and 7 to 150 of your coolest friends.

Please Compliment the Food Quietly. Our Musicians Are Starving. / It's Lindey's Starving Musician's Night.

They Seem to Play Better When They're Hungry. / It's Lindey's Starving Musician's Night.

Try to Keep Your Mmmmm's to a Minimum. / It's Lindey's Starving Musician's Night.

Halloween was the Beck Tavern, where we took a seat in the front window only to find that the window had been slightly ajar. It swung open and tumbled two of us out into the street. Brushing off our habits and our dignity, we proceeded to Lindey's where we blessed various friends and diners from our positions at the bar.

Tica Mitchell: One year, the Barnes's Halloween theme was "Fairy Tales," and my husband and I came as "fairy" and "tales." We rented a tutu for Bill, who wore a halo of flowers and nylon tights, and I rented a tuxedo with tails, and made a wrap around of various animal tails—anything resembling a store-bought fur. And we won first prize, even though one gentleman did come as the "Emperor's New Clothes," wearing absolutely nothing.

Above, from left: **Bonnie and Clyde** *(Mark Rinker and Stephanie Ford);* **Mae West** *(Mary Marsh);* **Scarlett O'Hara** *(Terri Dickie); at left:* **Jean Harlow** *(Janice Barnes); and below from left:* **Wonder Woman** *(Mary Marsh);* **Uncle Fester and Morticia** *(Gary Ross and Janice Barnes);* **cast member from Cats** *(Harlan Green).*

ON THE HOUSE

· ·

THE BAR AS DMZ

KEEPING TABS

BAR TENDENCIES AT LINDEY'S

THE BAR AT LINDEY'S—all of 12 stools and 6 deuces—has been the setting for many of our most unabashed moments. There was the woman who dumped our rather enormous coffee fudge sundae on a man who persisted in blowing cigar smoke in her direction. There were nights of dancing on the bar. There was the guest falling asleep at the bar with a little sign propped between his hands saying "Help me," compliments of friends who had gone on to another party but couldn't resist sending someone back to Lindey's every half an hour to see if their friend was still snoozing.

Server **Abby Pemberton:** I used to live a couple blocks from Lindey's. One summer night, a weeknight, no one was going out after work, so I went home. My bedroom window opened onto Fourth Street, and I could hear a bunch of laughter; somehow I just knew it was coming from Lindey's. It turns out that 15 minutes after I'd left, Nicole, Bob, Collin, and Eddie, who were the last ones there, had one guest, Mark, who'd had been encouraged to go home a few times, but ended up passing out at the bar. So the four of them picked up the barstool and carried him out, still sitting in the chair, snoozing away, and then locked the restaurant on their way out. "You just left him there on a tall stool, sleeping, drunk, four feet above a brick sidewalk? What if he wakes up and leans over?"

But my question was never answered; the next night, Mark was at the bar, ready for another round.

Yes, the Lindey's bar is a very comfortable place, in no small part because many of the bartenders have spent 7 or 12 or 16 years in that narrow, slippery, miracle .0004 mile.

General manager **Ian Brown:** You don't even have to know Tony to understand how he can make any stranger feel like an old friend at Lindey's. He's at one end of the crowded bar and sees four women—let's say they're just past middle-age—settle into a space on the opposite end. As he's walking over to take their drink order, he's holding conversations with at least two other parties, pausing to light someone's cigarette, grabbing the draft beer he'd been pouring, putting a fresh napkin underneath a sweating glass, reaching to shake hands goodbye with a guest, laughing, and, arriving in front of the new guests, turning his head at the last second, saying in his warm, baritone voice: "Now, what are you birds drinking tonight?"

Here's a range of memorable moments to toast this, our 25th year.

Your Place IS Mine

We'll always remember Neil Schultz, who thought of the bar at Lindey's as his own. The self proclaimed "King of Lindey's" for the last 10 years of his life, he was the sort of fellow you'd either want to sit next to or avoid at all costs. He tossed ashtrays to get a bartender's attention, and, at least one of the seven nights a week that he'd join us, Neil would slip behind the bar in his double-breasted suit to serve drinks. He'd get tired of waiting. Or tired of sitting on the other side of the bar. Sometimes bartender Tony Murray would tie his apron under Neil's arms (which gave him an even shorter appearance).

Usually, this would be quite late at night. He'd come over to the other people at the bar and ask, "What are you drinking?" and you could say a margarita or a Manhattan, and so Neil would make you a martini, since that was really all he knew how to make. All he really wanted to do was walk back and forth, shooting the breeze. He told Sue on a number of occasions that she should do a charity benefit and auction off a night as maître d' at Lindey's: "I'd bid a small fortune."

Other nights, Neil would come in, the bar would be packed, and he'd stand up on the barstool, and shout, *Who the fuck are these people and what are they doing in my restaurant?*" It was all in good fun, even if we found it difficult to explain his definition of "good fun" to some of the less familiar guests.

Charge!

Tommy Anderson: This one guy came in pretty frequently for about six months. He started a house charge, and he'd have a big time, buying drinks for everyone, Dom Perignon, the best of anything. He did some kind of business in town. All I remember is that he was a very big tipper and put everything on his house charge. At first, I gather, the guy was paying his monthly tabs, and then the tab got larger, and he floated it a couple months. Then his bill was close to $10,000, and I believe he just skipped town, never to be seen again. Skipped out on everything. Sure, it was great for us bartenders while it lasted, but...

Super Silly Server

How it happened, we don't know, but at one point, we had two ladies working at the host stand who weren't always generous. They could be very supercilious to people. (We're trying

"At the bar there were some guys, however impossible, that you put up with because they were...well...they were human."

—bartender Jim "Finn" Finnerty

to be polite; they were Hollywood überbitches.) But one hostess—we'll call her Misty, just to be snooty—decided that she needed to make more than hostess wages. For a few nights, she worked as a cocktailer, helping to serve the small tables that border the bar. It's an incredibly hard job, since the space between the bar chairs and the tables is typically packed with people. So Misty coped by taking drink orders both from the guests and from herself. In other words, by the middle of the shift, she fell out of control, and Jimmy, another server, found her under the coats in the staff room/coat check. But being a true team player, he went from Table 11 to Table 17, saying, "I'm sorry. Your server has had some female problems," patting his tummy in a sympathetic way. "So we don't know what you ordered. But you tell me again, I'll get whatever it was right out to you."

Unhappy Hour

Eddie Meecham: I had a customer sitting at the bar, who told me three times as the end of happy hour approached that he was going to want another drink before happy hour ended. I told him that was fine, but, at the time, you couldn't have two drinks on the bar at once—a state law—but I assured him that I'd take care of him. So five minutes until 7:00, the end of happy hour, I ask him if he wants another drink. And then he says no. Then ten minutes pass, so it's now five after happy hour's ended, and he says, "I'll go ahead and have that other drink now."

"I just asked you if wanted a drink, and you said no, and now happy hour's over, so if you—"

"Well, that's not what I meant," he tells me.

"I'm sorry, as I explained, I can't give you two drinks at once, and you said no—"

I try to explain. But he's run up to the front desk and is recounting the whole thing to the host there, and then he comes back, and now he's steaming, and he's looking and looking at me figuring out what he's going to do.

"Sir, I'm sorry, but..."

"I'm going to have your job!" he barks at me.

So once again I recount how I'd asked him, just as he requested, and how he'd declined.

"I want to talk to the owner," he demands. So in a moment, Rick Doody comes over, acting on Sue's behalf. And he explains the state's drinking policy about two-for-one drinks, just as I did, "I'm sorry, but these are the rules we have to follow."

The guy asks for his tab, pays with his credit card, and writes in "0" for the tip. He also puts a dime on the slip and waits for me to come back. "That dime's your tip," he tells me. "Why don't you go out and buy yourself a new sport coat."

I throw his dime in the air, and even manage to catch it. "You know, I bet I can get one just like yours."

Oh yes, this totally infuriates the guy. He runs back to the host stand, demands to see Sue, then repeats the whole story for a third time to her.

And Sue backs me up, telling him as everyone else had that his happy hour is clearly over.

The funniest thing: he came back in two months later to apologize. Lindey's was the kind of place where you wanted to be welcome among the attractive, well-to-do, hip people.

Got a Match?

Nicole Neamand: In 1988, I was a cocktail waitress at Lindey's—my very first job—and I worked the copper-topped tables, and began to learn the regular customers and what each drank. In one group of people who had become familiar to me—Sally Levy, Diana Block, and Jerry Simmons—appeared a man named Mel Kent. He ordered one scotch. He was very polite, and he always looked like he was having fun. After waiting on him a few times, I went up to Eddie, the bartender. "You know this guy, Mel? I really like him. I think I should fix him up with my mother." And Eddie replied, *absolutely.* (If he hadn't liked Mel, there was no way I could have introduced him to my mother. Eddie just knew people.)

So just as Mel's group was leaving, I asked him if I could talk to him a moment.

"Is there a problem with my tab?" he asked.

"No, no, I just noticed that you haven't had a date lately."

"Hey, thanks, lady."

"Well, I think I have the perfect woman for you."

He gave me a big hug. "Who is it?"

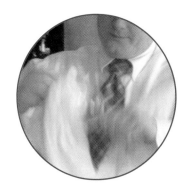

"Going from the bar to the bathroom, he looked as if he were on the QE II at high seas."

Joe Goetz, referring to a particular regular guest

I should say I was almost 21 at the time. (I may have lied on my application. I definitely lied, now that I think of it, because I celebrated my 21st a few months later at the Hi-Beck Tavern, and Eddie overheard me telling the bartender it was my 21st.)

"My mother."

I could see he was shocked. "How old is she?"

"Thirty-nine."

"Who in the hell has a 39-year-old mother? Give me her number."

So I did. But then I had an even harder conversation.

"Mom, just hear me out. I gave out your number to a customer last night."

"You did what?!"

"He's a good tipper. He's not a big drinker. He's Jewish. He's nice. Just go out to lunch with him."

So they went to lunch, while I worried, *What if he doesn't like her? What if he ends up rejecting my mother?*

The next time Mel and his friends came into Lindey's, I was really nervous going up to the table. But first thing, Jerry Simmons says, "Hey, Nicole, do you have another mother?"

And they got married at Mel's house in German Village, and then celebrated with a small dinner party at Table 34 here at Lindey's.

Powerbar

Eddie Meecham: There's always a little fight for power at the bar. The waiters need their drinks now: they have customers waiting. And customers who feel they've had to wait too much give worse tips. But you, the bartenders, are also making tips from your own bar customers, so you can't have them wait too long for the same reasons. But the waiters tip out at the end of the night, and even though it's supposed to be a straight percentage of their total, you'll get more if you were able to turn their drinks around quickly. So there's *that* tension.

But I'll tell you: the work side of Lindey's was all professional, and then the post-work side was all party: the Hi-Beck, Victory's, the original Short North Tavern, and clubs like the Eagle, Garage, or Wall Street. We were like an extended family. You went to work so you could make money to go and spend it with these same people after work.

Remember Me?

One uncanny ability that Lindey's bartenders seem to possess is a variation of the talent to remember names and faces. Here's how it goes:

Bartender **Jim Finnerty:** One guy came in on a Thursday, at the end of the bar, so I say, what can I get you?

"Chivas on the rocks with a twist,"

He nursed his drink for about 30 minutes. I asked him if he'd care for another, he declined, paid the check, and left shortly thereafter.

So about a month later, the man came back in, sat down at the bar, and I set down a Chivas on the rocks with a twist in front of him.

"What? Who bought me a drink?" he asks me.

"Isn't this what you drink?"

"But how did you know that?"

"You were in here a month ago, and I remember, you sat about where you are now, and we talked a little bit."

Once every couple of weeks, he'd come back to Lindey's. I'd made us a friend.

And that happened time and time again.

Serve Yourself

One other moment that, technically, did not happen at our bar—at least initially—gives the term "being served" a whole new twist.

Jimmy Strausbaugh: One weekend night, I was the on-call waiter, and when I called in, Ross said they didn't need me, so I had the night off. But then the restaurant had a last-minute party booking and they needed someone to work it. As I mentioned, this was now my night off, and I was at David's on Main, having a few drinks with friends. And I get a call: it's Ross, who obviously had been telephoning all the obvious places in town.

"Jimmy, I need you to work tonight."

"Hey, Ross, too late. I've been drinking for two hours. I'm drunk."

"But I need you, get in here."

I continued to protest. I'm willing to work hard and also play hard, but I don't mix the two. "Ross, I won't even be able to count money!"

But he insists. So I say, "Look, the only way I'm going to even get through the night is if you keep me drunk."

I arrive and the four tables in the back are already seated, waiting for me. I was so pickled. "Hello, folks, I'm not even going to pretend with you: I was on call tonight, then I was told I had the night off, and then the manager called and found me at a bar and said he needed me. So I'm liquored, and I'm not going to pretend otherwise."

Maybe they were surprised or just hungry, but they all just smiled and I took their drink orders and we were underway. Other waiters carried all the dinner trays, I believe. And I think I had a couple of the guests help themselves to more bread, and get the coffee pot for refills. We were in it together. And once an hour, Ross came over and set down a vodka and cranberry for me, and I'd toast my party.

The party and I had a great time together. They understood, and left me not a small tip for giving up my night off for them.

Looking back, I just can't imagine that Lindey's would solve a staffing shortage in quite the same way ever again.

After Dinner Selection

Chef **Matt Harding:** One New Year's Eve, the entire dining room is toasting one another, hugging, dancing—having a great time. We know how to put on a boisterous party, with a lot of guests who'd never dream of welcoming the new year anywhere else. One especially happy reveler is Andrea Cambern, who sees me by the kitchen, and calls to me: "Chef, come over, join us!"

I go over, and she's smoking a cigar—we used to offer a selection of great cigars for a time at the bar.

"Here, try this," Andrea says, handing me the cigar and pointing to a glass of brandy, "dip it in brandy first." So I go to dip the cigar into the glass. "No, not the lit end, the other end!" she says, jabbing me.

How was I supposed to know? Brandy already sort of tastes like an ashtray to me. Sort of embarrassing, I suppose, but who's going to remember anything from that night?

Finn

Jim Finnerty: I worked at Lindey's until 1985—four of the best years of my life. Eddie Meecham started soon after me out on the patio, and Tommy Anderson, who first worked as a busser, soon joined me behind the copper bar.

Folks at the bar would often ask me, "Finn, how did you get your name?" (Almost no one called me "Jim.") And even though I felt a certain twinge of guilt, this is how I would always conduct the rest of the conversation:

"I can't tell you," I'd reply.

"Well, why not?"

"Because you'll get mad at me."

"No, I won't, just tell me."

"Okay, well, the staff at the last place I bartended gave me the name because I've never had anyone leave me less than a fin."

"Oh, yeah? Tonight might be your first!" they'd reply. But by the end of the night...?

I've been out of the business for years now, but folks still call me "Finn."

Ballooning

When Ross started brunches on Sunday, we couldn't serve liquor until 1 p.m. But we opened at 11, and many guests waited as long as possible before coming in, and then hoped that someone wasn't watching the clock when they ordered a mimosa or a Bloody Mary.

Many people considered Ross family, and vice versa. One Sunday, a couple called in to ask about brunch, and despite the liquor license problem, Ross insisted they come in immediately—it was 11:30 or so—because he had just squeezed some "special orange juice" just for them. They did come in and brunch was lovely, as ever. They were joined at an adjacent table by Skip and Cherie, who sported a leather-with-chains skirt that might have been four inches from waist to hem. ("It was Jean-Paul Gaultier," Cherie recalls.) Ross had also decided that balloons were key to a festive Sunday brunch aura, and so multicolored balloons were tied to chairs, floating along the ceiling, and gathered at the host stand.

Cherie: I decided to write a little note and attach a menu to a helium balloon: "Whoever finds this balloon, please join us for brunch at Lindey's. Our treat! Skip and Cherie." Then I added our phone number. I walked out into the intersection of Beck and Mohawk, and released the balloon into the air—

Guest **Michael M:** —with *both hands*, as I recall, so that her four-inch skirt would rise an inch or two, much to the delight of the straight members of the community.

Cherie: Week after week, I "sent out" our "invitation," but no one ever found the menu and called. You see, this was part of my Save the Balloon Campaign, because all the brunch balloons had to be out by dinner. "You can't keep them captive. You can't pop them. We had to save the balloons! They have to go free!"

But there were problems with releasing several dozen helium-filled balloons in German Village. The neighbors complained about balloons getting tangled in their trees and in the electrical lines.

One Sunday, Cherie and a friend went out with something close to 60 balloons, and a police car whizzed by.

Cherie: So my friend Father P.J. says to me, "We can't release the balloons now. That would be littering." So I say, "No, littering is when you throw something *on the ground*." And we start laughing, and then Father P.J. says, "On the count of three..." Meanwhile, Skip is watching from the curb, in case we get busted, and all of sudden—I don't know how—but all the balloons lift off, and they miss all the wires, and they're up in the sky.

Skip: So I walk over and say, "Where's our evidence? Near as I can tell, there is none."

Cherie: I half expected a police helicopter to come along and shoot them down so that there would be evidence.

OUR LI'L PLACE
IN THE HISTORY OF LIBATIONS

GRANTED, WE'VE ONLY BEEN AROUND for a quarter of a century, while cocktails have been giving happy hour its sex appeal for nearly 7,500 years. Still, we thought it might be interesting to see our place in the Big Potatory* Picture.

Not to be boorish, comprehensive, or even informative, we've picked out a few notable moments in the annals of alcohol below, in hopes that one or another might make a good conversation starter the next time you're sitting at the bar at Lindey's.

circa 5,400 B.C.E.	2137 B.C.E.	800 B.C.E.	33 A.D.
Some kind of retsina-like wine is created in the mountainous regions of Iran. It was presumably meant for drinking, though it may have been an early version of Pine-Sol, retsina's closest relative and Lindey's favorite cleaning product.	Two royal astronomers of Ancient China, Hsi and Ho, having giddily consumed too much rice wine, fail to predict the first eclipse ever recorded. They are summarily executed. (To this day, Lindey's does not serve rice wine for this very reason.)	The first wines of France are produced in the Languedoc, home of the troubadours, the poet-musicians who weave the themes of love, war, and nature into their albas, dirges, pastorals, and *jeux-partis* (songs of dispute). The seeds of Lindey's Jazz Night are planted.	Jesus turns water to wine, performing the greatest food-friendly miracle of all time.

* That's "of or related to potables and potations," not potatoes. For potatoes, see page 82.

| 300 A.D. | 1516 | 1609 | 1775 | |

Before the cultivation of yeasts, the Japanese create *Kuchikami no saké*, or "chewing-in-the-mouth sake," for which an entire village, probably no larger than our own German Village (although comprised of individuals of Asian descent), gathered together to chew rice, millet, and chestnuts and then regurgitate the slurry into large vats. Enzymes in the villagers' saliva started a fermentation process, converting starches to sugars, resulting in an alcoholic rice wine.

The Reinheitsgebot law is enacted in Germany, specifying that only malt, hops, yeast, and water can be used in the process of beer-making. Someone is surely having the dream of coming to the New World, making little brick homes in central Ohio, tapping the pure waters there for beer-making, and establishing a series of saloons, one of which will become Lindey's.

Brandy arrives! Henry Hudson shares a bottle with the native residents of an island that will one day be called "Manhattan," derived from the indigenous word *manahachtanienk*, which means "where everyone got drunk." (Google it if you don't believe us!) While inspired, in part, by restaurants on Manhattan's Upper West Side, 372 years later the Doodys choose the name "Lindey's" over "Manahachtanienk's" for their new restaurant, feeling that local color would be more appealing than accuracy.

A year before America's independence, in an era when beer is consumed by men, women, and children as a healthier alternative to water, General George Washington orders Colonial soldiers to receive four ounces of either rum or whiskey as part of their daily rations. The precedent for shift drinks at Lindey's is thus established.

How to Tie a Knot in a Cherry Stem After Drinking a Manhattan

  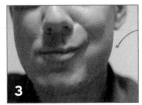 

Fig. 1 Take the cherry from the bottom of the glass. If it is not your drink, ask the drink's owner for the cherry. Do not fish out the cherry yourself. Worst case, ask the bartender for your own cherry.

Fig. 2 Holding the cherry stem, insert the fruit between the upper and lower incisors and bite down while simultaneously pulling on the cherry stem, thereby disengaging the cherry from its stem.

Fig. 3 Close the lips. Chew the fruit and swallow when the fruit is sufficiently crushed. Enjoy!

Fig. 4 Insert the cherry stem into the mouth as shown.

1776	1830	1830s	1838
A tavern keeper in New York garnishes his rum drinks with rooster feathers. The name "cocktail" is born. (His other decorations—pemmican swizzle sticks, rabbit's-foot charms, and a variety of marzipan figures inspired by Goethe's *Sorrows of Young Werther*—do not give birth to much more than nausea.)	The average American's consumption of alcohol rises to 7.1 gallons per year. That comes to more than 450 shots of booze, which is only about one of Lindey's generous ounce pours per day. (In 2005, we poured 83,599 ounces of liquor.) This is still years before the American Heart Association will claim that such imbibing has "medicinal purposes."	Louis Hoster arrives in Columbus. Having boarded a train near the ferry landing from Ellis Island, Louis disembarks at every stop in search of the perfect local water for brewing beer. He finds it at Pete's Run, one of the viaducts which conducts the local Columbus water supply. His family joins him in Columbus, and he builds his brewery right above the run. Within a few years, 85 percent of Columbus's population will be employed by the Hoster Brewing Company.	Tennessee bans alcohol, becoming the first state to which Lindey's, had it been around in 1838, would *not* have considered moving, even though Tennessee *is* the only state with four e's, plus two other double letters.

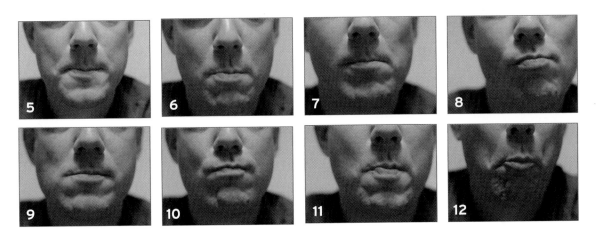

Fig. 5 through 12
Tie a knot.*

* Unfortunately, the actual tying occurs in the darkness of the mouth and is as undocu-
mentable as the Loch Ness Monster. All we can say is that there's a curling stage, an
insertion stage, and a tightening stage and that's probably everything you always wanted to
know about a bar trick but were afraid to ask.

early 1900s	1919	1921	

The Gambrinus Brewery erects the structure that will become Lindey's, a saloon at the corner of Beck and Mohawk streets called the Tide House Saloon. Shortly thereafter, the place is purchased by the King family, who decide to rename it. (Could it be that sober folks realized Columbus had no tides to speak of?) Now known as Kings Rose Garden Saloon, they enjoy a few years of prosperity before...

Prohibition begins, and Kings Rose Garden becomes a (wink, wink) hardware store. Across America, there are 1,600 breweries, each wondering what else it might do with storerooms filled with empty bottles. By 1961, only 230 will remain.

Ohio-born President Harding, who history will rank as one of America's lesser presidents, signs the anti-beer bill, closing the loophole in Prohibition that allows doctors to prescribe beer or liquor to their (wink, wink) patients. This is the same Harding whose language (he wrote his own speeches, having come to politics from journalism) the critic H.L. Mencken described as "a string of wet sponges...It drags itself out of the dark abysm of pish, and crawls insanely up the topmost pinnacle of posh. It is rumble and bumble. It is flap and doodle. It is balder and dash." (Sounds distinctly like the slurred speech of someone composing himself at the bar.)

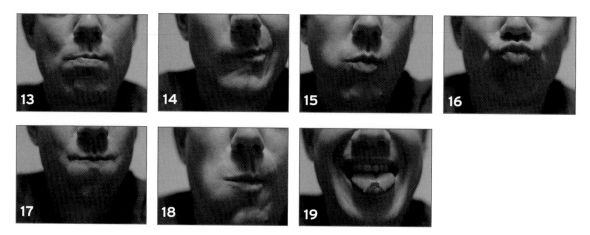

Fig. 13 through 18 Continue to tie a knot.

Fig. 19 Center the cherry stem on the tip of the tongue and open the mouth to reveal the finished knot.*

1931	1933	June 10, 1935

Rolla Harger, a professor at Indiana University, invents the Drunkometer, the first breath-testing device to measure alcohol consumption. An individual would exhale into a balloon, and the breath would be released into a liquid that would change colors according to the alcohol content of the breath. Patented in 1936, Harger's prototype inspired the Breathalyzer (1951) as well as our own PlasteredOmeter (1988): Order any drink that comes with a cocktail straw at our dimly lit bar. If, at any point, bending over to take a sip, you poke yourself in the eye or cheek, you may conclude that you've had enough.

Congress repeals the 18th amendment, which outlawed the serving of alcohol. Hardware stores become hardware stores again, and patients, patients.

Wilson and Smith establish Alcoholics Anonymous in Akron, Ohio. In other Ohio news, 200 miles away in Dayton, Lindey's founder Sue Doody is just three and a half months from celebrating her first birthday.

* **Note:** After a couple Manhattans skip steps 7 through 18 and remember: *in liquor lingua liberalis* (with booze the tongue becomes a liberal).

Photos by Darlene Snuffer. Talent: Dr. Douglas Zullo, Associate Professor of Art at Tapatio Community College. Hairstyling by Duane Ellis. Food styling by David White.

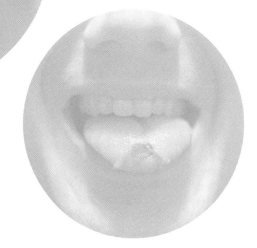

1942	1952	1963	June 7, 1981

1942

In the year that saw Bambi and Mighty Mouse launch their careers, War Ration Books issued to home-makers nationwide, and six million Victory Gardens planted, Sue begins her career in food service. With her brother Joe, she opens a lemonade stand in her front yard. After several slow days (and with only one sugar ration coupon left in her booklet), she closes her establishment and heads off to the swimming pool.

1952

The first sugar-free soft drink, No-Cal Ginger Ale, lines the shelves of America. Sue attends Ohio Wesleyan University. For her birthday in September, her parents send her a little spending money. Rather than load up with cases of the diet soda, the ever prudent co-ed gambles away her birthday money at the Little Brown Jug, the premier pacing event for three-year-old horses at the Delaware fairgrounds.

1963

The French Chef debuts on PBS; Weight Watchers is founded; self-cleaning ovens become the rage, and one of Lindey's future partners, Chris Doody, is born. His uncle, a catholic priest studying for his doctorate at King's College, returns to Ohio to baptize the child and toast him with a lovely bottle from the English college's fabulous wine cellar.

June 7, 1981

Lindey's opens, but the liquor license is held up. **Sue Doody:** A glitch in the transfer of the license from the Palmer Haus to Lindey's meant we need-ed a whole new license. Alton called in a favor with Mayor Rinehart to help us move quickly, and I remember we got finger-printed so the state could be sure we weren't con-victed felons suddenly operating a bar and pass-ing out liquor to fellow convicts! Every few years, we're still fingerprinted, just in case I become a felon or have acquired all kinds of outstanding arrest warrants.

179

mid-June, 1981   July 15, 1981   1982

The bartending staff, now complete, is composed of four women, only one of whom possesses any previous experience behind a bar.

Rick Doody: The idea behind that was to get businessmen in the bar seats, so we thought beautiful women might be the key.

Jim Finnerty is hired as head bartender, breaking the "skirt barrier" at Lindey's.

Guests Skip and Cherie receive an urgent message one evening from their answering service, relaying a message from Lindey's wine aficionado Emil Shedlock. "You've got to come in tonight. Please, just you two. I want you to have dinner with me: I have a wine…" Emil had ordered a case of Dom Perignon for a special event at the restaurant, only the supplier didn't have a full case, so the supplier substituted a couple other bottles.

Cherie: When we arrived, Emil was chilling a rare Dom Ruinart and a prewar 1930s-vintage Dom Perignon. As the monk says, it was the taste of the stars blinking coldly—simply the most spectacular champagne I've ever tasted. Emil told us, "When I saw what they'd put in to fill the carton, I ran down to Hausfrau Haven, bought whatever bottle of Dom Perignon they had to replace this incredible bottle, and immediately picked up the phone to call you."

For one **Blow Job**, which is, in essence, what's called a shooter shot: float 1/3 ounce each of these three liquors in a tall shot glass (pony glass) in this order: Kahlúa, then Bailey's Irish Cream, then vodka. Top with whipped cream. The idea is that the guest bends down to grab the glass with the lips, lifts up and swallows the drink in one gulp—the whipping cream holding back the liquid for a brief moment before it all rushes out—and then sets the glass back down, once again using only the lips.

In case you'd like to relive our foolish youth, a **Kamikaze** (to be downed in one swallow), is 2 ounces Stolichnaya vodka and 1 teaspoon Rose's lime juice, chilled in a cocktail shaker with a few ice cubes, and strained into a rocks glass.

1984

Just as Lindey's guests are being swept up in the wine craze, we also find ourselves in the decade of crazy shooters that have regrettable names such as "Surfer on Acid," "Zipperhead," and "Sex on the Beach."
Bartender **Eddie Meecham:** We went through a wave of drinks with suggestive names. The ladies liked to order them just to flirt with you or so that they could walk the drink back to the table and announce the name in a provocative manner to the gentlemen they had hopes of going home with.

Bartender **T.A. Anderson:** Ah, yes. Our crowd, especially the gay crowd, would love to call out, "Hey, Tommy, can you give me a Blow Job?" Thankfully, the novelty of that drink wore off in a few months (recipe above).

1985

Along with the craze for white zinfandel (Lindey's offered the Charles LeFranc, which moved 40,000 cases in its first year), the short-lived but plenty-potent Kamikaze era descends upon Lindey's.
Jim Finnerty: Once Jazz Night was well underway, we had Jimmy G., a patron whose son played in the original band, take over Lindey's on Thursday nights with his friends. During the evening, these guys would say "Let's meet the chief," which meant let's do a Kamikaze. So Jimmy would order a round of them, and when a server would come over to pick up drinks for a table, Jimmy G. might ask, "Have you ever met the chief?"

And the server would say, "You mean Sue, the owner?"

"No, no..." he'd reply. "I mean this!" and he'd pass over a shot so the server could partake.

I suppose we were all family then, with all the complications that love brings (recipe above).

June, 1985

The piña colada steals the show for one evening at Lindey's. Just imagine another ad we might have run in *Columbus Monthly*: "Lindey's now has a drive-through window! (At least, one person thought so: driving south on Oscar Alley, she crossed Beck Street, and barreled into Lindey's courtyard, crashing over the concrete fountain and ramming the car's bumper through the picture window, stopping just inches from the guests dining at Table 44.)" For further details, let's go to our on-site reporter (*Columbus Dispatch* columnist Mike Harden, who went undercover as a busboy to write a feature story, "Lindey's, Simply THE Place to Be." Above photo of Mike by Ken Chamberlain.)

Mike: It's inching up toward last call during my last shift out of five nights of busing tables—the zenith of my career at Lindey's—and we suddenly hear this crash that probably registered 5.5 on the Richter scale. We all rush through the front door and out into the street only to see a car smashed into the front of the building. Of course, the first thing we want to see is if anyone's hurt. There's a woman in the driver's seat and she has a pitcher of what turns out to be piña coladas between her legs. (Actually, the pitcher had probably kept her from accelerating more than she did–otherwise, she might have spilled more than her cocktails and ended up somewhere in the middle of the dining room.) She's looking up at all of us—Sue's there, as well as a couple other staff members—and she says, "You're Mike Harden! My mother is a big fan of yours." And to make her point, she proceeds to call her mother—this is well after midnight!—on one of those early cell phones that looked like a World War II field unit and made the voice on the other end of the line sound like a wasp trapped in an empty Cheerios box. So I'm trying to tell her mother that her daughter has just driven her car over a concrete fountain and into the window of a restaurant while under the influence of alcohol, while the mother, who has every reason to be concerned about her daughter on any number of levels, is saying, "I just love your writing...and my favorite column is...and where do you get all your ideas..." and on and on.

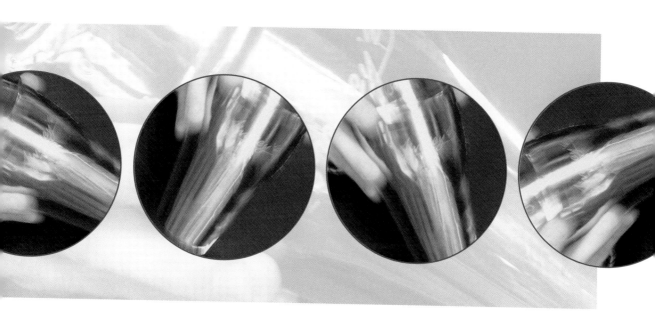

1986

America's passion for wine coolers reaches its peak, with over 122 million gallons consumed this year. Not a single ounce of which is poured at Lindey's. Instead, our wines-by-the-glass program takes off. The "Kendall Jackson chardonnay" phenomenon begins.

Wine purveyor **Dan Frey:** Columbus became the first Kendall Jackson town in the country because of Lindey's, which sold 16 or 17 cases of their chardonnay each week; at the time, no one else had that wine in the city. Sales exploded. All the other restaurants were asking for it. And it became the best-selling wine of its type in the state—and in the nation—at that time.

1988

Lindey's barters with Noni's, another local restaurant: each will host a holiday party for the other staff. At a managers' meeting a few weeks after the two parties, Sue mentions, "Noni sent me a bill for $2,000 for the bar tab from our holiday party! Could we have drunk *that much more* than their staff did at our place? *Is that possible?"* The answer was yes: Lindey's staff had much more holiday spirit! (Year-round.)

1989

Inspired by Oprah's announcement that Optifast had helped her lose some 70 pounds, various replacement meals find their way to Lindey's...and are promptly shown the way out.

Alice Mattimo: I'm bartending on a Friday afternoon in June. We had a regular lunch staff, which could serve about half the restaurant. One day, we were completely unaware that it was OSU graduation day; by noon, every table was filled, the bar was packed, and everyone was in the mood to

1990

2001

drink. So I'm cranking out drink orders at super speed, hardly looking up, just shaking, pouring, ringing in the drinks, uncorking—going nuts. And then a server brings over a packet of chocolate diet powder and says that a lady at his table needs it to be blended with water and ice. I quickly throw everything in the drink mixer, turn it on, and before I can even turn to pick up another glass, the powder thickens up so quickly that the mixer cup goes flying off the motor and this chocolate goo sprays everywhere...mostly all over me and my starched white shirt. It's cold, it's gross, but I can't even stop making drinks for a moment to go clean up!

Then I see this woman marching over to the bar from her table, and she says to me, "That's the *only* lunch I brought and *you've ruined it*."

"Ma'am," I reply, "Look at me. I assure you, I couldn't be more sorry. But if you'd like, you can wring me out into a glass."

She did not take me up on the offer.

Lindey's becomes the first restaurant in Columbus to put an end to white zinfandel. **Dan Frey:** No more. Sure, we appreciate that it welcomed new drinkers into the world of wine, but we decided to give the pink drink a rest. Meanwhile, at just about this time, wine comprised 26% of overall sales at Lindey's—the highest percentage in the city. This was, in part, because going to a varietals menu helped people understand that Montrachet, Mâcon, and Meursault were simply versions of the chardonnay they loved.

For its 20th anniversary, Lindey's pours more liquor in three hours for the thousand guests in attendance than in the prior three weeks of business.

Sue: Give people an open bar, and they drink like there's no tomorrow. Except there always is, and the next morning many of them are sure to have regrets.

2005

Along with all other restaurants in Columbus, Lindey's goes nonsmoking, losing a few people and gaining a few people in the transition. As a side benefit, servers' aprons clank less without the extra ashtrays.

Sue: But now I can't even smoke in my own restaurant.

June 15, 2006

For our silver anniversary, bartender Kurt Baughman creates a special martini that comes in a souvenir silver cocktail shaker engraved with the restaurant's name. The drink, the Socialite, inspires lots of toasting and getting toasted! Even the bartenders consider calling themselves "beverage specialists" or one of many other suggested titles: resident alconaut, swizzler, spirit savant, doctor of cocktails, and potable poobah. There will always a place for the overindulgent at Lindey's.

The Socialite

- 1 1/4 ounces vanilla vodka
- 3/4 ounce Frangelico
- 3/4 ounce triple sec
- 3/4 ounce champagne
- lemon twist, for garnish

Place the first three ingredients into a cocktail shaker filled with ice. Shake vigorously, then pour the contents into a chilled martini glass. Top with the champagne. Rub the glass rim with the lemon twist, then float it in the center of the drink.

A FEW TOASTS

FROM THE REGULARS' DRINK MENU

EVEN MORE THAN THE RECIPE for a drink, the length of a pour, or the ambience of a place, it's familiarity that makes you return, night after night, to a certain bar. Lindey's bartenders are legendary for creating that allegiance with a potent mix of generosity, jocularity, gossip, gentility, sexiness, and collegiality, with a dash or two of bitters. Remember Rodney Dangerfield's famous joke? "I said to a bartender, 'Make me a zombie.' He said, 'God beat me to it.'" That's the dash of bitters—or call it "irony" if you'd rather— that brings us all together to raise glasses in a toast, let loose with a couple of tequila shots, or settle into a long conversation and a short cry in our beers.

So while certain drinks may have come and gone, others have become as familiar as some of our longtime guests. Here's a healthy sampling of our regulars' favorites. Each recipe below will serve one, although you're welcome to put two straws in a glass and share.

The Birds' Cosmopolitan

Rhonda and Christy can be found on the two stools at the first corner of the bar, just inside the door, sipping their *Sex and the City*–style favorite, the Cosmopolitan.

Rhonda: We never drink it outside of Lindey's, but here, we don't know why, it's the perfect drink. Sometimes, the bar is crowded, and like Moses parting the Red Sea, we walk over and there are two pink martini glasses on the bar and two free stools...and it's our time to perch. The rest of the night is in Tony's hands. He refills our glasses before we can even drink the last sip. He makes sure we get something to eat. He signals the valets, just in case a drive home is in order. Once, we called Christy's sister to take us home, but she sidled up to the bar, ordered her own Cosmo from Tony, and, in short order, we were back in the same predicament.

- 1 1/2 ounces Grey Goose vodka
- 1/4 ounce triple sec
- splash of fresh cranberry juice
- 1 orange twist, for garnish

So here's Tony's secret for this, as well as all varieties of martini: "Use a cocktail shaker and fill it with small ice cubes. Small ice cubes mean lots of icy surfaces to chill the liquids. Then pour in your ingredients, and vigorously shake until you've done some real damage to the ice. When you strain the liquids into the chilled martini glass, you want ice crystals to float on the surface. It's that little slush that makes the difference."

Lindey's Dirty Martini

When FDR toasted goodbye to prohibition in 1933, he did so with a Dirty Martini, which was then enjoying its heyday during that swanky post-Depression era. Some 70 years later, we're still making heydays while the sun shines at Lindey's.

- 2 ounces Absolut vodka
- a little olive juice

Since everyone has a preferred "house" method for concocting martinis, we'll let you be in charge of the stirring and/or the shaking. But Tony can offer you one other tip (besides his first suggestion above). "All you need to know is that when most folks say they like it 'dirty,' that usually means they like it nice and dirty. I have some folks who tell me, 'Tony, you can't make it dirty enough for me,' and you know, I think some people might like a martini that's all olive juice with just a hint of vodka, the way we used to talk about vermouth."

Add a skewer of gorgonzola-stuffed olives for garnish—and that *extra* nice and dirty touch.

Tony's Famous Lemon Drop Martini, "Pucker Up"

For years, this recipe has been Tony's juicy little secret. On the occasion of our silver anniversary, we've convinced him to divulge the delicious truth. "It's an idea I 'stole' from the Ohio State Fair. I'd walk around the midway, and there were all these vendors serving lemon shake-ups for like five bucks—*five bucks* and there wasn't even any booze in them! So I thought to myself, I've got to do a version with vodka and without all that sugar.

"Now I have to give you a word of caution: this is *not* lemonade, even if it tastes that easy going down. That's why this recipe has been a secret for so long: you have to exercise some caution! I don't want to be held responsible!"

- 1 half lemon, cut into three wedges
- 2 ounces Absolut Citron Vodka
- splash of 7-Up
- 1 twist of lemon, for garnish

In a cocktail shaker filled halfway with ice, squeeze the lemons, and toss them into the shaker as well. Add the vodka and shake like there's no tomorrow: you want to release the lemon oil, shred a little of the lemon pulp, and really create a frosty liquid. Add your splash of 7-Up and pour into a chilled martini glass. Garnish with another twist of lemon.

Jim Barnes: You want German Village news? There's the *German Village Gazette*, the *German Village Society Newsletter*, and then there's Tony Murray, our favorite bartender, who actually has the real news:

"Actually T.D. and Rudy aren't coming back from their cruise on Sunday. They're stopping over in Dallas and will be back on Tuesday."

"No, no, he doesn't have cancer. All he has is an ulcer. He'll be home in a couple of days."

"No, that was *not* his sister he was here with last night."

"Yeah, lady, he really is good-looking, but trust me, it's not going to work. This is German Village, you know."

The Full Monty

A Lindey's tradition—at least it was for Monty Will—this drink is, per his request, "cheap scotch and city water." Monty ate lunch here most every day with his buddy Neil Schultz (see below). To make your own version exactly like ours, grab a highball glass, fill it with ice, and add:

- 1 1/4 ounces well scotch (if you don't have a well, well, just use any swell Scotch you have on hand)
- splash of water

Richard's Golden Margarita

Lindey's has never considered serving pitchers of margaritas. Nor have we ever tried to rival the world's largest one, a 5,861-gallon margarita, mixed in 2001 at Jimmy Buffett's Margaritaville in Orlando. But if you add up all the times bartender Richard Kullman has concocted his "signature drink" over the years at Lindey's, it would qualify as some kind of record—it certainly beats our inter-restaurant softball record.

A veteran of two Florida beach communities, Richard remembers that "a gentleman named Fast Eddie, one of the great bartenders, trained me 15 years ago, and he believed that every bartender should have a signature drink to bring back customers to your bar. And the margarita is mine. Now, I know some bar guides say orange juice doesn't belong here—oh, that's a sacrilege!—but relax, it's just a splash. It cuts a bit of the acidity and lets the tequila shine through."

- margarita salt (optional)
- 1 1/2 ounces Patrón Añejo (a blend of aged tequilas)
- 1/2 ounce Cointreau
- splash of Grand Marnier
- good splash of sour mix
- splash of orange juice
- slice of lime, for garnish

For a salted rim, dab the rim of the chilled stemmed glass onto a dampened towel, and then into a shallow saucer of the salt. Carefully fill the glass with ice. Pour the liquid ingredients into a cocktail shaker filled with ice, shake vigorously, and strain into the waiting ice. Garnish with a slice of lime.

Neil's Bullshot

Neil Schultz was one of Lindey's most loyal regulars: no matter what else opened in the city, he never shifted allegiance. Sure, he'd try the other places once or twice, but he always returned to Lindey's, where he held court. "If you want to see me, come to Lindey's," he'd tell people. Lindey's was his home office. His company, Columbus Window Cleaning, even did the windows!

Every day, Neil met friends for a power lunch at the bar. And he'd often be back at five to meet his buddy Marv Glassman. And his drink, almost invariably, was the Bullshot. We stocked cans of Campbell's beef bouillon behind the bar just for Neil.

- 3 ounces beef bouillon
- 1 ounce Smirnoff vodka

Fill a highball glass with ice, add the bouillon, and then pour in the shot of vodka.

Tony's Sexy South Beach Mojito

"You have to trust us on this one. Once you've tasted this refreshing drink, you'll want another." That's what we wrote on our drink menu more than 10 years ago. Tony brought this concoction back from South Beach. "I was there on vacation, and I'd never heard of the mojito. We were at Nikki Beach, blown away by the sun and the nudity, and I knew there was a place for this drink at Lindey's. Just don't ask me why I knew."

- 5 mint leaves
- 1/2 lime, cut into small sections
- 1/2 ounce of simple syrup*
- splash of sweet and sour mix
- 2 ounces of Bacardi light rum
- splash of soda
- sugar cane "swizzle stick," for garnish

Muddle the first four ingredient together in a cocktail shaker or large water glass. Fill with ice. Add the rum. Cover with a the top of the shaker and shake briefly.

Pour into a highball glass filled with ice. Top off with a splash of soda, and garnish with the sugar cane.

---

* To make a batch of simple syrup, pour 1 cup boiling water into 1 cup of granulated sugar. Stir to dissolve. Let cool, and store in the refrigerator until needed.

Jim & Jan's Sidecar

"The Doctors Barnes" rediscovered this drink at a WOSU fundraiser held at the Royal York penthouse. "The theme was the 1940s, and the guests wore antique clothing. Brice Lancaster from the classical music station played dance music of the period, while the bartenders served Sidecars, Wedding Bells, and Rob Roys—all these drinks our parents used to drink. I remember Jan had on an old, fragile black-lace dress and we could hear a little *riiiiip* each time we swiveled or dipped during a dance. By the end of the evening, poor Jan was wearing a body suit with disconnected sleeves.

"Since then, we took a fancy to those fashionable drinks of yesteryear, and I found a copy of the original *Old Mr. Boston's De Luxe Official Bartender's Guide*, which we shared with our friends behind the bar at Lindey's."

Guests at Lindey's have been sipping delicious nostalgia ever since.

- 2 ounces Hennessy Cognac
- 1/4 ounce triple sec liqueur
- splash of sweet and sour mix
- sugar, for coating the rim of the martini glass

Shake the first three ingredients in a cocktail shaker filled with small cubes of ice. Coat the rim of a martini glass with granulated sugar, and fill with the strained icy liquid.

Bananas Faster

In the early years of the restaurant, we offered a few ice-cream drinks by way of dessert. The Doody family, on visits to paternal relatives, often ordered the New Orleans classic, Bananas Foster: bananas sautéed in brown sugar and butter, flamed in rum, and served over ice cream. The dish is the 1950s creation of Brennan's chef Paul Blangé who was charged with creating a dish to feature bananas, the majority of which entered the States

from Central and South America through New Orleans. Years later, having made the dessert many times at her home, it was still a stretch for Sue to imagine servers rolling out the captain's cart to conduct this little bit of pyromaniacal wizardry in the narrow aisles of the crowded dining rooms. So, at Sue's suggestion, the bartenders created this version, which captures that French Quarter feeling in about one quarter of the time.

- 1 ounce dark rum
- 1 ounce DeKuyper's banana liqueur
- 1/4 cup banana (about half of a small banana), plus an extra slice for garnish
- 1/2 cup ice cream
- dash of cinnamon

Add all the ingredients to the jar of a blender, and blend until smooth but still thick. Pour into a stemmed glass. Garnish with the banana and another dash of cinnamon.

Now if you're planning to serve this at a party (rather than standing behind a bar waiting for a guest to order such a drink), you should consider sautéing the bananas in a little butter and brown sugar until slightly soft, and then refrigerating them until you're ready to make the drink. That will add the true Bananas Foster touch of caramelized sugar and gently browned bananas.

To complete the saga of this international favorite: in 2001, Shelia Wiley arrived from Commander's Palace (one of the Brennans' restaurants) and created the authentic "slow version" of the dessert for our guests, wheeling out her cart and preparing Bananas Foster at the table for guests using Ella Brennan's recipe. As it turns out, Shelia's dining-room treat was short-lived: flaming brandy tableside doesn't comply with German Village fire code. So, once again, Lindey's has left this dish to the Brennans, where, just at their flagship restaurant, the captains flame about 105,000 bananas each year.

The Hummer

Also known as The Doctors' After-Dinner Delight, this is another "blender drink," yes, made with ice cream, which is, in the words of an anonymous bartender, "the bane of every bartender because it creates all that whizzing noise and takes all that friggin' time amid the flurry of all the other fast-paced actions you've got to do in a cramped space on a hectic night with dozens of guests waiting for their nice-and-quiet drinks."

Among the Hummer's fans were Fred and Howard who both enjoyed a Hummer as a nightcap. But often, certain bartenders would say, "Oh, Howard, sorry, but the blender is on the fritz." It was sort of a standing joke.

Fred Holdrich: So one night, Howard put his own blender from home in the trunk, asked for a Hummer and simultaneously set his own blender on the copper bar. Gave everyone a good laugh.

Bartender **Eddie Meecham:** Actually, we all laughed the first time. But after that—Howard brought that blender time and time again—it actually made things a little easier.

If you're ever in Lindey's and would like to try a Hummer, you might take a cue from Jim and Jan: "Just start humming...the bartenders will know what you need."

- 2 small scoops premium vanilla ice cream
- 1 1/2 ounces light rum
- 1 ounce Kahlúa
- 1/2 ounce Myers's Dark Rum
- whipped cream, for garnish

Place the first three ingredients in the jar of an electric blender, and create a smooth, frothy mixture. Pour into a wine glass and float the dark rum on top. Garnish with a little squirt of whipped cream.

We All Scream

Our veteran bartender Eddie Meecham just detested the blender, as well as all frozen drinks such as frozen Strawberry Daiquiris and Pink Squirrels (they just weren't upscale and professional—in fact, an article in the *New York Times* mentioned that some of the toniest bars in Manhattan didn't even *own* a blender). A lady joined Eddie at the bar between shifts: Eddie had just arrived in his white socks and jeans, and Tony, then on lunches, was restocking the bar, shuttling back and forth between the basement and the bar with bottles of liquor. The young lady orders a frozen Strawberry Daiquiri and Eddie says, "I'm sorry, but the blender is broken." Eddie mixes her something else and goes out for a smoke. Tony returns to the bar, slides some wine bottles into the refrigerator, and the lady says to him, "Can you make me a frozen Strawberry Daiquiri?" and he says sure, and whips it up for her.

"I guess you have to know somebody here," she says to Tony, as he serves her drink.

Tony: I have no idea what she means, but just then, Eddie walks in, sees the dreaded blender drink, turns right around, and heads out. Then I knew what she meant.

Eddie Meecham: Lindey's was always upscale drinking. Scotch. Wine. If a guy asked for a martini up, you appreciated that. But a guy asking for some chocolate martini? If you want milkshakes, I figure you should go to a milkshake bar.

Bartender John Lee: The ice cream back in the kitchen is hard as granite. And as soon I'd make one ice-cream drink, which would be incredibly labor-intensive, someone else would see me serve the drink and say those dreaded words, "Oh, that looks good, I'll have one, too." And then I'd have to go back into the kitchen with my jackhammer and pry loose a couple more scoops...

Joan Flower: The servers didn't want to bother with blender drinks either. Like for Bananas Faster, you'd first have to ring in the drink order, then you'd have to run into the kitchen and scoop out the ice cream into a bowl. (And there would be the chef, guarding over the ice cream and his food costs. So you'd say, it's for a guest, not for my own snack.) Then you'd carry the bowl back over to the bar, set it down, and try to get the bartender's attention. "Hey, can you make this before the ice cream melts?" And, of course, there would be other servers with other drink orders, and other little bowls of ice cream waiting. And, of course, the other drinks for the guests at your same table would be ready in two shakes, sitting there. So it was always a hassle.

This is just a sampling, as we said. But when it comes to imbibing, it's always best to know your limits.

BACK OF THE HOUSE

· ·

COOKING, MANAGING &
KEEPING THE KITCHEN RUNNING

NOTES FROM THE BACK OF THE HOUSE
FROM THE MANAGERS' JOURNALS

AT LINDEY'S, as at most restaurants, chefs and managers keep a log or a journal to communicate with one another. The day shift leaves notes for the evening shift. The closing chef jots down a few notes for the opening chef. The owners read along. (And now, we get to take a peek.) These books help with organization, troubleshooting, inventory, and personnel issues, but as you can see from the more uncharacteristic excerpts we've selected, they also showcase the trivia, tedium, and tumult that fuels a restaurant. We've taken liberties with the chronology. Many journals weren't dated, but these seem to be from 1988–1992. So we distilled and jumbled the months into a chronicle of what goes on at Lindey's). We've left out a few names. Otherwise, these shorthand comments are reprinted as originally scrawled, albeit without the typical spills and typographical <u>OVEREXERTION!!!</u>

Saturday, December 2

...400 covers—things went well with 2 exceptions. 1. Problem with tables 71 + 72. They wanted 1 check for each table, should have been no problem—Les and Marion waited on them—I've already written a letter of apology. 2. A lady from table 20 parked illegally in the alley where Sue usually parks. She said the shuttle driver said she was parked OK and there would be no trouble. Well, 2 police cars and 1 tow truck later she was in tears at table 20 in front of everyone in the restaurant...More to follow—oh yes, I found 6–8 empty beer cans in basement trash can in employee's john—Dwight was just thirsty and full of the holiday spirit as well as 1 gallon of Colt 45. Just another Saturday night here at Lindey's—*Biff*

Friday, December 8

Great dinner—350 covers. Very smooth. No one had to wait more than 10 minutes, even the walk-ins!

Very interesting party in Mohawk Room. 80 sorority girls + guys getting rowdy on amaretto sours. Small part of chandelier was broken when slam dancing began. Building is intact though. Over and out. *SG*

Friday, December 22

Slow nite. 217 covers. The checkout is all messed up. Server X walked with all her charge vouchers: she owes us $320.42 in Visa/MC vouchers. And a customer walked on a $25 tab, but we had his Visa #. *SG*

Saturday, December 23

197 covers. Slow night for a Saturday. Holiday cheer seemed to be flowing. Only problem, a lady passed out on the way to the restroom around 11:30. [Chef] Jack and I gave her oxygen and some French doctor from #22 looked at her. She seemed fine and even finished her dinner and stayed around another hour. All is well with the world. *B*

Wednesday, February 7

Hectic morning. But lunch went well. Poor Sue has the flu along with about a third of the staff. Take two aspirins and call me in the morning. *B*

Saturday, April 22

Freezer went down. Called Edwards Services. All of the ice cream melted—that's all the damages so far. There were 3 ice cream cakes for a party that got 86'd. We made sundaes for them instead; they were fine.

Friday, April 28

Steam kettle needs an electrician. There is a little bit of arcing going on. I have a feeling the connections need to be cleaned.

Wednesday, November 6

Tilapia overbreaded—find culprit and train please. Also, You have cooked risotto and duck confit. USE! SELL!

Sunday, November 10

Hand mixer M.I.A.

Saturday, November 16

Talk to servers, team service will work better if they follow simple rule: "Full hands in, full hands out!" *

Saturday night didn't happen.

Tuesday, December 17

Why are potatoes sweet (Idaho)?

Friday, December 27

Dishwashers seem to be taking too much time to finish.

Tuesday, January 21

Smooth night, front sold well.

Hey Mark—Rob didn't know sheet trays cannot go in the dumbwaiter, so we are 86'd key lime pie and there are 24 pieces smashed in the bottom of the dumbwaiter!

Finally pried the door open, Rob will be cleaning this after his shift.

Noel can open the door tomorrow.

Friday, February 7

Found a very scary thing on the prep table.

---

* For those of you who have done "team service," this means that servers aren't merely in charge of their own station. Additionally, each server should enter the kitchen with dirty plates taken from the dining room, and every server should leave the kitchen with plated foods that are ready to go out to the dining room.

Thursday, March 6

Mark: I dropped the ball tonight—I forgot to have 20 cheesecakes cut, we had to sub desserts (brûlées, key limes).

I burned the brûlées, so they are now a priority.

We have bare minimum calamari, but I thawed 5 lbs. for tomorrow.

Prime rib is seasoned and seared on the rolling cart.

Sunday, March 9

Did you ever feel like you got into the wrong side of the restaurant industry? Two quotes for equipment repair: $1,500 and $2,000.

Monday, March 10

We have not sold a bone-in* for 3 days.

Saturday, March 25

Stinky water flooded neighborhood. Oil recovery team was dispatched. Small animals were saved. The rat man stood and pondered.

Wednesday, April 11

Our new G.M. starts today. The lamb is multiplying.

Tuesday, September 18

Strange night. Rob left because testicles hurt. Came back and worked 6:30-9:00 p.m. Got hit at once but pretty slow before 7:30.

Monday, August 28

We are dying for mop heads. If John comes in, see if he can bring in some.

Friday, August 1

Chef—I've been subpoena'd again. I'll find out if I can skip it.

Friday, April 19

Air conditioning never turned on, kitchen was 101 degrees!!!

Thursday, May 16

Tyson will need a day off in the near future to attend my uncle's funeral. I do not have a date (he is still living).

Thursday, June 6

Grimebusters turned off all gas lines. MAJOR fun getting all pilots lit. BOOOOM!! singed eyebrows only damage.

Thursday, June 27

Marshall, Ice cream coming from Abbott. Don't return!

Abbott called late at night and saw that someone ordered 33 cases of ice cream CONES! I cancelled the order. (OR maybe Sue's planned a kiddie party of 5,000 for the Fourth of July!) Please see what was mis-keyed and follow up.

Thursday, January 25

Give new guy kitchen approach and let him set up station with Jordan, and then we need to go over page 1 + 2 training materials.

Oyster gratin plate breaks in oven—cold to hot, no bueno.

Tuesday, November 15

Few (2) complaints that sweetbreads were "disgusting."

Wednesday, November 23

Slow night, tables are ready, light bulbs are all working downstairs, but Kurt tried to help me change one in the Mohawk Room and the whole entire fixture fell out with a bunch of

---

* **Speak Restaurantese:** "Bone-in" means a boneless chicken breast with the first joint of the wing—that little drumstick—still attached. Also called an airline breast.

drywall. Kurt shoved it back up in there and we said screw the rest because they'll probably just fall out too. At least we tried!!

Saturday, July 2

Neighbor complained again...about patio being seated without a permanent wall. Lance said don't seat it until the wall is up.

Thursday, July 7

E [a server] was complaining about tipping out 5% tonight. I was trying to explain everything. He didn't like my answers, got pissy and walked away. I told him not to come to me if he doesn't want an explanation.

Saturday, July 9

We got HIT! Busy non-stop. ☺ Missed budget by $162. ☆ Florists are in town!

Monday, July 11

Pre-shift topic: Chef noticed chilled forks are being placed on salad plates. The forks are to be placed on the table and THEN the salads.

Tuesday, July 19

In reference to what Andrew wrote, 6 ladies waited for their check to be divided until I went over and told them that we were unsuccessful so I put the same amount on each of their credit cards, and bought their appetizers and dessert. I know that Jess did everything to make them happy and I tried to explain everything to them. I know they loved him, I just hope I did enough for them to love me and Lindey's.

Wednesday, July 20

John X was served a steak that was overdone. We sent out a new one that was fatty and "covered in so much pepper that he almost choked." He felt the kitchen was pissed off and taking it out on him. I spoke with Alfredo who said most of the steaks had marbling and that we had switched the steak dust to a simple salt and pepper blend. I informed John of this and he said the second steak was nothing like the first. I apologized and bought his entire meal.

Monday, July 25

The pay phone was moved this a.m. We hung a picture over the hole in the wall.

We put screened pour spouts on all liquor bottles today due to increased fly issues. Flies continue to be a nuisance inside and out. Outside bar also has been getting ants. All bartenders need to wipe down areas better.

Thursday, February 3

Chad lost a guest's car keys. We had to pay $187 for new set plus $50 A&P G.C. for his inconvenience.* Also Will lost track of his tix times and the kitchen had some "opportunities" resulting in two $35 two tops being A&P'd.**

Friday, February 11

The highlight tonight was having John R pass out drunk at the bar and then spending the next hour trying to figure out where he lives and getting him home.

Friday, August 12

Got "suckered into" buying a table of 2 because no one greeted them for 20 minutes. After much kissing ass they were still upset. However, they were overheard saying that their intentions all along were to get free food. Very rude to everyone, though, and Tony helped take care of them.

---

* **Speak restaurantese:** A&P G.C. is "advertising & promotion gift certificates."

** **Speak restaurantese:** To "A&P" or "comp" a guest's meal is a form of "advertising & promotion," since we only want guests leaving Lindey's with good things to say.

Wednesday, August 17

My highlight tonight was unclogging the men's downstairs toilet and then finding a pair of fingernail clippers at the bottom of the bowl. I used a pair of kitchen tongs and chef Rob made me throw them away.

Saturday, August 20

Kurt's drawer was short $42 but the other was over $7, so I made him pay the difference. Lincoln's drawer was short $15, and without using the money from both Kurt and Lincoln we were still over by $462. Since we had a net overage, should I still accept their $$ to repay their individual drawers?

A woman dropped her cell phone, picked it up, but didn't realize the battery came apart. It's here and she wants us to mail it to her in Dayton. She'll reimburse us for the shipping. Card attached.

Marshall washed his check he needs a new one issued.

The Million Miscellaneous Things that Pluck at a Manager's Mind

"My 18 months as a manager at Lindey's were transformative. From the moment I parked my car on Fifth Street and strolled down the brick walks toward the restaurant—me, a kid from suburbia!—the air, the trees, the heavy wooden doors, the smell of the brass polish, the familiar faces at the door, it was exhilarating. I didn't run Lindey's, that place ran me."

No doubt, every manager has shared **Ian Brown's** sentiments, at least, at the beginning of a shift. But as an evening wears on, the number and the variety of concerns served up on the manager's plate—well, there's just not a platter large enough to hold it all! Here's a sampling from the journals:

"Started night with the wrong menus. I just grabbed menus that were on the shelf, but later found current menus under the phone books. No other problems."

"Talk to staff about the importance of a starched all-cotton shirt."

"The soda guns at the main bar aren't mixing the right ratio again."

"The steady drip, drip, drip of the upstairs into the downstairs ladies' restroom slowed things in there a bit."

"Had a problem with a blackened swordfish. It was burnt-blackened rather than spicy-cooked. Spoke with the kitchen about that."

"Caught [prep chef] stealing two 10-pound bags of shrimp, 2 veal chops, and 2 filets tonight. He denied everything, but the evidence was there, and we have a witness. Film at 11."

"Had some serious problems with [waiter]. He lied about doing sidework, etc., then we found a $300,000.00 over-ring on one of his checks. I believe he has been suspended."

"Two dishwashers were let go tonight due to lateness and being drunk. The actual kitchen did the dishes and cleaned up. It was nice to see people work together like that."

"Too many servers coming to me in tears because the chef is shoving food onto the floor because the dinners had waited too long in the window."

"There seemed to be some 'tomfoolery' going on tonight. First, as I went to answer the phone at the front desk, the phone cord was gone. Wendy found it in the kitchen. Later I was walking through the kitchen, and an unknown artist had highlighted the kitchen phone—I had it cleaned."

"Missing in Action: garde-manger lost a finger cot in a salad.* Not the first time! I've always wondered: for each finger cot lost, how come there's not a corresponding complaint from the dining room?"

"Taught the servers a little common sense: When you're trying to get a shift covered all week, and we all see you asking and we all see no one is picking it up for you, don't turn around and call in sick that day. We're not that stupid."

"Emergency brake on a car didn't work— although valet had put it on. During the night the car rolled and hit two other cars. So all three valet parked. Expect insurance will be happy."

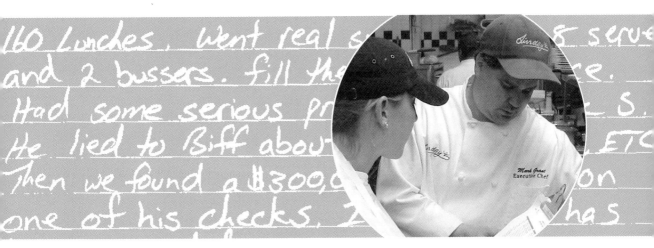

---

* **Speak Restaurantese:** a "finger cot," available at most drugstores and proctologist's office, is a very small condom, used in food service to protect cuts.

IT'S THE LITTLE THINGS THAT COST
TRY, TRY, TRY (EVERYONE'S PATIENCE) AGAIN

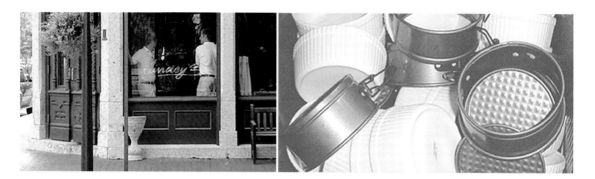

INTERVIEWING GUESTS AND EMPLOYEES for this book has often required that someone recall details and experiences that took place decades ago and, not too infrequently, under the influence of cocktails, romance, or multitasking zeal. But collectively, an oral history of Lindey's emerged, with many odd and priceless moments, including these short-lived and often wayward ideas we tried out at one time or another. As none other than Julia Child said while making French bread during an episode of *The French Chef*, "You must have the courage to fail." And did we ever.

Gifting

Manager **Freddie Cortez:** A mention of Lindey's gift certificates appeared at the bottom of the menu for many years. One December, we had a call from Grant Hospital: they wanted to buy $10,000 worth of gift certificates in increments of $50 and $100 for their staff members. Sue was so happy, she was chirping! The two of us, with our cigarettes and cups of coffee, sat in the office for hours one evening, writing out each certificate by hand—something like 150 individual certificates. I don't know who had more caffeine or nicotine, but I know she kissed me three times that night, saying it's only early December, and we've already made our numbers! It was thrilling.

Unfortunately, the December boon was followed by a bleak January and February because all those gift certificates came back...and most of the parties were first-timers. So all those dollars came directly off our sales. And a couple with a $40 bill and a $100 gift certificate received $60 back in cash, which killed us. Oh, Sue was not happy having negative balances for two months straight.

Sue: January is always bad. During the holidays, we have a full staff, with everyone working extra shifts and overtime hours, and then suddenly, January 2nd, things screech to a halt. Guests stay home, they're budgeting, they're vacationing. And we have to cut staff and cut hours, and that's never a pleasure.

Flower Power

Bartender **John Lee:** I was a bit of a bull in the china shop when I started at Lindey's, and everyone was patient with me. I'd bartended for seven years previously, but Lindey's was much more upscale. At the time, in the center of the bar, between the liquors and racks of wine, stood a humongous flower arrangement. The guys at the German Village Florist created them each week, and Sue must have paid a fortune for each one. But for the bartenders, they were a huge pain, sticking out into the narrow aisle in which we raced up and down, serving the guests. And when it was very busy, when you'd be hurrying and wedging past one another, you'd walk by and break off a bloom, or get a faceful of pollen, or poke yourself in the eye with a branch of pussy willow. One night, I'd had enough. I picked up this short knife and just started hacking at the arrangement, pruning it way back, out of our way. And just as I had finished my new arrangement, I turned around, and there's Sue at the foot of the stairs, staring over at me. And I knew she was thinking, "My god, I've put some crazy axe murderer behind my bar!"

Shortly thereafter, the flower arrangements grew a little "shorter" as well.

Let's Not and Say We Did

Some things are worth a try. Others are better served by the old expression, "Let's not and say we did." At two points in our history, we hired general managers from Commander's Palace in New Orleans, who had an exceptional spirit for testing new ideas. But both Ross and Shelia found that things that work on Bourbon Street don't always work on Beck Street.

For instance, Ross tried a raw bar, right inside the door, and we'd have a cook out there to shuck oysters and peel shrimp. But it took up the very bar space where the most regular of our regulars like to sit, the ice was always leaking across the coppertop and soaking stacks of napkins, guests at the bar just weren't coming to Lindey's to slurp oysters—well, all those were very valid reasons, but one other problem arose:

Sue: One day, a guy came into the restaurant and said he could get us a great deal on fresh shrimp, oysters, and crab claws. He had his own boat and he could bring us the freshest seafood, straight from Florida. And it worked for a while: the raw bar created a little drama right when guests would walk in the door. But then our "source" was thrown in jail for transporting other things besides "legal seafoods" in his little boat.

Server C: Ross also hired a magician to go from table to table on Friday and Saturday nights. Maybe it worked in New Orleans. But here? Some people liked it (the 1 in 100 parties that brought along a child), but what our guests liked most about the magician was when he took his deck of cards and shiny hoops and entertained the other dining room. Yes, we finally convinced Ross that for the Lindey's crowd, a magician felt as if a mariachi band had washed up on your table for eternity.

And then Shelia Wiley tried candlelight Sunday dinners. Now, in the late 1980s, our Sunday-brunch guests enjoyed the twinkling fingers of harpist Pegi Engleman as well as the occasional Jim Nabors–like vocals of server Randy Manypenny. But in 2000, Shelia hired a strolling violinist who would sidle up to a table and saw away until someone tipped him to go away. Mid-shift, one evening, the staff insisted that the violinist had to leave.

As for the accordion player Shelia tried one Sunday brunch? The poor man didn't even get to finish a chorus of "(Don't Mess With) My Toot Toot" before he was sent packing.

Cigar Dinners

Amy Goldstein: A few times a year, my husband Marc would be in heaven because Lindey's hosted a cigar dinner. The chef would have free rein to create a four- or five-course dinner with the sponsorship of a wine purveyor or a spirits company. First would be cocktails, hors d'oeuvres, and a pre-dinner cigar. Then the dinner courses, each paired with a wine. Then an after-dinner cigar, more wine, and maybe a different cigar for a brandy on the terrace. Each dinner had a theme—a bourbon tasting, or foods of Northern Italy.

But we had one rule: after dinner, Marc had to deposit his clothes in the laundry room, and he had to take a long shower *before* coming to bed.

Today, with the no-smoking ordinance, our chef offers quarterly wine dinners, in which guests need only shower before arriving.

Guilt-Ridden, as Charged

In 1995, oddly mixing business with pleasure, we actually printed this in the dessert listing on our menu: "Assorted Ice Creams & French-Style Sorbets (sorbet less than 90 calories per serving)." Yes, sorbet was all the rage, along with gelato, premium ice creams, and self-indulgent guilt.

"Care for Pepper?"

Remember back when pepper grinders were nothing to fear? What rude roué decided that a sign of class or fancy service meant grinders needed to be bigger and thicker and heavier, as if the inevitable outcome might be a device so large it would take two servers to wield it, battering-ram-like, over some wary guest's chilly baby greens?

If our pursuit of the ideal restaurant-size grinder contributed to that trend, we apologize. But we have to admit we had a few challenges while trying to offer guests this seasoning.

For a time, we had reasonably sized wooden grinders, about a foot and a half tall, that remained on the service stands, shared, more or less, among a few stations. Inevitably, water on the side stand (or something spilled there, or a few too many accidental bounces on the floor) would cause the bases of the grinders to clog or warp or crack. Then, on a busy Saturday, we'd suddenly be down to two pepper grinders in the entire restaurant. Come Monday, someone would go spend a small fortune buying another dozen grinders—better grinders, with lifetime warranties that we'd lose long before their short lives ended.

Then someone clever said, "You know what would be even classier? What if every member of the waitstaff sported his or her own grinder!"

And then some of the even more clever servers said, "In other words, you'll spend no money, and each of us will pay $25 for a new pepper grinder?"

The answer was affirmative: "You'll take better care of your personal grinder, and we'll all come out ahead."

The servers bought the grinders. "Next we'll be carrying around butter pats in our aprons," one begrudging server remarked.

As you might guess, things got worse before they got better. The staff wore the grinders on a little pepper holster that secured in the back beside the apron's strings. The grinders were always ready to offer, but it became a contest among the mischief-making servers to add additional items to other servers' pepper holsters: pens, bread sticks, table crumbers, sugar packets, and especially iced-tea spoons: one, two, three—the record was five, held by Brian Bailey, who seemingly possessed the numbest butt of any server. This juvenile amusement entertained both staff and guests alike.

Food runner **Jason Cull:** When I produce the pepper grinder from behind my back, there's at least one smart guy each week who says, "Hey, did you just pull that out of your butt?"

Tea Totaling

Server **M:** When Rick Doody returned from a trip to California, he decided that Lindey's should offer a selection of teas tableside. It wasn't enough that a guest who ordered hot tea meant assembling a pot of hot water, a tea bag, lemon slices on a plate, a selection of sugars, a cup, a saucer, and a spoon. Now, as if we weren't always crushed for time, we had to make *two* trips for one cup of tea: the first to point to eight different teas in a little coffin and often read aloud the selections for the farsighted or decode which ones were caffeinated and which herbal. Then the guest would fumble with the packets, pick one, put one back...and they were often tucked in so tightly that a few would pop out at the same time, and you'd have neatly repack one or another compartment after every selection. Then, finally, you could go and get the water, the—oh, never mind. Describing all this is going to give me nightmares about waiting tables again.

Who's Been Playing With the Lights?

Manager S: When Rick and Chris were coming in and out of Lindey's, we were always trying out improvements. One night, Rick, reprising his Captain Clipboard role, and his sidekick decided to change all the light bulbs in the restaurant to halogens that would shine directly on each table. This was a big project that took a few days: installing the new lights in the recessed cans and aiming them at the center of each table.

No sooner had we completed this than people started to move the tables. Closer to a friend's table. Farther from a loud table. Out from under the spotlight. I remember Sue came up to me and said, "I don't understand why people come in to my restaurant and move my furniture around. I wouldn't go into their houses and move their furniture around."

Jazz Nights, Crazy Nights

Singer Jeanette Williams: Lindey's on a Thursday night, say, 15 years ago, was a whole different restaurant. A different crowd gathered and mixed right in with the regulars. And they were as regular as I was: every Thursday night, and I mean, for a solid 10, 12 years. I sang with Tom Carroll, Seeds of Fulfillment, Kenny Banks, Bobby Floyd, Hank Mahr—we had a great time. I'd sing some Peabo Bryson, some Patti Austin, lots of Aretha. And we did plenty of requests, too. I remember the first time this lady asked me to do "Crazy" by Pasty Cline, I looked at her long and hard, and I said, "Honey, what do you think, I'm Jeanette *Wynette?*" But every Thursday, it was "Crazy" for Marianne, who became my dear friend, my drinking partner, and my occasional ride home.

Marianne McCarty Collins: Jeanette just knew how to work the room and get everyone participating. We'd get up and dance between the crowded tables (making the servers crazy, I'm sure), and some of us would go up and sing with her—even *I* would, and I can't sing. I remember one night, there were four of us women standing behind Jeanette, doing what we must have thought were backup vocals on "Crazy," and Susan Ricart, apparently feeling inspired, decided to grab the microphone from Jeanette and continue the song all by herself. Jeanette just stood there. In shock, I think. Crazy is right.

Band leader Tom Carroll: For a time, Lindey's was the premier jazz spot in Columbus. And I was lucky to work with great musicians. Not just fabulous vocalists like Jeanette, Mary McClendon, Michelle Horsefield, Kelly Crum, or Marie Walker, my first vocalist, who had worked the circuit with Etta James, but great players, too. I mean, the legendary Hank Mahr on piano, Sonny McBroom on sax, Bob Breighthaupt on drums, Gene Walker (who did the 1965 tour with the Beatles) on sax. And whenever there was a Broadway show or another performer in town, a few musicians always made a beeline to Lindey's to sit it for a set. We had Louis Bellson, who played with Duke Ellington; Gene Bertoncini, one of the most versatile guitarists around; drummer Jeff Hamilton, who played with Ella, Count Basie, the Ray Brown Trio; Casey Cherrell, who'd recorded with Chaka Khan—it's impossible to remember everyone, but I'll tell you, that was one mecca for jazz musicians.

Profile: Ross Hall
ONE OF OUR BEST

"My job is a cross between a high-class traffic cop and a politician."—*Ross Hall*

BY OUR IMPROMPTU CENSUS, Ross Hall was the most beloved maître d' Columbus has ever known. As a general manager, he faced the usual challenges—and then some—but when it came to knowing what guests needed, Ross possessed a certain genius. Not only did he have a memory for faces and names, but he also knew how to apply the same gift of welcome familiarity to first-time guests. As manager Jason Seigler recalls, "Everyone Ross met felt as if he were an old friend inviting a guest into his house. And he found a way never to say no to anyone. It was always yes, and later he'd figure out how to make yes happen."

Rick Doody: I met Ross with my grandfather and grandmother at Commander's Palace. Ross was our captain, and the three of us were totally swept away by Ross's charm, warmth, professionalism, and talent. "You're the most amazing person. If you ever leave here, call us," I told him, and gave him our card.

Sure enough, Ross flew up here, and we started him immediately as manager. We literally threw him the keys.

Server and manager **Tim Picard:** Ross was always up, always cheerleading—he was perfect for this place. I remember when he first arrived, this young Italian guy from Flint, Michigan, he was possibly the worst-dressed person at Lindey's. He'd have a black shirt with a purple tie and a jacket with sleeves that were too short. His suits were poly-blends that looked as if they were made of pot scrubbers. And Sue gave him an allowance and bought him a wardrobe.

Chris Doody: Ross took care of the kids. He took the reservations in a way that made people feel special. He was the first one to get us to open for holidays. Ross had this energy and talent, and all he needed was a few trips to Schottenstein's for some suits and ties and sport coats. He was a diamond in the rough.

Manager **Freddie Cortez:** I learned so much from Ross, but I also taught him a few things, even though my mother always said it's worse to correct someone's grammar than to have bad grammar. I suppose I couldn't help myself.

One evening, Ross emerged from the kitchen on a busy night with a plunger in his hand.

"Ross, what the hell are you doing?" I say to him, rushing among the crowded tables to intercept him.

"The ladies room is plugged up," he tells me. "How else can you get to the bathroom other than through the dining room?"

"Ross," I say, dragging him back into the kitchen, "at least you could shove the plunger in a to-go bag to disguise it!"

Chef **Gretchen Eiselt:** When Ross arrived, we experienced a big jump in sales. He charmed guests; he created lifetime guests. For instance, Ross would write his own name on a busy Friday night's reservation sheet. Four or five times. Then, when someone without a reservation would come in—someone he knew we ought to treat right—he'd say, "Let me see what I can do...." He'd take a pretend look around the place or shuttle them into another room, and all of a sudden he'd be carrying menus and escorting the party to a table.

On big nights, Ross would come back to the kitchen and say, "Chefs, what do you want me to sell tonight?" And we'd have made up 25 of one particular dinner special, so he'd go out to the staff and give the mother of all speeches, whipping the servers into a selling frenzy, and the special would be sold out by 7:30.

And when we'd be backed up and crazy busy, he'd pop back in the kitchen and say, "I'm buying you all drinks tonight, let's do it!" At the end of the night, we'd just feel great about what we'd accomplished.

Sliding Into Home

Assistant manager **Michael Mastracci:** It was a busy Friday night, and Ross was trying to see if the round table in the back room was ready to turn, because a walk-in party of six was at the door. I was working in the middle room as Ross breezed by me to enter the back room. A few seconds later, as Ross was run-walking down the stairs back into the front room, he tripped and did a Pete Rose slide head-first into the chair legs of Table 23. Keep in mind the restaurant was absolutely packed. Ross stood, brushed himself off, and escorted his guests back to the table. It is an image of implacable poise that's etched into my memory along with many others.

Well-Chilled

Regular guest **Michael Morris:** I always used to sit at Table 21 if I came with just one other person, and at 31 for larger parties. One night, during a fairly hot summer, the air conditioner in the restaurant was just not keeping up—it's always rather minimal. Ross was the manager then, and I called him over to ask if there wasn't something he could do since it was so uncomfortably hot. Ross nodded, walked up the stairs to Sue's office, hoisted the window air conditioning unit out of her office, and carried it down the stairs. Then he grabbed one of the folding tray stands and a tray, and balanced the unit on top. He plugged in the air conditioner and aimed it so that it was blowing right on us.

We thought maybe he was going to—we didn't know, but when we realized he was setting it up just to blow on our table, I said, "Ross, you can't do that, there are people behind it—they're not going to like it."

He replied, "I'm buying them a bottle of champagne." That's how Ross took care of people.

The Voice of Authority

One year, Jimmy, Allen, and Kip, all servers at Lindey's, were at Mardi Gras on one of their frequent group holidays. Allen had a fight with his boyfriend, and somehow, in the subsequent chaos, they all had to cancel their flights, leave their hotel room, and arrive home a day late—all missing a busy shift. Everyone on staff was adamant that Ross punish the merrymakers. On their return, Ross sent them upstairs to the Terrace Room, and, while all the other management watched from the back of the room to ensure that discipline was being carried out, Ross whispered to the three men, "Now, um, *I* am going to pretend to yell at you. And, then, *you* are going to pretend to be very sorry, got it?"

Mentoring

Kurt Baughman: One early Saturday afternoon in the spring of 1995, Ross was smoking in front of Lindey's, talking to a valet. I needed a job. I thought he was the owner. He looked the part: he had a thousand-dollar black suit, slicked-back hair, and a twinkling Rolex. The valet had just moved his Range Rover to an open spot in front of the restaurant.

That was 11 years ago. Ross hired me on the spot—I had no experience—but he had a certain intuition. I still work at Lindey's.

What's the proper way to carry a tray? What's the correct way to make certain drinks (mint juleps, Sazeracs, mimosas)? How do you fold a 50-dollar bill just right so you that can grease someone's palm and get things done? Ross taught me all the basics and more.

I've never known anyone with the people skills that Ross possessed. He was, simultaneously, a charmer, a street hustler, a polished professional, and a great boss. He only had to meet a person one time. He'd never forget your name, where you worked, where you lived, who you were married to, who you were cheating with, what you liked to drink, and where you preferred to sit. He had this immense Rolodex in his mind and he never stopped adding notes to the cards.

But the way Ross treated guests, everyone felt like a movie star. Whether you came to Lindey's once a year, once a month, or seven nights a week, he'd greet you, "Hey, baby!" I think he wanted everyone to feel sexy. You were the center of attention. You were going to get lucky—or at least think you could if you wanted to.

He was famous for talking on two phones at once. Yes, two phones, one held at each ear, and he'd have a conversation going on both lines, first talking into one mouthpiece and then into the other. "Y-y-y-yeah, b-b-b-baby!" (Once in a while, he would get going so fast he would, in fact, stutter.)

I only knew Ross for 18 months before his death. It's now been 10 years. Guests still come in and talk about Ross. Every once in a while, the few remaining members of the staff who worked with Ross will retell some crazy thing that Ross did, and we'll all just laugh and laugh. It's unfathomable to think how far he might have gone in the world.

How to Grease the Palm That Feeds You

Lindey's is a restaurant where reservations are usually all a guest needs to get a good table. Pestering, pouting, and pleading produce variable results. It's the rare guest who tries to grease a palm. But here's how Ross taught Kurt to fold a fifty. Of course, this method works with other denominations (once again, with varying results).

Fig. 1 Take one crisp or sort-of-crisp Andrew Jackson.

Fig. 2 Fold the bill in half lengthwise.

Fig. 3 Fold the bill in half lengthwise once again.

Fig. 4 Fold the bill in half, widthwise this time. You should now have a bill about the size of a large postage stamp.

Fig. 5 Hold the bill in the palm of your right hand and cup your palm slightly to keep the bill in place. Turn your hand over, to conceal the bill from view.

Fig. 6 Approach the maître d'. Extend your right hand to shake the maître d's hand. Maintain eye contact. Do not look at your hand. Smile. Make your request.

Fig. 7 Pull your hand away, discreetly leaving the bill in the hand of the maître d' who, likewise, will not look at or acknowledge the folded bill.

Fig. 8 Follow the maître d' to your table. Do not think about other things that $50 might have bought.

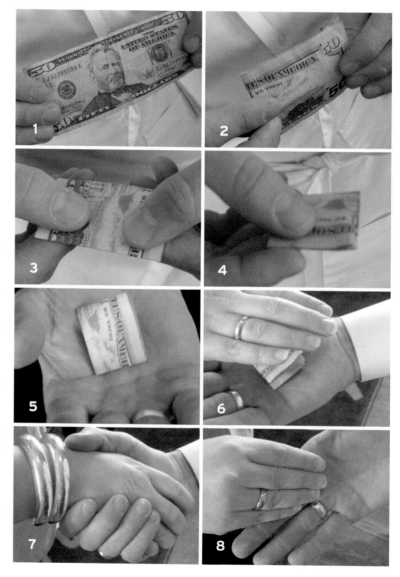

The Work Continues

Bartender **Tony Murray:** Ross rooted for the underdog. He hired folks because he just had faith they could come through if they had a chance. Sure, this probably had to do with his own story. He was an underdog. He'd been divorced before coming here, and when Rick hired him, he arrived without much of anything but whatever demons he'd tried to leave behind in New Orleans. He was earnest, humble, eager, generous—guests came back again and again just to see him.

He took care of people. Even first-time guests would be dazzled by his attention. He had a helium tank installed, and when a kid walked in the door, he'd run back, inflate a balloon, and deliver it to the table. He'd escort a little kid right into the kitchen—while we're busy as can be—to show him the kitchen and scoop out a dip of ice cream as a little appetizer.

I'll never forget, a couple came for dinner one Thanksgiving, asked for Ross as soon as they walked in, and when we told them that he'd passed away the month before, they looked at one another, said they were sorry, and then they hesitated and turned to leave. That probably ruined their Thanksgiving. While Ross was here, no one could imagine Lindey's without him.

Chefs **Matt Harding** and **Gretchen Eiselt:** At 6:30 one Sunday morning, we both go into Lindey's to change the brunch menu. We'd never worked together on a Sunday. And we aren't there more than half an hour when Sue calls. We know something's wrong immediately. She says that Ross had died. Almost at that same moment, Chris Doody arrives. Then, one by one, people come to the restaurant: staff, regulars, people in the neighborhood who loved Ross. We never end up opening that day, but as people arrive, we begin to cook food for everyone. It's like a wake, in a way: everyone weeping, sharing stories, eating together, just staying on and on because no one wanted to go home.

We closed Lindey's for the funeral as well, and we threw a big lunch afterwards. That night, we all went to Skip and Cherie's house in the village. Just to keep Ross among us for a while longer. None one could imagine his leaving us.

Sue: During his eulogy, the priest talked about the great composer Puccini and how he never finished his masterwork, the opera *Turandot*. Puccini would not rest, telling his friends that he wanted to work until he couldn't work anymore, and then they could finish the work. When Arturo Toscanini debuted the opera some time after Puccini's death, there's a story that the conductor put down his baton and stopped the orchestra during the premiere. And after a minute of silence, he said, "This is where the maestro stopped," and then he picked up his baton, "and this is where his friends continued." Toscanini then conducted the final part of the opera. I remember how much I cherished those words, thinking about Ross and about how we continued to serve our guests at Lindey's, amid all the sadness.

As the Tablecloths Turn
A Short History of Lindey's Linens

FOR MANY YEARS, crisp white tablecloths have been the blank canvas for every meal at Lindey's. But this was not always the case, especially in the early years. Here is a brief summary of our ever-evolving table toppings; we'll leave aside the ongoing reconsideration of things that go on the table (particularly the search for a vase that is both elegant and resistant to breakage, toppling over, theft, and horseplay), as well as things that go below the table (specifically, the various shimming devices—bev naps, matches, bottle caps— that tables require on wooden floors as well-worn and warped as ours).

Red-and-White Checkered Oilcloth

Wash 'n' Wear White Linen (Polyester) Tablecloths
(We did our own laundry in the basement.)

White Paper Placemats

Rented White Linen Tablecloths

(Washing and drying got to be a bit too much.)

Rented White Linen Tablecloths,
PLUS the Other Side of the Linen
If There Were No Spills,
Plus Nice White Paper Placemats

Linen Tablecloths Covered With Butcher Paper
and Crayons for the Kiddies[1]

Linen Tablecloths Covered With Butcher Paper
But No More Crayons Thanks to Those Few
Who Ruin the Privilege for Everyone Else

*(With Additional Thanks to Waiter Kevin Donoghue's
Rather Compromising Caricatures of Regular Patrons,
Colleagues, and, Most Damagingly, Management.)* [2 and 3]

Linen Tablecloths and
Just Forget the Butcher Paper,
What the Heck!

---

1   Just remember Robert Fulghum's comment: "If you want an interesting party sometime, combine cocktails and a fresh box of crayons for everyone."

2   Kevin's peers at Lindey's weren't the only ones to recognize his talent: he later worked at Pixar Studios, where he joined the animation team for *A Bug's Life*. If you're reading this, Kevin, have your people give us a call. We've been thinking there's a film—maybe a rockumentary? a miniseries?—based on *As the Tables Turn*.

3   Peter Max drew all over his table when he was in for lunch one day. Sue patiently waited for her guests' departure, figuring she might frame the drawing for the restaurant, which features nothing but paintings and drawings on every wall. Unfortunately, Max's host Roger Blackwell took the tablecloth for his own invidious purposes. Curses.

In the Laundry Room

Chef **Matt Harding:** When I arrived at Lindey's, it was super scary down in the basement. The place was run by Dwight and Neil. They were the dishwashers, and they had been for a long time. A long, long time. At the top of the stairs, the servers were supposed to bus their own trays and deliver them to the dishwashers to finish. But when it was particularly busy, some of the servers wouldn't do much in the way of cleanup. They would drop off the trays of food—as well as the wine glasses—and instead of dumping everything, Neil would make a sort of bus-tub punch: all the leftover wines in one inspired nightly blend. Some of the staff obviously knew about this—and helped with the winemaker's blend—but it wasn't exactly public knowledge.

But then one day I saw Neil come up to the service stand and fill a glass just half full of Coca-Cola. I thought that was sort of odd. And it was then I realized that the glass of soda he was always carrying around—the full glass—was half Coke and half wine. So it wasn't obvious that he was getting a little more and more inebriated as the evening wore on.

Some nights, I would be closing, and I'd give Neil a ride home. He'd hop in my car, since he lived in a nearby neighborhood—not exactly the best neighborhood. We'd stop at Jay's Drive-Thru on the way home, he'd get his 40, and then we'd be at his house. "You lock your door and get the hell out of here," he'd say to me.

Now, Neil would also bring his clothes from home and do his laundry in the washer and dryer at Lindey's. We knew, and we sort of didn't know: this certainly wasn't a policy we wanted to institutionalize. But one year, we got rid of the washer and dryer, deciding it was just more cost-effective and convenient to pay for a linen service.

Not to be inconvenienced, Neil would simply put his clothes into the dumbwaiter, which would deliver his laundry from the basement to the first floor and the dishwashing station. Then he'd come up and run his laundry through the dishwasher. Again, we knew and sort of didn't know what he was up to. Neil, bless his heart, was untouchable: an indispensable part of Lindey's.

George B. Myers: My first day working as a manager, I'm closing up for Ross, and I go downstairs, and there's one of our dishwashers, an older guy, doing his laundry in a five-gallon bucket in the prep kitchen, near where we have the bread ovens. So I go over and ask him what he's doing, though it's pretty obvious.

And he tells me Sue said it was okay for him to do his clothes after we closed.

Now I can tell he's drunker than a skunk, so I tell him, no, I don't think so, no one is supposed to be here at night doing laundry or doing anything. And I tell him to stop and get ready to leave. But he insists that he's allowed to be there. So I say, all right, I'll just go upstairs and call Sue and see what she says. (But I actually had planned to call Ross, since I'd never have called the owner that late.)

So I start up the stairs and he meets me in the kitchen by the phone, and he hauls off and punches me right in the face, and yanks the tie off my neck.

So my first day on the job, I arrive with a nice black eye, and a new appreciation for Neil's preferred status.

But then, one night, someone saw Neil go down the stairs to the meat locker with an empty duffel bag, and then come back up the stairs with a full duffel bag containing 10 steaks and a few strip loins. That, regrettably, was how we parted ways.

LINDEY'S ORIGINAL CRAB CAKES WITH CREOLE MUSTARD SAUCE

IF LINDEY'S MATERNAL INFLUENCE is upper-east-side New York, our paternal home is New Orleans. Alton Doody's side of the family hails from the Gulf, and Sue and the kids often spent vacations there with relatives. "And that's a profound influence," as Alton says, "since people from New Orleans are highly opinionated about food, even if it's something as plain as a crawfish boil or something as common as a crab cake. We may not be cooking professionals, but we all have an opinion about the right way to prepare something."

Our crab cakes have been a favorite appetizer or entrée for almost two dozen years. For a time, each executive chef considered tweaking the recipe, trying a second sauce, or adding a different garnish, but this is the original version. Even if you're not from New Orleans, you may feel free to say that a "true crab cake isn't anything like this because it does/doesn't have this or that," and then serve yourself a second serving of this version.

If you're looking for that extra Lindey's touch, try this suggestion from Chef Mark Grant. "Over the years, we've garnished this perennial favorite in any number of ways. For one recent menu, we breaded them with kadaife, which is related to phyllo but looks more like shredded wheat. We'd fry that quickly so that the pastry strands would stand straight up. The line guys called it the 'Don King Crab Cake,' but that never appeared in the menu's description."

In any case, some chopped fresh parsley and half a lemon with one of those lemon "hair nets" would also work.

**serves 4 as an appetizer
(two 3-ounce cakes each)**

for the crab-cake mixture

- 🦀 1 cup heavy cream

- 🦀 1/4 teaspoon cayenne pepper

- 🦀 1 teaspoon minced jalapeño pepper

- 🦀 1/2 teaspoon Tabasco,
  or to taste

- 🦀 1/2 cup finely diced bell peppers
  (a combination of red, yellow, and green)

- 🦀 1/2 cup finely diced celery stalks

- 🦀 1/4 cup chopped fresh parsley leaves

- 🦀 1 tablespoon chopped fresh chives

- 🦀 1 cup bread crumbs, preferably
  panko (crisp Japanese bread crumbs)

- 🦀 1/2 tablespoon Dijon mustard

- 🦀 1 pound fresh jumbo lump crab meat

- 🦀 1/4 teaspoon freshly ground white pepper

- 🦀 2 teaspoons kosher salt

- 🦀 2 large egg yolks, whites reserved for
  the coating

In a medium-size heavy-bottomed saucepan, combine the cream, cayenne, and minced jalapeño. Over a medium heat, reduce the liquid by half—about 15 minutes. Be careful not to scald or burn the cream. Stir in the Tabasco, and remove from heat.

While the cream reduces, combine all the other ingredients except the crab meat and egg yolks in a large mixing bowl.

Place the egg yolks in a medium-size nonreactive mixing bowl. Once the cream mixture has reduced, very slowly pour it over the yolks in a thin stream, whisking continuously. As the yolks warm, add the remaining cream in a faster, steady flow.

Pour the cream mixture into the breading mixture and fold together. Add the crab-meat, folding gently to keep the pieces as large as possible.

for cooking the crab cakes

- 🦀 3/4 cup Wondra or all-purpose flour

- 🦀 1 whole egg, and the reserved egg
  whites, lightly beaten

- 🦀 1 cup bread crumbs, preferably panko

- 🦀 1/4 cup vegetable oil

Place three wide bowls on a work surface, one with the Wondra or flour, one with the eggs, and one with the bread crumbs. Place a sheet of parchment paper on a half-size baking sheet.

Using a small scoop or your hands, lightly form 3-ounce portions of the crab mixture (about 1 inch thick and 3 inches in diameter). Set each cake on the prepared baking sheet.

Preheat the oven to 350°F.

One at a time, dredge each crab cake in the flour, dip it into the egg wash, and roll it in the bread crumbs, pressing to create a light coating. Return it to the baking sheet. Once all eight are ready to cook, place a large heavy-bottomed skillet over medium-high heat and add the vegetable oil. When the oil has heated, transfer the coated crab cakes to the skillet with a spatula. Cook for 3 minutes until golden brown, carefully turn each one, and cook the other side for an additional 2 to 3 minutes.

Return the crab cakes to the baking sheet and place in the oven for 5 minutes or until heated through.

Place a small pool of warmed Creole Mustard Sauce on each plate, and place 2 crab cakes overlapping the sauce.

Creole Mustard Sauce
makes 1 cup, enough for 4 servings

This mustard gathers its tangy, smoky, fiery character from the Indonesian chili paste and two kinds of paprika (both kinds made from varieties of dried and ground peppers). The Hungarian paprika is the sweeter variety, while the Spanish paprika is more pungent.

- 1 cup heavy cream
- 1/8 teaspoon sambal oelek (an Indonesian chili paste, available in jars at larger markets and Asian groceries)
- 2 tablespoons whole-grain mustard
- 3/4 teaspoon Hungarian paprika
- 3/4 teaspoon Spanish paprika

In a small microwave-safe bowl, bring the cream to a simmer. Stir in the remaining ingredients, and continue to cook the liquid for 1 additional minute. Allow the mixture to cool, and then purée with a blender.

Transfer the liquid to a lidded jar and chill. Reheat the sauce in a small saucepan or in the microwave. Check the seasoning before serving, adding salt or pepper as needed. Use any remaining sauce within 1 week.

EVERYONE'S A CRITIC

IT'S THE RARE GUEST WHO'S BEING PAID TO COMPLAIN

TODAY, WE CAN ALL FANCY OURSELVES Michelin amateurs, Zagat zealots, CitySearch assistants. We log in to restaurant review sites, voting for local favorites and commenting on topical threads. We write in our authoritative two cents on everything from the "best places to take your mistress for late-night bites" to the "best wines under five bucks."

But in the culinary dark ages (a.k.a. when Lindey's opened), the reviewing of restaurants was not a secular pastime but a higher calling reserved for those bred close to the T-bone, those able to pronounce "bruschetta" (the second syllable starts with "sk," not "sh") or eat a double-cut pork chop with a pink center without hesitation.

Over the years, we've gathered paeans to our pastas, lauds for our lamb chops, and accolades for all sorts of menu items—but to reprint nothing but praise would seem narcissistic (and the job of our marketing department). Instead, we wanted to share some of the more puzzling "choice cuts" critics have served up over the years.

(Plus, we were advised not to go off on why, in the *Zagat Survey of America's Top Restaurants*, Cleveland is represented with 40 restaurants, and Cincinnati—*Cincinnati!*—with 20 restaurants, but Columbus? Columbus is completely overlooked as if all the restaurants here had been summarily excused from the great table for blowing bubbles through our cocktail straws.)

In keeping with our longstanding policy that the guest is always right even when we know we can be wittier, we've given a former server the chance to answer the critics with a little *esprit de l'escalier*, or "staircase wit": that dazzling retort you only think of when leaving the scene. His remarks follow each excerpted review. Consider them like an after-dinner drink—on the house.

Gourmet: "...Lindey's [boasts] a laughing clientele and an eclectic menu..." (Previous restaurants in this space had boasted an eclectic clientele with a laughable menu; we learned from their mistake.)

Dayton Daily News: "At Lindey's, it's a total package that makes the impression. There's an eclectic menu, a pleasing setting, and a mixed bag of customers that adds vibrancy to the place." (We also tried a mixed-bag menu, an eclectic setting, and pleasing customers, but instead of vibrating, the place just sort of yawned. But then, remembering the wit who once suggested that the *New York Times* having a rock critic was like *Women's Wear Daily* having one for football, we realized that simply setting a table without a ketchup bottle wows a food critic from Dayton.)

Washington Post: "[A] first-class restaurant in Columbus, Ohio." (While we were certainly flattered to read this endorsement in a first-class newspaper, we've always been curious how the *Baltimore Sun*, whose food section once sported the headline "How to Put Pickles Up Yourself," might have characterized our German Village crowd.)

Mike Harden, the *Columbus Dispatch:* "[Lindey's is] a whole way of life—it's a theater, it's an art gallery, it's an Easter parade." (Unfortunately, in order to accommodate the newspaper's tight layout, the columnist's words were heavily edited. The rest of his sentence continued, "...it's a fashion runway, it's a PTA Fun Frolic, it's a weenie roast, it's a petting zoo with miniature ponies, it's a trip to the moon on gossamer wings, it's just one of those things.")

Jon Christensen, *Columbus Monthly:* "What's surprising is that Lindey's has seemed to improve in spite of, or perhaps even because of, the upheavals. It wasn't long ago that we couldn't get anything but excruciatingly slow service, or even surly service." (Just a tip: using the royal "we" when writing for a hometown publication that devotes serious column inches to buffalo wings tends to make waiters want to give you a wide berth. As for the "surly service," that was just an inspired moment.)

Jim O'Connor, *Downtown Alive:* "I will say that when Lindey's first opened I heard many complaints about the rudeness of some of the waiters. (Is there anything more cranky than a waiter who wants to be a dress designer?)" (In fact, Jim, the following things are crankier: children who untie their Lindey's helium balloon from the arm of the chair and aren't permitted to have another balloon even if the server offers one; regulars who find their regular table occupied; the paralegals from V.S.S. & P. who learn that the bar blender's on the fritz; either of the Doody boys on a good day; and of course, zaftig food critics who, having teetered on a tiny café chair for close to three hours, overhear their waiter suggesting that a dress with vertical stripes would slimmerize even the chunkiest restaurant critic.)

Detroit Monthly: "Dubbed the 'Stork Club of Columbus,' [Lindey's] attracts the city's 'beautiful people.'" (And the resemblance to New York's legendary bar is even more striking when you see your server leave the restaurant after his shift in a disco unitard.)

The Grumpy Gourmet, from Mariani's *Coast-to-Coast Dining Guide*, edited by John Mariani, with America's Best Critics, 1985: "While Lindey's is considered to be a classy 'wine bar' in the intended context, it ain't. It is classy, but wine choices are limited to less than the best available in the market. Servers know nothing about the wines, so trust your own opinions and the labels. You're dining next to a vodka martini drinker and being served by a St. Pauli girl." (We tried having the Blue Nun serve him, but she absolutely refused his excited suggestion that she sit on his lap.) "Avoid the house bread which is something akin to an Iranian terrorist—hard enough to break your face and flaky." (Funny he should say that, since conspiring Central Ohio servers have long had a fatwa on fatheads.) "There is zero parking in the neighborhood, so call a cab. If you are an experienced car parker in Times Square or downtown Beirut, then you may survive a trip to Lindey's." (Enough with the Middle Eastern aspersions! No matter. Considering that the Grump arrived on a broom, we had no trouble accommodating his vehicle.)

Carl Japikse, *Pigging Out in Columbus:* "On a crowded evening—and that can be any one—the decibel level can get a little out of control. It's the kind of problem every restaurant wishes it had. The best defense against it, I have found, is quite simple...bring your own noise with you." (Carl must have been here one of those nights when we had to seat one of the regular front-room bon vivants in the normally sedate back dining room.)

John Marshall, *Columbus Monthly:* "...the service is as good as any place in town. The staffers are friendly, helpful, even a bit gregarious. Although they do introduce themselves, they do not exhibit the all-too-common assumption that citizens go to restaurants primarily to meet waiters." (True enough. A server is trained to introduce him- or herself at each table, but, typically, the home phone number is not among the nightly specials unless the reviewer is particularly generous or handsome.)

Campaigns & Elections, "America's 50 Favorite Political Hangouts," 1993: "Columbus: Tucked away in German Village, where workers from the old breweries used to live, Lindey's is a Republican favorite. Party leader Bob Bennett has adopted it as his own stomping ground. Owner Sue Doody prides her 12-year-old restaurant for its great pasta and American Cuisine." (While we try to be nonpartisan at Lindey's, we certainly prefer our patrons to be liberal with their tips.)

Bob Bennett: Every chairman of the Republican National Committee has had lunch or dinner at Lindey's, at least once, and this is going back to Lee Atwater, G.H.W. Bush's campaign manager, and all the way up to Ken Mehlman, George W. Bush's manager for 2004. I just like entertaining at Lindey's; it saves the wear and tear on my house.

Dave Davis, *Columbus Underground:* "The setting is really quaint with a small fountain and I imagine it would be a pretty good place for a nice, romantic date. If you're into that sort of thing." (Memo to critic: If you're banking on an unsuccessful date, definitely refer to romance as "that sort of thing.")

Fodor's Guide reviewer: "The atmosphere is so homey…no matter if you're in the smoking or non-smoking part." (This is assuming that you share your home with 75 chain-smokers, which is roughly the capacity of the front room, our former smoking section.)

CitySearch reviewer: "Watch the gnocchi, though. I love gnocchi and always order it when it's on the menu at any restaurant, but Lindey's gnocchi is unconventional. The sauce is not what you typically associate with pasta, so be warned. Not bad but not wonderful." (With so much else going on at Lindey's, do you really want to spend your time watching the unconventional gnocchi? Why not ogle our overzealous onion soup or stare down our original rack of lamb?)

DRBLAB, Web site: "I highly suggest utilizing the valet parking; although my valet took the keys home for our car, and we had to wait on his return, management handled the situation with professionalism. To quote a friend of mine, 'Sometimes it's not the incident of error that matters but how we recover and reestablish the relationship.' (That's so funny, because our valets also have a saying: "It's not only finding a place to park the guest's car, but also remembering to recover the license plate that pops off when you establish its relationship to the bumpers of adjacent cars.")

Burton Cantrell, Business First: "Lindey's…is often filled with an air of buzzing excitement, like a house where a birthday cake is in the oven." (If there's a cake in the oven and a buzzing in the house, Burton, that means something is about to burn.) "I could dine at Lindey's every night for a week and find the setting as unique as seven different holes on a good golf course." (Perhaps you're thinking of Tavern on the Green. Here in German Village, guests are strictly prohibited from taking out their putters.) "I have a friend who goes to Lindey's simply because she gets a charge out of seeing so many lawyers trying to talk with their mouths full. If you continually run into your lawyer at Lindey's, I would recommend switching law firms rather than switching restaurants." (Would you rather be paying your attorney's hourly rate while he or she deliberately chews each bite the requisite 50 times before swallowing and only then answers your pressing question? We didn't think so.)

Peter Mandel, the Washington Post, in an article entitled "O-Hi-Germany: For a bit of Deutschland, a village in Columbus is (almost) the real deal": "There's no sauerbraten on the menu, but who cares. Despite its lack of German specialties, Lindey's…has some of the best cuisine in the Village… Plus, the dining room has a bustling, Paris brasserie air." (Point taken. But most nights, we can almost guarantee that you'll spot one gentleman or another wearing nylons and calling it "meine Lederhosen.")

M. Ruth Abbott, *CEM:* "You'll never find Lindey's deserted. At noontime, it's buzzing with Columbus's power players; lots of handshakes and slick Italian suits. It's all money, honey, and something's happening at every white-clothed table." (What's happening is that billable hours and talking with those mouths full guarantees us a lot of changing linen.)

Mark Bernstein, *AmericaWest:* "Lindey's staked its claim early and never yielded: For a quarter century, this restaurant has ranked among Columbus, Ohio's half-dozen best." (Actually we tried to stake our claim on the whole of our German Village block, but we conceded the idea that leaving other houses in the neighborhood makes the annual *Haus und Garten* Tour more interesting. And when you say "quarter century," you almost make us sound respectable. It's not as if we're one of the 13 original colonies. We're just a humble neighborhood bistro with an overactive pituitary.) "If you wish to extend the evening out a little, consider the cigar list, ranging up to the La Duc Cognac Torpedo ($220), which spent three years in a cask with 30-year old cognac. Cognac is not the only thing that ages well; so does Lindey's." (We also have a selection of regulars at our bar who have spent at least 30 years soaking in cognac, in case that's more in your price range.)

Gayot.com: "The loud, smoky bar is the hub of this upscale boîte in German Village—-a Georgetown-like red brick enclave that passes for 'old' by Columbus standards. The high ceilings and the multi-levels of dining areas that radiate from this bar's bustle are more Victorian than Old German, giving the feeling of a onetime town mansion that's been reconfigured into a business." (We don't know about Georgetown, but in German Village, one says "excuse me" after emitting a boîte.)

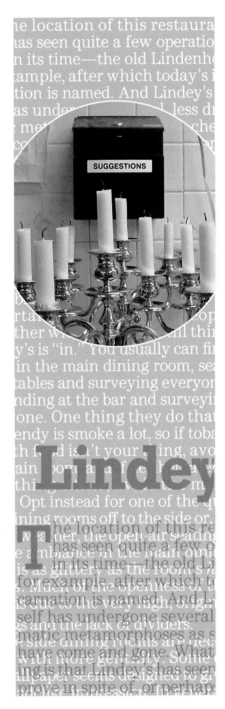

SOMETHING TO CELEBRATE
A YEAR OF SPECIAL EVENTS AT LINDEY'S

EVERY DAY AT LINDEY'S, several tables are filled with people celebrating one thing or another: an anniversary, a promotion, a mortgage closing, a political landslide, a fabulous haircut, the first time dear friends have hooked up in over six months.... But there are some occasions when the whole restaurant celebrates, when the host stand works double-time, the kitchen crew reveals dishes it's been prepping all week, and the dining room atmosphere seems composed of entirely different gases. More oxygen? A little too much helium?

In addition to events like holidays, prom nights, and OSU football games, there are the weeks of the Quarter Horse Congress when the faint aroma of hay and leather permeates the restaurant; Denison Parents Weekend, when the dining room has the appearance of a Ralph Lauren commercial; or the Arnold Classic when bodybuilders descend upon Columbus and our Bentwood chairs really bend under the weight of people who are actually in shape. (Some of the bodybuilders even require two chairs, one for each perfectly ripped gluteus maximus.) And then there are various German Village events like the annual garage sale, *Haus und Garten* Tour, and Oktoberfest, when Lindey's becomes each event's unofficial epicenter and afterparty.

Here are a few snapshots from these giddy moments, beginning with the craziest night of any year.

New Year's Eve

Server K: Lindey's *transforms* for New Year's Eve. One year, I swear we put a table anywhere a table could fit, and we probably considered stacking them two high. We had a band upstairs and a band downstairs, including a trombone player and someone at a table that I felt sure was going to have his head knocked off by one big sliding note. We took the Terrace Room and turned it into a second kitchen. Rented hot boxes, steam wells—it was amazing. And, for the most part, we got people their food, pretty much on time, table after table.

A veteran observer: I always thought it interesting that guests for New Year's Eve would be gorgeous, so fine looking, so refined. But by the stroke of midnight, they'd look as if they'd been in a train wreck: their stockings are run, they're shouting, they're completely disheveled. If anyone would show them a picture of what they were going to look like three hours later, they would be horrified. I bet the whole evening would be different.

Andrea Cambern: Our first New Year's Eve in Columbus, we assembled some friends to celebrate at Lindey's. There's something magical about New Year's Eve in this place. A lot of people know each other. It's not too big. It's not forced. It's comfortable, and the party just fills the place. And because our anniversary also happens to be New Year's Eve, it always feels as if the whole restaurant is celebrating with us.

This is 1991. We're all enjoying the evening; the champagne is flowing. There's a great buzz, and energy coming from friends as well as strangers, and one thing leads to another and Marcy Fleischer, a former reporter at Channel 10, and I begin a conga line in the main dining room. We snake through the aisles and into the other dining room, recruiting dancers and servers along the way, and we end up, a huge line of us, at the bar. Marcy turns to me and says, "Let's go," as if there's no place else but up, and we slip off our shoes and hop on the bar. Just the two of us. And we continue dancing and everyone else continues dancing below us, with the band playing chorus after chorus.

Brett Cambern: We had a very long table, and I remember whoever I was talking to saying, "Oh, look, Brett: there's your wife and Marcy dancing on the bar." I look over and, at the moment, I don't know, it just seemed right. And then the following year, Andrea says to me, "Brett, just *don't* let me get carried away again." And then after a few hours of eating and drinking and dancing, she just can't help it. She's up on the bar again. Without trying, it became a tradition, and it's hard to imagine starting the new year without Andrea dancing on the bar at Lindey's.

General manager Shelia Wiley: New Year's Eve, 2003, we were full. I mean full, as in I can't say how full in case the fire marshal is reading this and we can still get in trouble. We had two bands playing, one downstairs and one upstairs, where we were having a seven-course tasting menu paired with wines. People are laughing, dancing among the crowded tables, dancing on the bar, dancing along the foot-wide room divider that runs between the rows of banquettes. The ceilings of the restaurant are filled with black and silver helium balloons

with strings dangling down above the guests. It's a fabulous evening.

We all shout the countdown to midnight, with the kitchen crew in the dining room dancing and tossing back champagne with the guests.

Twenty minutes later, *ZZZROOOM!* All of a sudden, no lights, no amplifiers, no heat. The power's out. The room's pretty bright with all the candles, but we break out more candles.

People don't care! They're still dancing. The musicians are playing without electricity. The celebration continues while the managers finally figure out that one plug in the office—obviously on some other circuit—is still working. They run a few extension cords and process all the table checks so people can settle up and leave.

Meanwhile, I go outside, I see all the lights out on one side of the block, and then I look up and see a cluster of our New Year's Eve helium balloons all wound around the transformer. Did some stupid reveler from our party release the balloons and cause the outage?

We spent the rest of the night, cleaning up, waiting for the power to come back on, vowing that we'd fake a power outage every New Year's Eve if it got guests leaving a little early! Later, we heard that a transformer had blown, which had nothing to do with Lindey's guests.

Valentine's Day

This is not only one of the busiest nights of the year, but it's also the oddest one, since most every table is a deuce.

Server G: On February 14th, Lindey's becomes a romantic theme park: couples all want to share one side of a table as if they were snuggling in the bucket of a Ferris wheel. We send them around a couple times, they have their lovey-dovey dinner in the twinkling candle-light, and then it's out into the cold night for them and the next couple climbs into the booth.

Server A: Valentine's Day is amateur night, like Mother's Day and prom night, when we're serving a whole new set of people in the restaurant trying out "that crazy restaurant in German Village" for the first time. And the regulars? They stay in the safety of their own homes on those nights!

Prom Night

The mean age in the dining room drops about 30 years for prom night each year. The restaurant is booked solid, but only for the first turn; the high-school couples parade in shortly after they finish their homework, and shuttle off to their dance by 7:15. Trish, Sue's daughter, worked as a hostess for a few seasons at Lindey's. On one prom night, seating the dressed-up couples, it became increasingly clear to her that nearly all the kids were much bigger than what she remembered from her high-school years. The boys were all 6'3" and 6'4" and the woman were all well-endowed. "It's got to be all the hormones in the milk," she concluded. And from that night on, she and her husband Michael decided they'd only have organic foods in their house. They didn't want their children to be any bigger than their genes had already predicted.

Mother's Day

When is there a special occasion at every single table in the house? When are there more clusters of flowers on bosoms than table linens? It's Mother's Day, our busiest day of the entire year, and not simply because we serve close to 1,000 people and the kitchen is dipping giant strawberries in chocolate to give as a little gift to each and every mother. It's also a unique day numbers-wise: it's a day of almost pure food sales. (You have to show *some* temperance in front of your mom!)

Wedding Bells

Sous chef **Korir Russell:** In the bustle of a wedding a few years ago, one of our servers noticed that a wedding party had left without the top layer of their wedding cake, and during the cleaning up, he sliced it up for the waitstaff.

Sue: I walked into the kitchen, and everyone was eating little slices of the wedding cake, and I said to them, *"What are you thinking?* That's their *wedding* cake!"

Korir: But the next day, the bride—this was her second marriage—remembered that she didn't have her cake top, and she came back for it. And when we didn't have it waiting for her, she freaked out. "If my marriage doesn't work out, it's because Lindey's has put a curse on it, and...I'll come back to get you if anything goes wrong." Or something to that effect.

Sue: So I called the baker who'd made their cake and commissioned them to make another cake top, exactly like the first one, so they could have it for their first anniversary. The restaurant also gave her some Lindey's gift certificates, and even treated the couple to their first anniversary dinner. So the marriage lasted at least a year—so the "curse" has probably expired, hasn't it?

General manager Tom Harlor: On April 4th, the place was booked solid, with a rehearsal dinner upstairs in the Mohawk Room. Earlier that day, the snow started coming down—the wet, heavy snow—and 8 or 10 inches later, wires were dropping in the Village, and we lost power. We put a closed sign on the restaurant door, we called to cancel all the reservations on the books, but we couldn't reach the party planning to have the rehearsal dinner. Of course, they were probably rehearsing somewhere. So they arrived. And we didn't have a choice; we escorted them upstairs by flashlight, lit the party room and table with more than the usual number of candles, and the kitchen made their dinners by the light of the gas burners and flashlights. I don't think the party stayed quite as long as they might have, but it was the eve of a wedding, so no one was anything but happy.

Chef Gretchen Eiselt: The most fabulous party ever hosted at Lindey's—at least during my time at the restaurant—was Beth Doody's wedding. The ceremony was held upstairs, while we had food stations for the reception throughout the entire restaurant.

Beth Doody: When I got married in 1996, Lindey's had never closed on a Saturday night. I remember my dad called Mom: "What the hell are you doing closing on Saturday night! Do you know how much revenue you're losing?"

Gretchen: The place was filled with seafood. We had a raw bar with oysters and shrimp, we had caviar, and we had a centerpiece, our lobster Cobb salad, served in the shell of an 18-pound lobster. Yes, the family brought in a lobster that was so huge, I carried it around, clutched to my shoulder just like a toddler, to show everyone.

Chef Jared Bissel: Chef Matt ran the lobster head through the dishwasher and wore it as a hat. I shucked a million oysters for that night, at one point cutting my thumb right through the nail. I wrapped a towel around it and kept going. We pre-shucked 300 oysters, and then I shucked oysters to order—easily another 500 oysters—and I wasn't even working the whole time. So maybe it wasn't a million, but we had an insane number of oysters!

Halloween

Our first Halloween, in 1981, Sue dressed up as Suzie Chaffee, the "quintessential silver-sequined snow ballerina" (according to *Powder* magazine), who achieved another kind of

fame from her Chapstick ads on television. Sue wore long blond hair and made herself into a wind-burned skier. She walked into the dining room with her ski poles, and banged them on the floor, and the entire room turned to see her: "Hi, I'm Suzie Chaffee."

Chef **Tom Johnson:** Another waiter came as Hamlet, wearing nothing but pantyhose below his tunic, and a long sword that kept banging into the heads of the people at whatever table he was standing next to. And he had, well, his own sword sort of tucked in his britches. I remember we had to have him put on an apron for the rest of the evening, Halloween or not. I think that was the first and last time the staff dressed up for Halloween.

Sue: For some of our regulars, Halloween seemed to be the perfect time to cross the not-so-fine line into bad taste. One year, a neighbor's party theme for the night was "Outrageous," and their guests definitely rose to the occasion. We even had a group of hos and pimps, including a couple dressed in blackface, who stopped in on the way to the party just long enough to offend absolutely everyone.

Thanksgiving

In addition to 80 pounds of prime rib and 48 pounds of leg of lamb that we serve for Thanksgiving meals, we also cook: 620 pounds of turkey (120 pounds for the Salvation Army dinner), 250 pounds of cornbread stuffing, 48 pounds of cranberries for our relish, 90 pounds of green beans, (50 pounds for the Salvation Army dinner), 250 pounds of mashed potatoes, 150 pounds of sweet potatoes, and 300 slices of pie.

The Christmas Season

While Lindey's used to close by midafternoon on Christmas Eve for Christmas, the spirit of the holidays in all of German Village has always lasted for weeks: the wreaths and lights on all of the small homes, the snowfall on streets that aren't wide enough to clear, the people all bundled up and trudging right outside our front windows.

Jim Barnes: During the Christmas season, which begins mid-November, Lindey's would start playing carols and, forgive me, some of us had an incredible aversion to them. "Little Drummer Boy" is at the top of my list. Jan and I would walk into Lindey's, and the manager, Ross, would smile, run to the sound system, switch off the caroling, and rush back to seat us saying, "Do you know how many times 'Little Drummer Boy' plays during my shift? About 23 times!"

Server Erich Kraus: Desperate to earn enough money in order to move to Germany, I scheduled myself to work every shift that Lindey's was open in December. That was lunch or brunch and dinner, seven days a week. (Minus Christmas Eve and Christmas, that's 57 consecutive shifts that go roughly 10:00 to 3:00, and 4:00 to midnight—*at least*—in the busiest time of the year.) I didn't get much sleep, but the money I earned during those four weeks would shock most people. It even managed to shock Sue about mid-month.

"Now, hon..." she said to me one afternoon, "you can't keep working all these hours. I can't pay you overtime. My labor-cost percentages would go over—"

"Well, what if I clock out?" I offered.

"No, then you wouldn't be covered by workman's comp, and what if something happened to you?"

She had reasons that I really didn't understand. Finally, I explained to Sue that I only had this one month before my move and that I needed to earn as much as possible, so wasn't there some way that we could work it out? "After all," I said, "You don't want me calling you collect from Berlin begging for money, do you?"

Without looking up from her desk, she replied, "I wouldn't accept the charges, hon."

And that was the extent of her concern. We worked something out.

Ann Shay: Every year our family has held our Christmas Eve at Lindey's, during lunch, in one of the upstairs rooms. Last fall, we had taken our seven grandchildren to Disney World. During the welcome revue, the Disney dancers and characters came out with washboards that said "Columbus Washboard Company" on one side, since they're made here in Columbus. So my husband decided that he was going to order these washboards for our grandkids for our Christmas party.

There were 24 of us upstairs in the Mohawk Room, which hopefully meant some of the noise was confined to the second floor. He handed a washboard to each of our grandchildren—age 5 to age 15—and they took their spoons and scraped up and down on the metal, singing "Jingle Bells" and "Santa Claus Is Coming to Town."

A belated thank you (or apology?) to Sara, our server.

PROFILES IN COURAGE
...AND HEELS: SHELIA WILEY

NOW A DISTRICT PARTNER in Bravo! Development Incorporated, the restaurant group that grew out of Lindey's, Shelia Wiley was something of a force of nature during her time at Lindey's. She wasn't the first female general manager, nor the first from the South, nor the first African-American on staff. But she was the first to be all three. And did we say she was stunning, feisty, hilarious, dressed to kill, and pretty much always late?

Shelia Arrives

Server **Allen Jones:** When Shelia came for her interviews at Lindey's, she had her hair in major cornrows. I mean, like the kind the alien in *Predator* wore. But then the first day of work, her hair was done up beautifully, she had impeccable make-up, and a very gracious manner. However, sometimes she'd arrive at work right under the deadline, and not exactly put together. Never one to withhold comment, one day I said, "So...you expect us to come in here with four pens, a pepper grinder, a corkscrew, a lighter, and a crisp, clean uniform, and *you* don't even have *two eyebrows?*"

General manager **Rebecca Holder:** Lindey's staff had never worked for a powerhouse like Shelia. Both dead serious and seriously funny, she was a dynamo. Servers still laugh, telling "Shelia stories," and others still have Shelia nightmares. She expected—and she got—as much as she gave from everyone.

Now you knew you were in trouble, when, in the middle of service, Shelia grabbed you by the upper arm, and led you toward the side stand. She'd get right up in your face: "Tell me what you see!" she'd say, pointing back at the server's station. *"Be the dining room!"*

"Be the dining room!" That's what she'd say, and that meant that she had noticed things that weren't right, and you were supposed to turn around, find all the mistakes like in those kids' puzzle books where the artist draws things topsy-turvy and out of place—someone didn't have a napkin, a dead soldier was left on a table, a water glass was half-empty, or some other bit of inattentive service—and then report back to her with everything you were going to go fix, *immediately!*

Shelia: When I first started here, men would ask me to come over to their table. Sometimes it was because they actually needed the manager, but sometimes it was just to flirt. It ended up being rather time-consuming and tiresome. So I finally said to the staff, "You find out what a man wants before you ask me to go over to his table, you understand? If a gentleman wants to get my attention, tell him to send me flowers. I mean, I can't get my meat where I get my bread! Not while I'm working."

Fast(-Talking) Food

Shelia: A party of eight sat down at Table 33, including a gentleman who'd just come home from a stint overseas. He ordered a steak, but I could see something was wrong—this man was pouting. I went over and inquired if everything was all right, and the man says he didn't want to be at Lindey's. "I got outvoted," he tells me. "All I wanted was Wendy's. I was craving Wendy's. I've been gone for months, and now I'm stuck here for the evening."

So I squat down next to the man. "What would you have wanted? A double cheeseburger?" (The man nodded yes.) "And those big-ol' fries, too?" (The man nodded yes.) "And for a beverage, were you thinking of that big lemonade they have? That sound right?" (The man nodded yes.) "All right, I'm going to get as close as I can to your Wendy's, so you stop your pouting," I said, and left the table.

So I called over to the Wendy's and got the manager. (A hundred years ago, I was a G.M. at a Wendy's down south.) "I need a double cheese dressed up to the nines, know what I'm saying? I need to be able to present a very beautiful burger to a guest here. Put it in the salad box so it won't be smashed. And give me a big order of fries, uncooked—I'll cook them here. And your giant lemonade *without* the ice; I don't want it watery by the time I serve it."

We ran and got the order, including a nice, flat foil wrapper, and prepared everything perfectly on Lindey's plates. When I brought out his dinner with the other dinners, he almost cried. The whole table was in shock, laughing. At the end of the meal, he couldn't thank me enough. But I said, "You might not thank me when you see the bill. Even though we didn't cook the steak you ordered originally, I'm still going to charge you for that. You just ate the most expensive Wendy's meal you'll ever have."

Heels' Kitchen

Chef Matt Harding: Shelia is a marvel. She wanted to entertain the guests and make them come back, but she also took care of the staff in similar ways. For instance, instead of staying in the front of the house, she'd join us in the kitchen and fry up some chicken, or make homemade candy, or gumbo, or her fabulous bread pudding.

One day, my chef Mark Grant comes up to me: "Do you realize how much of my vanilla she's using?" At the time, the vanilla crop in Madagascar had jumped to something like $200 a quart, and Shelia was using up a cup or more every week!

Sous chef **Léon de Leon:** On a slow day, Shelia would waltz into the kitchen through the side door, holding two shopping bags from Big Bear. She'd strap on an apron and squeeze herself in between the line cooks on the sauté station. "I'm making fried chicken for the staff."

"How the hell are you going to make dinner and also run all around and do whatever else you got to do?" I'd say. We'd all say something like that, kidding her. And she'd say. "You-all are gonna miss me one day."

She was in everyone's way, but she was making a staff meal, all by herself: fried chicken and peach cobbler to die for—you didn't want anything else.

But her favorite treat was bread pudding. And she'd make it for her favorite guests. She'd bring in her Wonder Bread or brioche and wedge herself right into the line, grab a pan, a free burner, and a new bottle of well bourbon. She'd look over at me, doing whatever I was doing: "Léon, you know how to make a good sauce for bread pudding?" And I'd nod and she'd go on: "You've got all the butter and sugar and then you add bourbon—oh, honey, did I tell you about the new shoes I found?" (She's inverted the bourbon and deliberately not looking at how much she's pouring. The bourbon is flooding the pan, and she's talking and talking, and then she takes a quick look—a third of the bottle's gone—and keeps talking.) "And you know what I paid? You don't want to know what I paid for these shoes!" I'm telling you she'd serve half a bottle of bourbon in a sauce that would serve six people. You had to be 21 to have this dessert!

And P.S.: Shelia wouldn't let you reheat the sauce because that would burn off the alcohol and ruin the whole dessert.

Another thing you need to know about Shelia: she had shoes. Shoes like nobody else had shoes. She had shoes for the dining room and shoes for the kitchen. When she wanted to cook, she'd slip off her fancy pumps and slip on some flip-flops. And she'd *never* wear the one pair of shoes in the other room. So the staff liked to hide her "dining room shoes" when she was in the kitchen. Or put them in the freezer.

Or say Shelia wanted you to do something you didn't think was quite right, and say you weren't all that eager to give in. In just about two seconds, Shelia would say, "Look, I'll tell you what," and then she'd kick off her shoes, flinging them across the kitchen straight toward you: "*You* try to walk in them! *Go on!* But let me tell you, if you stretch them out, mister, *I'm gonna fuck you up!*"

Laundry Day

General manager **Rebecca Holder:** One day the staff walked in and Shelia had Lindey's entire supply of napkins on the bar. And she was going to have everyone fold napkins until they were all folded because—well, maybe one side stand ran out of clean napkins at lunch or there were napkins folded inside out. Whatever it was, it's what was on her mind and had to

be done *that minute*. The whole waitstaff was going to fold, *and fold neatly*, while she marched up and down the bar, cajoling her team into folding every napkin just right.

Twenty minutes of folding later, one server came up to me and said, "Since when do we work at Lindey's sweat shop?"

So DON'T Take the Money and Run

Shelia: For whatever reason, this guest just didn't enjoy his meal, so I arrived at the table, told him I was taking care of his check this evening, and then, thinking that was that, I see that the "conversation" is continuing, with the man extending his credit card toward me.

"No, I'm paying for my meal."

"No, you're not. We didn't live up to our reputation, and—"

He interrupts. His credit card is pointed at me like a sword. So I dodge, and parry:

"No, I appreciate that, but I'm not going to take your money."

"*Yes*, you *are*. I pay my way through life."

"That's good," I say, smiling back at him, since we both see how foolish this is getting. "But we didn't take care of you. And that's that."

"But I'm still paying."

"But just how are you going to make me take your money?" I say, turning on some Southern charm.

It dawns on him that no one here is going to run his credit card. But we have this funny few seconds where he's trying to figure out how he can force the money on me. Finally he smiles back. "Okay, I'm paying for the service, and I'm paying for the wines," he says.

"You're just hard-headed, aren't you?"

We agreed to disagree, I suppose. The guest may always be right, but at Lindey's, I always liked to be righter.

TOO MANY CHEFS SPOIL THE JOKE

COOKING UP A STORM

"The kitchen in a restaurant is like backstage at a theatre. Everyone's working to put on a show that the patrons have come to see, and behind the scenes, water is flooding in from the patio, the grease trap has stopped up, the dishwasher didn't show up, the cooks aren't speaking to one another, and the sous chef just cut himself and is debating about whether or not to go get stitches. Meanwhile, out in the dining room? It's all pomp and circumstance and glitter." —*Chef Bob Keane*

WHEN LINDEY'S OPENED IN 1981, if you felt hungry, you weighed the fridge's prospects against the possibilities offered by nearby restaurants. Then, if dining out sounded more promising, you thought about what *food*, not what *chef*, you wanted to try. Dining pleasure had to do with qualities such as taste, price, atmosphere, length of the bartender's pour, and whether or not you were willing to wait for a table. Yes, you might have debated about one cuisine or another, but rarely did you consider the individuals creating the menu. (And let's remember, even "cuisine" in 1980s Columbus mostly meant chains, Chinese-American, Italian-American, casual, or fast food, with very few ethnic offerings unless you counted every Zantigo's and Taco Bell drive-thru as a Hispanic restaurant.) Ninety-nine-point-nine percent of any restaurant's guests probably never knew the chef's name, even when the place was called "Mama Leone's Kitchen." And even a place with that name usually indicated the original owner's family name, passed on along with the business.

But today we dine under the glow of star chefs, where we even know the names of chefs in other cities—in restaurants where we haven't even eaten. Our appetites are at least partly satisfied now by a chef's apprenticeships, aspirations, and even social conscience. (Okay, coupons and portion size are still key happiness factors.) Our culinary curiosity, our expectations for a dining experience, and our general food savvy has grown keener in the last quarter century, even here in a "meat-and-potatoes town" where, as chef Kent Rigsby points out, most people prefer their steaks cooked into medium oblivion.

It's hard to say with any accuracy how many chefs Lindey's has hired over the years. At any time, we have an executive chef, a few sous chefs and line cooks, apprentices, chefs training at Lindey's to work at another restaurant in the group founded at Lindey's, and, of course, prep cooks and dishwashers.

But just counting chefs, we're going to throw out the number 25. That's 25, or maybe 30, chefs who have left their mark on Lindey's, whether by dint of dazzling innovation or sheer duration. And that still leaves us room for a few tales of chefs whose kitchen stints were little more than a flash in the pan.

It's often said how tough a chef's job is, and how improbable it is that anyone could manage to keep up the hours, the intensity, the responsibility. If a chef's job were just inventing recipes, or merely preparing those recipes for table after table of appreciative and/or impossible diners, that would be reasonable. But a chef's job also includes staff management, public relations, food- and labor-cost analysis, inventory control, sanitation supervision, daily and ongoing ordering, and plenty of sheer physical labor in a kitchen where the temperature is likely to be a bit warmer than the comfortable dining room where the rest of us are lucky to sit.

And the hours are long—often very early and very late. Weekends are days on, rather than days off. There's the demanding need for perfect timing and precision teamwork among the kitchen crew (many of whom work two shifts on too little sleep). There's the pressure from servers, owners, managers, guests, and even from within the hierarchy of chefs. And don't forget the heat. All this combines to create a pace that recalls what race-car driver Mario Andretti once said: "If things seem under your control, you're just not going fast enough."

And did we mention the great pay? We didn't think so.

Think of the following pages as snapshots from the album of chefs who have posed behind the stove at Lindey's.

Our First Dishes

Sue Doody: In our first several months, Lindey's had to figure out which dishes were feasible in terms of preparation time, guest appeal, and cost. Everyone had ideas for me. Alton wanted more of one kind of dish, but Rick and Chris suggested something else. I had delicious recipes that I'd developed from various cookbooks, but I soon realized they weren't adaptable to production cooking. You don't just multiply by 6 if you want 24 dinners out of a recipe that serves 4. Not if you ever want to make money.

Chef Tom Johnson: Lindey's began with something like an encyclopedic approach to cuisine. We could do quite fine food, but it was sometimes a New York bistro item and at other times a New Orleans pastiche, a French classic, or something entirely American. Meanwhile the specials could be something Chinese, osso buco, a lovely risotto, or just a pan-seared fresh fish.

Alton Doody: One of our original menu items was linguine with clams. The Grumpy Gourmet, Doral Chenoweth, absolutely loved that dish. But when chef Tom Johnson arrived, he said it had to go, and then Doral had a fit when it wasn't listed on the menu. There's no pleasing everybody, even though that's exactly what we tried to do.

Tom: Once Sue and I were preparing a lunch for 150 people, which was huge for us at the time, and some of the staff didn't show. Right in the middle of the lunch, Alton walked into the kitchen with a dish of cole slaw in his hands. We were up to our asses in alligators, we couldn't even look up, and he said, "Sue, this isn't how you make it at home." I don't know how Sue dealt with it. He simply didn't understand how you had to concentrate.

Suzanne Karpus, owner of Cornucopia Catering: Before Sharon Reiss and I opened our business, we worked at Lindey's, mostly doing pastas, desserts, and prep work with Tom Johnson in the basement kitchen.

In the early years, Lindey's didn't have a real system. Tom would be preoccupied with one thing or another, and he'd give us the night's specials very late in the day, and then we'd all be scrambling to create the specials, even as the guests were coming in.

We were still improvising to get each evening's meals on the table. One time, I made pâtés and I forgot to remind Tom that they were in the oven; I thought he knew. So when he discovered them in the oven at closing, they were no longer pâtés. But the next day, we used them as the stuffing for the cannelloni. You have to work efficiently, fearlessly, and, if the restaurant is going to stay afloat, you need to use most everything you've purchased. Cooking is an imperfect world. If only cookies didn't burn, things weren't forgotten, things didn't break. If all you were doing was cooking for people, being a chef would be pure joy. It would be ideal. But when you own a restaurant, suddenly the business challenges come in. You find out that you can't take two hours to make a tart. And rather than lose the joy, there's a different fun that comes from speeding up and getting the same results. You learn

to do two or three things at once. The whole day becomes denser and packed with activity. You can examine the day, see where you were efficient, and learn where you could improve. Lindey's taught me how to see a wider world even in the specific tasks of creating one dish.

Tom Johnson: Sue had hired Walter to prepare the recipes she'd developed. He was still working there when I arrived, and I let him do the ordering, since I just hated all that. Had we only understood that he used the "one-for-the-restaurant-and-one-for-me" method! But his pilfering managed to go undetected for quite some time. His career finally ended with us when he decided to sue Lindey's after he fell and hurt his back.

Sue: Yes, Walter fell, after having half a water glass full of vodka for his "shift drink." The poor man had been robbing Lindey's blind for months and, apparently, was in cahoots with the meat salesman because we'd order all kinds of things that never appeared in the delivered orders.

Chef **Kent Rigsby:** A kitchen is really based on the whole brigade system: the uniforms, the hats, the chain of command. It's derived from the military. And that chain of command can't be compromised: if all of a sudden, in the middle of service, someone thinks he or she knows better—it's just *not* the time to stop the flow of service. Bring it up at a meeting after the shift, but *not* in the heat of the moment. I'd have to say that's what would infuriate me at Lindey's—and still does: trying to keep a dozen things flowing, on time, up to speed, with good quality and great efficiency, and suddenly screeching to a halt because someone's missing or someone decides to change something without me knowing.

Bartender **T.A. Anderson:** During the "reign" of some chefs, if I went back into the kitchen, there'd be plenty of yelling and arguments, and heated negotiations between the cooks and the waiters a plate smashed or flung across the room on occasion. And the waitstaff, they'd come to me at the service bar, and complain about the kitchen. And then, at the end of the evening, the chef would come out, stand at the end of the bar, and have a cocktail, and sometimes, give me his side of things. I came to think of the bar as a kind of DMZ, midway between the front and the back of the house.

Chris Doody: Before I knew much of anything about the restaurant business, I worked as a busboy at Lindey's. I was a freshman in college. Kent was the chef then, and one day I'm walking through the back door, near the dumpster, thinking I'm hot shit, Sue's son, and I say, "Kent, it smells like hell out here. Can't you get that cleaned up?"

He gets so upset, he takes all the dinners that were ready to go out and tosses them all on the floor, breaking a bunch of china. And then he storms out of the kitchen and goes to find Sue. Eventually, my mom comes into the kitchen and says to me, "Chris, don't piss off the chef unless you can do his job." From that moment, I figured I had better learn the business before I made any more comments.

Two Very Brief Courses

Sue: We managed to hire a chef we'll call Chef M. We were very excited about this man: we sent out cards announcing his arrival and ran an ad in *Columbus Monthly* that read, in part: "It's a fact, something new is cooking at Lindey's." The ad mentioned that our new chef had worked with renowned chef Wolfgang Puck at Spago and that he'd be bringing an "unprecedented culinary style of mesquite grill cooking, innovative pastas, and gourmet pizzas to Lindey's already popular menu. Fact is…there's still nothing quite like Lindey's." This was going to be some coup to have a chef from one of Wolfgang Puck's restaurants!

We needed to do several things to woo Chef M. He wanted large plates. Huge plates inscribed with the Lindey's logo. And we bought Villeroy & Boch china. Previously, we used plain white plates that made portions look substantial, but the new chef wanted dramatic plates.

Then after six weeks, he made an equally dramatic exit.

Server Bob Bergandine: We had this chef from Texas for about two months. He was clearly not happy at Lindey's and he did not make anyone else happy. He was supposed to be a big score: he'd come from Wolfgang Puck's restaurants, and Sue had bought the new plates for him—which I remember he placed in the oven so he could have warm dishes to serve on, and promptly broke an entire oven's worth. He liked the idea of sizzling hot plates maybe just so that they would burn the waiters' hands.

Part of his trouble, I think, was that by the time Kent Rigsby left, the waitstaff really had a lot of clout, but this chef wasn't used to the idea of the waiters speaking or holding any sway at all. And we weren't meek little mice who didn't know a thing about Lindey's. (Not that we didn't *have* meek little mice—that was the exterminator's problem.) Some of the restaurant's success was the rapport we'd built up with the guests in the dining room. We had a lot of collective intelligence, and we didn't hesitate to say what we thought. Unlike some restaurants, Lindey's didn't have a class system of chef versus waitstaff, front of the house versus the back of the house. I'm sure I wasn't the only server who loathed him, but it might have been harder for me to keep a lid on it.

One night, the last night he worked at Lindey's, he put up my food for Table 26, my deuce, and I carried the food out to the table: a pasta dish and the pork chop. The chef followed me out into the dining room. I set down the couple's entrées, and asked if they needed anything else. Just then, I see the chef reach down his hand and turn a plate around so that the pork chop is at *this* angle rather than *that* angle.

I followed him right into the kitchen. *"Don't you ever..."* and you can fill in the rest. No chef is about to humiliate me in front of guests—especially over some stupid idea about what "hour" you're supposed to position the meat. For that night, I was the staff's hero; I got up in his face and made it clear we weren't going to take his crap.

Was I nervous the next day when I found out that he didn't show up and that Rick Doody was on the phone with him, pleading with him to come back—he was boarding a plane to Texas—you bet. But another chef stepped in, and another one after that.

Manager Tim Picard: When the new "star" chef arrived, he insisted on tongs only at the grill: no meat was ever to be pierced with the fork tines. One of the line cooks, Craig, was very accustomed to using the forks—that's how he was comfortable working, how he kept up his speed—and there was honestly a kitchen revolt brewing. But then the chef didn't stay long enough for that to happen.

Chris Doody: Chef M. was living in the two-bedroom apartment behind the restaurant with my brother Rick while the chef's wife was still in Houston. We'd play singles tennis on his day off. We'd have good three-set matches, and he'd beat me every time. One night I beat him two out of three sets. And then the next Saturday evening, the chef just didn't show up. So Rick went over to see what was up: "His tennis racket is gone, and I think he is, too."

I know his losing a couple tennis matches couldn't have been the reason Tim Zahler and I got to take over as sous chefs, but it's a funny coincidence.

Server T: Taking on the staff at Lindey's had to be a challenge for every chef that came in from about 1986 until about 1996. We were the backbone of experience at that place. We had been here, we knew the customers and the management. It might have been easier to reroute the OSU marching band to spell "California" instead of "Ohio" than to get us to give up all the things Lindey's fans had been expecting for years.

A Selection of Fine Chefs

"Lindey's is the Chez Panisse of Columbus: so many culinary luminaries sprang from Lindey's kitchen. It's a credit to the good management that they could nurture so much talent."

—*cookbook author Betty Rosbottom*

Chef Jack Cory: A Canadian chef named Gene became chef when Chef M. left. Gene's wife also worked at Lindey's as a server. But when I arrived, a couple months later, the kitchen was in disarray. We had no specials. We were plenty busy, even though lots of guests had followed Kent to his new restaurant, Rigsby's.

The next day, we'd scheduled a kitchen meeting, and Sue says to me, "Jack, you run the meeting." Maybe Gene had felt the place was slipping away from him, I don't know, but he'd just evaporated, and Chris Doody, still working at Mr. B's in New Orleans, hadn't come home to join our kitchen. So I suggested some specials and stepped in. At the time, Sue said, "We're going to hire another executive chef like Kent Rigsby for the kitchen," while I'm saying, "I got it, I can do this." I was headstrong, like most 24-year-olds.

So Lindey's began the quest for a chef. Sue would bring in guest chefs to audition, basically. I recall a husband and wife team—Anne and David Gingrich—they were great, but I gather their price tag was too steep. Then I worked for three days with someone from Paul Prudhomme's, who was fantastic. To this day, I credit him with teaching me about Creole cooking. He sat down with the Lindey's owners on Sunday, having cooked for three days straight. He reviewed the experience that he'd had here and said, "I will work both day and night for you, I'll oversee every meal that comes out of this kitchen, but I need *one* day off, and the restaurant has to close that day because the quality will change if I'm not here." But Sue wouldn't agree to that. She called me into the office and said, "You're the new chef. Here's the job, and I'm going to bring in Chris to help you."

Chef **Bob Keane:** We had a microwave in the kitchen when I started at Lindey's. Why? Just to heat the brownie for the Post Mortem. A big fat microwave to heat up a tiny brownie, and it occupied a significant bit of work space in that crowded kitchen. After a few days, I just decided it had to go, so I lugged it downstairs to the chef's office. I just couldn't see

having a microwave in our kitchen. The brownie could be served at room temperature. It could be chilled—it was going under ice cream and hot fudge anyway. Two weeks later, the microwave is right back on the work table beside the ice cream. The owner's son simply insisted that the brownie had to be warm and that we had to warm it with the microwave.

Too many chefs....

General Manager **Tom Harlor:** There was always a new chef, and that was always a pain in the ass. They'd always want a new menu, a chance to show their chops, a whole special way of doing this or that, and when they'd leave in the middle of the night, there'd be no one there to continue cooking their recipes. I remember suggesting once that we needed some way to decrease our dependence on the actual chef. If we could decide things on a committee level—choose the dishes and have them standardized and ready to execute, no matter who was behind the line. But there was something volatile and energetic that Lindey's must have enjoyed about all that improvising.

Manager and server **Michael Mastracci:** So here comes the next chef, tooting his horn even before he's even proven himself. Sorry, but at the time, you couldn't just stand in Lindey's kitchen without first earning respect. Lindey's wasn't a place where the chef was the restaurant. The restaurant was the restaurant, and the chef was there to satisfy the guests who were people who wanted to eat, yes, but they also wanted to be seen, they wanted to have fun, they wanted to network and climb the social ladder. The food just had to be consistently good, and the staff was hell-bent on doing whatever it took to bring that out to the table.

Employee of the Mouth: SOME Discovery

Server **Mark Svede:** One pre-shift meeting, the new chef put out the night's specials for us to taste, and I don't recall what the dish was exactly, but someone on the staff made a comment along the lines of, "Now, *that's* a combination I'd never have expected to be on the same plate." Or something like that, hinting that the special might be a bit hard to sell at the table.

The chef replied, "Trust me: you're looking at the Christopher Columbus of cuisine."

He may have been smiling and only half serious, but I couldn't help replying, "Oh! So you 'discovered' something that's been around for thousands of years and claimed it as your own."

Which prompted my friend, bartender Mark Ronckovsky, to add, "...and brought pestilence and disease upon millions of innocent people."

A Tale of Two Pizzas

When Jack Cory was chef, he inherited a kitchen crew, another chef's menu, and a waitstaff that had a solid following out in the dining room. And this was his first job as executive chef. Understandably, there were any number of regrettable evenings.

Jack decided that the servers couldn't take special requests on Saturday nights since the kitchen was too busy. (He didn't like them on other nights either—no chef really does. However, Lindey's reputation was based on accommodating guests' whims: substitutions, special requests, etc.) So servers weren't supposed to go back and request something for a customer that wasn't on the menu.

Server P: One Saturday night, I forget if there was some reason, such as bad weather, but we weren't doing much business. I had a nice table who wanted the plain pizza instead of the one on the menu, so I asked the chef, very nicely, hey, since we're slow at the moment, could you just fire the pizza with only the tomatoes and cheese—or whatever it was. And he shouted back at me, "Absolutely not!" embarrassing me in front of the entire kitchen. "Absolutely not! Tell them this isn't Domino's!"

"That's *obvious*," I yelled back. "Domino's would never hire *you!*"

Bad timing on my part. We had a new general manager, and the chef complained about my "insubordination," so I got suspended for a few days, which was my cue to say, maybe I'm ready to move on.

Speaking of pizzas, another server remembers what are now affectionately known as "e-meals": the suppers the chef offers the waitstaff before service. At times, they were leftovers from parties. At times, fairly simple pans of pasta with a sauce and salad.

Server A: And at other times, the chef just couldn't be bothered. We had a period when our employee meals grew progressively worse, and became a renewable source of contention between the waitstaff and the kitchen. I remember Andrew Bessey became so angry about the "dog food" the chefs were serving us that he ordered a pizza and had it delivered to the kitchen door on Mohawk. As he paid the pizza guy and brought in the pizza boxes, he flipped the kitchen staff the bird and announced, "Now for some *real* food!"

HUNAN BARBECUED PORK CHOPS

SINCE THESE PORK CHOPS NEED TO MARINATE for two days, make the marinade ahead of time (it will easily keep for a week). Likewise, you can grill the pork chops ahead of time and finish cooking them in the oven. Prepared this way, it's an ideal dish to serve to a crowd, since the final cooking is really just heating the meat to the correct degree of doneness (an interior temperature of 145°F).

You might also try this marinade on chicken or beef ribs. Who knows, it might even do wonders for tofu, although it's no wonder that Lindey's has never served it.

- 8 center-cut pork chops (about 7 ounces each)
- 2 cups Hunan Barbecue Marinade

Prepare the marinade. Pour 1 cup into a resealable bag or plastic container, and allow the pork chops to marinate for two days. Reserve the other cup of marinade for the final cooking.

To cook the chops, brush off most of the marinade. Preheat a grill to a medium-hot temperature and brush it lightly with vegetable oil. Grill the chops for about 3 minutes, then rotate each chop 45 degrees and continue to cook another 2 minutes; you're creating that oh-so-appealing cross-marking on the meat. Flip the chop over, and repeat the previous step for a total cook time of 10 minutes. The chops will still be slightly undercooked.

Thirty minutes before serving, preheat the oven to 450°F and place a rack in the middle of the oven. Place the grilled chops on a baking sheet lined with aluminum foil or parchment paper. Brush the tops of the chops with some of the reserved marinade. Bake for 3 minutes, turn the chops, and brush once again with the marinade, and bake for an additional 3 minutes.

Serve immediately, two chops on each plate. If you're going for the 100% Lindey's presentation, you'll want to nest some onion straws on top of the chops (they are very thin onion rings), and accompany the chops with Garlic Mashed Potatoes (see page 82) and your vegetable of the day.

Hunan Barbecue Marinade
makes 2 cups

- 1/4 cup sesame oil
- 1/2 tablespoon minced fresh ginger
- 3/4 teaspoon red pepper flakes
- 1 large clove garlic, minced
- 4 whole scallions
- 1/2 tablespoon dry sherry
- 1/2 tablespoon rice vinegar
- 1/4 cup chili garlic sauce (see Note)
- 1/4 cup ketchup
- 1/4 cup hoisin sauce
- 1/4 cup sweet red bean paste (see Note)
- 1/4 cup soy sauce
- 3/8 cup applesauce

Place the sesame oil in a small heavy-bottomed skillet over medium heat. (Watch carefully: this oil will begin smoking at a low temperature, and you don't want it to burn.) Add the ginger, pepper flakes, and garlic to the hot oil and stir them for 2 or 3 minutes, until golden brown. Do not put your face near the volatile oils as they cook.

Empty the contents of the skillet into a bowl large enough to hold the pork chops. When the oil has cooled, add the remaining ingredients and stir to combine.

Note: *Chili garlic sauce is also known as Vietnamese chili sauce with garlic. Sweet red bean paste, made from adzuki beans, is often used as a filling in Japanese pastries and savories. Both ingredients are available at larger groceries or Asian supermarkets.*

Lindey's as Avalanche

Chef **David Tidd:** This is what I understood about Lindey's in the 1980s—now, granted, I was a 23-year-old chef. *We were a freaking giant snowball flying down the hill, completely out of control, and all we could do was keep it going and stand out of the way.* We had no time to revisit what we were doing, rethink anything. We were plowing ahead, rolling with every problem, putting food under the lamps and yelling for folks to carry it out to the dining room.

From the line cooks to the dishwashers, everyone was a loaded gun. You never knew what would set someone off. We had to keep the ranks full—you can't run a busy kitchen if you've suddenly lost your grill man or if there's no one expediting. So we were always hiring. We always had guys coming to the back door—mostly for handouts. And I'd say, come on in, bust some suds, and I'll make you a sandwich. Most of them didn't want the work. But some did stay on. We had this one dude who had real aptitude, and I was grooming him. I had hopes he'd be on the line soon. Well, one night, I went down to the ice machine, and he'd buried 15 pounds of shrimp under the ice, knowing that the freezer got locked at the end of the night, but the ice machine didn't. I had to fire him. And then he came back and threatened me.

Others would come in, we'd pay them at the end of each shift, see if they were going to work out or not, and then we'd do an application and all the official stuff, since it was pointless to do all that every week for nothing. It would have been great to have had a training camp where everything could be calm and orderly. Not possible: every new hire got thrown right into the fire, and we'd figure out, as quickly as possible, what he could or couldn't do, hoping he wouldn't just blow up in the middle of a crowded night.

Like one night, we had an older cook—older, meaning in his 50s—who was an architect, but he had fallen behind in his computer skills and sort of fallen out of work. He'd cooked in the army, and so he came to rely on his cooking skills for work. But grill and sauté [stations] were too much for him: up and down all night. And even the pizza station I could see he

246

was struggling. One busy night, I'm firing an order—I need a this, and a this, and a this, and one pesto pizza—and the cook yells back, "Hey, I got a *better* idea, why don't *you* make the pesto pizza," and he peels off his chef's jacket and walks out.

A Side Trip to New Orleans

Chris Doody: I had a short reign as chef at Lindey's. Here's the basic story. I started out at Ohio Wesleyan, and my fraternity got in trouble and we were kicked off campus. My dad was a trustee of the university. "Son, your frat has made it all the way to the trustees' meeting, and I'm not happy with the education you're getting," he told me. "If you want to work, you need to go to New Orleans and you need to work for the Brennans." Now I don't think I was the reason for my fraternity being thrown off campus. (I could have been *part* of the reason.)

So I do go to New Orleans, enroll at Tulane, and head straight to Mr. B's, an older restaurant in the French Quarter. I had no experience other than waiting tables at TGI Friday's. Cindy and Ralph Brennan sit me down at the bar. I fill out an application. I wait an hour, and then the chef comes out, a piece of paper in his hand: it's a cooking test. *How do you make this. What goes into that. How can you tell when...* I start answering questions, but I'm sure I don't get 10 percent of them right. Then I turn in the test and wait some more.

Now Mr. B's has an open kitchen. So I can see all the cooks and chefs laughing. There's a ruckus going on. I later find out that they are looking at my test. The chef, Gerard Maras, comes and sits down. "So you're from the cooking school."

"No, I'm from Tulane's business school, and my mother owns a restaurant in Columbus. My dad told me I ought to go to Brennan's restaurants and learn how to cook."

Immediately, he asks me how many hours I can work. And that's the end of our interview.

I worked at Mr. B's 50 or 60 hours each week. Gerard took me under his wing. He never lost his cool, although I gave him plenty of reasons to.

For instance, I'll never forget the day they charged me with making the hollandaise. Now a restaurant goes through a lot of hollandaise down there. It's the basic sauce at Sunday brunch, which is a celebration where the rich New Orleans families eat and drink for most of the day. So Chef Gerard tells me to get a case of eggs. That's 12 dozen eggs. Since the hollandaise was made in the steam kettle, my first task was just to crack the eggs into the kettle.

Finally I'm ready for the next step. I go get the chef, and he says, "Now, you didn't turn the kettle on, did you?" And we go back to the kettle, and sure enough, I'd made a huge vat of scrambled eggs. Chef called the dishwasher over to clean it out, and told me to go get another case of eggs. He could have bit my head off—I'd wasted all that money, all that time—but he believed in coaching and teaching. (My mom would have done the same thing.) When I came back to Lindey's, I was unsure of what role I was going to play. I started out in the front of the house, but a month later, the chef walked out, and I put my whites back on and helped. I've always thought of it as a watershed day: the day that Lindey's was freed from the Tyranny of the Chefs.

This recipe for Shrimp and Angel Hair Pasta is very similar to one I brought with me from Mr. B's, adapted for the home kitchen.

LINDEY'S LEGENDARY
SHRIMP & ANGEL HAIR PASTA

THIS IS A RECIPE THAT'S EASY TO PULL TOGETHER, but it does require some initial preparation—what chefs call the *mise en place*, which comes from the French for "misplaced," if we remember our high school French correctly, which we might not. In this case, all it means is that you should read through the directions completely, do the little bits of chopping and cleaning, and blend the Cajun Seasoning ahead of time. You'll have plenty of seasoning left over, so you can make the recipe even faster next time. You can also use it to rub grilled fish or meats, to season stews or rice dishes or dips, or to sprinkle on steamed vegetables or anything else that needs "a swift kick in the pans."

serves 4

- 1 3/4 pounds dried angel hair pasta
- 4 ounces olive oil, half used in each of two steps
- 28 raw shrimp (21–25 count, about 1 1/2 pounds before peeling), shells removed, deveined
- 2 teaspoons chopped fresh garlic (about 3 cloves)
- 1/4 cup dry white wine
- 3 cups heavy cream
- 1/4 pound (1 stick) unsalted butter, room temperature
- 3 tablespoons Dijon mustard
- 4 tablespoons Cajun Seasoning
- 1 cup diced, seeded Roma tomatoes (2 to 3 tomatoes)
- 1 small bunch of fresh parsley, stems removed, half chopped finely, half chopped coarsely and reserved for garnish
- 4 large fresh basil leaves, sliced into thin strips (chiffonade)
- 2 teaspoons capers, drained
- 2 tablespoons diced pimentos (roasted red pepper strips)
- 3/4 teaspoon salt, or to taste
- 1/4 teaspoon pepper, or to taste
- 2 tablespoons grated Parmesan

Set a large pot of salted water over high heat. While it is coming to a boil, prepare the other individual ingredients: clean the shrimp; chop the garlic; dice the tomatoes; clean and chop the parsley and basil; dice the pimentos; grate the cheese. Also prepare a bowl of ice water large enough to hold the colander in which the pasta will be drained.

Once the water is boiling, add the pasta and cook according to package instructions until the angel hair is not quite al dente (about 4 to 6 minutes). Immediately drain the pasta in a large colander, then return it to the stock pot—off the heat—and toss it with 2 tablespoons of the olive oil. Set the pasta aside, covered, where it will keep warm.

Add the remaining 2 tablespoons olive oil to a very large heavy-bottom skillet or casserole pan (large enough to accommodate all the pasta as well as the shrimp and sauce), and set it over medium heat. When the oil just begins smoking, add the shrimp and garlic, stirring for 1 minute to quickly sear the shrimp. Deglaze the pan with the white wine, and continue stirring for another minute, scraping the bottom of the pan and turning the shrimp.

Add the cream, butter, mustard, Cajun Seasoning, diced tomatoes, the finely chopped parsley, basil leaves, capers, pimentos, salt, and pepper. Stir well for 1 minute to combine and heat through.

Add the angel hair pasta, tossing it to coat each strand, and evenly heat the entire dish. Taste, correcting the seasonings if needed.

Serve immediately, dividing up the finished pasta among four large warmed bowls, twirling the pasta to create a swirl of angel hair in each bowl. Check to see that the shrimp have been distributed evenly. Garnish each dish with the grated cheese and the roughly chopped parsley.

Cajun Seasoning
makes 1/2 cup (enough for 2 recipes)

- 1/4 cup Hungarian paprika
- 1 tablespoon dried cayenne pepper
- 1/4 teaspoon ground cumin
- 1 1/4 teaspoons ground bay leaves (about 20 bay leaves, ground)
- 1 tablespoon dried thyme
- 1 tablespoon dried oregano
- 1 tablespoon garlic powder
- 1 1/4 teaspoons onion powder

Combine all the ingredients in an airtight jar. At the restaurant, we make up a fresh batch of Cajun Seasoning each week; in your kitchen, the blend should last for several months in an airtight container, although its pungency will begin to fade.

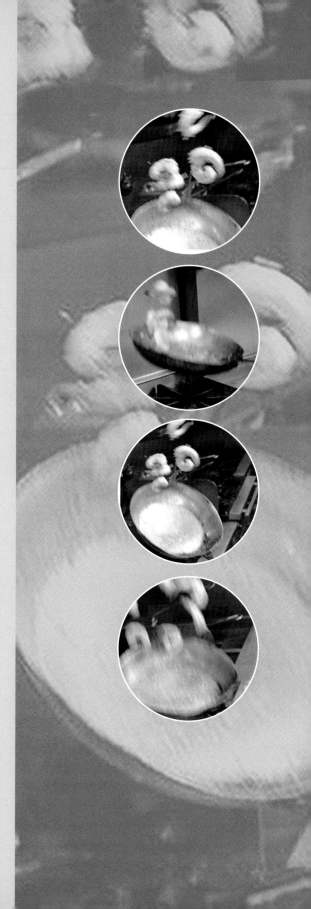

Special Treats

Chef **John Martin:** As garde-manger I was responsible for the cold items coming from the kitchen: salads, cold appetizers, and desserts. I didn't get any pastry experience in my apprenticeship (except one class). In order to expand that experience, I took on a part-time job with a caterer on the east side. I developed many desserts there and would also do the same at Lindey's, making dessert specials and trying out my latest creations on the staff and patrons. I did a Blackberry Drambuie Cheesecake, Apricot Baklava, and, since chocolate always seemed to sell well, I made a Chocolate Raspberry Brownie Torte, and a Chocolate Mousse Tart that was decadent (and, according to Tom Harlor, a bit too decadent, as he kept asking me to cut the serving size).

    I had also made a deep-dish apple pie that was very popular. At the time, we were changing the menu daily, and one evening Tom and I were writing up the dessert menu. I'd had a very busy weekend and I was kind of scrounging for that last item. I spotted part of a deep-dish apple pie in the back of the reach-in. Tom eyed it suspiciously. "How old do you think it is?" I replied that I didn't think it was *that* old. So he said he wanted to try a piece. I cut a wedge and made a nice presentation for him. Tom tried it, mumbled something about it tasting like the reach-in cooler, and then left to finish the evening's menu. I thought nothing more about it until I saw the finished menu. Tom had renamed the item "Delfield Deep-Dish Apple Pie," which made me laugh that night, each time I saw the manufacturer's emblem on the reach-in cooler: DELFIELD.

Toasted

Chef **Jason Wright:** I had a guy working the grill, a really good guy, 6'3" and no more than 150 pounds, with dreadlocks that weighed as much as the rest of him. It was obvious he consumed more than just food. Once he claimed that someone had stolen $5,000 worth of pot plants from his apartment. One night he comes in, and he's clearly lit up on something. His eyes are open about a millimeter. I figured we couldn't count on him for anything, so I put him on pizza station—not a lot of work, just firing a flat bread or two, ladling out soup. Not taxing. Early in the shift, I call out, "*Fire a soup.*" The soup had a crouton and a dollop of goat cheese heated quickly under the broiler. The soup went out. The soup came back. The server said it was cold. "*I need another soup, super hot, get it going, get the crouton going.*" A minute later, I turn around, and look over at the pizza station, and no one's there. He's gone. I find him over at the sink, washing the goat cheese off the crouton, in very slow motion. "What are you doing? You're washing the toast? How is the toast going to be toasty if you do that?" He just stares back at me as if he actually didn't know the answer to those questions. "All right, never mind," I tell him. "Time to go." As much as I wanted to keep him on, I just couldn't cover for him, couldn't be responsible for someone working stoned in front of an inferno of flaming pans, a 750°F pizza oven, and vats of boiling oil.

Chef **Matt Harding:** Before I worked at Lindey's, I'd never heard a member of a kitchen staff say, "You'll have to cover my shift because I'm going to jail." I'd never met a cook who could say, "I'm the only the person you'll meet who can smoke a rock of crack *and* eat a sub." The people behind the line in other restaurant kitchens were responsible. So it took a little getting used to.

You Know I Can't Hear the Water Running When You're Screaming

Chef **Gretchen Eiselt:** Matt and I were co-chefs for a time. The first married couple who ran Lindey's. I did the lunches, I did the pastries. Matt did the dinners, and Matt did the ordering. We collaborated a lot. And we both brought our passion for food to the job. Which meant that from time to time we'd have a disagreement. I'd yell at Matt, he'd scream at me, and we'd retreat to the chef's office, shut the door, and go at it for 30 minutes.

Chef **Matt:** And then, at the end of the 30 minutes, I was going to be sorry.

Manager **Jason Seigler:** I needed to do some wine inventory one afternoon, so I was in the wine room, which you get to by going through the chef's—I mean, chefs'—office. So I'm putting away wines, and I hear Matt and Gretchen ramping up. And then comes this fury of expletives and screaming.

Chef **Gretchen:** We'd completely forgotten that Jason was back in the wine room, so I go back to tell him, come on out, we're done, and he's all, "I'm okay, I'm okay," but he's completely weirded out and calls the vice president of the company (at this point, Lindey's was part of the BDI restaurant group) who calls me and says, "What were you two doing? Jason was afraid to come out!" Of course, the answer was, "Nothing, really. Just working out some details for the evening."

Chef's Knife

Manager **Todd Cumbow:** One late afternoon, we were closing up lunch. This is about 2002. It's 4 p.m., and there is only Skip and Cherie at Table 10, and another couple at the bar. I was coming downstairs from the office with a new cashbox. So I walk through the room, and I see a man—not a chef—with something like a 12-inch chef's knife in the dining room.

"Get up. Get up!" he keeps saying to Skip and Cherie. I put down the cashbox and rush over. Skip is standing up, and as I'm walking over, the man stabs the chef's knife into the ledge by the host stand, and I grab it and throw it down the aisle away from everyone.

Then the man grabs Skip by the shoulders, and throws him against the banister, and there's Léon beside me, and we both jump on this crazy man and hold him down. He was 210 pounds, maybe, about 6'2". His pupils were really dilated.

Eventually, five police cars pull up, and we're still holding him there.

They took chef Leon's knife (we ended up buying him a new one), and Skip insisted that he would have kicked the guy's ass. But after that day, Skip and Cherie switched from Table 10, right by the door, to Table 30.

Gretchen: We had a cook that was not quite right—I don't know, his eyes weren't quite right. Very Type A. He was incredibly diligent: "How exactly do you want this cut?" He took his work very seriously. When he left Lindey's, he did some part-time construction work on our house. Then one day, he arrives at the back door to Lindey's at prep time. He has on chef's whites, and he grabs a long chef's knife and heads into the dining room. The next thing I hear, he's shouting, "You killed Ross Hall!" Ross was Lindey's much loved general manager for many years.

Sous chef **Léon:** I see this guy come in through the kitchen door, and I recognize him, so I say, "Hey, what are you doing here?" He mumbles something and heads out the double doors into the dining room. Next thing I know, the hostess is in the kitchen, telling me to get out into the dining room. This guy is flinging Skip's head over the banister. And I bolt out there and grab the cook and throw him against the wall and then Todd and I just pin him down until the police arrive.

Cherie: I don't recognize the man: he just walks up and says, "Pardon the language, but stand up, motherfucker, we're going to do this the Chechen way." I don't know what nationality he was, but Skip sees the knife, stands up and lunges across the table.

"*Fuck you*, we'll do it *my* way," he says, and the fight begins.

Now the cook is 30 years younger and 30 pounds heavier than Skip, and they're fighting and I'm screaming and Jenn the assistant manager is screaming and finally Skip pins the cook against the wall, and hits him in the eye—something like four times—and he never blinks. I don't know what he's on.

Eventually, Todd jumps on Skip's back to break up the fight. Michael, a waiter, and sous chef Léon join in: it takes all three of them to pin this guy on the staircase. Then all the cops in the world show up, and get him outside. And he's still shouting, "This is for Ross Hall."

The cook was charged with assault, found guilty in front of a jury, and sentenced to a

mental hospital where he ended up being released accidentally. For months afterwards, he drove by Lindey's in various vehicles—despite two restraining orders: one from Lindey's, one from us—making various threatening gestures at us.

Léon: So then I see the cops bagging up my knife. My 10-inch Wüsthof Grand Prix. It's evidence! But, I'm saying to them, look, that's my favorite knife, it's the first knife I bought myself—I mean, I started at $9 an hour on the grill, and a $100 knife was something I had to save up to buy. Plus, I grew to depend on its feel, on how it worked in my hand. Sure, Lindey's bought me another knife, but that's not the same.

Cherie: We switched from Table 10 by the door to Table 30 by the emergency exit after that night. I don't think we've ever experienced anything scarier.

Monkey See, Monkey Cook

Baryea Oberting: My first day of work in Lindey's kitchen, I was 17, a student from the Northwest Career Center, and my task was to peel a 10-pound bag of onions—onions that weren't quite as small as pearl onions, but that weren't much bigger either. Three hours later, finally finished, I brought them up to Chef Matt. "Am I really that slow? Will I get any faster?"

"No, they just take that long," he said. And that was my first hint of what I was in for.

I immediately became attached to Chef Gretchen, who took me under her wing. (Later Chef Matt told me, "I was just waiting to see if you were going to stay or drop out." But eventually, Matt, too, took a genuine interest in helping me along.)

One thing I'll never forget is Monday morning inventory. It starts at 4:30, every Monday. You go in and count every piece of food in the entire building. Dry storage. Walk-in. The herbs. The line. You mark down pounds, or pack size, or tubs, or "each"—whatever unit is

on the printout of what's supposed to be in the house. It's just you and one other person, and it takes a couple hours, marking the printout with an count of each item. But that's part of your apprenticeship.

After several months, I earned my own name. I really was one of the basement dwellers, doing prep. Another cook, Justin, asked me to take something downstairs, and I said something like, "What do you think, I'm your lackey?" And Chef Matt overheard me, or misheard me: he thought I said "...I'm your monkey?" Almost immediately, Matt took masking tape, and wrote "Justin's Monkey" and adhered it to my back. And that became my nickname. And when Justin left the kitchen, I became "Matt's Monkey," and even when he didn't use my name, he would come up behind me, and do these incredibly realistic monkey sounds. Everyone in the kitchen had nicknames—that's just a sign of being comfortable with people you're working with, day in and day out.

Sister Cities

Chef **Mark Grant:** For more than 15 years, the Lindey's kitchen staff has come from Capulin, a small town near Guanajuato, Mexico. Pecho and Piojo were the first to be hired. They'd cooked in Pasadena, and then in Chicago, and when they arrived at Lindey's their English didn't exactly come through, but their experience spoke for them. Since then, we've hardly had to post a job in the paper. Lindey's has its own built-in Mexican HR department. If someone in the kitchen wants a longer vacation or to spend a season in Mexico, his friend or cousin or brother has already filled out an application to stand in—and maybe stay on.

Manager **Rebecca Holder:** Standard turnover in our industry is 110 percent—that means if you have a staff of 50, you'll hire 55 new people in one year. When I got to Lindey's, the turnover was 230 percent. Now it's 45 percent. Most of our prep cooks, line cooks, dishwashers, bussers, and sous chefs grew up in the same neighborhood, knew one other as kids, or married into one another's family. So Columbus must have something like a sister-city program with Capulin.

Noe Hernandez: Today, if you look around Capulin, all the license plates are from Ohio. Franklin County. At least all the nice cars. Most people in landscaping or restaurants in Columbus have a car. And you can take a car across the Mexican border and pay a border tax, and then if you bring your car back, the money is refunded to you. But many people leave their cars for their families in Mexico.

Chef **Mark Grant:** Fifty percent of our cooks start out as a dishwasher and move up. An ambitious guy will hang out by the plates, watch how everything's being prepped and plated, and the moment someone needs to leave, he'll move right in. We cross-train everyone, and the guys mentor one another, teaching, translating, making sure the jobs are done right.

Our line cooks work 35 or 40 hours a week, and the really good guys are averaging $15 an hour. And most of them also work a second shift at another restaurant before or after Lindey's—so they're averaging $1,000 a week.

During the games of the FIFA World Cup, someone brings in a portable television to ensure that Lindey's will have a kitchen staff.

We've never had a cook advance to sous chef or executive chef—partly because the restaurant can't offer a chef a starting salary of $50,000, and that's what they're bringing home for the two jobs they're holding down. So our line cooks are motivated to stay at that position. Some have shown a little interest in becoming a chef, but the extra reading, mathematics, and computer skills—all in English—are bigger challenges. Plus the crazy public!

Noe: I came straight to Columbus from Mexico. I was going to school here, and also working, but then I started to like the money more than the school. From dishwasher, I went to cold appetizers, pasta station, pizza station, then the line: grill, and then sauté.

In the beginning of the year, it's slow, and we don't work that much. But then it's December—the busiest time of the year. And all year, we save money from our paychecks: this much for rent, this much for car insurance, this much for living, and the rest goes home to Mexico. Then, finally, when you go home, you can live for free a little while and everything is sweet. You're not working all day and night. You're not paying for meals or rent—and even though the cost of life is expensive, you can live nicely.

Mes Nombres

One funny thing: when the kitchen paychecks come, it's always hard to distribute them among the Mexican staff because almost no one in the kitchen goes by his or her real name. It's all nicknames, changing nicknames, and never last names, while the checks, of course, are all official first and last names. At various times, we've had cooks named Pulque (a milky drink made from fermented agave), Frijoles (beans), Pingüino (penguin), Pasmada (the village gossip), Gato (cat), Wamisha (the fruit of an enormous Mexican plant that resembles a pineapple), Motor (also known as Tractor, names that are English cognates), Bisho (a little whining kid), Nacho (not referring to cheesy tortilla chips, but short for "Ignacio"), Pecho (chest—apparently, when Pecho's first child was born, he walked around with his chest puffed out), Piojo (lice), Canicas (marbles), and then there's Vicente, the senior member of the restaurant crew, who's "the Major," or "Presidente of the slums"— just out of respect.

And then, for a long time, all the Mexican cooks had animal nicknames for one another: Llegua (miniature horse), Camello (camel), Jirafa (giraffe), Burro, and then a few other odd names such as Abuelo (grandfather, a younger cook who had gray hair), Chamoros (the calf muscles), and a whole group of Mariposas (butterflies), the gay waiters.

Lindey's Legacy

Sue: When I think of all the chefs who have cooked for us at Lindey's, and then look around the city, it fills me with such pride to see how many of our chefs—let alone our managers and servers and bartenders—have helped to create such a vital restaurant community.

In the '80s, of course, our first chef Tom Johnson took over the kitchen at L'Armagnac, then Kent Rigbsy's left Lindey's to open Rigsby's Cuisine Volatile. Our chef Jack Cory opened Bexley's Monk and Bistro Roti. Chef Ricky Barnes created the wonderful Galaxy Cafés around town. There are so many! Mamma Mimi's Pizza, Elemental, Thom's in Grandview, the Yard Club, Carsonie's—I hardly know where to stop.

And then, around the country, Lindey's chefs like Michael Tsonton at copperblue in Chicago and Todd Atcheson at California Cuisine in San Diego have made names for themselves, inspired, in no small part, by their early experience at Lindey's.

Chef Matt Harding: If you add in all the cooks from the dozens of Brio and Bravo! and Bon Vie restaurants we've trained in Lindey's kitchen, Lindey's just might be the mother ship of Columbus cuisine.

THE DUMB-AND-DUMBER-WAITER
MECHANICS OF A MISHAP

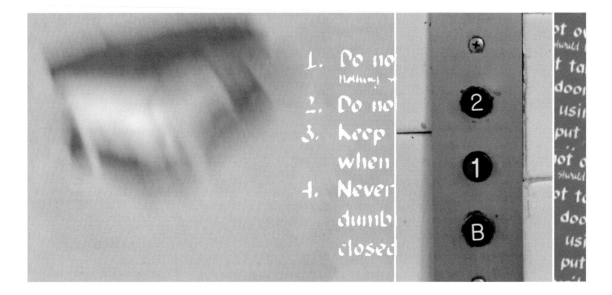

AMONG THE HUNDREDS of servers we've worked with over 25 years, we may have hired a few who were just shy of brilliant, but we've only had one dumbwaiter throughout our history—and no staff member could ever have supplied the aggravation this one piece of machinery has afforded the restaurant.

The size of a large dishwasher, our dumbwaiter is an ancient box that shuttles from the basement (where we have the prep kitchens and walk-in refrigerator) to the first floor (with the main kitchen and dining rooms) and then to a second floor (with the small prep kitchen, party rooms, and the terrace). It can hold a small cart of trays, dinners for a large party, or one scrunched-up drunk or truly dumb waiter. (It has shuttled both.)

The real trouble, for something which seems like a rather simple device, is that the doors jam, the call buttons fail to work, and the elevator stalls between floors as if out of gas.

Bartender **Eddie Meecham:** To open the second-floor bar, we used the dumbwaiter to send up beer kegs from the basement. But a 125-pound keg had a good chance of stalling between floors, which would not only tie up the dumbwaiter, but also require me to find someone to help me pull the keg up three floors, where someone's waiting for a beer.

This would be irritating enough if the dumbwaiter were only carrying dirty dishes, beer kegs, or buckets of ice. But we sort of pride ourselves in delivering meals, too—*and* in a timely manner. Not infrequently, the dumbwaiter will suspend an entire tray of entrées between floors while diners look anxiously at one another, waiters make apologies even as they recalculate their plummeting tips, and the chefs start going through their seven D's of restaurant grief:

1) **DENIAL** "This *can't* be happening two Saturday nights in a row!"

2) **DEFENSIVENESS** "Don't look at *me!* I called in the repair twice last week, and it was fixed twice!"

3) **DOODY-BASHING** "How could anyone expect to run a restaurant with equipment that has more days off than the owner's son?"

4) **DILLYDALLYING** "Give me that cleaver: maybe I can pry open the doors."

5) **DESPERATION** The staccato sound of fists punching buttons, hammering doors, and punching walls.

6) **DEFEAT** "Let's just re-fire the entire order."

7) **DREAMING ON** "Well, now that we've had our little trauma this evening, the rest of the night should be hassle-free."

And all this takes place within about seven minutes, ending with the entire waitstaff parading through the dining room with the waiting party's dinners.

Dumbwaiter v. Dumb Waiter

Server **Bob Bergandine:** One evening, Randy Manypenny had a party upstairs, and needed to send a rack of glasses up with the dumbwaiter. Somehow, it got wedged in the shaft just as it started to go up. Steve Moore tried prying open the door a little bit, and stuck in his arm to unwedge the glasses. But then the dumbwaiter started up, with his hand pinned inside. He had thick bones—not thin little bones, like some of us. One person thought very quickly, ran downstairs, and flipped off the power. The rest of us looking on moved in to pry open the door that was clamped right at his wrist. As soon as his arm was free, I remember Sue standing behind us, exasperated. *"Hon!* Don't you *ever!"*

Midwestern Style

General Manager **Biff Eschenbrenner:** We were having a tour group from the Metropolitan Museum of Art in the library room—they were in town to see our museum and tour Columbus. And they had what you'd call "an attitude" about visiting Cowtown, USA. For instance, one woman asked, "Do you have skim milk here in the Midwest or just whole milk?" As if being a cowtown meant we only had whole-milk cows?

So they had preordered the rack of lamb for their main course—about 40 of them. And, wouldn't you know, their dinners got stuck in the dumbwaiter: all 40 rack of lamb dinners jammed between floors while the New Yorkers sat there, reaffirming their low expectations about restaurants outside their beloved Manhattan.

Lindey's Fables for the Famished

The New Yorker and the Long Island Duck:

A fable inspired by chef David Tidd

Once upon a time, guests would come to Lindey's to show their friends how much they knew about cooking, which was always more than the server, and sometimes even more than the chef.

Some evenings, guests would come in just to see how much they could get away with because they were regulars and knew that Lindey's would go out of the way to please them. "I want my cream soup hotter, *scalding hot!*" one guest would demand, forgetting that a chef can only heat such a soup so hot before it curdles.

Another guest would refuse to eat the Peruvian blue potatoes the restaurant served for a short time. "They're *obviously* dyed, and I *won't* eat dyed things," the knowing guest announced, despite the staff assuring her that these potatoes were indeed naturally blue. ☞

When we finally got the dumbwaiter doors open, the people were so anxious to eat, the servers just rushed the plates to the table. Of course, as the manager on duty, I went up to make apologies and thank everyone for their patience.

When I walked in the room, I knew something was wrong beyond the fact that this party had been waiting for the dinners. The look on the guests' faces was—well, they were horrified. Then I looked at the tables. On their plates, the entire rack was standing there—all five chops still connected, rather than fanned out into individual chops. (When things go as planned, the kitchen sends up one of the line cooks to do the final prep on the racks, cutting them into individual chops—but after waiting and waiting, he'd run back down to the kitchen.)

So I had to explain that the humongous slab of ribs on their plates was "our Midwestern way of presenting things. We don't do the little lollipops like you do in New York." Whether they were amused or miffed, I don't know, but they all picked up their knives and forks and went at it.

There's one other troublesome thing about the dumbwaiter: things that seem to fit initially don't always fit on the journey between floors. In other practical terms, there are taped lines inside the dumbwaiter, and anything that extends over the lines...

Chef Gretchen Eiselt had just joined the company. She and her husband Matt Harding were sharing the head chef position, and Gretchen also took the role of pastry chef. She'd had experience working at Blair House, our government's official guest house in D.C., in Bavaria, at Ziggy's very upscale restaurant here in Columbus, and at restaurants in San Francisco where's she'd mastered a flourless chocolate cake.

(Remember, in the late 1980s, how that dessert was all the rage—only to be nudged out of the spotlight by the late 1990s "molten" chocolate cake?)

Gretchen Eiselt: I'd only been working for a couple of weeks, and on a Saturday night, we had a party upstairs for which I'd made my flourless chocolate cake. It's two layers of cake, with a white chocolate mousse sandwiched between. Sue just loved this dessert, and was very proud to have offered it to the party. I made it in a huge sheet pan, and we were going to cut it into individual portions upstairs in the second-floor prep kitchen. So I put the tray in the dumbwaiter, and I see this black-tape line there, and I remember that nothing's supposed to hang over the black line. I look again, and I shift the tray a bit—it's hanging over a little, maybe, but it clearly fit. So I closed the cake inside, hit the second floor button, and walked up to retrieve the cake and slice it for the party.

I'm waiting and waiting, and the dumbwaiter never arrives. I hit the call button. I hit the other buttons. I try again and again. So I rush down to the kitchen and say to Matt, who's in front of the line expediting orders. "Matt, the dumbwaiter won't deliver the cake—it won't come up and their desserts are trapped in there."

"Did you make sure the tray could fit?" he asks me.

And I say, "Of course it fit—it was barely hanging over that tape line—"

"But it *was* hanging over? Even *a little*? Then forget it!" and he rushes down the stairs to the basement. We open the dumbwaiter door. The sheet pan had tipped up and over, falling down the elevator shaft. And then, each time I'd pressed the button, I'd managed to send the car up and down again, compacting the cake.

In record time, Gretchen managed to send up another chocolaty dessert for the waiting guests. (Actually, the waitstaff was asked to prep Post Mortems for the whole party.) After the guests heard about their dessert's less-than-happy ending, they were quick to forgive the delay. Chef Eiselt, however, took a bit longer to forgive herself.

Unless you have a dumbwaiter at your house, Gretchen's recipe for "Elevator Cake" should be, let's say, "foolish-proof."

Then one weekend, the chef featured Long Island Duck in one of the evening's specials. When the server brought the entrée to the aforementioned knowledgeable diner, she dismissed the dish instantly. "That is certainly *not* Long Island Duck." She was from Long Island, she informed the waiter, and she knew.

The server returned the plate to the kitchen, explained the problem to the chef, and asked that he confirm that the dish was what he had said it was.

And he said it was.

The server reported this to the guest, but returned to the kitchen a moment later to report to the chef that the lady didn't believe that it was what he had said it was, since she herself was from Long Island.

Too busy to take the time, but too proud *not* to prove a point, the chef grabbed another duck from the walk-in and carried it out into the dining room. He arrived at the disgruntled guest's table. Preferring youthful churlishness over maturity's charms, he pointed to the large letters printed on the bird's plastic package, LONG ISLAND DUCK, and asked the guest, "Maybe you recognize it now?"

Moral kindly provided by the writer Helen Rowland: *"Love, much like chicken salad in a restaurant, must be taken with blind faith or it loses its flavor."*

ELEVATOR CAKE

THIS RICH CAKE, DIVIDED INTO TWO LAYERS, is spongy and intensely flavored, sandwiching a thick layer of flavored white-chocolate cream. While it is delicate, with almost no "cake crumb" texture since there's no flour, it's not a difficult cake to create. Don't be intimidated by the length of the recipe. The three components are simple to execute. That said, the filling does need to be made a day ahead, and the cake needs a short refrigeration to chill the glaze and to set up. But since the final result is served at room temperature, your battle plan is manageable: concoct the filling the night before; make the cake and the glaze in the morning; allow the cake to chill all afternoon; and bring it out before the guests arrive for dinner so it will be at the perfect temperature at which to enjoy this rich and delicate "truffle" of a cake, held aloft by the mere foam of egg whites and your proud, beaming smile.

makes twelve 3 x 3-inch squares

for the filling

- 🐾 1/8 pound decaffeinated coffee beans, crushed or pulsed into small chips (do not substitute caffeinated beans, which can curdle the cream)
- 🐾 3/8 pound white chocolate, finely chopped
- 🐾 1 1/4 cups heavy cream

Bring the cream just to the point of boiling in a medium heavy saucepan. Remove from the heat, add the coffee, cover, and allow the cream to steep for 20 minutes. (Any longer will provide a disagreeable, burnt taste.) If the cream is still fairly hot, strain it through a fine mesh strainer over the white chips, discard the grounds, and stir the white chocolate-cream mixture until smooth. (The cream's heat should have been enough to melt the chips; if it's too cool, microwave it briefly before pouring over the chips.)

Cover and refrigerate overnight or until ready to use.

for the cake

- 🐾 4 ounces semi-sweet chocolate, chipped into bits
- 🐾 1 ounce unsweetened chocolate, chipped into bits
- 🐾 10 large eggs, separated
- 🐾 1/2 cup plus 1 tablespoons sugar, half used in each of two steps
- 🐾 1/4 teaspoon salt
- 🐾 2 teaspoons brewed espresso
- 🐾 3/8 teaspoon pure vanilla extract

In the top of a double boiler, melt the two chocolates. (Alternatively, you can use the microwave by adding the chocolates to a microwave-safe bowl, and using half power for 1 minute. Stir the chocolate, and microwave for additional seconds until the chocolate is nearly all melted. It will finish melting once removed from the machine and stirred.) Allow the chocolate to cool slightly.

Preheat the oven to 350°F and adjust a rack so that it rests in the centermost position of the oven. Spray a 17 x 12-inch sheet pan with cooking spray. Line the bottom with parchment paper and mist the top of the paper with the cooking spray. (This is *not* the time to decide to go *without* the parchment paper; you'll never remove the cake without it.)

Separate the eggs and reserve the whites. In the bowl of an electric mixer fitted with the paddle attachment, beat the egg yolks with half the sugar (1/4 cup plus 1/2 tablespoon) at medium, then medium-high speed until the mixture is pale and forms light yellow ribbons, about 3 minutes. Add the salt and the coffee, and mix briefly.

In a second mixing bowl, using the mixer's whisk attachment, beat the egg whites on low, then medium-high, then high speed until they form soft peaks. Add the remaining sugar (1/4 cup plus 1/2 tablespoon) and continue to mix on high until stiff peaks form.

Fold the egg yolk mixture into the lukewarm chocolate mixture, using large strokes to blend. Stir in 1/4 of the stiff whites to lighten the mixture. Now fold in the remaining egg whites, using large strokes, folding only as much as needed to incorporate the whites.

Pour into the prepared baking sheet; the mixture will not rise significantly, and should almost fill the pan.

Bake for 15 to 20 minutes, rotating the pan from front to back halfway through. The cake is done when your finger makes a slight dent in the surface, which should be slightly springy.

Allow the cake to cool completely. Using

a small knife, cut around the side of the pan to loosen the cake and slice through the cake and the paper liner to create two 8 1/2 x 12-inch cakes. Using the parchment, lift one half of the cake onto a large, flat cake plate or foil-wrapped piece of cardboard.

To finish the filling, place it in the bowl of an electric mixer fitted with the paddle attachment. (The filling may have separated into layers; this next process will homogenize it again.) Whip the filling on medium, then high speed until just stiff, about 4 minutes. Use a spatula to scrape the filling into a pastry sack fitted with a very large, round tip or into a large zip-lock bag from which you can snip off one corner; you'll be piping out a layer that's to be as thick as each layer of cake. Pipe the filling in inch-thick "ropes" across the surface of the first layer of the cake. The cake will be too crumbly to spread the filling with a knife, but placing the second layer on the filling will help it spread evenly.

Lift the second half of the cake with the parchment, line it up carefully to one side of the iced cake, take a deep breath, and—*go for it!*—flip the cake onto the filling. Here's an example where Julia Child's admonition, "You must have the courage of your convictions," certainly applies. Peel away the parchment. If your alignment is a bit off, simply trim the edges to create straight sides since the top layer can't be moved without crumbling.

for the glaze

- 3/8 cup heavy cream
- 1 1/2 tablespoons cognac, brandy, or Kahlúa
- 2 teaspoons light corn syrup
- 4 ounces bittersweet chocolate (not unsweetened), preferably Callebaut
- 3 tablespoons unsalted butter, cut into pieces

This makes enough glaze so that you can pour rather than spread the glaze; you'll have enough left to dip strawberries for an extra garnish or to use as a chocolate sauce. (Or simply refrigerate the remaining glaze, and warm it with either of the methods mentioned earlier.)

Heat the cream, corn syrup, and your choice of alcohol in a small saucepan or a microwave. Place the chocolate and butter in a medium mixing bowl. Once the liquids just reach a simmer, pour this over the chocolate and butter, and whisk until smooth.

Ladle half of the glaze over the top of the cake. Spread it with a palette knife if you like, or just pour the glaze in strips and allow its flow to cover the cake. Place the cake in your walk-in freezer for 3 minutes or until almost set. (Lacking a walk-in freezer or space in your own crowded freezer compartment, you can, of course, chill the glaze in the refrigerator for about 10 or 15 minutes.) Ladle the remaining glaze over the chilled glaze and smooth gently, if needed. Chill again until the glaze is firm, or overnight. You can wrap the edges of the cake with a band of folded plastic wrap, but do not cover the top.

Bring the cake to room temperature before serving. Since this is a delicate cake, cut squares with a sharp knife, cleaning in hot water after each cut, and then carefully slide an offset spatula between the bottom of the cake and the parchment, lifting each serving onto a dessert plate. Store any of the remaining cake under a cake dome at room temperature.

HOT ENOUGH FOR YOU?

TEMPERATURE TANTRUMS

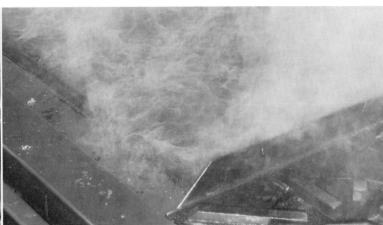

AT LINDEY'S, ON ANY GIVEN DAY, we're operating quite a lot of machinery: 2 dishwashing stations, 1 dumbwaiter with 3 entry/exit stations, 1 walk-in freezer the size of your entryway, 1 ice cream freezer, 2 upright-piano-size ice makers, 13 refrigeration units, 1 plate chiller, 1 side-by-side dessert refrigerator, and 1 salad refrigerator. There's 1 ancient microwave, 24 gas burners firing up blue flames, 1 grill, 2 broilers, 3 ovens, 1 pizza oven with two compartments, 2 Frialators (those are deep-fryers), 2 griddle flat tops, and 2 salamander broilers. We've got a few coffee makers, 1 large espresso maker, 2 iced-tea machines, a large bread warmer with two drawers, a few scales, warming units to keep sauces and soups warm, chilling units to keep garnishes and cold sauces chilled, plate warmers, plate chillers, ticket printers, beverage guns, several air conditioners, ventilation hoods, water softeners, and a variety of smaller appliances such as mixers, blenders, food processors, and portable radios. And let's not forget that downstairs we have steam kettles for making stocks, electric convection ovens for toasting flatbreads, mammoth mixers, beer keg hookups, a walk-in refrigerator similar in size to your bedroom, 1 walk-in freezer similar in size to your tool shed, and a single ancient computer that the chefs have to share for ordering, menu-writing, and inventory.

And this leaves out the zillions of interior and exterior lights, the heating and cooling units, plumbing machinery, cash register systems, phone and alarm system, photocopiers, time clock, and all the office computers, modems, and whatnot that keep our staff running so smoothly and cursing so frequently.

Oh, wait, and then there's another bar and side stand on the terrace and on the patio.

In case this inventory doesn't make the point, our average monthly electric bill over these last five years has been about $3,600. The average gas bill has tripled in five years to almost $3,315 per month, and the water bill has doubled to $1,215 per month.

That's a lot of energy. And if we remember the rules of thermodynamics we learned in restaurant management school, we understand that all that Energy, once it puts on a capital letter like that, will be converted into one or more of the following: Heat, Light, Work, or a Constant Source of Aggravation. All things considered, this old building, with all of its ongoing improvements, has held its own.

> "Contrary to popular notion, truck drivers know nothing about good
> restaurants. If you want a reliable tip, go to the nearest appliance
> store and seek out the dishwasher repair man. He spends a lot of time
> in restaurant kitchens and usually has strong opinions about them."
> —**New York Times** *restaurant reviewer Bryan J. Miller*

But if we were to pick our biggest challenge, whether in the kitchen, in the dining rooms, or even outside the building, it would have to be heating and cooling. And this doesn't even cover the hotheads that we've employed and/or served over the years.

Is It Warm or Is It Just Me?

It's 8:00 p.m. in the middle of summer in central Ohio, and someone who's chosen to sit out on our patio complains about the heat, as if the server might have a small air-conditioning unit rather than a pepper grinder in his apron. Finally, the guest cries, "—and can't you do *something* about the mosquitoes!"

We've also had these pouting summer requests on the patio and terrace:

- 🐾 *"The ice has melted in my drink."*
- 🐾 *"The lettuce is wilting."* (The waiter's reply: *"And so's my hope for a decent tip."*)
- 🐾 *"Can't you get rid of the bees and flies when we're eating?"*
- 🐾 *"Are the people across the street going to be running that noisy leaf-blower all day?"*
- 🐾 *"Aren't there fans you can set up out here?"*

Wedding Cake Blues

Sue: One of the first wedding receptions we ever hosted was held upstairs on a particularly hot night. The couple had brought in a beautiful cake in the afternoon, and we made a special place for it. Everything seemed to be in order.

Chef **Tom Johnson:** But apparently the woman who had created the cake had used little more than butter to create her exquisite scrolls and flowers: an hour or so before the party began, the icing started rolling off the cake in sheets. The whole thing was moving in slow motion, like time-lapse photography of an avalanche! Sue and I had to keep hoisting the icing back onto the cake (parts of it had already slid to the floor and had to be pitched). Even with the air conditioning cranked up, we had to perform a second round of impromptu decoration, shifting rosettes and smoothing edges. The whole cake was disintegrating under its own richness! We stood there fanning the cake until the moment the guests arrived, and then just prayed they would decide to cut the cake first thing!

Lindey's Inferno

Chef **Matt Harding:** In the early days, before the Lindey's kitchen was completely renovated, working the line during the month of August was unbearable. I hope it's safe to admit this now, so many years later, but we kept five-gallon buckets of ice water all along the grill-, the sauté-, and the pizza-oven stations, and the line cooks would all wrap their heads in towels or aprons and dip their heads in and out of the water all night to keep down their body temperatures. On a busy night, the heat could reach 130°F. If anyone from OSHA (Occupational Safety and Health Administration) is reading this, that's a typo.

One night, even though we had electricity, the huge ventilation hoods went down for some reason. And we kept cooking, even without the cooling system. The thermometer read 138°F—that's basically the temperature of a medium-rare steak! So the cooks took turns working 15 minutes beside the flames and then rotating out. That night, driving home, I wasn't feeling right, and I veered over to St. Ann's Hospital, where, on arrival, they treated me for heat exhaustion. If anyone from the Ohio's Workers' Comp is reading this, that's *also* a misprint.

Cold Air Return

Banquet manager, **Stephanie Walsh:** The air conditioning went out upstairs during a long hot stretch, and we had a large reception booked for that space in the evening. By midafternoon, it was hotter than blue blazes up there and we fell into a complete panic. We had no idea what to do. I'm not sure who suggested it or who paid for it, but I remember I ran over to the nearest Best Buy, bought six window air conditions, ran them back to Lindey's, and the entire staff hauled them up the stairs into the banquet room. We unpacked the units, pried open six windows (that I don't think had been opened in years), and cranked up the air conditioners full blast until the moment the party began. They did manage to cool off the room, and by then the sun had gone down beyond the trees, so, miraculously, the room stayed cool enough that we didn't have to have all six noisy machines running during the event.

In the morning, the staff repacked all six units back inside their boxes, and I gather someone returned them to the store.

Temperature Control

General Manager Rebecca Holder often greets guests at the host stand. Remember, this is six feet inside the double doors that open into the vestibule, which opens directly onto the street. "Not infrequently, a guest walks in with a friend, looks around the air-conditioned dining room and asks, 'How hot is it out on the patio?' as if *I'd* just come in from the street and *they* had been standing here in the air conditioning for the last four hours!

"Come wintertime—and once again, we're still in Central Ohio—someone calls for a reservation and asks, 'Is the patio open?' The guest is asking just in case we've installed some kind of weatherproof dome over the courtyard? (We *would!* Of course we *would*, if that would make a guest happy, but the German Village Commission just won't permit it.)"

The Social Event of the Summer

Host **Corrina Starbuck:** All the tables on the patio were full, and all the people with inside reservations wanted to be outside. We don't take reservations for the patio, but people didn't mind waiting—with drinks, of course—at the bar upstairs. As the only hostess outside, I was running up and down the sidewalk to let the inside hosts know about the people who were waiting for outside tables, adding names to my growing waiting list, and running up and down the stairs to take guests to their table or update them on their table status. On one trip up the stairs, I noticed a strange smell, a little like burning rubber. When I reached the top, I noticed a group of Asian businessmen happily puffing away at cigars. I figured that had created the smell, so I didn't run in to grab a manager to double-check things—especially since I was just seeing the light at the end of my waitlist tunnel.

General manager **Rebecca Holder:** First I called the fire department from the host stand. "We have a fire here at Lindey's at Beck and Mohawk, but please don't turn on the sirens. We don't want to disturb the diners."

And then I called our GM at the time, Shelia. Her home phone's answering service picked up. After the beep, the voice stated, *"The mailbox of Shelia Wiley is…full."* Then I tried her cell phone. After her message, the cellular service said, *"The mailbox for the party you are calling is full. Please try your call again later."*

So then I called our corporate manager vice-president, who told me, "Yes, we always set the building on fire for the first Saturday night of a new manager. It's a test."

Corinna: In the next 20 minutes, I was able to seat all the waiting parties and even bus a table before Andrew Day, one of the managers on duty, tapped me on the shoulder and informed me, as calmly as possible, that the front dining room had filled with smoke.

"There's a fire somewhere, but we can't find it." Before I could even react, the fire trucks were blaring down our street.

Discreetly, I told the patio staff what was going on (not that I actually knew): "Don't ring anything else in, the building's on fire." The servers seemed surprised, and maybe even a little thrilled at the sudden change in the evening's direction. Then Andrew and I went to

all the tables and explained that there was, maybe, we weren't sure, a small fire somewhere and everyone must abandon dinner and step out to the street, away from the building.

"Can I take my drink?" more than one party asked me.

"Um, sure." How was I supposed to say no?

By now the firemen had everyone in the building moved outside while they stormed the place in full uniform. All the guests and staff stood on the sidewalk, watching and wondering.

Server:	"Will the building just burn to the ground right in front of us?"
Guest 1:	"Oh poor Sue."
Assistant manager:	"Do I have to look for another job now?"
Guest 2:	"This is the first restaurant I've ever seen on fire—I mean, *while* it's happening."

Corinna: Me? I was confident that nothing was going to happen. There weren't any flames! Meanwhile, the poor managers, both of them new and completely alone, looked crazed. People from the corporate office were on their way.

Sous chef **Léon de León:** The firefighters were about to yank all the equipment out of the kitchen and start chopping at the walls, and we're saying, "It's nothing big, it's an old building, it's just some makeshift electrical thing—" and the next thing you know, they tell us to get the guests out of the dining room, to drop whatever we're doing, and go outside. So it's 7:45, we're cooking a full board, and all the sauces, all the foods on the grill and in the oven—all lost. Along with the rest of the evening's revenue. But the fire department, they're saying that if they don't find the source of this smoke within the next minute, they're going into the wall. And they've got these huge axes.

Not two seconds later, they're chopping the lattice over the ventilation systems—it's this 4-foot-wide by 20-foot-high box, and they're convinced that's the source of the smoke now. On the terrace, they're ripping open the floor. They knock over the railing, pull up the floorboards. It's like they're taking Lindey's down to the street level.

But they found leaves smoldering in the ventilation shaft.

Chris Doody shows up, cigarette in mouth, and says, "We're putting this back together right now." And he had two guys, right then, start repairing everything.

Corinna: Meanwhile, the guests, most of them, were happy to be a part of all this excitement. Drinking wine, standing in the middle of the road as if this were a festival, chatting on their cell phones: "Yes, we didn't even finish dinner. Uh-huh, *on fire!* The whole place!"

A few other guests thought that the situation entitled them to request whatever they wanted and that their requests would be fulfilled instantly.

Guest 1:	"Ugh, I just want to pay my tab and go. Why is that too much to ask?"
Server:	"Well, ma'am, the building may be on fire, and we can't go inside to use the—"
Guest 2:	"But I want my car right now! This is ridiculous!"
Valet:	"Unfortunately, you and about 30 other cars would all like to leave right now, so it might be a few minutes."

On the fortunate side, the fire team had eliminated the possibility of there being a fire in the front room. They tore down the nice little cover that had been built over the outside ventilation system. A few thwacks with a pair of axes revealed a large, ugly, silver structure that was supposed to have something to do with circulating air but was mostly rumbling as if it were about to blast off. And that, apparently, was the source of the smoke: a smoldering fire of leaves in one of the vents, which the firemen quickly extinguished.

The guests returned to their tables to collect their belongings. A few left a little cash on the tables for the servers. (We'd comped the entire restaurant's meals.) We thanked everyone for being so understanding, said good night, and then began the cleanup.

SALMON CHANTED EVENING
SPAWNING A QUARTER CENTURY

YES, LINDEY'S HAS CREATED "salmon chanted evenings" in every possible fashion over our 25 years. And while we can't remember if it was Mary McClendon, Kelly Crum, or another singer on Jazz Night who shared that classic tune with our guests, we do remember how diners have always sung the praises of the seafood items on our menu.

(Okay, let's make believe it's Jazz Night, we've all had a few cocktails, and someone in our party decides to go over and snatch the microphone from Jeanette Williams and break into some fishy song...can't you just hear..."That's a Moray," or "My Foolish Carp," or "It Haddock Be You?" Can't you just imagine the entire front room joining in on "Clam Every Mountain," or standing for a rousing patriotic rendition of "A Barracuda Beautiful"? And then, not to be outdone, can't you just see Jeanette grabbing the mic again for her favorite gospel number, "Nearer My Cod To Thee," and then, setting caution and cocktail aside, delivering her show-stopper, "Oyster Parade.")

Now back to dry land. No fish has traveled the ladder of years with us like the salmon. First, let's remember, this rich pink or orange fish hasn't always been the warhorse of the seafood offerings. Twenty-five years ago, finding salmon on a menu in Ohio would have been remarkable, while the preparation itself would not. Then came a time when chefs and fancy grocers could offer this great fish a few weekends each year.

Now, of course, the salmon, once the regional and seasonal exclusive of the Pacific Northwest or Norway or some other non-Ohio waters, is considered the default seafood offering at steak houses, at banquets, and even on airplanes.

Just looking at the salmon entrées we've prepared over the years provides a mini gastronomical history of our taste buds. The dishes below, culled from 25 years of menus, are not in chronological order. We're happy to offer a free salmon entrée to the first five guests who send in this list with all the dishes in the correct order. (We'll just take your word for it.)

Fresh Grilled Coho Salmon with capers, red onions, and parmesan

Salmon Streudal stuffed with spinach and Boursin cheese[1]

Fresh Grilled Salmon Steak Painted Desert

Fresh Marinated and Grilled Norwegian Salmon with Bermuda onions, capers, and fresh parmesan

Norwegian Salmon and Mouseline Encroute with basil sauce[2]

Chilled Poached Salmon with asparagus and saffron mayonnaise

Chilled Poached Salmon with dill cream and marinated cucumbers

Oven-Poached Norwegian Salmon with Bermuda onions, capers, and fresh parmesan

Poached Norwegian Salmon Spirals with dill beurre blanc

Grilled Salmon with wild rice soubise and red wine mushroom veal jus

Grilled Jail Island Salmon with thyme-scented succotash and roasted red pepper jus

Poached Norwegian Salmon with exotic greens in a lemon caper vinaigrette and garnished with crème fraîche

Grilled Salmon with black beans, scallions, and a summer vegetable vinaigrette

Grilled Salmon with tabbouleh, cucumber, and lemon

Grilled Salmon with white bean hummus, tomato vinaigrette, and pickled Napa cabbage

Grilled Salmon with roasted potatoes and a citrus pesto sauce

Sesame crusted salmon with spinach, shiitake mushrooms, and a warm miso emulsion

Grilled Salmon with caviar, fresh spinach, and champagne butter sauce

Atlantic Salmon with roasted Yukon Gold potatoes, shallots, bacon, and spinach

Grilled Salmon Salad with a soy glaze, avocado, cucumber, and toasted sesame

Grilled Salmon with white corn, lobster fritters, and a red pepper jus

Panned Atlantic Salmon with white truffle and red skin whipped potatoes

---

1 You get a bonus point for spelling "strudel" correctly, because we didn't.

2 Another point for you if you recognized that we meant "mousseline" rather than something that sounds like a piece of exterminating equipment—not that we'd know anything about that at Lindey's.

CAN WE GET YOU ANYTHING ELSE TO SEND BACK TO THE KITCHEN?

25 YEARS OF EXTRA-SPECIAL REQUESTS AT LINDEY'S

LINDEY'S HAS ALWAYS TRIED to prepare anything and/or everything a guest wants. (The "and/or" seems to be the operant word in this case.) This is regardless of whatever we might be offering on an already ample menu, and regardless of what the chef or server believes to be a sorry compromise, ridiculous dietary notion, or complete waste of ingredients. We have even managed to do this without offering an opinion on some occasions. (The "some" seems to be the operant word in this case.)

But our occasional generosity has only required more generosity on the kitchen's part, and, a few times, maybe things have gone a little too far. (We leave it to you to decide in which direction.)

The Password Is...

On a busy night, server Randy Manypenny was trying to move past another waiter and a couple taking off their coats and being seated, and a guest at yet another table hailed him. Randy, on his way to pick up drinks or something else important, tried not to make eye contact, but with all the "Behind you...," and "Excuse me," jostling his way through the crowded aisle, the guest had several chances to catch Randy's eye, and finally did:

"Coffee...?" The customer asked, raising his voice at the end of the word as if to coax the correct reply from the server.

"...Cream?" Randy answered back, drawing out the word as he continued to walk past. "What's the next word? I love this game!"

Asking for coffee does not typically qualify as an extra-special request. So forgive us for entertaining—and being entertained by—some remarkably peculiar exchanges between guests and servers.

Eye-Popping Entrée

John Martin: Once, on a very slow Sunday night, we had time to swap stories. A favorite category: patrons who try to impress the staff with their travels or food knowledge. Randy trumped all the other stories. "I had this woman who ordered the swordfish and then commanded me to have the chef remove the sword in the kitchen." When Randy enunciated the punch line I began laughing so hard that I doubled over and ejected my contact lens into the holes of the rubber matting below me. With the help of five servers and two cooks, we managed to locate it—how, I'm still not quite sure.

And for Starters...

Gentleman: I'd like to have the Caesar Salad, let's see, with French dressing...and....

Gracious Server: Oh, you know, I don't think the chef made French dressing tonight. He makes all our dressing from scratch, and I don't think he's offering that tonight. But you could try our green salad, it comes with a nice vinaigrette?

The Great Missed Steaks

General manager **Shelia Wiley:** I had a gentleman at Table 82 who calls me over and says, "My steak just isn't cooked right: I wanted medium well and this is cooked medium."

So I assure him that we'll cook him another right away.

"No. I don't want another steak," he declares. "I don't want anything else."

Despite his claim, I offer him any number of items and options. He won't budge.

(Now, for all you listening out there, cooking a steak past medium is really hard for our chefs—for any chef. They know the meat is going to dry out, and they know you're not going to like that, even though that does get rid of the pink or the red you also don't like.)

So before he can march out of the restaurant unhappy, I have the chef make me another steak—only cooked medium, not medium-well—for a carry-out order, and I go back over to the table and I set the steak on the adjacent table. Before I can say a thing, the man says,

"Just so you'll know, it's my birthday and my fiancée brought me here for a great dinner, but now the evening is ruined."

"Here's the thing," I tell him. "We didn't know you were coming and so we couldn't have set out to disappoint you. That's first of all. Second, both of your meals are on us. I understand: I'm finicky too, and I like my meals cooked the way I like them. But I don't want you to leave here hungry or be hungry in an hour. So here's a steak," I say, pointing to the carry-out container. "It's only cooked to medium. So when you get hungry, you heat it and bring it up to whatever kind of medium well you want."

Well, that caught him by such a surprise, his entire mood changed. Suddenly, he was all appreciative and comfortable. So comfortable that he says: "By the way, my fiancée is an artist, a vocalist. Do you ever have singing here?"

When I tell him we do, on Thursdays, he asks, "Can we give you one of her CDs? You might want her to come sing."

So a moment ago the world had just come to a horrible end, and now it was all beautiful. As it turned out, we did listen to her CD, and his fiancée came to sing at the restaurant, and we happen to be best friends to this day.

While Shelia's steak-to-go idea couldn't solve the kitchen's ongoing trouble with well-done steaks, she also knew how to create a thoroughly cooked piece of meat that was moist.

Shelia: What I tried to do was to steal a steak off the grill, wrap it tightly in Saran Wrap with a little water, and pop it in the microwave to finish cooking. That would seal in moisture even as the meat cooked all the way through. Plus the steak would still have the grill's taste and char marks. I knew a few guests who liked well-done meat, and I'd sneak into the kitchen and do this little trick. But Chef Mark Grant wouldn't hear of this. He threatened me with bodily harm, told me to keep my hands off the grill. True enough, that is the chef's, not the manager's, territory.

But then, one night, a certain guest sent back a steak three times. Each time, it just wasn't cooked enough. So the third time the steak comes back, Chef Mark says to the server,

"Go get Shelia." So I sashay into the kitchen.

"What do you need with me, chef?"

"Um, Shelia, you do your secret method...with that steak."

And the guest loved it—it was perfect—and we still treated him to dinner, of course.

On a Winning Steak

One of our most devoted regulars, who dined with us several nights a week, had a favorite dish which has never appeared on a Lindey's menu, and never will: a filet, wrapped in bacon, and cooked "Pittsburgh," which means charred outside and left entirely raw inside. When the waiter would come to the table, Neil Schultz would have this conversation with any server who didn't know the drill—as in, *his* drill.

"Do you have bacon back there?"

"Yes, sir, we do."

"Do you have a steak back there?"

"Yes, we do."

"Okay, you go back there, wrap that bacon around the steak, and have the chef just char the outside, and then bring that back out to me immediately. *No* potato and *no* vegetable and certainly *no salad.*"

And a few minutes later, the nervous server would return with the bloody offering on the plate. "But Mr. Schultz, the steak was only on the grill for, like, 10 seconds."

And that was perfect.

Chef **Kent Rigsby:** You'd think that for being such a meat-and-potatoes town, Columbus would know how to eat great beef. But, no. The national standard—look anywhere!—says a steak is best served medium rare, and I bet 75% of the steaks in Columbus are cooked well or medium well.

Go Fish

Most restaurants do most everything they can to accommodate a guest's special needs. But while the staff in the front of the house may behave as if "it's no problem at all," the back of the house—depending the number of tickets on the board, the time of the evening, and so many other factors that the mood is rarely relaxed—usually has a very different attitude. But that's why you tip the server: to face off with the brutes in the kitchen.

For instance, a nice lady and her son come to our restaurant, sit down, and hand the waiter a list of 15 ingredients that includes everything from dairy to nuts, from wheat to garlic: "Can you show this to the chef and ask him what on the menu doesn't have any of these things in it? My son has a few allergies."

Or, at Thanksgiving, the mother of one particular family comes in to discuss what her family would like. (Our set menu with three or four variations doesn't work for them.)

Chef **Matt Harding:** I think I have this right—the daughter's vegan; the son is allergic to peanuts and needs low fat; the husband's on a high-carb diet; and the wife is interested in low *everything*: no seafood, no chicken, low protein. So we have a pre-holiday meal conference where I play a game of "Go Fish." "How about risotto?"

"No, I'm trying to limit my intake of simple grains."

"How about a vegetable plate with—"

"Well, I don't really like many vegetables."

I think we served her a baked sweet potato, a slice of turkey, and three miniature carrots. (Why she needs Lindey's for this kind of meal is not for the chef to ask.) Not that she isn't gracious or appreciative. But each Thanksgiving has become more difficult and now, for those four people, it probably takes 30 minutes per person just to prep *their* meals.

On the Side

Server **Jim Borden:** We've had so many guests from the Bexley neighborhood over the years who seemed to be in cahoots with each other. One woman would adopt some new dietary rule or decide some special food was or wasn't "allowed," and suddenly everyone in Bexley would want the same thing. Instead of *this*, they all want *that*. They need the sauce on the side. They need extra lemon slices. More times than not, this applied to salads, which made John Martin, who worked as our garde-manger, especially crazy. Out of nowhere, balsamic vinegar became the craze. This was the one and only thing the ladies wanted on their salads: "I'll start with the three-green salad, but with balsamic..." or "Could I have the Caesar salad, but instead of the..." or "I'll have your wedge of iceberg, but substitute the balsamic..." Over and over and over, the tickets would come through, "balsamic only," until one night, we're crazy busy, and the whole kitchen is tense and backed up, with the servers going nuts waiting for their food. And the tickets are being called out, and suddenly John just screams out, *"NO TABLESIDE DOUCHING! I mean it! No more!"*

The whole kitchen broke up laughing. It calmed us down and got us back on track.

Chicken Scratching

We don't mean to come off as self-righteous: we know that, on occasion, guests do have reason to complain. Chef **Jason Wright** remembers a little slip that created an immediate, but remediable, concern:

Shortly after I'd started at Lindey's, I was the chef on duty one Sunday. In addition to the brunch crowd, we had a large private party of thirty-some women in a party room. They'd ordered the chicken breast, which I'd prepped beforehand, searing the chicken in the main kitchen on the grill, and preparing the rest of the items for the plates. (We could then finish cooking the chicken in the ovens downstairs, and send the dishes upstairs in the dumbwaiter just before serving.) Since we were hit with a good crowd for the downstairs brunch, I asked Léon, one of the line cooks at the time, to take care of the party's food downstairs and send

Lindey's
Fables
for the
Famished

• • • • • • • • • • • • • • • • • • • •

The Twins
and the Birthday Gaffe:

A fable inspired by managers
Todd Cumbow and Shelia Wiley

Two ladies, twins, decided to
celebrate their birthday together
at Lindey's. Somehow, for all the
restaurant's attention to detail,
the staff forgot to offer the
ladies a free dessert at the end
of their meals. Very upset, one of
the twins complained to Todd,
the spry, youthful manager on
duty. Very contrite, Todd offered
not only apologies but any
dessert they might like from the
menu. However, the ladies had
paid their check and built up a
good head of indignation. They
preferred to leave the restaurant
in a miffed state.

The next day, Todd explained
the whole situation to the general
manager Shelia, and they decided
that something must be done. ☞

it up to the second floor. Which he did. Unfortunately, no
one remembered that the chicken had only been
"marked"—just seared on the grill to give the exterior
a nice look. The servers working the party saw the food
arrive in the dumbwaiter, and served the dishes immediately. A few moments later, the entire room of ladies
was absolutely mortified: *they had been served rare
chicken*. They all felt certain they were going to succumb
instantly to some rare disease. Five or six waiters ran
up, collected the lunches, paraded them through the
dining room, and we prepared everything again.

Executive Chef Mark Grant: And I remember walking in
just as all those chicken breasts were coming back
across the dining room. I said to Jason, "You're the chef
on duty. It's not Léon's fault, and it's not the servers'
fault. But everyone's entitled to make a mistake. I just
don't ever want you to make that one again."

Thanks(Indian)Giving

Jimmy S: When Ross was our general manager, we had
one family who joined us for Thanksgiving and required
no less than a dozen calls in the three days prior to the
holiday to ensure each aspect of the menu. She's
reconfirming. She's switching from five to six in her
party. She wants to make sure we know she wants Table
32. She wants to go over the ingredients in the stuffing.
And the cranberry sauce. Over and over, making us crazy.
And Ross is assuring us that everything will be fine.
Don't worry.

But I'm the closer that night, which is the day from
hell since you start at 10 and end at 10, with a final turn
at 7:30...so here this family comes, and I brace myself,
ready to give them my all. But all of a sudden, the 86
board* starts ripping. "This cannot be happening for

---

* **Speak restaurantese:** The number 86 has come to mean items from the
menu that have sold out, typically an evening special. Servers check the
86 board throughout a shift to prevent ringing in a guest order that the
kitchen can't fulfill. Guests can also be 86'd, as in refused service. (But
not at Lindey's.)

this family! The host will lose her mind, she's been freaking for a week!" We're out of everything she counted on! Now I *had* put their order in, but it was impossible to tell if my order had been covered or not.

I race over to Ross: "You've got to rescue me. I'd put another deuce's order in at the same time as Table 32, their food is coming up any minute, and there's not enough for the six-top, can you—" and someone has already run my food for the deuce out to the table and they're about to set down the plates and Ross bolts out and says, "Could I offer you a bottle of our finest wine for your meal?" and snatched the food from the runner. "I'll make it worth your while. Let me keep this hot..." It was classic Ross Hall work. They were more than happy to be "treated" to his largesse; meanwhile, Ross divided up their two portions to cover Table 32's special requests, substituting other things the other couple would hardly mind, and we were able to serve everyone a Thanksgiving dinner without any further negotiation. But the plates were literally one inch from being served, and then, ever so suavely, they were removed, re-plated, and re-served, and no one knew the difference. I don't think I'd ever seen anything like that happen before—or after.

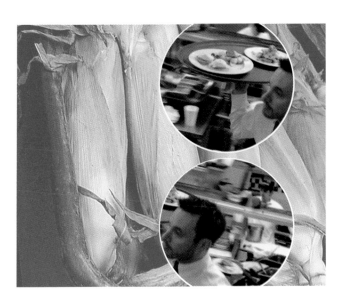

"I mean if no free sundae with candles is enough to spoil two adults' birthday..." Shelia said, "well, we can't have that!"

They hopped in the car, drove to a florist's for a bouquet, a candy store for chocolates, and a gift boutique to buy two small pendants.

They then had everything gift wrapped. They found the address for the twin who had made the reservation and drove to her house. Through the screen door, they could hear the guest talking on the portable telephone. In fact, they could hear her bitching to her mother about their dinner at Lindey's. "And you won't believe this, after we spent all this money, they didn't even—"

But then she saw Todd and Shelia with their arms holding the little birthday gifts, and she began to scream with delight: "Oh my god! Oh my god!" as if the pair from Lindey's were Ed McMahon and a camera crew bringing her a million dollars.

"It's just a few things," Shelia said, "since we dropped the ball last night at Lindey's, and we do apologize. Happy birthday."

Moral: *The whole idea of a birthday is that you should now be old enough to know at least a little better.*

NUT-CRUSTED CHICKEN SALAD

FOR 25 YEARS, Sue has been known for being "hands-on" wherever and whenever a hand was needed (and only rarely when "hands-off" might have been a better idea). Here's an instance of the latter, as recalled through the fond haze of bygone years.

During one busy lunch party in the upstairs library, there was something of a back-up downstairs in the kitchen, so Sue washed up, rolled up her sleeves, and tossed and plated Lindey's popular Nut-Crusted Chicken Salad in the small upstairs kitchen.

Chef Gretchen Eiselt: Sue came back from delivering the salads to the ladies in the library room, looked down at her hand, and realized that her diamond ring was not on her finger. "My ring got tossed in one of those salads!" she exclaimed. So she turned right around, walked right into the party and said, in her typically charming manner, "Hi, everyone! So how's your lunch today?" Everyone mumbled, *oh, delicious, yummy, very good,* etc., etc. without a moment's hesitation, so Sue added, "Oh, good...and if any of you find a ring in your salad, it's mine, so just let the server know."

Sue: Someone did find the ring, although it was just an inexpensive little diamond-and-sapphire pinky ring that, I'm embarrassed to say, I got in Japan.

Here is the recipe for the entire dish, sans ring, which probably accounts for a third of Lindey's present lunchtime business. It has an uncanny appeal. As Chef Matt Harding quipped, "If we called it Fried Chicken Salad with Bacon and Cheese, I bet it wouldn't be quite so popular—but that's what it is—and it's delicious."

serves 4 as an entrée

- 12 ounces mesclun greens (your choice of assorted seasonal baby greens)
- 2 slices Roma tomato (about 3 whole tomatoes)
- 1/4 teaspoon kosher salt
- 1/4 teaspoon freshly ground black pepper
- 1/2 cup Honey Mustard Dressing
- 1/4 cup chopped bacon bits
- 20 Granny Smith apple slices (about 2 apples)
- 1 recipe Nut-Crusted Chicken Breast
- 2 tablespoons grated smoked gouda

In a large mixing bowl, toss the mesclun greens with the tomato slices, salt and pepper, and 1/2 cup Honey Mustard Dressing. Divide the salad among four large salad plates, and sprinkle each with a portion of the bacon bits.

Slice the Nut-Crusted Chicken Breasts into thin strips and alternate them with 5 apple slices on each salad. Ladle the remaining Honey Mustard Dressing over the salads (or serve on the side) and sprinkle each with the shredded gouda.

Honey Mustard Dressing
makes about 1 cup

- 6 tablespoons honey mustard (such as Honeycup)
- 1 small shallot, peeled and chopped (about 1/2 ounce)
- 1 1/4 tablespoons red wine vinegar
- 1/4 cup canola oil
- 1/4 cup extra-virgin olive oil
- 2 tablespoons walnut oil
- salt and freshly ground black pepper, to taste

Place the honey mustard, chopped shallot, and vinegar in the jar of an electric blender. (If you have a submersible blender, you can use this, placing the ingredients in a steep-sided bowl or large jar.) Mix until thoroughly blended. With the mixer running, gradually add the canola oil, creating a thick emulsion. Continue the same process with the two other oils. Season with salt and pepper, to taste. If the dressing is too thick, thin it with 1 or 2 tablespoons of water.

Nut-Crusted Chicken Breast
makes 4 portions

- 🥄 ¹/2 cup whole walnuts
- 🥄 ¹/4 cup whole almonds
- 🥄 1 cup panko (coarse, crunchy Japanese bread crumbs, available at larger grocers or Asian markets)
- 🥄 1 ¹/3 pounds boneless, skinless chicken breasts (about 4 medium-size breasts), blotted dry with paper towels
- 🥄 salt and freshly ground black pepper, to taste
- 🥄 1 cup Wondra (a fine-grain flour ideal for coating) or all-purpose flour
- 🥄 2 large eggs, lightly scrambled
- 🥄 2 tablespoons unsalted butter
- 🥄 2 tablespoons olive oil

To make the nut-crust breading, place the walnuts and almonds in the bowl of a food processor and pulse until they are finely ground. Pour the ground nuts into a shallow pan or onto a large plate, and add the bread crumbs, stirring well to combine.

Set up two additional pans: a shallow one with the flour, and a slightly deeper one with the eggs. Spread a large plate or baking sheet with waxed paper.

Season the chicken breasts with salt and pepper. Dredge each breast in the flour, shaking off the excess. Then dip in the egg. Finally, press each side of the breast in the nut-crumbs, coating well. Set aside on a piece of waxed paper until ready to cook—no more than 8 hours (after which they'll be too soggy, and you'll want to rebread the breasts.)

Add a tablespoon or so of both the butter and the olive oil to a large heavy-bottom skillet set over medium-high heat. When the oil begins to simmer, carefully add the chicken breasts. Cook for about 3 minutes until a crisp, lightly browned crust forms, then carefully turn the breasts and cook for an additional 3 minutes. When cooked through, any juices will be clear.

Remove the breasts, place on a cutting board, and allow them to cool to room temperature before slicing.

(Note: If there is leftover nut-breading, place it in a locking plastic bag in the freezer, and use it within 2 months in this or any other recipes that involve high-temperature cooking.)

WE'VE GOT SOME EXPLAINING TO DO
MISTAKES THAT MADE IT ONTO THE MENU

THE MENU AT LINDEY'S has always enjoyed a certain fluidity. Sometimes the flux was "seasonal." At other times, the flow was "chef-able," as in one chef just left and another was taking over. At still other times, the owners' travels or a new culinary trend stirred in a few suggestions. We have always hoped to be a bistro where chefs can test, explore, and tempt guests with novel dishes. But with all this creativity, there's been a bit of trial and error, a serving or two of confusion, and the very infrequent "86 it this instant."

But consider, for a moment, the recent revolution in America's passion for food. In the early 1980s, when Lindey's first opened its doors, cuisine was suddenly and all at once nouvelle and fusion and Chino-Latino and New American and Volatile and several other concepts that hovered over our imaginations and stoves like a thick cloud of steam. So…we may have offered a few things that might have been slightly out of keeping, or out of whack. Forgive us. Fran Lebowitz was right: "People have been cooking and eating for thousands of years, so if you are the very first to have thought of adding fresh lime juice to scalloped potatoes, try to understand that there must be a reason for this." But those were the exceptions that success permits us to admit in retrospect.

Server **Collin Smith:** When I started working here, Lindey's offered Overglazed Onion Soup and Shrimp and Angel Hair Pasta and the Post Mortem every day. But every two or three days, the rest of the menu—and we're talking thirty-some items—would change. As a server, if you didn't yourself know how to cook, you couldn't really explain the menu. It was that adventurous.

Employee of the Mouth: Redonions

Server, then manager, **Tim Picard:** One chef used to give us the day's specials written out in his handwriting, which I have to say was almost impossible to read. I was an innocent young server, and one day, reading the specials, I walked over to the chef and said, "Sorry, but what's the liver have with it? It says redonions? What's that?"

"It's *red*…[big pause] *onions* [another big pause]…and you're…[a third big pause] a *dumb ass*, Picard." The scowling look of the chef lasted the night. Funny—I don't think I sold a single order of liver that night.

CAN YOU SPOT THE SPELLING ERRORS?

You could say that Lindey's "catch of the day" was all too often filet of solecism. That is, we *didn't* catch quite a few spelling errors before printing up a menu. This menu cobbles together some doozies.

Start With

Chilled Cream of Avacado Soup
Spicey Manhattan Clam chowder
Parmesian Scallion Souffle
Parmesiano reggiano
Calimari Fritti

Specialties

Cajun Crawfish Etoufeé
Margret Duck Breast[1]
Sole Baked in Parchment with Rock Shrimp and Maderia
Day Boat Scallops with a Potato-Cellry Root Napoleon and Burgandy Butter
Sauteed Scallops and Langastinoes with apple and gruyere in a cream sauce
Lindey's Famous Tournedoes of Beef

Pastas

Linguinne & White Clam Sauce
cherry stone clams sautéed in olive oil & butter w/ parsely, seasonings
& a touch of garlic served over linguine [2]
Pasta Cabonara
the popular Italian dish, pasta tossed w/ proscuitto cheese & cream

Desserts

Crème Carmel
Cream Caramel
Kaluha hot fudge sauce
Banana's Foster
Cappucino w/ Brandy

Lindey's Gift certificates make great gifts for all occassions.
Lindey's can accomodate parties from 10 to 150.

MORE TASTY BLUNDERS AT RIGHT

Lindey's Mispronunciation Guide

hollandaise sauce / HOL-i-day soss [3]
beef tournedos / beef tor-NAY-doe [4]
bruschetta / broo-SHET-uh [5]
Sue Doody / Soo DOW-dee [6]
vichyssoise / vish-y-SWA [7]
salade Niçoise / SAH-lad knee-COYZ [8]
Crème Brûlée / CREAM-y BROO-lee [9]

[1] Now this one's a humdinger, since a "magret" *is* a filet of duck breast, so this joins "shrimp scampi" as another favorite culinary redundancy. We're not sure who "Margret" is.

[2] Yes, we also had a hard time spelling those other pastas: "fettucini" and "bucchatini" and "canneloni."

[3] Of course, it's always a holiday when egg yolks and butter get together!

[4] Just picture the cow and Dorothy and her little house spiraling away in *The Wizard of Oz*. Now wake up and pronounce the word correctly, "beef TOR-nah-doze." Yes, it's French, from the verb "to turn" (tourner) and the word for "the back" (dos). Granted, to our Midwestern eyes, "tournedos" looks plural, but, as noted on the Lindey's menu, you may order either one or two of these small filets and the same word, spelling, and pronunciation applies. (The price, however, is different.)

[5] Although we can only speak a few words of Italian (we can order different pasta shapes and deli meats), we've been corrected enough times to know that the "sch" in "bruschetta" makes a sound as in "school."

[6] See "Oh, We're Good Friends of the Owner," which begins on page 84.

[7] Go on, pronounce the final "s" like a "z" and smile with confidence as your dinner companion takes the other side in the tiresome bet. Likewise, make the "z" sound at the end of "Niçoise" and double your winnings.

[8] More French! As in the previous note, the penultimate "s" sounds like a "z," while that "c" with the fishhook stuck on its bottom gets the "s" sound.

[9] Yes, still more French. You'd think a dinner at Lindey's was a field trip in your conversational French course. But no, it's just that a typical Ohioan's sense of France's global contributions pertains to junior high school kissing. "Brûlée" means burnt. (See page 310.)

Lindey's

IN THE EVENING

APPETIZERS

OVERGLAZED FRENCH ONION SOUP
OUR CRITICALLY ACCLAIMED FAVORITE SCRATCH MADE AND GLAZED WITH SPECIAL CHEESES
2.50

LINDEY'S PÂTÉ
OUR OWN TERRINE OF VEAL, PORK, & COGNAC, SERVED W/ CRUSTY FRENCH BREAD & CORNICHONS
3.50

PETITE MARMITE
RICH BEEF BROTH W/ JULIENNE OF FRESH VEGETABLES & CHICKEN
2.50

BAKED & BUTTERED BRIE WITH ALMONDS
THE CHEESE IS BAKED CRUSTY OUTSIDE, CREAMY INSIDE TOPPED W/ TOASTED ALMONDS GARNISHED W/ FRESH FRUIT
3.95

NEW ORLEANS SHRIMP BISTRO

ENTREES

NEW ENGLAND SOLE
BROILED FRESH FILET PREPARED W/ BUTTER & FRESH LEMONS
8.95

SAUTEED TOURNEDOS OF BEEF TENDERLOIN
WITH BEARNAISE SAUCE
ONE 8.95
TWO 11.95

NEW YORK STRIP STEAK
HICKORY BROILED W/ FRENCH FRIED ONION RINGS
12.95

ENGLISH CUT LOIN LAMB CHOPS
BROILED & SERVED W/ A SAUCE PALOISE (A MINTED BEARNAISE TYPE SAUCE)
ONE 10.95
TWO 12.95

SCAMPI
GIANT PRAWN SHRIMP BROILED IN WHITE WINE & FRESH GARLIC BUTTER
11.50

ITALIANO

CANNELONI
A ROMAN CLASSIC—TUBES OF HOMEMADE PASTA, STUFFED W/ A RICH MEAT AND SPINACH FILLING, TOPPED WITH TWO SAUCES AND FRESH CHEESES
APPETIZER SIZE 4.95
DINNER SERVED W/ SMALL GREEN SALAD 8.95

FETTUCCINE VERDE RAGU
BOLOGNESE GREEN NOODLES WITH A RICH NORTHERN ITALIAN MEAT SAUCE
APPETIZER SIZE 4.95
DINNER SERVED W/ SMALL GREEN SALAD 8.95

SALADS

SALADE VERTE
A CLASSIC FRENCH GREEN SALAD SERVED WITH OUR AUTHENTIC FRENCH VINAIGRETTE DRESSING
2.50
WITH CRUMBLED GENUINE ROQUEFORT ADDITIONAL 1.00

CAESAR SALAD
A CALIFORNIA FAVORITE WITH ROMAINE

Detail from architect George Acock's "Starving Artist" menu cover. Above and right: part of our first Fall menu, 1981.

FROM THE WINE BAR

(NV), MARTEAU BORDEAUX BLANC
(NV), CANTEVAL WHITE, NICOLAS
1981, JOHANNISBERG RIESLING, SAN MARTIN
1980, ZINFANDEL, FETZER VINEYARDS
(NV), CUVEE CABERNET, J. LOHR VINEYAR
(NV), MOREAU BLANC, MOREAU ET FILS

DOMESTIC WHITES

CHARDONNAY
#1 1980, WENTE BROS. VINEYARDS
#2 1981, BERINGER VINEYARDS
#3 1981, ROBERT MONDAVI VINEYARDS
#4 1980, CUVAISON VINEYARDS

SAUVIGNON BLANC
#5 1982, McDOWELL VINEYARDS

OUT OF THE HOUSE

····································

DRAMA IN THE NEIGHBORHOOD

A BRIEF HISTORY OF LINDEY'S, THE BUILDING

WITH HELP FROM GERMAN VILLAGE HISTORIAN and realtor Pat Phillips, and the good folks at the German Village Society, we've put together a short chronicle of Lindey's neighborhood and actual structure.

Columbus's German Village is a unique example of a 19th-century working-class neighborhood that deteriorated with the 20th-century's urban decline, and then revitalized to become a thriving community listed on the National Register of History Places. Unlike Mt. Adams in Cincinnati, or Georgetown in the District of Columbia, the broad-scale restoration in German Village was not financed by foundation grants or government funding. Instead, individuals took on the project as a fledging neighborhood organization.

The buildings within the neighborhood include gabled, story-and-a-half brick cottages, dating between 1840 and 1870; Italianate Vernacular Houses, popular between 1860 and 1890; Vernacular- and High-Style Queen Anne Houses erected from 1880 and 1900, as well as bungalows and row houses built in the 20th Century.

1814	1865	1900s	Prohibition Era
An area that will become German Village is added to the original boundaries of Columbus, which, just two years earlier, had been designated Ohio's capital.	Fleeing wars, famine, persecution, and limited opportunities in the Old World, an increasing number of Germans arrive in Columbus. By 1865, the city is one-third German.	The Gambrinus Brewing Company erects a building at Beck and Mohawk, the Tide House Saloon. It's name is a homonym of "tied house," a saloon financially tied to a brewery.	Anti-German prejudice reappears. German street names in the Village are given more American names. The passage of Volstead Act, outlawing the production and consumption of alcoholic beverages, closes the local breweries, further dooming the Village community. Kings Rose Garden Saloon becomes a hardware store, and, according to some accounts, a speakeasy.

As soon as the law is repealed, August Wagner, owner of one of nine breweries in Columbus's south end, buys all of the saloons in the area, and serves only his beer, essentially making "last call" for the other breweries. He is shown at left posing as King Gambrinus on his stead.

With its pedestrian scale and distinctly urban character, German Village has several identifying features:

- closely spaced buildings with small or nonexistent front yards, often enclosed with wrought-iron fences
- a preponderance of brick, not only used in houses, but also as streets and sidewalks
- commercial buildings interspersed among residential buildings
- a wealth of gardens: private gardens, small neighborhood plots, and the grander scale of Schiller Park

The timeline below suggests a few landmark dates in the development of German Village and its oldest fine-dining restaurant, Lindey's.

1923

Zoned for manufacturing and commercial use, the structures of the Village lose their exclusive residential character.

1930-1940

The Great Depression takes its toll on the neighborhood. Likewise, World War II furthers deterioration: wrought-iron fences are removed for scrap metal to serve the war efforts. Many dwellings, owned by absentee landlords, fall into neglect.

Pat Phillips: Once the breweries closed up, the next generation was moving to other neighborhoods. The Village became an inner city. Most streets had so many boarded up properties, that someone could buy a house and not even have to pay the back taxes owed on it. Eventually, properties were auctioned. If no one would bid on a house, the lucky ones were boarded up, the unlucky ones, torn down.

At the time, the Kings Rose Garden had a rooming house upstairs: six or seven bedrooms and a shared bath: it was called light housekeeping, a kind of license most bars had at the time.

1950s

Under the Federal Urban Renewal Program, the northern third of the district, which contains the most blighted, derelict buildings, is bulldozed.

Pat: The Kings Rose Garden was a beer, pool, and euchre joint, and not the safest place in town. In about 1953, on the school bus going home, we stopped at the corner of Beck and Mohawk, and the driver yells, "Everyone get down." There was a gunfight right outside the

Above: the Tide House Saloon and a horse-drawn beer cart.

	1959	**1960**

restaurant with the police on the scene and something like thirty shots fired.

A few years later, my friend Joe and I would go in. We were 16 and 15 respectively. (Back then, you could send your kid to the bar to bring home a bucket of beer.) So we were drinking a Gam (Gambrinus Beer being the only beer on tap), playing euchre, a quarter a game, and a dime a set, maybe the equivalent of $10 and $5. We were playing men from Kentucky or West Virginia who'd come to Columbus looking for work. And in the middle of a game, a woman walked in and said to a guy at another table, "Loosing your paycheck again?" And the guy answered her, "Aw, go away." She took out a shot gun and shot him in the head. Dead. I jumped under the table, Joe jumped out of the room. And I stayed there, under the table until a policeman knocked me on the shoulder, and told me to get the hell out of there.

In 1959, Frank Fetch, the person considered the founder of the Village's renewal, purchases a single brick house on Wall Street for less than $1,000.

1959

Ted Dawson and Bill Kerr completely remodel the saloon at Beck and Mohawk streets and open the Lindenhof, an elegant restaurant serving German classics such as Sauerbraten, continental specials like "Chateaubriand for two, Bauquetiere, $11.50" and other items that were considered fine dining for Columbus: "Lindenhof Feuerdegen Flaming Sword $4.50," and "Caesar Salad for two expertly prepared at your table, $1.25 per person," and a "Delicious Fruit Plate with Cottage Cheese or Sherbet, $1.75."

1960

The German Village Society forms, with Frank Fetch leading the way to designate the area as a protected historic preservation district.

Pat: People who bought property in German Village in the 1960s could sell it for twice what they'd paid for it in the 1970s. Real estate quadrupled in value from 1965 to 1970. Prices in the Village were inflating 1.5–2% per month. (Just for comparison, housing in Florida rose about 3% per month in 2005.)

Above: the Lindenhof dining room. At left: the Lindenhof, showing corner entry, macrame spider-plant holders, and walled-in dining room. Lindey's retained only the corner entry.

1970-1980

Barry Zacks buys the Lindenhof, changes the concept to create Albert P. Grubbs, changes it again to create Barney's, and finally sells the business to Palmer McNeil who creates yet another restaurant concept, The Palmer Haus.

1974

German Village is listed on the National Register of Historic Places. For the next several years, more homes in the Village undergo extensive restoration. By the time Lindey's opens in 1981, German Village is a leading historic preservation district.

1984

The Doody family buys the building from Bill Scheurer; two years later, they purchase the two buildings behind the restaurant to create the courtyard.

2005

After almost twenty years of planning meetings, commission hearings, neighborhood negotiations, and architectural refinements, Lindey's opens the courtyard, and finally offers outdoor seating on the street level as well as on a newly remodeled terrace.

AT THE CORNER OF BECK AND MOHAWK
LINDEY'S NEIGHBORHOOD

THE INTERSECTION OF A LIVELY RESTAURANT and a quiet neighborhood can be the playing field for any number of incidents and ongoing negotiations. One Village resident summarized it this way: "Some people, when they move into the Village, don't realize what it means to live in a city. A city where buildings have various uses, streets are narrow, parking hardly exists, and everyone's yard is shared. Area realtors should have a CD-ROM that they give out to anyone who comes looking."

Indeed, there are the issues of loud voices, litter, the noise of frequent trash-collection trucks, wafting smoke, the occasional less-than-sober person on the street, and parking. But it's always been Lindey's hope that we offer the community other things to offset these inconveniences, which are often beyond our control.

Let Them Eat Bricks

Pat Groseck: The old brick streets in German Village are an ongoing challenge. And in Lindey's early years, the streets were in terrible condition, with missing or loose bricks and large potholes. Now the usual political M.O. of the time was to load senior citizens onto a bus and crowd the city council meeting on the evening of a vote. Instead, we tried lobbying to get the streets fixed. To no avail: historic brick streets cost more to repair, and Mayor Rinehart thought it would be simpler to pave them. His director of public services was Gisela Rosenbaum, who was unpersuaded by our arguments. She earned an extra-special place in our hearts the day she tried to demonstrate god-knows-what by riding on a truck with a team of trash collectors for a few hours, *wearing her mink coat.*

So, we German Village residents took things into our own hands. I was doing PR for the annual *Haus und Garten* Tour, and I spearheaded a group that decided to plant a tree—a large dead tree—in the enormous pothole that had erupted in front of Lindey's. We brought in bags of dirt. We called all the news teams in town. This was Memorial Day weekend, a slow time for news, so besides the protestors and the police cars circling the area, we had a group of reporters covering the event including channel 10's Sharon Kornugay.

And Sharon took up our charge, following up with Gisela on her day off at the golf course.

"So what do you make of the citizens planting this tree in front of Lindey's?" she asked. (I believe she did not ask this in the middle of Gisela's swing.)

"Those people—they can go eat bricks," Gisela replied.

Shortly thereafter, the morning paper ran an editorial that asked, in essence, is adapting Marie Antoinette's apathetic dismissal of starving peasants any way to treat a taxpayer?

That's all we needed! We decided to lay the bricks ourselves! Neighbors gathered and divided into teams. Some scraped, some dug, some poured cement, some (Tony and Ray, to be specific) served Bloody Marys to the laborers. Greg Lashutka (this was before he became mayor) joined in the bricklaying. Congressman John Kasick. Even Mayor Rinehart showed up in his Navy Reserve uniform, all in white, trying not to get dirty.

And the results of our efforts? The City Council set aside a budget for brick street repair throughout the city. It's now a part of the yearly maintenance budget.

Attorney Skip Van Dyne: When the city decided to repair the street, they poured fresh cement before they laid the brick. One evening, we were sitting at Table 10, as usual, and Cherie was like a little kid who just couldn't resist the chance to carve her initials in the wet sidewalk. She got up and decided to leave her own mark in the street: her butt print. Beneath the bricks, even today, there's our own Grauman's Chinese Theater star sidewalk: a nice pair of cheeks, compliments of Cherie.

Pat Groseck: Lindey's was our window on what was happening in the Village. Before most every event in German Village—Halloween, Fasching (the German pre-Lenten Carnival with all its attendant revelry), the *Haus und Garten* Tour, Oktoberfest—people would gather at Lindey's first. It was our staging area.

Wheels of Missed Fortune

During Dana "Buck" Rinehart's terms as mayor, he established the short-lived Columbus 500. The first one was held in 1985, a street circuit race that had Grand Prix autos buzzing around a few downtown city blocks with bleachers erected along them. It drew crowds, gathered national publicity from ESPN, and lost money. Buck told the *Virginian-Pilot*, 10 years later: "An enormous amount of money came into the city. You know cars just don't fall out of the sky. The people came here and rented hotels, ate in restaurants, spent money. Plus, you had people who came here for the race." But the race drew as much opposition as it did spectators: downtown streets had to shut down for a weekend, the race had yet to turn a profit—and then the race's chief promoter, Jim Trueman, died unexpectedly.

Fred Holdrich: Meanwhile, the creative people in our neighborhood decided to host the German Village 500. Our version came together rather quickly. We announced the competition in our column in the alternative paper. Basically it said all you need is a vehicle. Any kind. The event involved carrying a bucket of water in your lap while driving your vehicle across the German Village brick streets. The winner was the person with the best time and the most water left in the bucket. The starting block was Lindey's and the finish line was Lazelle Street, which meant quite a distance on a bumpy track. And thanks to Chris King, the spectators, aside from the entrants' friends, were a bunch of mannequins handsomely dressed in upscale women's clothing that Chris had assembled on the porch of the dilapidated house across the street from Lindey's.

Among the contestants, I remember Tony and Ray had a wheelchair with an IV drip and an attending nurse. Phil Keitz wore a Viking helmet on a rollaway bed, I believe. We only had 15 entrants, but that still meant we had to run two heats because of the narrow streets. We also had to block off the track—just like the city did for the Columbus 500, only German Village traffic is nothing compared with downtown's.

When Monday morning arrived, we received a citation for closing the street. But Gisela remembered our last encounter—she knew we were doing all this just to call attention to the Village—so instead of letting us get a lot of capital out of that incident, she accompanied us to the courthouse and expedited the whole process and had the fine removed.

Parking Privileges

Chef **David Tidd:** While working at Lindey's, I had a Subaru that was pretty busted up: the front had been wrapped around a pole and had a huge V smashed into the center, and the hood had to be chained down or it would fly up. One evening, Sue called me into the office to go move my car. She'd had a call from the house where I'd parked my car that day. "The woman says you're bringing down the property value. Can you find somewhere else, David? Or maybe just hide your car?" At the time, Lindey's had no parking places for the staff. Some 30 employees, and we all had to find some place within walking distance to park, but out of sight, and not in front of someone's house who didn't have a garage, and try not to antagonize the neighbors. And be on time.

Al Fresco Dining

For nearly two decades, Lindey's tried to receive a zoning variance to serve food in the courtyard they'd built in 1984 after acquiring the two buildings behind the restaurant. In 2002, the German Village Commission finally granted the variance.

Architect **Lajos Szabó:** Over the years, it was always trouble. We enclosed the patio behind the restaurant, and the neighbors didn't want us to do that. We wanted to add a fountain and a garden. No, they said, not unless you set it back from the street. We tried to put a terrace on the back of the building, overlooking the patio, and that wasn't approved. Why? Because that could lead to outdoor dining...and outdoor dining could lead to...what? People having food with their cocktails? We wanted to build a fancy octagonal bar with a roof, like a gazebo, for the patio and they vetoed that. Can we extend the outside bar across the new roof of the addition we'd built over the courtyard? No. Year after year, we went back and back to the commission, having made each change they'd specified at the last meeting—and then they'd find something more they didn't like at the next meeting, just to keep us from improving the building. I think Lindey's, being one of the most successful businesses in the neighbor-hood—bringing no small amount of tourists and revenue into it!—was a big and easy target.

A German Village resident: The real issue has always been the size of the restaurant. First, the building was a two-story corner bar with two dining rooms and an upstairs bar. Then they built a terrace upstairs, under the tree. Then they enclosed the outside patio. And then they made the back yards of two adjacent properties into a garden area to look out on. We all remember Sue coming to the German Village Commission with those plans, month after month. But the outcome seemed clear: they'd work and work until there would be outdoor dining.

Southern Charm

In 2001, when general manager Shelia Wiley began her tenure at Lindey's, she inherited years of this tension between nearby residents and the restaurant.

Shelia: Basically, Fifth Street had become our personal parking lot, leaving some neighbors without spaces at their own homes. And some members of our staff didn't see that it was their job to build community relationships: they're rushing to work, there really aren't other spaces to find that wouldn't bring up the same issue with yet another neighbor, so the servers countered hostility with hostility. The first time I got a call from a neighbor who said one of our employees had just flipped her off, I greeted the server at the door. "Number one, turn right around and go apologize to the neighbor. Number two, move your car. And number three, come back and see me: you don't work here any longer."

I had just come from Commander's Palace, which is part of a neighborhood, too. I figured I should knock on doors up and down our neighboring streets and introduce myself. After three doors were slammed in my face, I knew Southern charm wasn't going to do it.

We distributed a flyer within a five-block radius, calling for a neighborhood meeting. The Mohawk Room filled: Sue, her sons, the lawyers, people from the German Village Commission, the city council, neighbors. I had hors d'oeuvres, but we didn't serve cocktails since I didn't want to give anyone liquor-courage.

"Folks, I want to apologize," I said. "Some of the trouble I don't even know about. And I don't know how the problems got to be this way. But I do know we're going to correct things. We won't park on Fifth Street. We're going to pay to have trash collections moved from 6:00 a.m. to later in the day, and it will come after 10:00 on Saturdays and Sundays." I went on and on, addressing the problems: noise, litter, smoking on the roof.

Then, after the meeting, I made good on our promises. When the trash people went and did their own thing every so often, I sent flowers and apologized every time. As for our most critical next-door neighbor, I left her flowers, I gave her my home and cell phone numbers, and I thanked her for allowing us to earn our living in her backyard. I was committed to making it better. Unfortunately, I misspelled her name on the flowers' gift card, and she wasn't inclined to forgive me.

Léon: Shelia took such an interest in making our neighbor a happy person. She made pralines and took them over. She sent over dinners. Every morning, during the summer, she'd send the dishwashers with a Shop-Vac over to the brick sidewalk in front of her house and have them sweep the walk and vacuum the water that our neighbor felt sure the restaurant was responsible for, even if, say, the slope of the street or the weather might have had something to do with the problem.

Sue: One of our neighbors has lived next to a restaurant ever since moving to the Village. Lindey's is just the most popular of them. Her mother understood this and was very sweet, as nice as can be. I went to her funeral. But the daughter, who continues to live there, has rarely been happy with us. "Mother said I should be nice to you," she told me once. But mostly she told me how she can hardly walk from her house to her garage for the cigar smoke, how leaves from Lindey's blow into her yard, how people wander near her property, how swizzle sticks and cigarette butts litter her yard, how the noise bothers her. I tried to buy her house, just to put her out of her pain. But we've made plenty of strides. I think things are better.

Before we had completed all the variance work to have dining on the outside patio, we made a couple exceptions, and hosted a few private events out there. Quiet events. Small events. Things that weren't meant to attract attention. And one afternoon, a wedding gathered on the patio. Our neighbor brought a chainsaw out into her backyard, started it up, and set it on her picnic table, where it ran for the duration of the wedding. At least, that's the story I've heard for years. Our only question: What does any citizen of German Village, where the backyards are the size of a garage and Duraflame® logs are the idea of firewood, need with a chainsaw? And how does a somewhat older woman wield such a machine?

Abbey and Sean Cowan: For a Buddhist wedding ceremony in May, Lindey's courtyard in spring bloom was ideal. A string quartet started the afternoon, but then, just as the sensei (Reverend Koshin Ogui, who is now bishop of the Buddhist Churches of America) started the ceremony, chanting and ringing a bell to signify the clarifying of the mind, Lindey's next-door neighbor revved up her hedge trimmer. At *the* exact moment the ceremony began. The Reverend tried to chant over the din—meanwhile, a friend ran over to ask if she could possibly trim her hedges half an hour later. "I'm not asking for the restaurant, just for the 64 people who are trying to celebrate a wedding...." "They don't do weddings over there," the disbelieving neighbor insisted. But after several minutes, our friend finally prevailed.

The L Word

The house cattycorner to Lindey's sold to a couple who were not thrilled to live cattycorner to Lindey's. (It's not as if the house moved at some point during the financing.) Weeks pass, and then one of the new neighbors walks across the intersection and asks our hostess to summon the manager because he wishes to discuss a problem. She informs him that the day manager has just left and that the night manager is due in at five. Not satisfied with this answer, the man begins to make a fuss just as Sue Doody walks into the room from the upstairs office. Seeing her, the hostess suggests that the irritated neighbor might wish to speak with the owner, and introduces Sue.

For the next longish interval, the man basically says that Lindey's is too noisy, disturbs the neighborhood, hosts loud and obnoxious people, etcetera, etcetera, essentially stating what must have been obvious when he bought the home: that he lives across the street from a large, two-story restaurant that's a neighborhood institution.

Nothing Sue can say seems to placate the man, although she tries to suggest how hard the restaurant works to improve the neighborhood, how we work to resolve issues ranging from parking to littering, and how we want to treat our neighbors like family. She says how much she appreciates "his concern" and values his taking the time to address the problem with her. She says we'll certainly try to do a better job—and even points to the brass plaque on the door that says "PLEASE BE QUIET AND RESPECT OUR NEIGHBORS." None of this is adequate. The man remains angry.

"If you don't stop the noise, we're going to close you down," he concludes.

"I'm sorry," Sue replied, "I realize I'm not giving you the satisfaction you want. Can you call here tomorrow at 10:00? My sons will be here, and they're the ones who have worked so hard with the Village over the years. Maybe they can help."

The neighbor walks the 20 steps back to his home.

The next morning, Chris Doody takes his call, and listens to the neighbor repeat his diatribe about the noise and his threat to "close you down."

Chris replies, "You know, my mom and my brother Rick and I had a chance to discuss the matter together because we'd like to resolve the situation to everyone's satisfaction. And what's we've decided is this. We'd like you to fuck off."

(It should be said that this was the first and only time we've resorted to using profanity in a reply to a neighbor. And it should be said that Chris did not, in fact, discuss his "resolution" with "my mom and my brother Rick." And it should be said that we are, none of us, proud of this part of the story, however much it makes us laugh. Really laugh. As in, tears-running-down-our-cheeks laughing.)

The next Thursday night, a special duty police car is stationed outside our neighbor's home for the entire evening. Likewise Friday and Saturday. Likewise those same nights during the next week. For a few months, our neighbors paid to have an officer sit across the street from the main entrance, hoping, we suppose, that some particularly loud disturbance would burst forth into the street and herald the beginning of the end of Lindey's. No such thing occurred.

Andrea Cambern, who lived next door to the troubled neighbor: They hired a police car for weeks on end. It sat right outside our door, as if protecting us. From what? I just felt bad that our corner was so uneventful!

Another evening, Jan and Jim Barnes knocked on the officer's window on their way to Lindey's. "You must be hungry…can we bring you a hamburger or something? We can get one for you at Lindey's."

"That is, by far, the sweetest thing anyone's offered since I've been on this job," he replied. "No, thank you. I just ate with my wife and kids before the shift."

Walking away, Jim muttered, "Yes! That's 1 for Lindey's, 0 for the bad neighbors!"

One night, the police car was not there. One month later, the neighbors weren't either.

Like a Thief in the Twilight

Marilyn Vuteck: I got off work at dusk—it must have been about 6:00—and I was unexpectedly greeted by my springer spaniel in the alley (our home was just a block and a half away from Lindey's). Jim, my husband, wasn't home and so I went into the house, totally stumped because the door was open and all the lights were on.

It took me about 30 seconds to figure out that I was in the process of being robbed. And the fact that my belongings were stacked in piles meant *they were coming back!*

I flew out the door and ran back to Lindey's where I told Rick Doody and Gene, the chef at the time, and—I don't know what they were thinking—they went tearing back to my house to catch the bad guys. And, sure enough, the guys were loading their van again with our TV and other stuff.

So the thieves took off and Rick tore off after them, chasing them out to Livingston Avenue and then flagging down a car—a women actually stopped and let Rick jump into her car, and they both flew off after the thieves. A few rounds of the Village later, they ended up finding the van, abandoned. I lost some of my jewelry but everything else could be replaced. Rick gets the medal for heroics—or for stupidity, I'm not sure which.

Rick Doody: So the chef and I race over to Marilyn's, and there's a loaded van, abandoned in the alley. "What the fuck are you doing?" we shout, and these kids scatter. Meanwhile, the hostess has called the cops, who are on the way over. So the restaurant is three people deep at the bar, it's 6:00 at night, and the chef and I are standing out at Jackson and Mohawk, waiting for the cops. After 10 or 15 minutes pass, this little punk walks up, and he's crying.

"I just got beat up by these three big black guys and they stole my wallet and beat me." And we're listening, and then he bolts for the van, starts it, and peels off.

Maybe I'd watched too much *Mannix*, but I chase after the van, running over to Livingston. and the van flies around the corner. *What do I do now?* I think. And this woman sees me in the road, and I say "Stop, stop!" and she drives me around and around looking for the van, and we end up finding it at a gas station on Parsons Avenue. The kids had managed to strip the van of everything they'd grabbed from the Vutecks'.

It's a Wrap(per)

Sous chef Léon de Léon: When you clock in and out at Lindey's, you get a time chit, which prints out who you are and what hours you worked. Employees stuff them in their pockets. And employees eat the mints by the front door on their way in and out of Lindey's, and stuff the wrappers in their pockets. Then, somehow, the chits and the wrappers end up on the streets and in the neighbors' yards—whether accidentally or on purpose, isn't the point.

One gentleman, an older man, has a little swimming pool and brick house in the Village, and every once in a while he'd come to the restaurant with a paper bag and leave it with the host. Finally, one day someone showed me what was inside: all the cooks' time chits and mint wrappers that he'd gathered from around his house.

One look at his house and anyone could see how much care he took in that place. And he's elderly. I grabbed that bag and decided I had to do something. I made the next week's schedule: every cook had to come in at 8:00 in the morning. Every cook. That meant 13 or 14 people who shouldn't have been in at that hour. But they all arrived, and I told them first thing: you're not punching in. You owe something to somebody.

I took the crew outside where I had a bunch of brooms stacked up. "Come on," I told them, and I walked all these guys over to that man's street, and they started at one end of the block, everyone sweeping, all the way past this man's house and down the rest of the street.

When the old guy came outside to see what was going on, he looked like he was about to cry. "You didn't think anyone cared," I said to him. "But we do." And I told my cooks that day, "You have to think. Think about how hard *you* work; don't make more work for others." And I think we made a real change—for everyone—that morning.

10 Advantages to Living Down the Street from Lindey's

1 Terri Dickie: "You're cooking—and you suddenly realize you're out of eggs or vanilla extract...you can call over to Lindey's, and, yes, they've got that. "Or, you're having a party and suddenly everyone's drinking B&B! So you call Tony, borrow a bottle from Lindey's, and replace it first thing Monday morning."

2 Marisa Cinson: "During winter storms, the snowplows can only get through on certain German Village streets; there's nowhere to put the snow! But if you live in the same building as a Lindey's manager, he can open up the restaurant and make you dinner."

3 Fred Holdrich: "It's always best to drink in your own zip code."

4 Linda and Steve Bagley: "When you suddenly realize that your oven isn't large enough for the enormous turkey you've bought, you might be able to cook it at Lindey's."

5 Lynn Elliott: "My husband Neil considered Lindey's his Coleman cooler. Most Fridays, he'd go to Thurn's, the German butcher shop, and buy an entire sack of sausages, smoked meats, and ham. On his way home, he'd stop at Lindey's and have the staff stash the bag in the walk-in. And then, after Neil had held court over cocktails and dinner and after-dinner visits with whoever had gathered at his bar, he'd ask for his sack of pork products and tote it the rest of the way home."

6 Bartender Tony Murray: "One of our regular customers asked me if I could work a party at his home, which I do every now and then for our good guests. As it turned out, everyone at his party knew me, and they were all drinking and talking and visiting with me, having a great time...and the party went later and later and really later. The next day, the host comes back to Lindey's. 'You won't need to worry about working parties for us again, Tony. Our friends only wanted to talk to you! They didn't even come out from the kitchen! And nobody wanted to leave, you were giving them such a good time.' I guess I take satisfaction in my work!"

7-10 Brett and Andrea Cambern: "'How can you live on that busy corner across from Lindey's?' friends were always asking us. But that's why we liked our house. We had a second-floor balcony, so we could sit outside with a glass of something, do a crossword puzzle, and watch the theater below."

"And the valets—they're like family—were always there, watching over our property all night. They've brought us dinner when we've been sick in bed. They've parked the cars of all the guests we've had over for a Christmas party."

"Or just before 7,000 people paraded through our house for the German Village *Haus und Garten* Tour, we needed something sewn, and we remembered Bill, a server at Lindey's, is a master sewer; he zipped right over. Lindey's is full service!"

VALET TALES

AND OTHER TOURS OF DOODY

THERE'S NO GREATER CHALLENGE for a popular establishment such as Lindey's than to coexist with the residents of a small neighborhood in which few properties include a garage, let alone a driveway. In other words, where can 125 cars (on average) arrive each night and find a place to park on the narrow streets of German Village, where nearly every linear foot of curb is someone's sacred turf?

In the early years, Lindey's had no parking solutions to offer. "And the staff had to park at least two blocks away," remembers server Joan Flower, "and that meant that Andy or Emil or Tommy—one of the men on staff—would have to escort every waitress back to her car after closing."

Eventually, we tried any number of solutions before renting multiple lots and hiring our own troupe of valets. But even now, it's an ordeal. One evening, for example, the city decided to tow all cars parked too close to a corner—just to teach the drivers a lesson. And when the valets ran out to find various guests' cars that night, we had something of a major problem.

Another night, we had a bar mitzvah party in the upstairs party rooms, and the kids decided to toss slices of pizza out the window onto the parked cars (not normally a part of any Jewish rite of passage that we know). That evening, our valets shuttled a caravan of vehicles through the nearby car wash.

It's been an amusing, frustrating, ongoing struggle. The sampling here, about and by our valiant—*and* artistic, as you can see from the key racks above—valets, is merely a hint of the logistical fun.

Early Valet Days

At one point, Lindey's had a shuttle van. Not valet parking with valets, just a brown van with our logo painted on the sides. Patrons would pull up in front, and the shuttle van would follow them until they found a place to park—somewhere in the neighborhood—and then the van would bring them back to the restaurant.

Then, after dinner, guests would climb back into the van and try to remember where they'd parked their car...and try to tell the driver where that might be...and the driver would cruise around the neighborhood. An imperfect system.

Manager Biff Eschenbrenner: There was another problem. Our guests parked in front of some neighbor's houses, and the van—with Lindey's logo—drove them to the restaurant. This just wasn't helping our image. So I suggested valets and a parking lot for employees. I arranged with Franklin Art Glass and St. Mary's School so that we could park there at night.

Then we ran an ad, hired some OSU kids, ran to Yankee Trader to buy some little cards to clip to the keys, arranged for the insurance, and put a board inside the front door with hooks. We now had valet parking. The moment we set our sandwich boards on the sidewalk, we were inundated with cars.

Collin Smith: When I applied for a job at Lindey's, I had three interviews: one with each manager, and then one with Sue. You'd have thought I was applying to be bank president! This was a job with a salary of $2 an hour! But *after* the interviews, I was just expected to know what to do. "We open at 11:30 and we stop serving at 10," and that was the extent of the training. It was the interview process that showed if you had the polish necessary, and the rest, I guess, the other servers or the managers pointed out as you went along.

It was hard to get a job as a dinner waiter at Lindey's. Someone had to quit or die for a new person to get on at night, and then you'd only get one night and three lunches. (But in one night you'd make as much at you did in the three lunches.) So for a time I drove the Lindey's shuttle. In fact, I did 89 shifts as a valet. Before Lindey's rented various parking lots in the village, we had a different system. Our van would wait right in front of the restaurant, and a guest would follow the van to the parking lot at St. Mary's Church, and then we'd drive the guests back to the restaurant in the shuttle. At the end of their meal, they'd hop in the shuttle again, I'd run them back over to the parking lot—and back and forth most of the night.

But primarily, what I did was wait and wait for one of the snooty regulars to say, "Park this, boy," which would mean see if, within the space of three short blocks, I could race their car up to 100 mph. Or someone would drive up and park illegally on the corner or in another space that was clearly designated no parking. Then as I'd hold the door to the restaurant open, the driver would say, "If the cops come, come get me." I'm sorry? What good would that do at that point?

But what was my unofficial job as I stood there on the corner, looking vaguely official? I was the perfect person to ask for directions to Schmidt's Sausage Haus. Car after car would roll down a window, and ask me how to get to Schmidt's. I began to think that Schmidt's deliberately chose their location just to torment the Village with bewildered tourists.

In a Pinch

Allen Jones: I started at Lindey's as a busser, shortly after Ross Hall became manager. One evening, the valets were just swamped at the start of dinner rush. Cars were piling up at the door and blocking the intersection. Ross grabbed me: "Allen, we'll get someone to cover your station. You've got to valet for a while."

"Um, Ross, I don't have a driver's license," I replied. "It's...been suspended."

"Okay," he replied, "then be *very* careful."

Slippery Conditions

Jim Barnes: One couple would come into Lindey's every Friday and Saturday evening, sit at the bar, eat and drink—actually more drinking than eating—and slowly but inexorably slide into a miserable stupor.

One memorable icy winter evening, the lady of the couple was assisted (euphemistically speaking) to their car, which the valet had parked curbside, and gently lifted into the passenger seat. Her inebriated husband, declining help, unsteadily made his way toward the car, only to slip on the ice, fall, and disappear—completely—under their vehicle. Did I mention the man stood 6'4"?

The valets all ran around the car trying to figure out what to do. Finally one innovative lad prostrated himself on our street while his friends stopped traffic. Then he reached under the car and extricated the unstruggling patron from his predicament.

The gentleman—with help—stood erect, brushed the snow from his jacket, shook his head like a cartoon character reviving himself, opened the driver's door, climbed in and drove off before the dumbfounded valets even realized that the guest had had the audacity and wherewithal to take the wheel in his state. (The couple made it home without mishap.)

Valet Extras

For certain regular customers and close neighbors, the valet system offers more options than merely parking cars.

Manager B: For many years Tony and Ray drove their Rolls-Royce to Lindey's. All of one short block from their house. The valets would park the car in front of the restaurant, under the street light, and often, after their evening at Lindey's, one would drive them up the block to their home, repark the Rolls on the Oriental carpet they'd spread on the floor of the garage, and then jog back to the restaurant. It almost makes you to want to slap these people across the face, but they were the most fun-loving and generous guys, always having the staff over after work. Flaunting the car was just part of their unself-conscious way of life.

For regulars, such as **Terri Dickie**, who happens to live very close, as in directly across the street: The valets used to take our car from the garage and park it in the lot Lindey's rented, and then use our driveway as a limbo for VIP cars or cars that were ready to return.

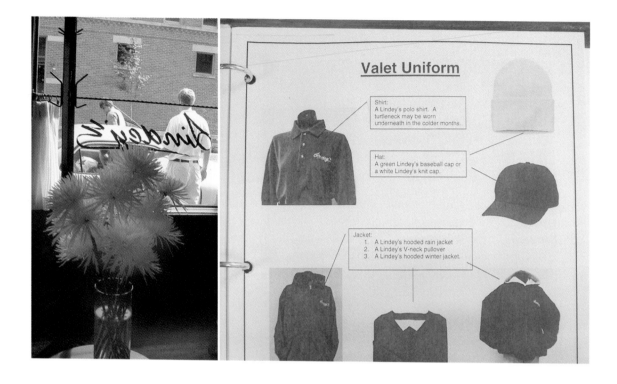

Of course, we could just walk over to Lindey's for dinner, and by the time we were ready to retire, the rush would have passed, and our car would have been returned home, safe and sound, where it belonged.

For a regular, such as **Stephanie F.**, who lives within a few blocks: On many occasions, we'd drive to Lindey's, and then the valets would drive our car home, run back, and hand us the keys. Then we could enjoy an evening at the bar and totter home without the least worry about driving. Other nights, we'd hand the keys back to the valet, who'd run back home, get our car, drive over to Lindey's, pick us up, take us home, repark the car, and then jog back to the restaurant. That was always worth a sizable tip.

For a couple with larger social plans than the street can accommodate, such as **Andrea** and **Brett Cambern**: When anyone has a party in the Village, there's no place for your guests' cars. But we're so lucky to have the Lindey's valets almost across the street. So we'd often try to time our dinner parties outside Lindey's rush, so we could co-opt the valets for our guests' cars as well.

Additionally, our guests make frequent requests of valets:

> Here's $20—can you start my truck every 15 minutes and get the A/C going, and also climb in to pet my one-year-old chocolate Lab for a few minutes each time?

Hello? Is this one of the valets? Great, I seem to have driven the wrong car home. I guess you gave me someone else's car and keys when I said I had the BMW, and I wonder if you can come trade cars with me? I know I should have recognized that it wasn't my car, but I guess I wasn't paying attention.

Can you drive us over to Rigsby's for a nightcap? We shouldn't be driving. We'll give you $50, and you can take a cab back.

Can you run and get me a disposable camera? I forgot it's my mom's 80th birthday dinner tonight.

Can you get us...a bouquet of roses, in any color but red / two cappuccinos from Starbucks, one with two sugars / a banana / a couple of burgers from Club 185 / my purse, which is on the kitchen counter, I think, and here's the key and the alarm code is... / our babysitter / a couple joints?

And finally, for people who have had a little too much alcohol with their evening of fun, the valets have a few other offerings.

Marianne Collins: For my 50th birthday party at Lindey's, my friend Maggie rented a cape and a crown so I could be queen for the day. We closed the place, dancing with all the guests we didn't even know, long past the usual closing time. But one friend, who'd had too much to drink, gave her ticket to the valets, and they came back a moment later, saying that they'd lost her car. They got her a cab home, and then next morning, she called me: "I can't believe Lindey's lost my car!" But as soon as she hopped in the cab, the valet told me they hadn't wanted her to drive home. Miraculously, when she called the restaurant the next morning, they'd found her car.

Parallel Universe Parking

Mark Rinker: We were all at a wedding upstairs, and somehow the valets lost the keys to my Jaguar. Or they gave the keys to the wrong person. I can't remember. (We were all partying rather hard at the wedding.) In any case, we looked up and down the nearby streets for my car and simply couldn't find it. At that point, we were all so happy, I just said to hell with it, the car was incidental at that point, and I went off with a friend to an afterparty.

   The next day, I think, I found another set of keys and we went back to Lindey's to start the search all over again. We drove up and down the side streets and finally located the car.

Lynn Elliott: As I remember that night. Mark was in a complete panic, walking up and down the street, convinced that the valets had lost his wonderful car or that someone had stolen it. And, yes, it wasn't until the next day that he found his car: someone else had driven him to Lindey's for dinner the night before, and his Jaguar had never left his own garage.

That Girl Valet

Attentive, marvelously funny, and just a little mishap-prone, Stephanie Barton worked as our banquet manager for a number of years. One story from her time has lived on and on, even though she might like to be remembered for her more stellar accomplishments.

Stephanie: Lindey's was hosting a dozen or so ladies, the Corporate Sisters, for a private party upstairs. It was an early gathering, an 8:30 breakfast, which was before the valets arrived—but as it was a Sunday, there was free, unrestricted street parking all around Lindey's. The guests start arriving, and they're all in big fur coats, large hats, lots of jewelry. They're driving Lincolns and Cadillacs. These are people turning out for a fancy brunch. One woman pulls right up in her BMW. She's got braids and Gucci glasses—it's a glam slam and it's only 7:30 on a Sunday morning.

"Good morning, Donna. How are you?" I lean out the door to greet her.

"I'm doing fine, I'm doing fine."

"You're here for the brunch, right? You're welcome to park anywhere," I say, gesturing up and down the empty block. "You can even take Sue's favorite spot, right there in the alley."

And Donna looks around. And she looks at her nails. "Is there someplace where I don't have to back up and stuff? I don't really like to back up and stuff."

Being the gracious employee, I step outside and say, "Well, I'd be happy to park your car for you, if you like." And I walk over in my heels, without a coat, and drive the car a couple doors down the block.

I put the woman's keys in my pocket, and greet a few other guests, and resume my other duties as banquet manager.

The party takes place, the ladies enjoy their brunch, conduct whatever business they'd planned, collect their coats, and head toward the door.

Then Donna stops at the host stand and tells the server standing there, "Could you have the valet bring my car around?"

"I'm sorry? We don't have a valet this morning, could you—"

"Yes, you do. That *girl* valet."

The server has no idea what the woman is referring to, especially since all the valets we had at the time were male. He runs up to the office, finds me—the only female staff member present—and asks about the car.

"Oh, shoot, *I completely forgot*. I have her keys. I'll go get her car...but I have to run to the bathroom first."

While the server runs back down to tell Donna that her car is coming right away, I run to the ladies room, and, unaccustomed to having that odd set of keys in my skirt, accidentally drop her keys into the toilet as I sit down.

Panicking, I rush back out of the rest room, grab my coworker Jimmy, and the two of us manage to fish out the keys with a bent coat-hanger, thanks to Lindey's 500-year-old plumbing system. We wash and dry the keys, I race out the back door to grab the car, and pull it up to the front door as if nothing had happened in the 15 minutes while Donna was waiting for that pokey girl valet.

Duty Calls and Keeps Calling

Collin: I had just started working at Lindey's and one evening Sue comes up to me—I'm having a drink with my girlfriend at the bar—and says, "Hon, I know it's your night off, but Alton is arriving for a dinner with five businessmen, and he wants you to go pick them up at the airport in the van, and bring them here." I'm not exactly delighted, but I figure this must be important. So I leave my girlfriend behind, take the Lindey's shuttle van, and rush over to the terminal. Here come some 25 businessmen—so I go up to each cluster and ask if they're here for a dinner at Lindey's, then I race back and shove money in the parking meter. I do this back and forth a few times until I find a ticket on the windshield and no arriving guests expecting me.

So I race back to Lindey's and my girlfriend, who is not exactly pleased. As I walk in the door, the Lindey's phone rings, and the host says, "Collin, it's Alton on the phone and he wants to know why you're not at the airport."

So I drive back, gather the group into the van, and conduct everyone to Lindey's via Broad Street rather than the more expedient Cassady because Alton doesn't want me showing his guests "any bad neighborhoods."

I drive as thoughtfully as can be, avoiding potholes, et cetera, but I'm steaming inside, of course, since this has taken about two hours of my night off.

When we arrive, I race into Lindey's to the bathroom, since I'd also been feeling a certain urgency ever since leaving the restaurant. I'm not two minutes inside the stall, and Alton is outside the door, knocking: "Hey, are you going to be much longer?"

"Um, I'll be out in just a moment, I'm sorry, but nature—"

"Well, we need the van keys," he tells me. "We've got to get to dinner."

They weren't even eating at Lindey's! They were going somewhere else?

I had spent two hours of my day off while my date waited for me at the bar so I could play taxi driver for the owner's ex-husband?

Yes. And I had also managed to forget that this is the way of restaurant life.

Something of a Parking Jam

Manager **Steve Gifford:** One Sunday in 1990, Herb Lape and his wife Jo came to dinner with Ed and Barbara Jennings. Herb was head of development for OSU's business school, and Ed was then president of the university. So dinner was a social occasion, but one that promoted a good working relationship.

I was stationed at the host stand, business as usual. The two couples valet parked, came in on time, and I seated them right away at Table 31. (I liked to put some of the more prominent patrons at tables 10, 20, 30, and 31, near the front windows.)

Since they were happy with their dinners, I was the happy host. We exchanged pleasantries again as they left, and I thought nothing more of their experience at Lindey's.

Two days later in the *Lantern*, the OSU student newspaper, among the op-ed letters, one writer began, "I'm a student and also a valet parker at Lindey's." After complaining about the recent increase in tuitions, he wanted to add insult to injury: "and I was just stiffed at work by the president of this university!"

Now I know for a fact that he received a tip from President Jennings—maybe he was expecting a five-spot, I don't know. How did I learn this? Because Herb Lape returned to the restaurant on Wednesday, *Lantern* in hand, asking to see the manager.

General Manager Biff Eschenbrenner: When Lindey's arrived on the restaurant scene, not many places offered valet parking in town. Our system was working pretty well. Then, one weeknight, Herb and Jo Lape made a reservation for four. Herb called me: "I'm bringing over Ed and Barbara Jennings next Sunday night, and I'd like to have Table 31—and Eshenbrenner, don't screw up, I want you to take care of us."

Sunday, it started snowing and snowing, and the valets parked both their cars. We served them a great dinner. No problem. Great time. The valet even kept Ed's car up right in front of the restaurant, and took a broom to brush the snow off a few times. When Barbara and Ed walked out the door, the heater had warmed the car, the doors were open just as they approached the curb. The valets did a good job.

We all concluded it was a successful night.

Tuesday morning I got a call from my dear friend. "*Goddamn it*, Eschenbrenner, I'm coming over this afternoon, you better have your ass there."

Herb arrives after lunch and grills me. "What the hell is going on? Your valet writes an article for the *Lantern* saying the president of the university is a lousy tipper: 'He only gave me $2, after I took care of his car all night.'" Herb throws down the paper, tells me I'd better fire that kid right away, and walks out. I was completely mortified.

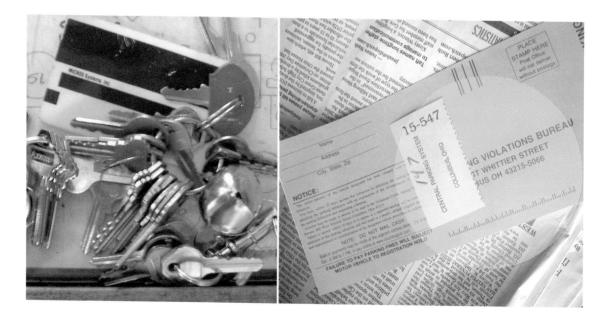

So when the valet showed up for work that night, I terminated him. You just don't give out that kind of information to the public—especially in that manner.

The next day in the *Lantern*, a cartoon appeared. It showed the front of Lindey's, renamed "Snooty Restaurant," with Ed Jennings walking out and the valet being fired.

On Friday, it's business as usual. And then Saturday night, we're packed with a full house, and all of a sudden, Freddie Cortez, one of the managers on duty comes up to me: "Biff, we've got a problem."

Freddie Cortez: A gentleman comes past the host stand and stops to tell me he'd had sensational food and great service, and then he looks down and says, and I love your loafers. (They were brand-new black Cole Haan, and I mention this not simply because I'm something of a clothes horse.) Not two minutes later, he comes back inside and asks me if the valet could get his car. So I tell him the valets are just outside the door, where he'd been, and that they must be off getting other guests' cars. He goes back out. Ten minutes later, he comes back in. He has yet to see a valet. So I go out, it's snowing, and there are no valets. And there are no keys in the valet box. And the snow is coming down.

Biff: Eventually, we hear that one of the valets, on his way out, said that they'd locked all the keys—oh, about 100 sets of keys—to all the cars in the trunk of one car. Good luck figuring out which. It was like some ridiculous television game show!

So we scoured the neighborhood, the parking lots, looking for cars with tags in the windows. Everyone is looking: Sue, Freddie, Alyson, Steve, me, a few bussers and waiters. We have a handful of keys, with no tags, that we're trying in every car that seemed to have been parked within the last few hours. Meanwhile, we're sending people home by cab. Finally, by dumb luck, we find the right car, and bring all the keys back to the restaurant. There was not one happy valet customer that evening. A hellacious night.

Freddie: As for my new shoes? Ruined from the hour of racing around in a panic through the slush and snow.

Biff: The next day we began to hire all new staff. But it was hard not to admire the incredibly sophomoric mind that had thought out such a good payback.

LINDEY'S CRÈME BRÛLÉE

CRÈME BRÛLÉE, which has three different French diacritical marks (none of which we could figure out how to type on our menus—heck, we even called this dessert "cream carmel" a couple of times!), simply means "don't worry about what it means, because you know it's just whipping cream and egg yolks." Okay, the literal translation is "burnt cream," and there's hardly anything that makes a better finale to a great meal than a luscious custard with a crisp caramelized crust. If we had a dessert motto at Lindey's it would be, "What good is indulgence if it's not overindulgence?"

A double-blind tasting by a sequestered bipartisan jury of local foodies voted the above milk-chocolate-and-orange version the all-time best Lindey's crème brûlée of all the many variations that we've featured over the years. Some kind of custard, mousse, or "crème" has certainly always enjoyed a position on the menu, no matter which chef was in charge. Perhaps you remember some of the following flavors, which, in retrospect, seem to range from the wondrous to the what-were-we-thinking: Classic Vanilla Bean, Caramelized Fennel, White-Chocolate-and-Espresso, Paw-Paw, Crystallized Ginger, Caramelized-Banana-and-Spiced-Rum, Pumpkin-Ginger, Eggnog—and the jury's second favorite, Butterscotch.

Milk-Chocolate-and-Orange Crème Brûlée
makes eight 1/2-cup ramekins

- 🍌 2 cups plus 1 tablespoon heavy cream
- 🍌 3/4 cup whole milk
- 🍌 6 tablespoons sugar
- 🍌 pinch of salt
- 🍌 grated zest of 1/2 orange
- 🍌 7 ounces chopped milk chocolate
- 🍌 6 egg yolks
- 🍌 2 bananas, sliced into very thin coins
- 🍌 1 cup additional sugar, preferably a mixture of granulated sugar and turbinado sugar (also called raw sugar), for creating the burnt sugar "crust"

Preheat the oven to 300°F. Position a rack in the middle of the oven, but low enough to accommodate a roasting pan or other shallow, oven-safe dish.

Place the cream, milk, sugar, and salt in a small saucepan over medium heat, and bring it just to a simmer. While it heats, grate the orange zest into a medium mixing bowl and add the chopped chocolate. When the liquids have reached a simmer, pour over the chocolate and orange zest. Stir until you've created a smooth mixture (this can take a few minutes).

When the chocolate mixture is still warm to the touch, add the yolks, one at a time, while stirring continuously. (If the chocolate mixture is too hot it will curdle the yolks; too cold, the final mixture won't be homogenous.) Strain the mixture through a fine sieve.

Place the empty ramekins in a deep pan, such as a roaster, and fill it with hot water so that it reaches halfway up the sides of the ramekins. Fill the ramekins with the chocolate-orange mixture. Cover the top of the entire pan with a sheet of thick plastic wrap (thick wrap won't melt) and bake for 30 to 40 minutes or until the cream has set at the sides of each ramekin but still jiggles in the center. (*Be confident!* If you overbake them, the custards will lose their delicate texture. You can do it! Besides, the chocolate, as it cools, will help the custard set up.)

Remove the ramekins from the water bath, let them come to room temperature, and chill for 2 hours or overnight. (Individually sealed with plastic wrap, the custards can be refrigerated for up to 3 days.)

When ready to serve, preheat the broiler to low to caramelize the sugars. Cover the surface of each ramekin with the thin banana slices, sprinkle the sugars to create a solid but light coating. Set the ramekins on a baking sheet. Heat the surfaces of the custards with the broiler just until the sugar begins to brown. Immediately remove the baking sheet from the oven, and serve. (Alternatively, you can finally use that acetylene torch you bought from the gourmet emporium.)

This entire dish can be made ahead of time. The sugar crust will retain its crispness for a few hours in the refrigerator, and then you can re-caramelize the surface by placing the ramekins for a few seconds under a broiler set on high.

Butterscotch Crème Brûlée

Simply proceed with the recipe above making just two changes: Replace the chopped milk chocolate with an equal weight of butterscotch chips, and omit the orange zest. Feel free to add the banana slices (now you have Butterscotch Banana Crème Brûlée—see how easy it is to be a pastry chef?) before you sugar the top and caramelize the sugars.

WILL THAT BE ALL?

AN APPENDIX WITH TOASTS

DESPITE THE ENORMOUS CHORUS OF VOICES assembled for this bistro oratorio, so much of the past 25 years at Lindey's has been lost to the memories of individual guests, employees, neighbors, and friends. As for what the next 25 years will bring, as for the progeny Lindey's has had some hand in fostering—we'll have to be all the more sketchy.

> If the world seems like it's getting smaller and smaller in 2006, by 2031 Lindey's menu will be global since diners will be as fascinated by cuisines from the far reaches of the globe as we are by the dynastic influences of France, Italy, and Asia today. But what I don't have to guess is why people will continue to come to Lindey's: for the warmth and the cozy, comforting feeling of eating in a place that makes you deposit whatever burdens you have at the door. Home away from home, that's Lindey's now and 25 years down the road—no matter where in the world the menu takes its inspiration!"
>
> —*Cookbook author and teacher Betty Rosbottom*

Consider these next few pages like glimpses into Lindey's largest reach, outside the bounds of a dining room and beyond an evening's reservations. Consider them celebratory toasts that have been sealed in a time capsule—or just stuck in our dumbwaiter between floors—ready to be opened, along with a few cases of champagne, on our 50th or even 100th anniversary.

LINDEY'S FIFTIETH
BY THE NUMBERS

Guests each week who approach the host stand, saying
"I went to school with the granddaughter of the lady who opened this place
back in the late 1900s, you know, Sue Dowdy": **7**

Years that Allen Jones, our longest-standing (now mostly-sitting) employee,
recently celebrated, proving that one can never be too old, too thin,
or too medicated to wait tables: **42**

Number of separate checks possible with our new iris-scan ordering system: **24**

Years until Sue Doody's name is etched in stone atop a culinary school in Columbus: **25**

Doral Chenoweth, the *Columbus Dispatch*'s Grumpy Gourmet: Ever since
my first dinner at Lindey's—opening night—I have referred to Sue as the
"Ella Brennan of Columbus." (If Ella's Commander's Palace exists in 2031,
it will be on a barge tied dockside in Baton Rouge, and the original Palace
in New Orleans will be a spawning reef for the fishes.) I see generations of
culinarians, back of the house and front of the house, in caps and gowns,
picking up degrees at the Sue Doody Culinary Institute. German Village
and Columbus are on high ground, like the Doody legend.

Orders of our calamari appetizer needed to receive a complimentary bucket of
frying oil for bio-diesel conversion: **10**

Chefs who have managed to convince patrons that the kitchen will not
prepare meat well-done: **0**

Channels on the bar television over the entrance
(even if only ESPN is the only station anyone ever watches): **32,200**

Shades of green that Lindey's has been repainted,
each one an attempt to recapture "the original green": **17**

Number of times that a bartender has told a customer
"I'm sorry, our blender is broken": **87.003**

Scoops of ice cream served in our Post Mortem in the last 50 years: **1,000,000**

Percent of the valets' tips from "parking" guests' jetpacks: **87**

Average temperature in Central Ohio thanks to global warming: **65**
*Lindey's Shrimp and Angel Hair Pasta is now made with crustaceans
harvested from our expanded courtyard fountain.*

Generations of next-door neighbors who continue to scowl over the parking, the noise,
and the people having better food than they are: **3**

Number of clothing stores, pizzerias, and antique shops that have come and gone
in the building across from Lindey's: **35**

Times that the 200-year-old bricks that compose the "drunken sidewalk"
in front of Lindey's have been pried loose and reset: **7**

Bail bonds posted by Van Dyne and Vamoose for extracurricular activities
of the kitchen staff: **34**

Children conceived on premises who are named Lindey: **0**

Years until Lindey's 75th year and, not coincidentally,
the bicentennial of Sigmund Freud's birth: **50**

Katherine Moore of the German Village Society: The good doctor preached that the ego, unlike the id, functions according to the reality principle: "Take care of a need as soon as an appropriate object is found." Wait, it gets better: "The organism is...guided toward those ends by its needs hunger, thirst, the avoidance of pain, and sex." That's in the Lindey's mission statement, yes? So how should this significant bicentennial be celebrated? With painted barns and limited-edition quarters? No, this will call for one hell of a patio party! Form a committee now.

Lindey's Extended Family

Sue: I believe that I've always had a true feeling about people. I've never treated my staff as if they were merely employees. I want to know about their families and their life outside of Lindey's—as well as their life here. But I also hope that my interest in them communicates that I hope they will treat our guests with similar interest and compassion.

Tony Murray: I'd only been bartending at Lindey's for three years, and was about to have my first child. Frank Cipriano got a group of the regulars and Ross and Sue, and had a shower for me at the German Village Meeting House. Everyone brought a gift, as well as a check for $100. This was early June, and the most fabulous party, with food and drinks and this whole Lindey's family that I'd been taking care of at the bar. When was all said and done, there was close to $3,000. You can't guess what kind of difference that made in my life at the time. Plus, I've always treasured the gifts we received. Even today—that's 14 years since Hannah was born—someone will come in and ask me, "Tony, tell me what Hannah's doing, how is she?"

Lindey's began the year that the first cases of what would come to be known as AIDS were discovered. In the coming years, our restaurant, like most, suffered many tragedies as the epidemic traveled through the community. Among the most cherished and devoted members of the staff lost to AIDS were Randy Manypenny, Steve Hempling, Craig Hardesty, Danny Burns, and Richard Freeman.

Sue: When Richard's health worsened, we wanted to find a way for him to continue to be with his friends at Lindey's, to earn some money, to feel needed. For a time, he served and the other waiters carried his trays and pitched in however they could. Richard had such regular customers, and they all knew he was sick, very sick, and they appreciated that he was here and they could come to dinner as a way of showing their love. When Richard grew even weaker, we found office work he could do. And then, after he passed away, when the quilts from the NAMES Project came to Ohio State, I read names in Richard's honor. And I continue to think about these sweet, devoted souls even today as this disease continues to reshape the world.

Sautéed and Served

Nineteen years ago, the Ohio Cancer Research Association, searching for a way to create awareness for cancer research and prevention, considered the idea of roasting a public figure. "We all thought of the Dean Martin roasts," remembers Executive Director Dennis Zack, "but they were too blue and bawdy for our purposes. So we came up with the idea of a sauté—we only wanted to lightly singe our honorees—and serve them up with lots of toasts.

"The event committee asked Sue if she'd be the first recipient of our sauté and help us call the community to our cause."

Sue, who has been honored by any number of civic associations and colleges, the Ohio Chamber of Commerce, and the German Village Society, declined.

Dennis persisted. "We are going to call our program 'Grand Illusions,' to celebrate a person that creates a special magic in the community and in the state of Ohio."

Sue declined.

But after the sixth or seventh petition, she finally agreed. "I just didn't want to call attention to myself, even though I realized the Association was such a good cause."

Dennis: That first event in 1988 with 350 people present (many of whom were at tables Sue helped us sell to her patrons and vendors), we cleared $46,000. And in the 19 years since that inaugural benefit, we've hosted 132 events in five Ohio cities. And Sue has remained Columbus's event chair, while we've sautéed the city's luminaries.

Since the beginning, Lindey's has been a supporter and patron to nearly every nonprofit in the city, with particularly generous contributions to Action for Children, Columbus Symphony, BalletMet, Opera Columbus, and the Columbus College of Art and Design. Donations to every sort of health, human rights, education, and community fundraising efforts feature into the ledger every day at Lindey's. As part of the 25th anniversary, Lindey's has identified a range of local beneficiaries, each of which will receive a donation during one month of the celebration.

Lindey's Offspring: Bravo!, Brio, and Beyond

1992

Having helped Sue start and build the business at Lindey's, sons Rick and Chris venture off on their own to open Bravo! Cucina Italiana, an Italian eatery that resembles the courtyard of an Italian ruin.

Alton Doody: I remember when Rick went to the bank to see about buying the building that had housed the Cadillac Café—with that ridiculous car sticking out of the front of the building. The financial officer said *"Great, but get your mom and dad to sign on the note."* And Rick said, "Look: I'm 33 years old, I have 10 years of business experience, and you don't have another buyer."

1999

....

The Doody brothers follow the success of Bravo! with Brio Tuscan Grille in Columbus's Easton Town Center: Tuscan tastes, fresh fish, and wood-grilled steaks and chops. It is an overnight success and Brio receives the prestigious "Hot Concepts!" award from *Nation's Restaurant News*.

Sue: The opening day of Brio it was such a hot summer night that Rick kept opening the doors, because otherwise people wouldn't realize that the restaurant had opened, and Chris kept closing the doors because of the terrible flies. (That sort of sums up how two brothers work together, doesn't it?) At one point, a waiter asked one of his tables, "Are you finished with your salad?" and the guest replied, "No, don't take it; it's for the flies, so they don't bother us."

Jeff Ramm, V.P. of training for BDI: Very quickly, management learned that if you don't want to get all of Rick's grunt work when opening a new store, you grab a broom. Rick's frugal philosophy, which started when he and Chris first opened Bravo! and re-tarred the roof and repaved the parking lot and drove Bobcats to re-grade the landscaping themselves, is that everyone pitches in.

By the seventh or eighth restaurant, we'd learned to hire out most of that work, of course, but in those critical days just prior to opening, the policy is there's nothing beneath anyone: scraping the fresh paint from the panes, dusting barware, polishing copper…or just grabbing a broom and looking busy. We're all there.

2001

Four days before 9/11, Chris and Rick open an entirely new kind of restaurant at Easton Town Center: Bon Vie, a bistro with French comfort foods. In November of that year, they open Lindey's Polaris in Columbus's Polaris Fashion Place, recreating much of German Village's culture and foods in a casual atmosphere.

Diane McLauglin, a trainer for BDI: The biggest difference between Lindey's and the other restaurants is Sue's remarkable sense of Lindey's as a family. She's always known everyone's name on staff. And most of the guests' names, too. She knows her employees, she cares about them, she remembers their history and their families. And in a sweet kind of way, she believes that's how the other stores operate. Once, at a training meeting, Sue spoke to a group of employees from the thirteen Bravo! and Brio restaurants we had at the time. Suddenly she stopped and asked me, "Diane, what's the name of the server with the long curly hair at our store in Dayton?"

I had absolutely no idea. Yes, I had traveled to most every store, but I hadn't been to Dayton in some time, and I didn't know all the hourly employees by name. But Sue just assumed that I knew everyone, the way she knew everyone at Lindey's, the way you know everyone in your family.

2005

BDI now includes restaurants in Orlando, Atlanta, Birmingham, Cincinnati, Richmond, St. Louis, Cleveland, West Palm Beach, Houston, Kansas City, Naples, and Dallas, with multiple new locations on the horizon.

Diane McLauglin: For many years, I was something like a floating manager for the company. At Brio and Bravo!, most guests want their meal—a good meal—and then they want to be on their way. They're headed to a movie. They've been shopping and they're beat.

As a manager at those restaurants, you fight the clock. Tables are constantly turning: you just jump in, seat guests, bus tables, serve wine, make sure a guest's meat was re-cooked to his or her satisfaction, solve check problems, help restock the bar, check that the ticket times aren't too long, run hot food to a waiting party—and, of course, of course, touch every table and make lifetime guests!

But at Lindey's, guests are having an event, even if they're going to or coming from another event. They're wearing pearls. They're ordering a nice wine. They're at a table to enjoy the night—the babysitter knows they might be late.

So my first night as a manager at Lindey's, I circled the dining rooms 50 times in the first 15 minutes, just looking for things to do. I was used to such a frantic, frenetic pace I didn't know how else to operate. I remember starting to bus a table and one of the bussers said, "I know my job, let me do this." I stood corrected.

June, 2006

BDI takes on an investment partner to further expansion. By November, 2006, the group will consist of 60 restaurants, with ambitious plans to open more Brio and Bravo! restaurants in each of the coming years. The Web site, **www.bestitalianusa.com**, lists addresses of all existing and forthcoming restaurants.

Bravo!'s Dipping Oil

Possibly the most requested recipe at the dozens of Bravo! restaurants around the country, this infused olive oil is a balanced mix of herbs and savory flecks of garlic and tomato. Now you can cut up a loaf of crusty bread, close your eyes, pretend you're at Bravo!, and dunk until you're too full for whatever you'd planned to serve.

makes 1 quart

- 1/4 cup canola oil
- 1/2 tablespoon each of dried rosemary, dried thyme, and dried basil
- 1/2 ounce sun-dried tomatoes, softened for 5 minutes in a few tablespoons of boiling water
- 1 teaspoon chopped fresh garlic
- 1 1/2 tablespoons tomato paste
- 1 tablespoon salt
- 1/2 teaspoon freshly ground black pepper
- 1 tablespoon fresh parsley, chopped
- 3 1/4 cups extra-virgin olive oil

In a small saucepan over medium-high heat, bring the canola oil and dried herbs to a simmer. Lower the heat, continue to simmer for 3 minutes, then strain the oil into a tall mixing bowl and discard the herbs.

Add the softened sun-dried tomatoes, garlic, tomato paste, salt, and pepper to the strained oil. Using a submersible blender, purée for 15 seconds. Add the parsley and olive oil, and blend for an additional 5 seconds.

About the authors

Sue Doody, the proprietor of Lindey's, was born in Dayton, Ohio, in 1934. A graduate and longtime supporter of Ohio Wesleyan University, Sue taught public school for several years, operated a small catering business, and conducted cooking classes in her home before opening Lindey's in 1981.

Since opening, Lindey's has remained one of Columbus's Top 10 Restaurants, and its chefs and managers continue to transform the culinary land-scape of Central Ohio. Moreover, Sue nurtured and supported her sons Rick and Chris as they created Bravo! Development Incorporated, one of the nation's most successful restaurant groups.

Sue's personal board activities and community commitments have included leadership roles with Action for Children, American Heart Association, Association for the Prevention of Blindness, Columbus Chamber of Commerce, Franklin University, Columbus State Community College, German Village Business League, United Way, Buckeye Boy's Ranch, Central Ohio Workforce Investment Corporation, and many others.

In her spare time, Sue is an avid reader, world traveler, and, of course, passionate cook.

Michael J. Rosen, a Columbus native son, is the author of more than 60 books, including cookbooks, poetry, anthologies of contemporary American humor, children's books, and a variety of philan-thropic books whose profits supported nearly 100 animal welfare agencies over a dozen years. He served as literary director of The Thurber House for nearly 20 years, and served for 14 years on the national board of directors for Share Our Strength, creating seven books to benefit the organization's pledge to create a hunger-free generation in America.

Photo Credits

All photography with the exceptions noted below are by Michael J. Rosen. Will Shively: color photography on the cover and back cover.

Chet Hay: spine, 14 [left], 44 [left], 71, 78, 84 [left], 90–94, 104 [left], 150, 183, 212, 216 [left], 218, 224, 226, 244, 248 [bottom], 273 [left], 279 [inset], 280 [left], and 320.

George Anderson: 16 [top], 50, 123 [right], and 160 [center]. Darlene Snuffer: 176–178.

Ken Chamberlain: 182, reprinted with permission of the *Columbus Dispatch*. Additional photographs have also been provided from the Doody family's personal collection (22, 25, 27, 30, 33, 291–293), Jim Barnes (page 164), Jack Cory (36, 47 [left], 109 [center]), the Wagner Collection of the German Village Society (30, 33, 288–290), and from the *Columbus Citizen-Journal* (27 [left], 92).

Excerpts from Mike Harden's work are reprinted courtesy of the *Columbus Dispatch*.

A few toasts: to copyeditor Francis Heaney, whose unfamiliarity with restaurant work rivals my own with proofreading; to designer Gregory Hischak, who might have felt like the grill cook on Mother's Day for the endless stream of special requests he accommodated; to Mark Svede, whose assistance on this book revived his dormant waiting-table nightmares; and to Sue Doody, who never once, in our joyful months of working together, uttered "What was he thinking!" at least when I was within earshot. —MJR